VICTORIAN VISIONS OF WAR & PEACE

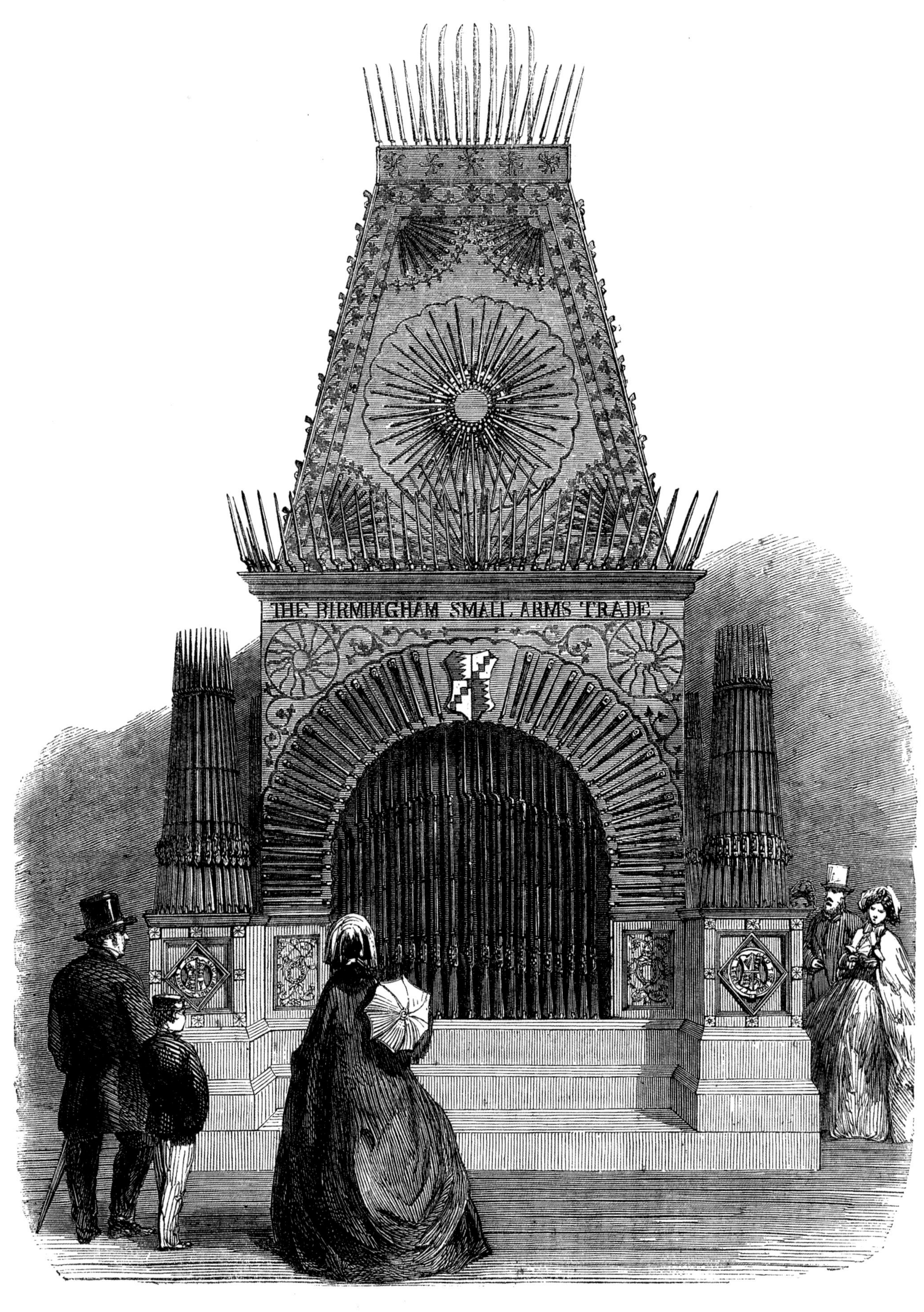
THE BIRMINGHAM SMALL ARMS TRADE.

Sean Willcock

VICTORIAN VISIONS OF WAR & PEACE

Aesthetics, Sovereignty & Violence in the British Empire, *c.* 1851–1900

The Paul Mellon Centre
for Studies in British Art

Distributed by Yale University Press
NEW HAVEN & LONDON

First published in 2021 by the Paul Mellon Centre for Studies in British Art
16 Bedford Square, London, WC1B 3JA
paul-mellon-centre.ac.uk

ISBN 978-1-913107-24-6 HB
Library of Congress Control Number: 2021935707

British Library Cataloguing-in-Publication Data
A catalogue record for this book is available from the British Library

Designed by Dalrymple
Origination by DL Imaging
Printed in China through World Print Ltd

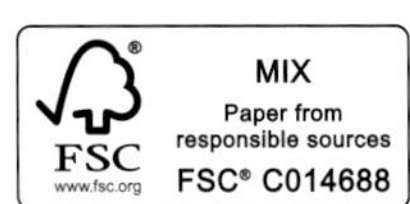

Frontispiece 'Birmingham Small Arms Trophy', *Illustrated London News*, 14 June 1862. Wood engraving. © Mary Evans Picture Library

Contents

ACKNOWLEDGEMENTS

This book developed from research undertaken for my PhD thesis at the University of York and during my time as a Leverhulme Early Career Fellow at Birkbeck, University of London. Both of these institutions provided highly supportive and stimulating academic environments that have shaped my thinking in profound ways.

I sincerely thank my PhD supervisor, Sarah Victoria Turner, for her invaluable encouragement and guidance over the years. I also thank those who offered such helpful feedback and support in various capacities during my postgraduate degrees: Jason Edwards, Sarah Monks, Mark Hallett and Natasha Eaton, among others. I am supremely grateful to Lynda Nead for guiding me through the arduous process of postdoctoral fellowship applications and for her mentoring at Birkbeck. The History and Theory of Photography Research Centre at Birkbeck has provided a helpful and supportive forum for discussing ideas, and I am very thankful to Patrizia Di Bello and Steve Edwards for fostering this research culture. And I would like to acknowledge my myriad debts to the scholars whose names populate the endnotes of this book; their work has provided the inspiration and the foundation for this study.

I am grateful to the many archivists who have provided assistance to me over the years, in particular those at the British Library, National Army Museum, Yale Center for British Art, Alkazi Foundation for the Arts and the Victoria Memorial Hall. Particular thanks must go to Peter Harrington at the Anne S. K. Brown Military Collection, who was so generous in sharing the fruits of his own significant research on William Simpson.

I would like to thank the Paul Mellon Centre for Studies in British Art for supporting the publication of this book, with particular gratitude to Katharine Ridler for her attentive editing and Emily Lees for her calm guidance throughout the process. I also thank the two anonymous peer reviewers of this book for their thorough and constructive reader reports.

None of this research would have been possible without funding from the Arts and Humanities Research Council and the Leverhulme Trust. It also benefited greatly from additional research and travel funding from the Yale Center for British Art, the Paul Mellon Centre for Studies in British Art and the Indian National Trust for Art and Cultural Heritage.

And, finally, my deepest thanks to my parents, for their support, and most of all to Josephine, for that and everything else.

INTRODUCTION

Visual Culture in the Global Field, *c.*1851–1900

IN AN ERA THAT SAW THE BIRTH OF PHOTOGRAPHY (*C.*1839) AND the rise of the illustrated press (*c.*1842), world events became increasingly entangled with the processes and products of image-making. New modes of popular visual imagery structured the Victorian experience of international crises and moulded Britain's sense of its identity as an imperial nation. This book considers how emerging forms of mass visual media intersected with the practices and discourses of the fine arts in ways that came to profoundly shape British visions of war and peace during a period of unprecedented global imperial dominance. In particular it examines how artists and photographers operating 'in the field' were instrumental in constituting the colonial encounter and guiding both the perception and management of conflict and diplomacy in the second half of the nineteenth century. Overseeing protean colonial regimes – formal empire, indirect rule, unequal treaties, gunboat diplomacy and punitive expeditions – the Victorians increasingly began to turn to pictorial reportage and visual spectacle to help them make sense of the modern world system and compose modes of imperial sovereignty that were intelligible to coloniser and colonised alike.

THE WORLD AS EXHIBITION

The Victorian era witnessed a major transformation in the relationship between visual technologies and imperial violence, but the wide-ranging intersections of these domains have remained largely unexplored. In a scene published in the *Illustrated London News* during the 1862 International Exhibition in South Kensington, middle-class visitors were shown admiring the 'Trophy of Armstrong Guns and Coils from the Royal Gun Factories, Woolwich' (fig. 1), one of a number of displays of British-manufactured weaponry on show at the World's Fair.[1] Other scenes

John Dalbiac Luard,
A Welcome Arrival, 1855, 1857
(detail of fig. 4).

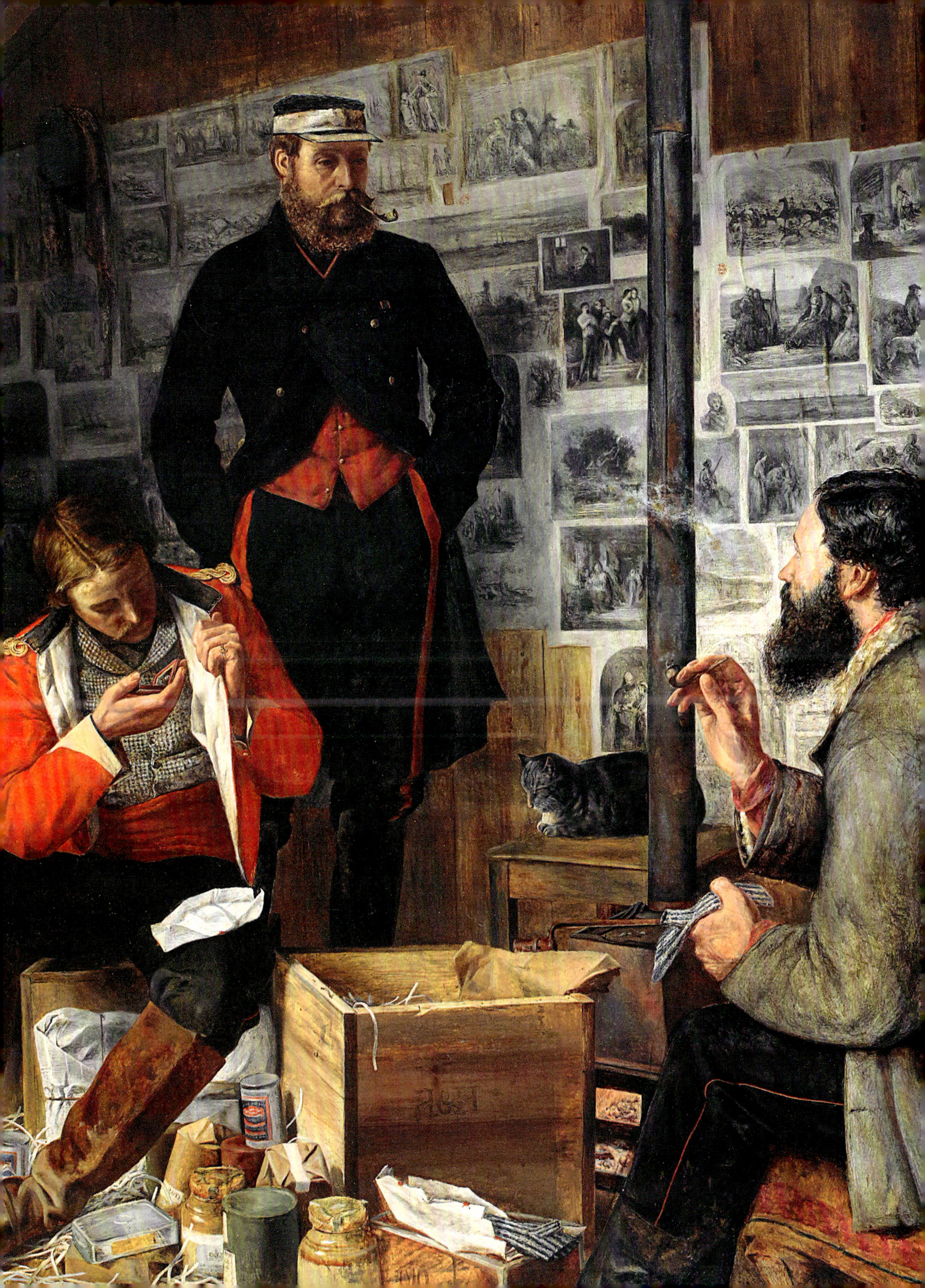

in the same supplement depicted visitors admiring works of art (fig. 2), thus registering an equivalence between a military way of seeing and the urbane viewing practices that had become a fundamental feature of Victorian metropolitan culture since at least the Great Exhibition of 1851, when millions had descended on Hyde Park to admire the art and industry of 'all nations'. Yet the equivalence between militaristic and artistic spectatorship was jarring; the Military Court was a controversial new addition to the 1862 show and it was seen by some as a corruption

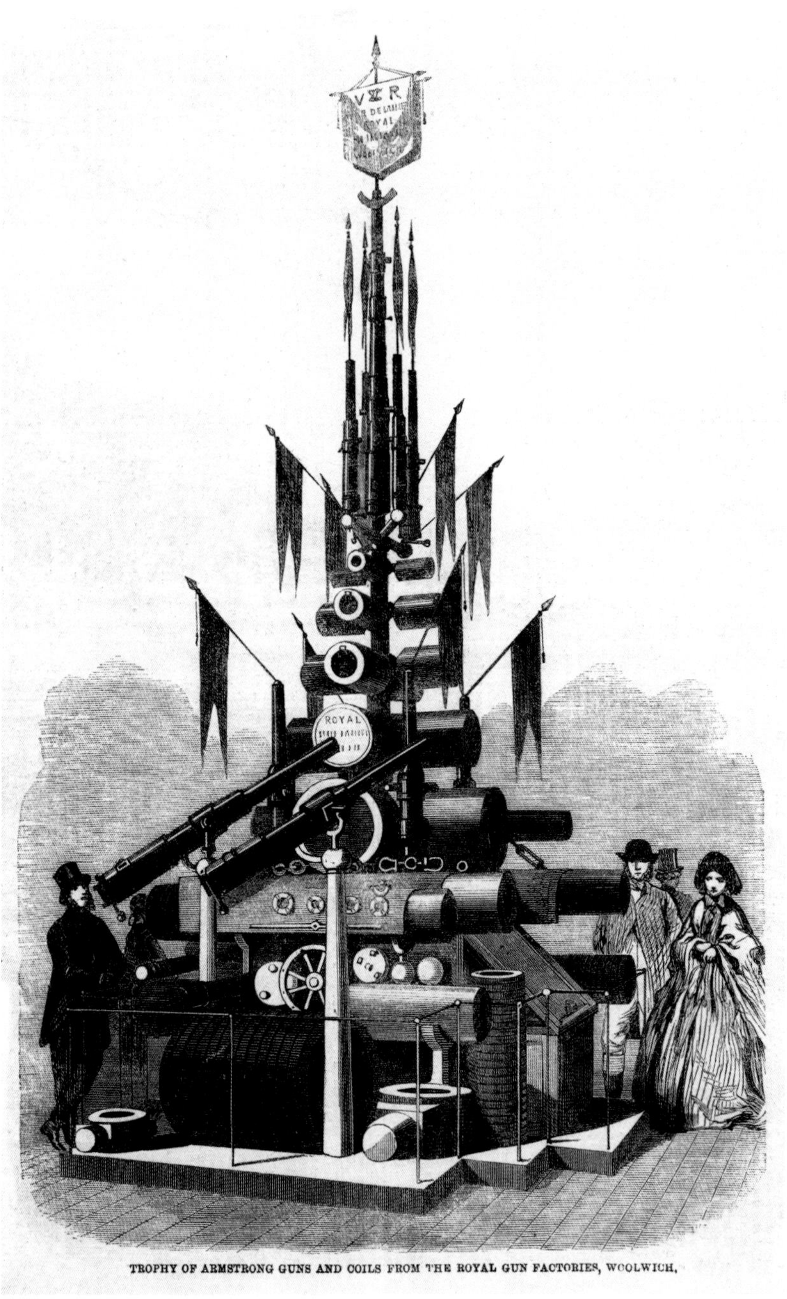

1 'Trophy of Armstrong Guns and Coils from the Royal Gun Factories, Woolwich', *Illustrated London News*, 14 June 1862. Wood engraving. © Mary Evans Picture Library

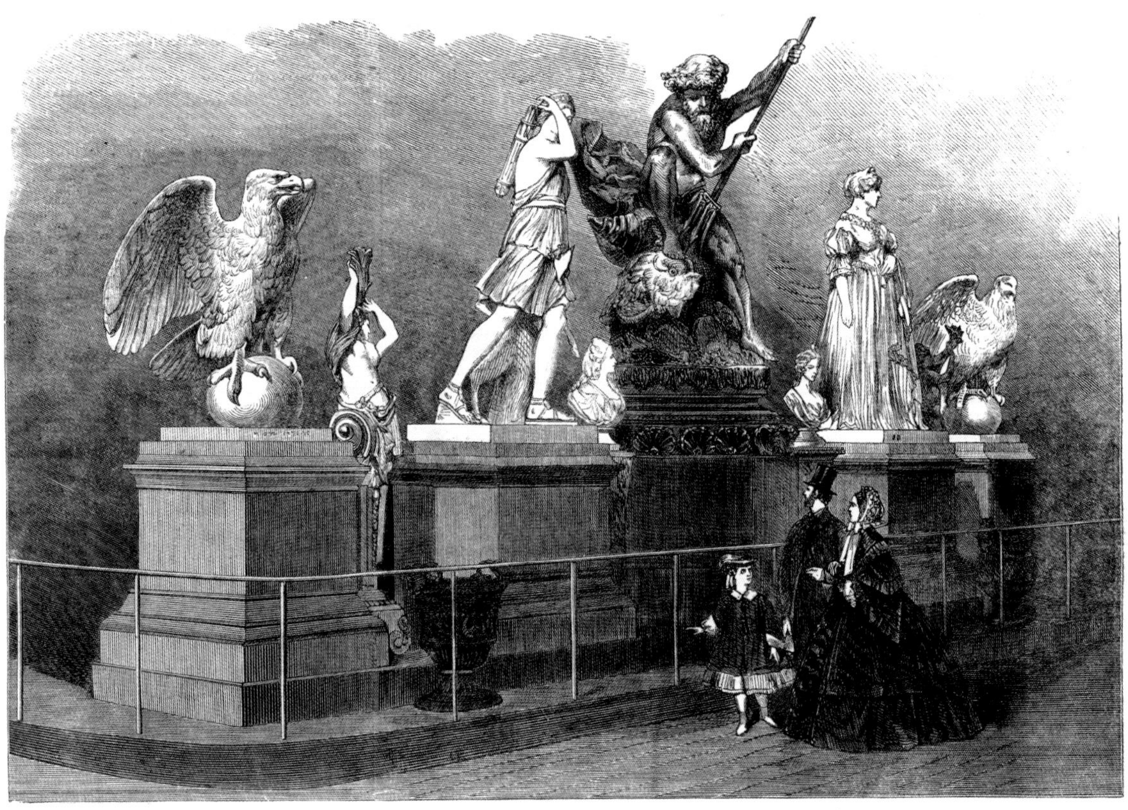

2 'Iron Figure Castings by M. Ducel, of Paris, in the International Exhibition', *Illustrated London News*, 14 June 1862. Wood engraving. © Mary Evans Picture Library

of the Great Exhibition's famously pacific ideals. 'No wonder the ghost of 1851 is so restless', wrote one reviewer. 'Peace, so loudly invoked in the first Exhibition, scarcely expected to see *this* as a result of it in the second.'[2] So what had happened?

The global events of the years linking the world's fairs of 1851 and 1862 sorely tested the geopolitical optimism of the Victorians. The Great Exhibition was supposed to substitute economic and aesthetic interchange for international conflict, but the years that followed saw a surge in both intra-European and colonial violence, changing Britain's outlook and reformulating the terms of its self-projection on the world stage. Russian expansionism had upset the balance of power in Europe, leading to warfare in the Crimean Peninsula; meanwhile, further east, an insurgency motivated (at least to the British mind) by Islamic fanaticism had launched a bloody challenge against the regime of the English East India Company in India. Such instability mocked the starry-eyed rhetoric of the 1851 spectacle; the mid-Victorian 'age of equipoise' was thus marred by a series of violent international crises that led to urgent questions about the nature of Britain's global role.[3] This book is concerned with the imperial imagination that emerged in the fallout of 1851's failure, when ideals about the civilising and peaceable nature of the world's fairs and their associated modes of visual education and consumption were put under extreme pressure by the realpolitik of maintaining a global empire.

In the decade separating the two exhibitions, numerous new modes of visual practice became entrenched in British culture in ways that would radically alter the Victorian relationship to their geopolitical present: there was a global explosion of amateur and professional photographers operating in war zones; newspapers began running illustrated reports on international conflict and foreign affairs that were unprecedented in their scope and popularity; war artists like William 'Crimea' Simpson became household names; and military aggression began to be staged for both the camera and the pencil. A wide-ranging traffic was developing between global violence and visual imagery, spanning 'high' and 'low' culture, and cultivating what Rudyard Kipling would eventually call 'the blind, brutal British public's thirst for blood'.[4] By 1862, with British culture newly inundated by images of global conflict, the presence of strange temples of military ordnance like 'The Birmingham Small-Arms Trophy' (see *frontispiece*) in the refined space of South Kensington made a certain kind of sense. The preceding years had seen warfare become thoroughly integrated in bourgeois spaces of metropolitan visual consumption, from the gallery wall to the pages of respectable illustrated periodicals. The leisure-time spectatorship of modern urbanites was regularly brushing up against the violent convulsions of empire.

Some elements of the Great Exhibition's confident former vision of the world remained. Above all, the 1851 show had been an exercise in the cognitive mapping of an increasingly complex global economic framework, positing Britain as the imperial centre into which flowed the arts and manufactures of the periphery; it 'symbolically enacted the idea of London as the heart of empire.'[5] Such an enterprise inaugurated what Timothy Mitchell, adapting Heidegger's notion of modernity as the 'age of the world picture', has termed the 'the age of the world exhibition, or rather, the age of the world-as-exhibition', in which the world was 'conceived and grasped as though it were an exhibition'.[6] The vast array of wares on show inside Joseph Paxton's custom-built iron and glass Crystal Palace in 1851 embodied a new, modern disposition that approached the world as a visual spectacle to be consumed (fig. 3). The British duly treated military invasions and diplomatic missions to foreign states not only as spectacular events in themselves but also as opportunities to 'collect' (this was the preferred euphemism) interesting artefacts and, in lieu of physical acquisition, visually to document a region's material culture.

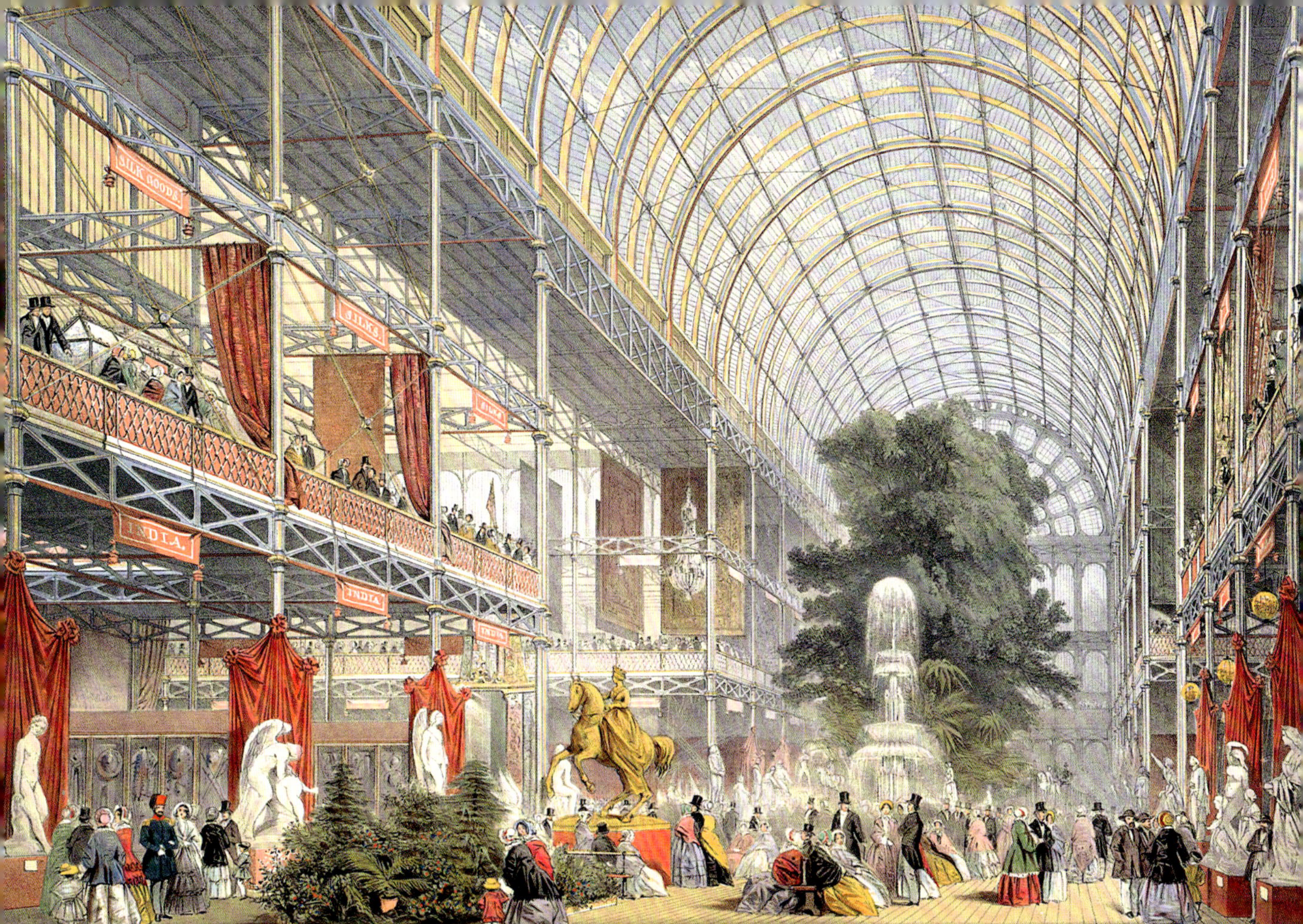

3 Joseph Nash, 'The Transept', *Dickinson's Comprehensive Pictures of the Great Exhibition of 1851, from the originals painted for H. R. H. Prince Albert by Messrs Nash, Hague, & Roberts*, vol. 2, 1854. British Library Creative Commons

Those Victorian visitors who left the virtual world tour on offer at the Crystal Palace and really journeyed abroad may have had a notion that they were moving from image to actuality, but 'they went on trying' (Mitchell again) 'to grasp the real thing as a picture.'[7] This is a book about such pictorial grasping, exploring how the modern enthralment to visual spectacle shaped the phenomenology of imperial conquest, occupation, governance and diplomatic relations in the nineteenth century.

MASS MEDIA

The Victorian experience of war and peace was increasingly mediated by new international networks of mass-produced imagery. This is indicated clearly by John Dalbiac Luard's *A Welcome Arrival* (fig. 4), in which three British officers are shown receiving supplies from England during the Crimean War (1853–6). The men unpack their parcel against the backdrop of a mess-hut wall plastered with press engravings, which function to domesticate the military dwelling with pictures of art, theatrical scenes and nature. Yet these reminders of peacetime in Britain are situated alongside numerous images of seafaring vessels that gesture towards an

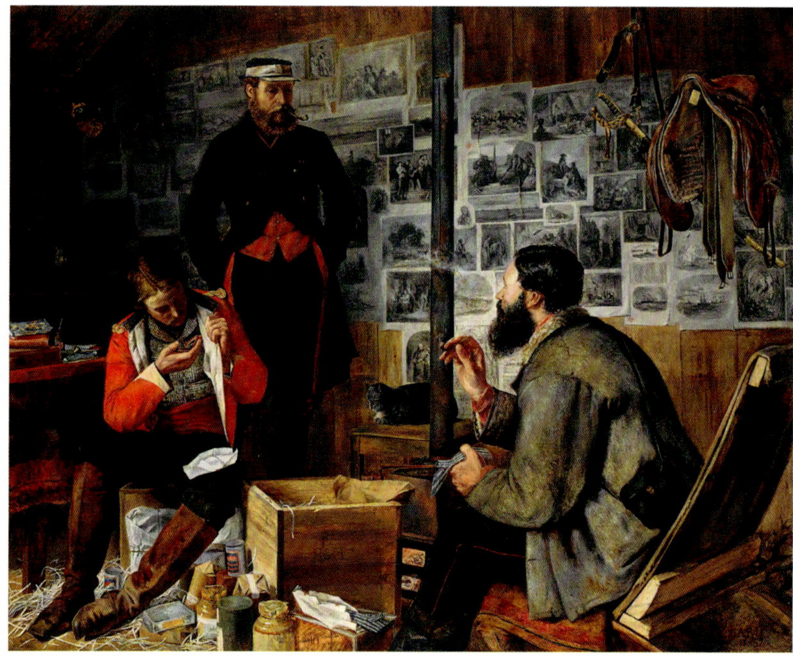

4 John Dalbiac Luard, *A Welcome Arrival, 1855*, 1857. Oil on canvas, 76.2 × 100 cm. National Army Museum, London

expanded geographical horizon and possess clear military connotations in the context of the naval battles then taking place in the Black Sea.

Such officers would have been well aware that a new breed of 'on the spot' artists like Constantin Guys (1802–1892) and Joseph Arthur Crowe (1825–1896) were with them on the Crimean Peninsula producing popular visual reports for the *Illustrated London News*. Founded by Herbert Ingram in 1842, the newspaper doubled its readership from 100,000 to 200,000 per week during the campaign. Luard appears to include one of the newspaper's wartime front pages in the bottom right-hand corner of the officers' wall: a slightly truncated version of a 2 September 1854 illustration of a fire at the naval base at Varna.[8] The lived experience of a military campaign was thereby shown to be shaped by the consumption and display of journalistic imagery.

The rise of the illustrated press – a process eased by the abolition of the newspaper duty as a 'tax on knowledge' in 1855 – profoundly impacted the Victorian engagement with global events. Wars in particular were increasingly brought to the attention of the British public via the visual serials of the *Illustrated London News*, which, in its first decade, had pivoted from its originally intended emphasis on domestic crime to expand its international coverage of British engagements in Afghanistan, China and Ceylon (Sri Lanka).[9] As a phenomenon, however, the rise of the 'special artist' working for the press has received limited attention, with existing accounts characterised by the positivism of traditional military history and sealed off from wider scholarship on Victorian visual culture and colonial politics.[10] Artists like William Simpson (1823–1899), Melton Prior (1845–1910) and Frederic Villiers (1851–1922) were once popular and prolific journalists whose names, images and articles were known to the reading public as well as to many of the men involved in the military and diplomatic events being reported. They leave an extensive but little-studied archive of sketches, prints, diaries and autobiographies – material which, along with the rise of photography as a visual technology increasingly embedded in military and diplomatic campaigns, helped to transform the modern experience of global war and peace.

The images produced in the field by such men were intended primarily for a British metropolitan audience. However, following publication as prints or press engravings, the images frequently circled back to their location of origin by way of railway and steamship to be consumed by soldiers and colonials alongside a multitude of other visual and textual narratives on domestic and international affairs. The historical agents of such events were thus doubly exposed to pictures, consuming the finished versions, as we see in Luard's vision of the image world of Crimean officers, but also, as this book will show, bearing witness to and posing for the plein-air practices that were increasingly responsible for feeding the Victorian military imagination in the first place: to the paintbrushes and easels, pencils and sketchbooks, cameras, tripods and tableaux vivants that now interpolated – and constituted – the imperial field. Producing visual and textual reports 'on the spot' or 'in the field' (hereafter lacking quotation marks) was not a neutral method of documentation but was formative of imperial ways of seeing and being, shaping the geographies, epistemologies and temporalities of the Victorian empire.

In a crucial sense, the illustrated periodicals publishing such imagery offered a similar visual experience to the world's fairs: they too responded to the increasingly networked modern world by making ever grander claims to representational comprehensiveness.[11] As the first editor of the *Illustrated London News*, F. W. N. Bayly, proclaimed in 1842 to his new readers:

> In the world of diplomacy, in the architecture of foreign policy, we can give you every trick of the great Babel that other empires are seeking to level or raise. Is there peace? Then shall its arts, implements, and manufactures be spread upon the page. The literature – the customs – the dress – nay, the institutions and localities of other lands, shall be brought home to you with spirit, with fidelity, and, we hope, with discretion and taste. Is there war? Then shall its seat and actions be laid naked before the eye.[12]

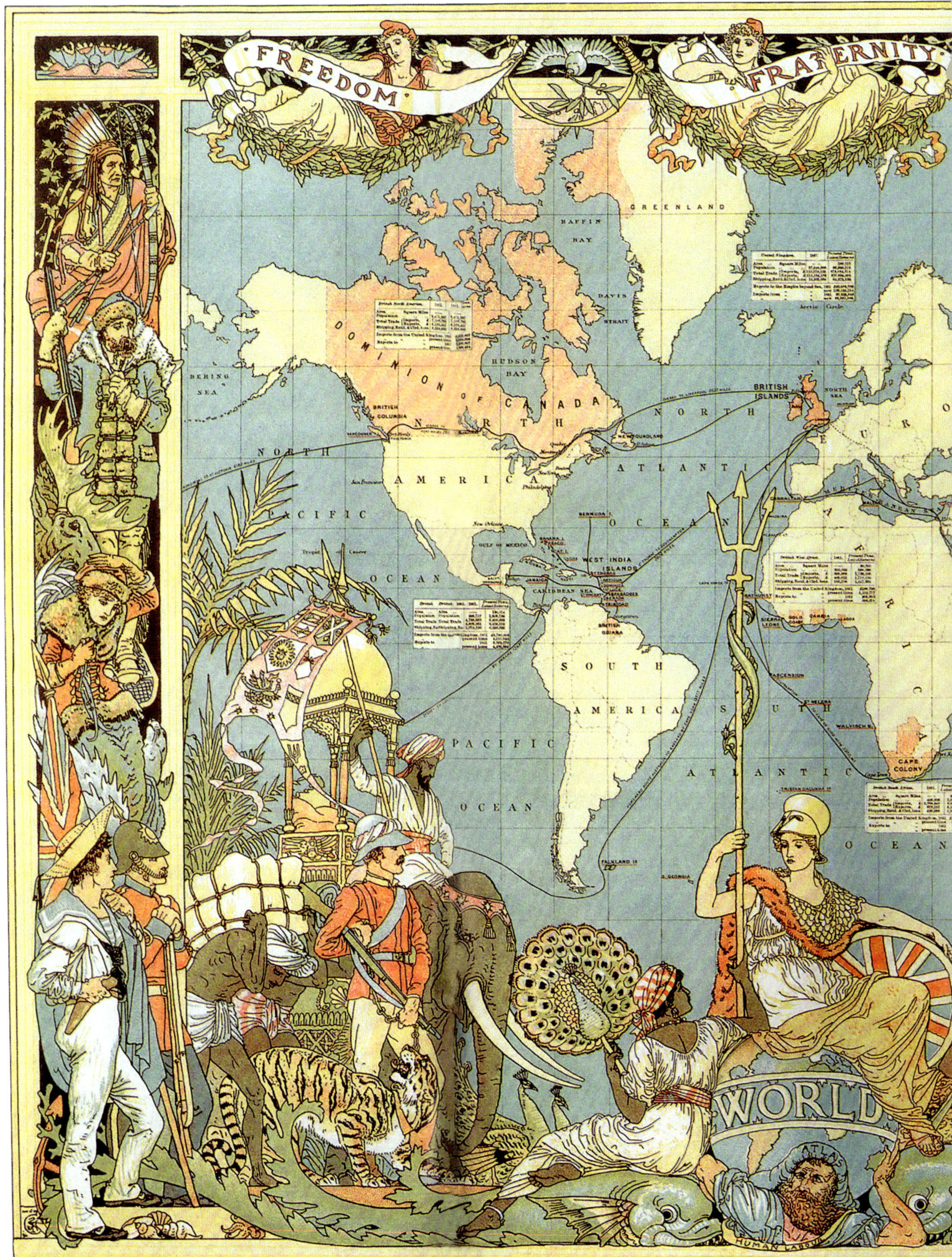

FREEDOM
FRATERNITY
GREENLAND
BAFFIN BAY
DAVIS STRAIT
HUDSON BAY
DOMINION OF CANADA
BERING SEA
BRITISH COLUMBIA
NORTH AMERICA
NORTH PACIFIC OCEAN
NORTH ATLANTIC OCEAN
BRITISH ISLANDS
GULF OF MEXICO
WEST INDIA ISLANDS
SOUTH AMERICA
PACIFIC OCEAN
SOUTH ATLANTIC OCEAN
FALKLAND IS
CAPE COLONY
WORLD
ATLAS
HUMAN LABOUR

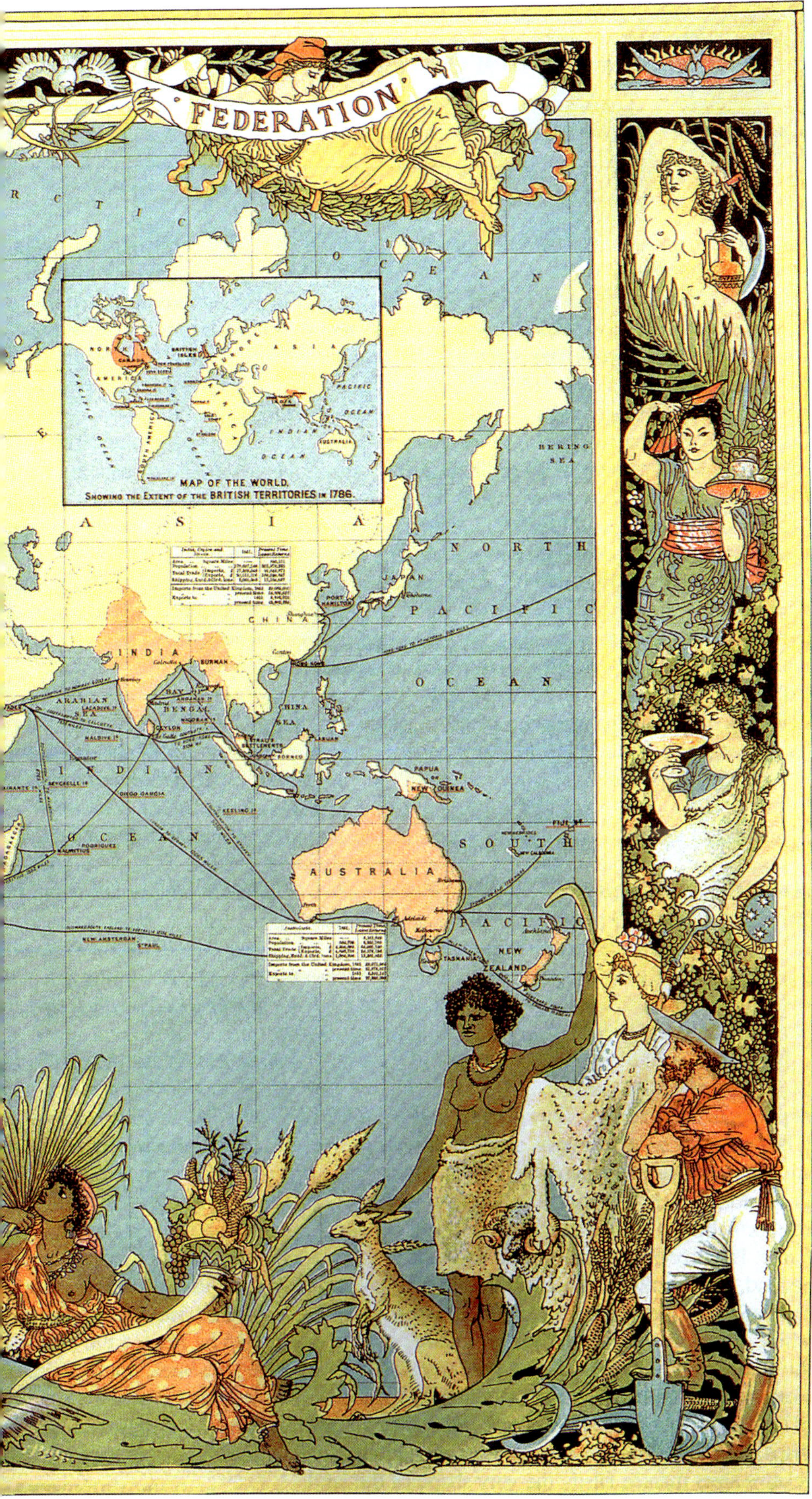

5 Walter Crane, 'Imperial Federation Map', *The Graphic*, 24 July 1886. Lithograph, 58 × 77 cm. © Mary Evans Picture Library

Such a totalising approach to the geopolitical landscape was later distilled by *The Graphic* (founded in 1869) when, in response to the popular imperial bombast of the Indian and Colonial Exhibition in South Kensington in 1886 (yet another iteration of the world-as-exhibition ethos that defined the Victorian age), it offered its own completist vision of the world by publishing Walter Crane's 'Imperial Federation Map' (fig. 5).[13] A large colour supplement intended as a wall chart for schools, Crane's map functioned as a form of imperial pedagogy, showing the British Empire in its global context, replete with ethnological figures. The modern spectator, writes Patrick Collier, was being trained in a 'new kind of seeing' by the illustrated press, one that imposed 'the impossible duty of maintaining surveillance over multiple, non-contiguous territories.'[14]

Mass print media, steam-engine transport and telegraphy thus formed 'an information network of political, military and commercial intelligence', writes Chandrika Kaul: 'They brought into being for the first time what Marshall McLuhan was later to call the "global village" – or in our case an imperial village.'[15] Such infrastructure provided a new context of experience for the Victorians, in which events were situated in an expansive geopolitical present – 'bringing near us a vast world beyond our limited circles', as the journalist and author E. S. Dallas wrote in 1866, 'and giving us a present interest in the transactions of the most distant regions.'[16]

THE GEOPOLITICAL AESTHETIC

Walter Crane's map has since become an icon of High Victorian imperialism. Yet its depiction of a clearly demarcated and unified empire belied the messy realities of Britain's global reach. It was a 'fiction of geopolitics', to use Christopher GoGwilt's term, producing 'an imaginary coherence of organised world political relations.'[17] Absent here is a sense of how these British territories were administered by radically different and even incompatible forms of imperial sovereignty, from ideals of a 'Greater Britain' consisting of white settler colonies like Canada, Australia and New Zealand, to the 'civilising mission' rhetoric and neo-feudal rituals that sought to legitimise the governance of large and highly diverse populations in India, as well as the indirect rule exerted over other nominally sovereign states.[18] Ann Laura Stoler, drawing on Giorgio Agamben's influential analysis of the logic of sovereignty as a 'state of exception' in *Homo Sacer: Sovereign Power and Bare Life*, has described imperial formations not as 'clearly bounded polities, but scaled genres of rule that produce and count different degrees of sovereignty and gradations of rights.'[19] Empire was defined by partial or attenuated sovereignties, ambiguous and contingent borders, coercive diplomacy, suspensions of rights, states of emergency, temporary occupations, punitive expeditions and the reduction of some subjects to what Agamben calls 'bare life' – abandoned by the law, exposed to violence, deprivation and death.[20] In imperial discourse these situations were 'framed as unique cases – but they are "exceptions" in a context in which such exceptions are a norm.'[21]

Painting the map an imperial pink obscured the myriad 'exceptions' that constituted British power on the global stage. Yet these exceptions were recurrent and urgent concerns for artists and photographers in the field seeking to make imperial machinations legible to British governments and publics. The imperial imaginary of the Victorians was suppler than the abstractions of such cartography suggest, accommodating multifarious forms of sovereignty, suzerainty and subjection, as well as their associated logics of explicit and implicit violence. The 'geopolitical image' of the Victorian world system pivoted on 'the split imperatives of national sovereignty and imperial power': far from envisioning a homogenous and stable world, writes GoGwilt, imperialist geopolitics presupposed an 'anarchic' mode of international relations that treated the nation-state as a contingent and thus alterable form of political organisation.[22] This study is concerned with how artists and photographers composed imperial power during its 'anarchic' moments of transition and crisis, when such contingency was most in evidence.

In his seminal 1992 study of the 'geopolitical aesthetic' in twentieth-century cinema, Frederic Jameson posited a 'geopolitical unconscious' by way of which the globalised structures of capitalism came to be encoded in (post)modern representational forms.[23] Lauren Goodlad has recently applied such an approach to nineteenth-century British literature and its depictions of imperial sovereignty, demonstrating 'how realist fiction altered in its multiple efforts to craft aesthetic forms receptive to the dynamism of a fast-globalizing world.'[24] Her exposition of 'the Victorian geopolitical aesthetic' goes beyond Jameson in its attempt to encompass not only 'the formal capture of geohistorical processes' through literary realism but also 'literature's links to the embodied features of lived experience.' I share Goodlad's concern with what she calls the 'sinuous interchange between embedding structures and embodied ethics', focusing on how aesthetic forms moulded the corporeal habits and moral sensibilities of the colonial British.[25] The fine arts, photography and the illustrated press were adaptive in their formal responses to the evolving techniques of imperial rule; in turn, the visual narratives and aesthetic conventions which arose in such spheres informed the affective, ethical and embodied engagement of the Victorians with those very techniques.

'Aesthetics' here refers not only to theories regarding formal properties, beauty and taste (although I do sometimes engage with such themes) but also to an embodied structure of feeling and perception. In this I follow scholars who have revived the meaning of the original Greek term *aisthetikos* as a discourse on, and organisation of, the senses in order to highlight how culture – in particular visual culture – shapes a *habitus*.[26] This book thus both considers how imperial sovereignty was made visible (and viable) to coloniser and colonised and, 'thinking geo – and body-politically', explores how such imperial designs were inscribed in the senses and sensibilities of colonial subjects by acts of image-making and their associated modes of spectatorship.[27] A colonial system, writes Walter Mignolo, 'orients both geopolitical designs and body-political subjectivities ... affecting our senses, driving our emotions and desires'.[28] There is a 'geopolitics of sensing and knowing'.[29]

Stated crudely, the argument is this: there was literally an art to imperial statecraft. The Victorians relied, to an extraordinary degree, on visual spectacle to help them envision acceptable (to the British) states of war and peace, particularly when peace had to emerge out of febrile international relations. Artists and photographers operating on the spot would increasingly chronicle – but also, I argue, constitute – the shift from one state of affairs to the other. By the time the 'New Imperialism' emerged in the 1870s, empire was explicitly conceived as a mode of image-management in which colonial relations were formalised through portrait sittings and other such embodied performances; international compacts, alliances or polities often had to be staged in order to be seen as credible. Yet acts of image-making occurring in the field were not merely producing representations of such events; they were cultivating ways of seeing and styles of comportment that were designed to help colonials navigate the politically fraught and often violent cross-cultural encounters that took place during moments of upheaval.

For the Victorian, however, there existed a paradox in which, as Jameson writes in *The Geopolitical Aesthetic*, 'information technology will become virtually the representational solution as well as the representational problem of the world system's cognitive mapping.'[30] This tension between technology-as-solution and technology-as-problem is a key theme of the chapters that follow. Practices of fieldwork and visual forms like the newspaper, the album and the exhibition space provided a means through which the Victorians could render their imperial project intelligible and therefore manageable; yet the aestheticisation of imperial sovereignty was unpredictable in its effects, trailing its own ethical, political and representational problems. This was particularly the case, I argue, during the image-making event itself, when the bodies of compatriots, allies and enemies had to be marshalled into politically resonant poses under conditions of significant violence and stress.

THE ART OF THE 'GREAT GAME'

This book's key area of focus is India – regarded as the 'Jewel in the Crown' of Britain's empire. I situate this most prized of imperial possessions both within and against a protean network of colonial regimes spanning Afghanistan, Burma, China and Tibet. For the British, holding onto India also meant no end of imperialist wrangling beyond its borders as they pursued the 'Great Game' of protecting trade routes and buffer states from the real and imagined ambitions of their rivals. British imperialism in Asia incorporated diverse political formations involving many gradations of sovereignty, but it was informed by a common set of Orientalist suppositions regarding the susceptibility of such populations to governance via spectacle ('the further east you go,' wrote the Viceroy of India, Lord Lytton, 'the greater becomes the importance of a bit of bunting'[31]).

Since the East India Company had morphed from a trading entity trafficking in opium, indigo, tea and spices to a quasi-governmental power with vast armies and the power to raise tax revenue (while also trafficking in said commodities), India had become indispensable to Britain's global hegemony. Over the eighteenth century, the Company had repeatedly taken advantage of the waning fortunes of the once formidable Mughal dynasty, reducing the Delhi-based emperor to a puppet figure and fighting a series of wars against the Maratha Empire, the Kingdom of Mysore and myriad tribal populations. By 1800 the British were the dominant power on the subcontinent; India's riches were being syphoned off into the hands of Company men, leading to periodic corruption scandals in which the British government sought to rein in excesses through regulation.[32] Yet the Company continued to expand aggressively throughout the early nineteenth century, until the bloody upheavals of the Indian Uprising in 1857 – a major insurgency against British rule that was termed a 'mutiny' by many colonials at the time – shredded its political legitimacy. The Crown took formal control of India the following year, forcing Britain to reassess the nature of its rule over its richest colony.

A key strand of this book will involve an extended consideration of Britain's post-1857 process of reconceptualising imperial sovereignty in India. This process was explicitly conceived as a visual project with ramifications across photography, the fine arts and the illustrated press. The photographic culture of the Raj – subject to pioneering archival research by John Fraser and John Falconer in the 1980s – has since become the focus of numerous critical studies by scholars including James R. Ryan,

Christopher Pinney and Zahid R. Chaudhary.[33] Such scholars have brought a range of disciplinary approaches to bear on the colonial camera, from the geographical and anthropological to the critical theoretical, and their research will be touched upon throughout this book. My own approach to this photographic material differs, however, in that it seeks to situate it within the broader art histories of British India, from which it has so far remained relatively isolated.

This isolation is perhaps due to the fact that photography initially met with an emaciated colonial art scene when it was first introduced to the subcontinent shortly after its invention was announced in Europe in 1839. India was no longer the profitable theatre for European artists that it had been in the eighteenth century, when oil painters like Johan Zoffany (1733–1810) and William Hodges (1744–1797) had enjoyed successful periods in the service of the Company and Indian royal courts.[34] While Lucknow held out as a bastion of Indian royal patronage for European artists – with George Beechey (1797–1852), Alexandre Benoit Jean Dufay (1770–1844), William Florio Hutchisson (1773–1857) and a German miniature painter, C. Muntz (dates unknown), all finding work there in the 1830s and 40s – the commissions that were received were seemingly not enough to sustain a career.[35] Artists faded into obscurity, returned to Europe or, like Hutchisson, moved into more profitable colonial trades like indigo farming.[36] The heady days of the 1770s and 80s, when the foreign policy of the Company had involved sending European artists to Indian courts, were long gone.[37]

Such was the pitiful state of the colonial art scene on the subcontinent at the dawn of the photographic age that, in the 1830s, the *India Review* went so far as to claim that a recently established artist – who at the time appears to have been doing little more than contributing some lithographed portraits of colonials to periodicals – was somebody that could be credited with 'laying the foundation for the fine arts' (a statement that implicitly denied that mantle to any Indian traditions).[38] The artist in question, Colesworthy Grant (1813–1880), had arrived in India in 1832 at the age of nineteen and was still in agreement with the *India Review* about the 'almost non-existence of the fine arts in the country' more than a decade later.[39] Even his attempts to foster a more artistically literate colonial public through his twice-weekly evening classes in drawing in Calcutta (Kolkata) during the 1840s came to little when the wider project of which they were a part – the short-lived Mechanics Institution and School of Arts – was abandoned.[40] This book's claim – that the Victorian experience of the colonial encounter was profoundly shaped by image-making practices – appears to find limited evidence in the commercially unrewarding colonial art scene of early nineteenth-century India.

Yet if one turns to how a once popular and important (but now almost entirely overlooked) colonial artist like Grant survived in this difficult market, a slightly different picture emerges.[41] Illustrated narratives were his forte and most of these attempted to capitalise on moments of political crisis in India and its borderlands. Following the First Anglo-Afghan War (1839–42), Grant published *Dost Muhummud Khan, and the Recent Events in Caubool* (1842), a collection of portraits of the exiled ruling elite of Afghanistan with notes detailing the disastrous British campaign there.[42] In the wake of the Second Anglo-Burmese War (1852), the artist was commissioned to accompany the British embassy that was sent to Burma to formalise conditions of peace, documenting everything from local dignitaries (fig. 6) to sites of conflict (see fig. 62).[43] Grant was explicit about the commercial advantage offered by colonial warfare. Sketches that he had made of Rangoon during the 1840s had languished unseen for years, he noted, until the Burmese had been 'considerate enough' (his words) to engage in the 1852 war with the British, drumming up enough colonial interest to make it worthwhile publishing the old imagery.[44] Moments of upheaval stimulated a desire for some sort of visual record, even if colonials remained stubbornly indifferent to the more refined offerings of the 'fine arts' whose relative absence Grant had lamented.

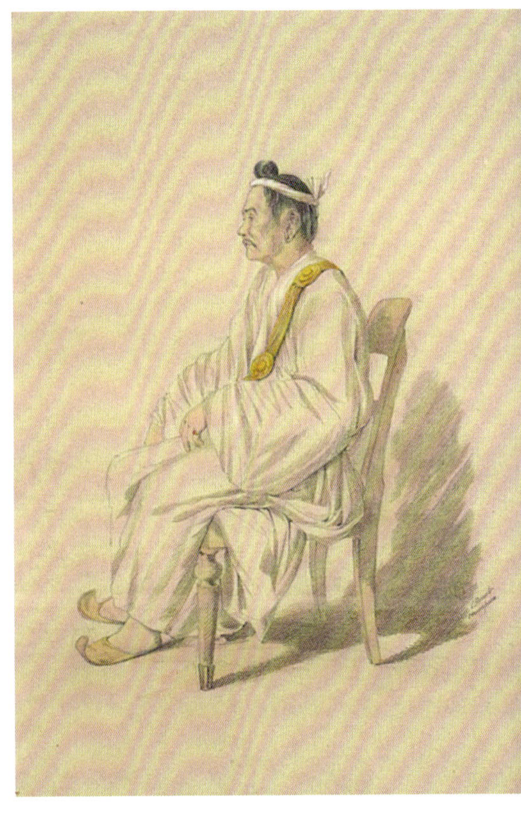

6 Colesworthy Grant, *Moung Mho, the Myadoung Myotsa. Second Woongee*, 1855. Watercolour with pen and ink, 27.7 × 37.9 cm. © The British Library Board, London

The market for colonial images in early nineteenth-century Britain was not much different. Prior to the more jingoistic mood of the 'New Imperialism' of the 1870s, the Empire was notable for its relative absence within British arts, education and political discourse, so much so that in 1849 there had even been a debate in Parliament on the lack of debate on colonial issues.[45] Yet this apparent indifference was punctuated by moments of heightened public concern brought on by news of rebellions or the prospect of significant imperial gains or losses. Not only did the interest of the British public spike under such circumstances but colonial governments, anxious to consolidate their power, were significantly more likely to extend patronage to artists and photographers in the aftermath of conquest, in order to document post-conflict diplomatic processes, survey 'discovered' antiquities and map new territories.[46] Empire thus became most visible to the British during its moments of crisis, when the tectonics of power threatened to shift under the pressure of border wars, insurgencies, invasions or the military-diplomatic hybrid of the imperial 'mission' sent to negotiate with foreign courts.

Myriad forms of pictorial material – journalistic, ethnographic, topographic, diplomatic, military – thus arose in response to international crises. Edward Said's well-known words from *Culture and Imperialism* (1993) continue to resonate: 'the struggle over geography ... is complex and interesting because it is not only about soldiers and cannons, but also about ideas, about forms, about images and imaginings.'[47] Yet when Victorian 'images and imaginings' have been considered in scholarship, they have generally been examined in a compartmentalised manner according to colony, event, genre, medium or style; there has been no extended study that looks to analyse the intersections of new forms of mass visual media and more traditional realms of the fine arts in shaping Victorian visions of their empire.

This book thus follows Deborah Poole's approach to the 'visual economy' of the Andean 'image world' by considering diverse forms of aesthetic practice 'as part of a general economy of vision.'[48] Only such an approach can yield a proper understanding of the centrality of empire to Victorian culture – more specifically, I suggest, it is only through such an approach that we can begin to appreciate the extent to which that culture was increasingly laced with colonial violence. Victorian visions of imperial war and peace emerged in a feedback loop with protean and evolving sovereign formations, but they also formed in the crucible of the new colonial military doctrine of counter-insurgency, a particularly violent method of conflict that came to be known as 'savage warfare'.[49] Graphic and photographic media raised different affective and ethical issues about such military engagements; any understanding of the Victorian perception of colonial violence is thus incomplete without considering its vexed inscriptions across multiple aesthetic registers.

This book does not claim to be a comprehensive account – it focuses on British imperialism in Asia from about 1850 to 1900, while recognising that the processes of colonisation were also deeply intertwined with image-making practices in other parts of the world, with artists and photographers responding to specific political and cultural exigencies. But I do aim to produce a transnational account which is sensitive to the visual strategies that helped the Victorians to maintain sovereignty over a longstanding imperial territory like India, as well as the ad hoc artistic interventions (in situations both military and diplomatic) into surrounding regions. I am concerned, then, with how Victorian visions of the imperial world system managed to encompass both formal imperial possessions governed by colonial British administrators and territories that were not (yet) under direct imperial control or which were ambiguous in their sovereign status, such as Afghanistan, Burma, China and Tibet, as well as the semi-autonomous 'princely states' of the subcontinent. The dynamics of settler colonialism in the 'White Dominions' and the vicious imperial landgrabs associated with the 'Scramble for Africa' raised their own issues about how to represent imperial sovereignty and its logics of violence, but these are outside the scope of this study. The visual politics of such imperial modes, while having much in common with the material examined here, were subject to particular discursive, aesthetic and political regimes that warrant in-depth consideration of their own.

ART HISTORY OF EMPIRE

The discipline of art history has recently experienced what Natasha Eaton has termed an 'Imperial Turn'.[50] Following decolonisation in the mid-twentieth century, the married couple of Mildred Archer, a curator of the Print Room at the India Office in the British Library, and W. G. Archer, a one-time officer in the Indian Civil Service and Keeper of the Indian Section at the Victoria and Albert Museum, together engaged in extensive work cataloguing the art of the Raj, whose visual archives had come to rest in the pair's respective London institutions.[51] As noted by Tim Barringer, Geoff Quilley and Douglas Fordham in their introduction to a 2007 collection of essays on art and empire, the Archers' writings, while valuable, are best conceived as '*late imperial* rather than post-colonial documents, in which the official language of mid-century art history shields a tender elegy for a lost empire.' Barringer, Quilley and Fordham called instead for imperial concerns to be brought in from the margins of art historical scholarship in a manner that 'destabilises stock assumptions' about the story of British art and of Britishness, which, far from being insular phenomena, were in fact always marked – in aesthetic, economic and political terms – by the imperatives of global imperialism.[52]

Subsequent art historians, spurred by postcolonial theory's concern with 'cultural hybridity', have shown that British art and identity were deeply affected by the imperial context.[53] The impact of the Empire on Victorian culture was perhaps never more visible than in the 'world-as-exhibition' approach embodied by the World's Fair and also apparent in an assemblage of museums and public exhibition spaces that together functioned to enshrine an imperial world-view. Such institutions were not passive receptacles of global goods but the beneficiaries and the exponents of a highly interventionist imperial agenda, not only through the aggressive practices of archaeological excavation, rapacious trade and ethnographic collecting that fed the complex in the first place, but also through government-funded programmes that sought to implement the perceived lessons of the objects.[54]

Following the success of the India Court at the 1851 Great Exhibition, for instance, Indian design became fundamental to the curriculum of the South Kensington Museum, founded the following year. From this new institutional base, the Victorians created a pedagogical network in India via which it sought to refashion Indian artisanal labour practices and thus 'save' traditional industries from the cheap mass-produced imports coming from (and here things became a little awkward) Britain itself.[55] The British thus sought to counter the culturally emaciating effects of their own imperialism by positioning themselves as custodians of the very arts that their empire was responsible for destroying. Yet British ambivalence about Indian art ran even deeper than this: colonial attitudes oscillated between a desire to use colonial art schools to preserve native craft and a wish to spread European artistic techniques as part of a broader 'civilising mission'. The complex and contested nature of such art institutions has been the subject of numerous in-depth treatments by scholars who have pioneered a transnational approach to the history of British and Indian art and highlighted the agency of the aesthetic within both colonial and anti-colonial politics.[56]

This book is indebted to – and it proceeds from – the findings of such institutional critique. But, as the chapters progress, I increasingly move beyond the relatively structured frameworks of the art school and the museum in order to assess how practices like sketching and photography mediated embodied colonial interactions in an expanded field. While scholars have subjected eighteenth-century colonial artists like Zoffany and Hodges to theoretically complex treatments,[57] accounts of colonial artists working in India and its borderlands in the nineteenth century have so far remained largely summary, with little interrogation of the agency of image-making practices as a significant zone of political encounter and a means of shaping the contours of conquest, pacification and imperial statecraft.[58]

The exception to this is Romita Ray's complex study of 'picturesque' visions of India. Complicating Jeffrey Auerbach's influential thesis that the picturesque style of landscape painting functioned to 'homogenise' the diverse territories of the British Empire by submitting them to standardised visual schemata, Ray reveals the picturesque to be an unstable and hybridised expression of colonial identity. Not just a feature of landscape conventions, the picturesque aesthetic functioned as a 'mobile repository of cultural values, beliefs, and imaginings ... a dynamic and portable constellation of ideas and interventions, its concepts and paradigms enmeshed in the unpredictability and open-endedness of travel.'[59] I follow Ray in emphasising the role of aesthetics in shaping 'the phenomenological experience of colonial geography', but I wish to consider different political geographies from the ones she analyses so well.[60] Rather than the relative stability of the colonial capital's urban landscape or the cultivated tranquillity of the English-style garden, I am interested in the fractious borders of the Empire and the moments of rupture within it. These crises of sovereignty rendered the very existence of bodies on contested sites a peculiarly fraught (beyond the already charged symbolism of white colonial bodies in Asia) and peculiarly newsworthy phenomenon.

What did it mean to experience such historical events in the shadow of image-making technologies? I believe that the answer to this question is not exhausted by the colonial apprehension of 'picturesqueness', although this was undoubtedly a core aspect of the imperial imagination. The artists and photographers who chronicled conflict and rapprochement – mobilised by newspapers, governments or simply their own entrepreneurial aspirations – deployed diverse and overlapping visual strategies, from detail-obsessed realism to the grand conventions of classical history painting, in order both to record and mould colonial experience. Aesthetic genres shaped expectations of how to process and manage international events while foreclosing the possibility of them taking shape in alternative ways for participants.[61] The 'becoming-historical' of an event is, Lauren Berlant suggests, a function of its capture by genre conventions, which, 'amid pervasive uncertainty', stabilise contingencies and provide a horizon of expectation for 'ideology, normativity, affective adjustment, improvisation and the conversion of singular to general or exemplary experience.'[62] It is such moments of capture that I seek to explore here, instances when visual practices interpellated the colonial experience of geopolitical upheaval.

Yet such image-making activities also shaped the perceptions of the Indian, Afghan, Burmese, Tibetan and Chinese peoples who, having witnessed an intervention into their homeland, were also therefore exposed to the acts of sketching, photographing and painting that followed in its wake. The extent to which such subaltern experiences can be recuperated from the imperial archive has been a key concern of South Asianist historiography: 'even as the impossibility of recovery is articulated,' writes Anjali Arondekar, 'the desire to add and fill in the gaps ... remains.'[63] The approach I take in this book – reading the visual archive as an index of image-making events – is perhaps particularly susceptible to this desire, for it conceives of the material not only in terms of pictorial motifs but as traces of embodied encounters, thus raising questions that touch on issues of corporeality, subjectivity and agency. What was it like to be posed on sites of colonial violence in moments of counter-insurgency? What was the significance of watching an image of oneself emerge slowly from the visual technologies of an invader (be it a glass-plate wet-collodion negative or an oil painting), knowing that the resulting portrait would circulate in imperial visual networks? How did such processes impact the sitters' own conceptualisation of their political status – and safety – within the imperial order? Such questions provide some of the recurrent concerns – and epistemological problems – of the following chapters.

CHAPTER OUTLINES

This book begins with an account of the 1850s as a transformative historical moment in the development of the modern spectator. Chapter One shows how, in spite of the 1851 Great Exhibition's emphasis on fostering peace, the following decade witnessed the militarisation of British spectatorial culture. An influx of images of international conflict – made possible by the new technologies of photography and the illustrated press – caused the British to reflect on the role of vision in the comprehension and conduct of war. The chapter considers how the Crimean War and the Indian Uprising were exhibited in London and how the critical responses to such wars entailed an evaluation of the role of naturalistic representation and close visual scrutiny in fostering a modern subject capable of understanding conflict – and engaging with it – without becoming overwhelmed by it. Vision was increasingly posited as the privileged means through which warfare could be rendered intelligible. More than this, when practised in accordance with Victorian values of empiricism, vision was a key precondition for exercising agency within a situation, enabling the Victorian subject to interpret properly the information of, and to stage interventions into, global war.

Chapter Two, 'Mutinous Vision: Indian Photography, Colonial Insurgency and the "Civilising Mission"', shows how Britain's faith in the military value of certain ways of seeing led to anxiety over the enemy utilising photography, which embodied the Victorians' empiricist ideals. I tell the story of Ahmad Ali Khan, an educated Lucknawi architect and amateur photographer who joined the Indian rebels against the British during the 1857 Uprising. A rumour spread in the colonial press that Khan was using his photographic practice against his colonial foe, producing a form of visual reconnaissance that not only posed a military threat but also disrupted supremacist Victorian narratives that pitched British rationality and progress against Indian superstition and technophobia. I thus situate these rumours in terms of a broader wartime breakdown in imperial hegemony. The British were haunted by the prospect that photographs of them and their fortresses were circulating among hostile insurgents; yet in order for this to be a threat at all, the British had to grant a level of ocular sophistication and rationality to Indians which had previously been denied to them under the guiding assumptions of colonial art schools and the wider 'civilising mission' that those institutions embodied.

Colonial anxieties over insurgent photography were the by-product of the rising British excitement over the potential of photography to represent reliably – and even shape the outcome of – a military campaign. Yet photography's engagements with Victorian warfare were not without controversy. As Chapter Three, '"Additional Horrors": Photography, Colonial Violence and the Archive', demonstrates, the new technology negotiated a complex and evolving ethical and military terrain. Over the late nineteenth century, spectacular displays of violence became increasingly fundamental to what colonials termed 'savage warfare', yet such performative brutality remained under-represented in the photographic medium compared to the pencil-based war reportage of artists. I explore the peculiarly fraught ethical resonance of photographing military violence, drawing on the most extreme examples from the camera's early history. Photography's engagement with the killings and punishments of colonial populations pushed against the limits of acceptability and legality for the Victorians. In doing so, it created a body of imagery that was the source of both intense excitement and deep anxiety for colonials, and which remains an ethically and politically sensitive subject matter for post-colonial scholars, publics and archives.

Chapter Four continues to explore the visual consumption of colonial violence from the perspective of the graphic arts. 'Sketching "On the Spot": Shaping the Victorian Experience of Colonial War' considers the phenomenon of the 'special artist' sent out by newspapers like the *Illustrated London News* to produce visual reports in the field. Such artists relied on what I term an 'epistemology of exposure', in which the authenticity and accuracy of their images was the product not of Cartesian detachment but of their embodied immersion in the cut-and-thrust of a military campaign. I am interested in the effect that such journalistic immersion had on colonial soldiers' perception of combat, suggesting that the processes of image-making – in which soldiers sometimes even staged tableaux vivants for the benefit of artists sketching in the field – structured perceptions of warfare's hardships and violence.

Overall, however, violence is often conspicuous in its absence from the visual archive of empire. The Victorians' favoured official means of representing their imperial project was not by recourse to an imagery of aggression – no matter how important its place in the visual economy of the press was becoming – but through an aesthetic of diplomacy. It is towards such an aesthetic that Chapter Five, '"Save Me From My

Friends!": The Art of Diplomacy in the Age of its Technological Reproducibility', turns. Here I consider the phenomenon of the imperial diplomatic embassy and its associated rituals of power, which relied on a series of aesthetic conventions rooted in European history painting that were designed to transmute violent conquest into a vision of gentlemanly ethics and cross-cultural consent. The process of posing for artists and photographers was an important part of imperial diplomatic theatre, helping to mark the transition from a state of war to a state of peace. Picturing the event became part of the event itself: diplomatic rituals occurred in a complex feedback loop with commemorative acts of image-making. This chapter involves an in-depth engagement with what Ariella Azoulay terms the 'event of photography', assessing how cross-cultural encounters with the camera and its images documented, instantiated and dissolved imperial sovereignties.[64]

The shaping of events by the processes and products of image-making – the ways in which the actual or potential presence of visual technologies like the camera and the artist's pencil increasingly constituted the Victorian experience of waging war and making peace – remains a key thematic concern of the following chapters. Also subject to such processes were the local populations of invaded regions, whose early experiences of British imperialism were often characterised by their exposure to the varied practices of visual fieldwork. Chapter Six, 'Negative Histories: Encountering Colonial Photography "in the Field" in Burma, China and Tibet', considers colonial photography from the perspective of the technical procedures necessary to prepare, expose and stabilise light-sensitive compounds in the field. This, I suggest, was how the colonised often encountered imperial photography: not in terms of static positive prints but as a durational performance of chemical and corporeal processes that yielded spectral images defined by their delicate and singular materiality as salt-paper negatives or collodion glass-plates. I consider what it meant to encounter photography via such negatives, suggesting that their delicate yet volatile chemistry catalysed interactions between self, other and environment that challenged Victorian photographic fantasies about the camera as cannon (the instantaneous 'shooting' of docile bodies) and the photograph as mirror of nature (a transparent reflection of the real).

The ability of colonial discourse to objectify and 'other' colonised populations has been well documented in scholarship but the efficacy of imperialism as a mode of governance was not just about constructing divisive racial hierarchies; it was also dependent on imagining shared political horizons. The final two chapters therefore consider the visual strategies used by the British, with varying degrees of success, to conceptualise and construct their multiracial empire as a workable political entity. 'Specimens, Suspects, Citizens: Photographing an Imperial Polity in Cawnpore' focuses on an album produced by the amateur photographer Dr John Nicholas Tresidder in the aftermath of the near-total annihilation of his colonial hometown, Cawnpore, amid the vicious Anglo-Indian violence of the Uprising. I argue that Tresidder's photography attempted to play a palliative and socially reconstructive role; he used the medium to process the racial violence that had deeply scarred the colonial community. More broadly, this chapter explores the visual politics of imperial citizenship, situating Tresidder's photographic survey of his British and Indian neighbours and colleagues in Cawnpore in terms of a recurrent liberal desire for a mode of imperial belonging that transcended the Victorian racial taxonomies that were deeply entrenched in imperial thought.

In the final chapter, I ask what it means for the aesthetics of an imperial regime to fail. In the aftermath of 1857, colonial governance in India had become increasingly wedded to the logic of the spectacle, with the grand 'coronation durbars' of 1877, 1903 and 1911 seeing the British adopt neo-feudal rituals and symbols of power. Yet the 'visual turn' of imperial governance was, I suggest, always haunted by failure, even or especially on its own terms. Focusing on the vast official group portrait of British and Indian rulers produced by Valentine Prinsep for the 'Imperial Assemblage' in 1877, I show that the pageantry of empire, far from consolidating power, registered instead as a crisis of governance. The colourful heterogeneity of the Indian rulers' dress stood in contrast to the monochromatic palette that dominated Victorian portraits – an aesthetic uniformity that had worked to picture a fractious parliamentary system in terms of an overarching national unity. A key reality of empire – highly visible cross-cultural differences – therefore undermined acceptable aesthetic conventions for picturing political systems, detonating the visual cohesiveness of an imperial project that had just turned to spectacle to help it envision stability.

In their fetishisation of hierarchy and their emphasis on collective performance, Julie Codell writes, such imperial spectacles 'anticipated the mass political rallies of European totalitarianism and the aestheticisation of politics in the modern world'.[65] The art of running an empire in the latter half of the nineteenth century meant navigating a complex feedback loop between events and the visual technologies deployed to document them, as the processes and products of image-making embedded themselves more and more into the fabric of geopolitical experience, providing the coordinates for interpretation and action in fraught moments of international crisis.

1 · EXHIBITING GLOBAL CONFLICT

Metropolitan Spectatorship and Military Sights from the Crimean War (1853–1856) to the Indian Uprising (1857–1858)

THE WELL-TO-DO VISITORS STARING DOWN THE BARREL OF HEAVY artillery at the Military Court of the International Exhibition in London in 1862 (see fig. 1) arrived at the display as a different kind of spectator from the crowds who had first admired global art and industry at the Crystal Palace a decade earlier. 'That generation may be said to have had a dream of peace', said the historian Sir Henry Maine in his Cambridge lectures on international law in 1887, 'It seriously believed that wars had ceased; strife in arms was to be superseded by competition in the peaceful arts ... But the Temple of Peace had hardly been removed when war broke out, more terrible than ever.' The Crimean War, the Indian Uprising, the Franco-Austrian War, the American Civil War: 'Not only is war to be seen everywhere, but it is war more atrocious than we, with our ideas, can easily conceive.'[1] While the Great Exhibition had signalled the birth of a modern culture of consumerist spectacle, it was only in the breakdown of that show's geopolitical utopianism that the modern spectator came of age after a period of relative innocence.[2] The new Military Court that greeted visitors in 1862 displayed the dark side of the globalisation that had created the staggering material wealth of the world's fairs. Art had manifestly failed to supplant war, said Maine, but war had become 'the mother of new arts': the 'art of explosives' and long-range guns.[3]

The arrival of weaponry at the World's Fair represented a radical shift in the tone of what Tony Bennet has termed the 'exhibitionary complex'. This privileged sight as an educative tool and had developed in earnest in Britain in the late eighteenth and early nineteenth century; the Great Exhibition was its triumphal expression. It was predicated on the transfer of objects from private collections into public arenas, wherein they could be seen as expressions of national wealth. Art, commodities and machinery were all exhibited as signifiers of progress and

Sir Joseph Noel Paton, *In Memoriam*, 1858 (detail of fig. 11).

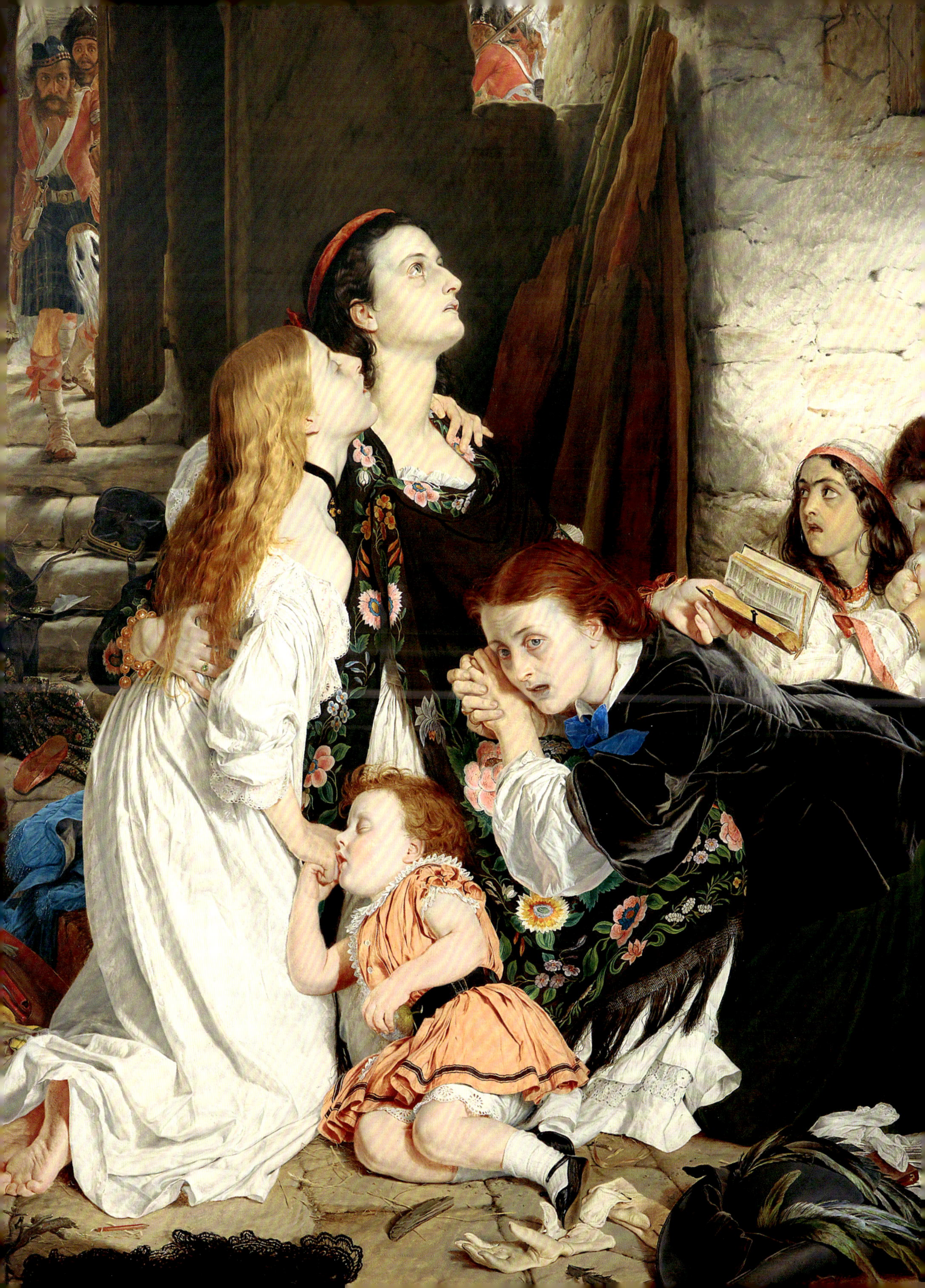

edification; the public display of such material helped to foster citizenship, enabling Britons to 'identify with power'.[4] On a more fundamental level, as Peter H. Hoffenberg writes, such shows were 'about teaching vision and the ways to manipulate the processes and products of sight.'[5] The wide-ranging Victorian preoccupation with the faculty of sight was 'politicoperceptual'; when properly managed, argues Chris Otter, vision 'provided the phenomenological structure' for the rational and self-governing liberal subject.[6] The Victorian spectator was thus not conceived of as passive but was expected to possess the capacity for 'visual discernment' and critical judgement.[7] Yet while such traits were promoted in 1851 as ingredients of global peace, by 1862 they were presented as part of the arsenal of war.

International exhibitions were part of a broader Victorian culture of spectacle, encompassing museums, arcades, department stores, dioramas, panoramas and the popular press. In his visual history of the Crimean conflict, Ulrich Keller identifies the 1850s as the moment at which 'the modalities of cultural consumption, notably spectatorship, began to penetrate and subsume all other social processes, including the conduct of war.'[8] Spectatorship radically altered public perceptions of geopolitical conflict but so too did conflict transform Victorian perceptions of their modern spectatorial culture and its supporting technologies. In 1854 an editorial in the *Journal of the Photographic Society of London* responded to reports that the military intended to recruit a photographer for the campaign in the Crimea: 'Hitherto Photography has flourished as one of the arts of peace, lending its aid to the direct advancement of civilisation in various ways. It seems not unlikely that it may now be pressed into the service of war.'[9] The author's reference to the civilising influence of the 'arts of peace' reproduced the rhetoric surrounding the Great Exhibition; yet here we see how readily such arts could be reframed as military tools.[10] Not just photography, I argue, but wide-ranging practices and discourses of vision were 'pressed into the service of war' in the years following the Great Exhibition. Over the next two chapters I explore how an assemblage of image-making activities and cultures of spectatorship which had once been touted as engines of peace came over the course of the 1850s to be subsumed under a rubric of war.

This chapter begins with a consideration of two important early photography exhibitions in London: Roger Fenton's (1819–1869) photographs of the Crimean War and Dr John Murray's (1808–1898) photographs of sites related to the Indian Uprising. The new visibility of distant warfare in metropolitan spaces prompted critics to reflect on the role played by visual realism in furnishing the spectator with an adequate – and actionable – understanding of conflict. The privileging of vision within the modern epistemology of war was soon to be theorised explicitly by the pre-eminent art critic of the period, John Ruskin (1819–1900), when he gave a speech in January 1858 at the new heart of the exhibitionary complex, the South Kensington Museum. Ruskin adopted a dramatic, clash-of-civilisations rhetoric to condemn the institution: he claimed that the Uprising was, literally, a war between different visions of the world; and the South Kensington Museum, in promoting Eastern-style aesthetics through its Indian collections and associated educational programme, was threatening to tarnish the 'naturalistic' way of seeing that the British relied on to ensure both military and moral victory during times of crisis. The aestheticisation of warfare rebounded as the militarisation of aesthetics within Ruskin's thought: 'It was very strange to me to discover this, and very dreadful', Ruskin later said to an audience of young cadets during an 1866 speech at the Royal Military Academy in Woolwich, '[but] all the pure and noble arts of peace are founded on war.'[11]

DISTANT WAR

Just two years after the Crystal Palace had been hailed as a harbinger of peace, a clash between Russia and the Ottoman Empire in the Balkans raised serious geopolitical issues for Britain. If Russia were to capitalise on the long-term decline of the Ottoman Empire by gaining significant territory in Eastern Europe, then Britain's Mediterranean ports – and more importantly its overland route to its most prized imperial possession, India – would be compromised. The prospect of a fight proved popular with a British public stirred up by a jingoistic press and so, on 28 March 1854, Britain and France (also concerned about the ramifications of Ottoman decline) entered the fray on the side of the Sublime Porte. The Crimean War was the first major European conflict since the Napoleonic era, and soon became what Keller has described as the 'ultimate spectacle', its traumas and triumphs packaged for popular consumption across various forms of old and new media to an unprecedented degree: from panoramas to theatrical re-enactments and from photography to the woodblock engravings of the illustrated press.[12] 'The English government seems to have declared war with Russia expressly for the benefit of the *Illustrated London News*', quipped *Punch*, 'inasmuch as that paper is evidently deriving the greatest advantage from its prosecution.'[13]

The conflict marked a radical transformation of the visual culture of the Victorians and of the public sphere more broadly. This was a new kind of war: 'The newly introduced rifle proved itself to be a formidable weapon; the electric telegraph linked the front line with London and Paris; William Howard Russell of *The Times* emerged as the first recognizable war correspondent; and Roger Fenton became the first war photographer.'[14] An array of technological innovations meant that the campaign was able to be experienced at a distance with more immediacy than ever before: telegraphy, railways and steamships were radically altering the temporality of conflict.[15] With the British public kept abreast of developments in what became an increasingly disastrous military campaign, where ill-equipped soldiers were suffering and dying from hunger and disease in appalling winter conditions, the war – so popular at the outset – quickly became a national political crisis in Britain, and 'a decisive moment in the reconfiguration of the responsibilities of the state to its subjects.'[16] In shaping public opinion against those responsible for the conduct of the war, the popular press played a key role in the collapse of Lord Aberdeen's coalition government in February 1855. Being an informed spectator of geopolitical events was thus to participate indirectly in those very events; reactions of outrage, anger, sympathy or other affective states could be translated into demands for change.

Yet, by the time the Victorian public were introduced to the first photographs of the Crimean War in the autumn of 1855, it was already in its final, victorious stages. Critics thus responded to the imagery in an elegiac mode: 'Men will fall before the battle scythe of war, but not before this infallible sketcher has caught their lineaments and given them an anonymous immortality more lasting perhaps than "storied urn or animated bust".'[17] The most celebrated Crimean photographer, Roger Fenton, was originally a painter who had exhibited many works at the Royal Academy. Impressed by the photographs he saw at the Crystal Palace in 1851, Fenton began experimenting with the new medium and became a founding member of the Photographic Society in London. He escorted Queen Victoria and Prince Albert round the society's first exhibition in January 1854, leading to his invitation to photograph the royal household the following May. Such establishment ties have raised questions over whether his aim in Crimea was to present a positive vision of the campaign to counter the shocking missives of the war journalist William Howard Russell,[18] whose articles in *The Times* had described dismal wartime conditions in which 'the wretched beggar who wanders about the streets of London in the rain, leads the life of a prince, compared with the British soldiers who are fighting out here for their country.'[19]

Fenton's presentation of the war differed widely from such graphic textual descriptions. He tended to show well-equipped and well-clothed soldiers in relaxed poses (fig. 7) and depicted officers such as Lord Raglan – much criticised in the press for his murderous incompetence as a leader – engaged in dignified council with his French and Ottoman counterparts (fig. 8). Even Fenton's most dramatic photograph, *Valley of*

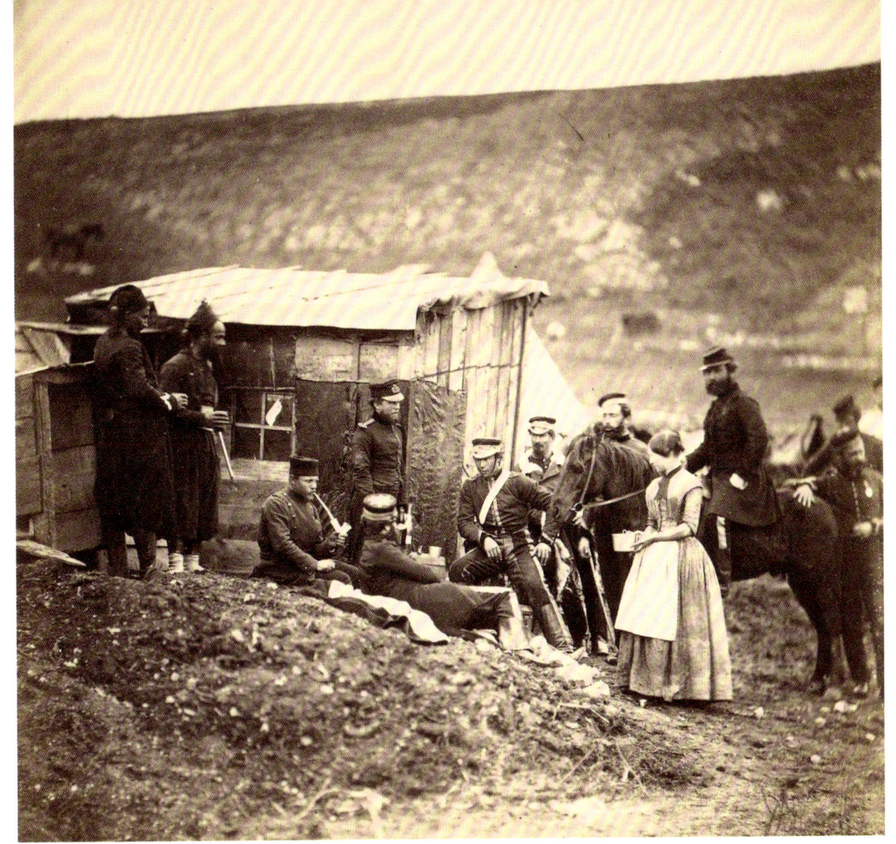

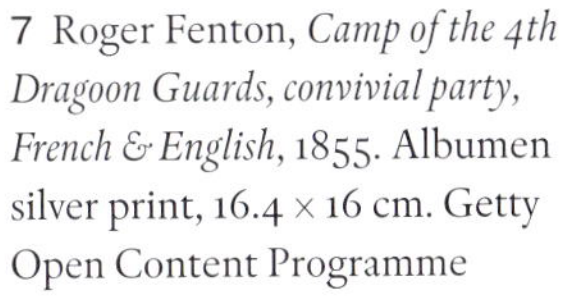

7 Roger Fenton, *Camp of the 4th Dragoon Guards, convivial party, French & English*, 1855. Albumen silver print, 16.4 × 16 cm. Getty Open Content Programme

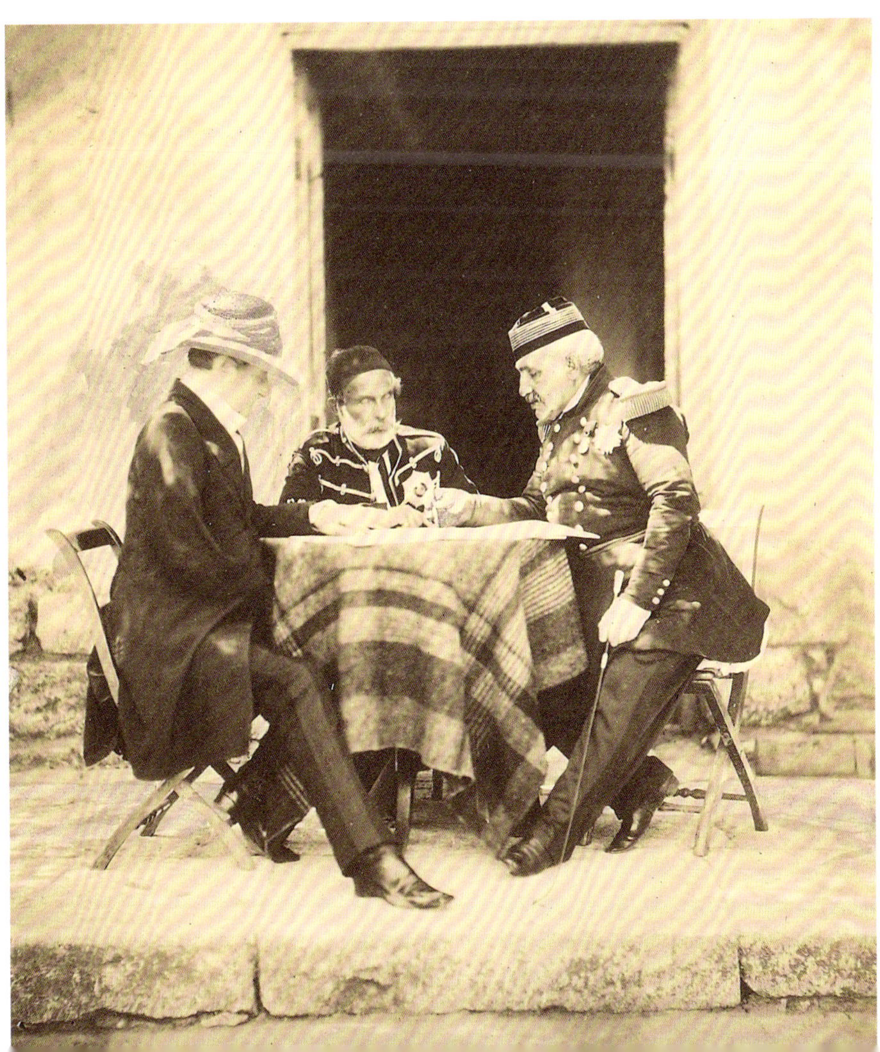

8 Roger Fenton, *The Council of War held on the Morning of the taking of the Mamelon*, 1855. Salted paper print, 18.4 × 15.6 cm. Getty Open Content Programme

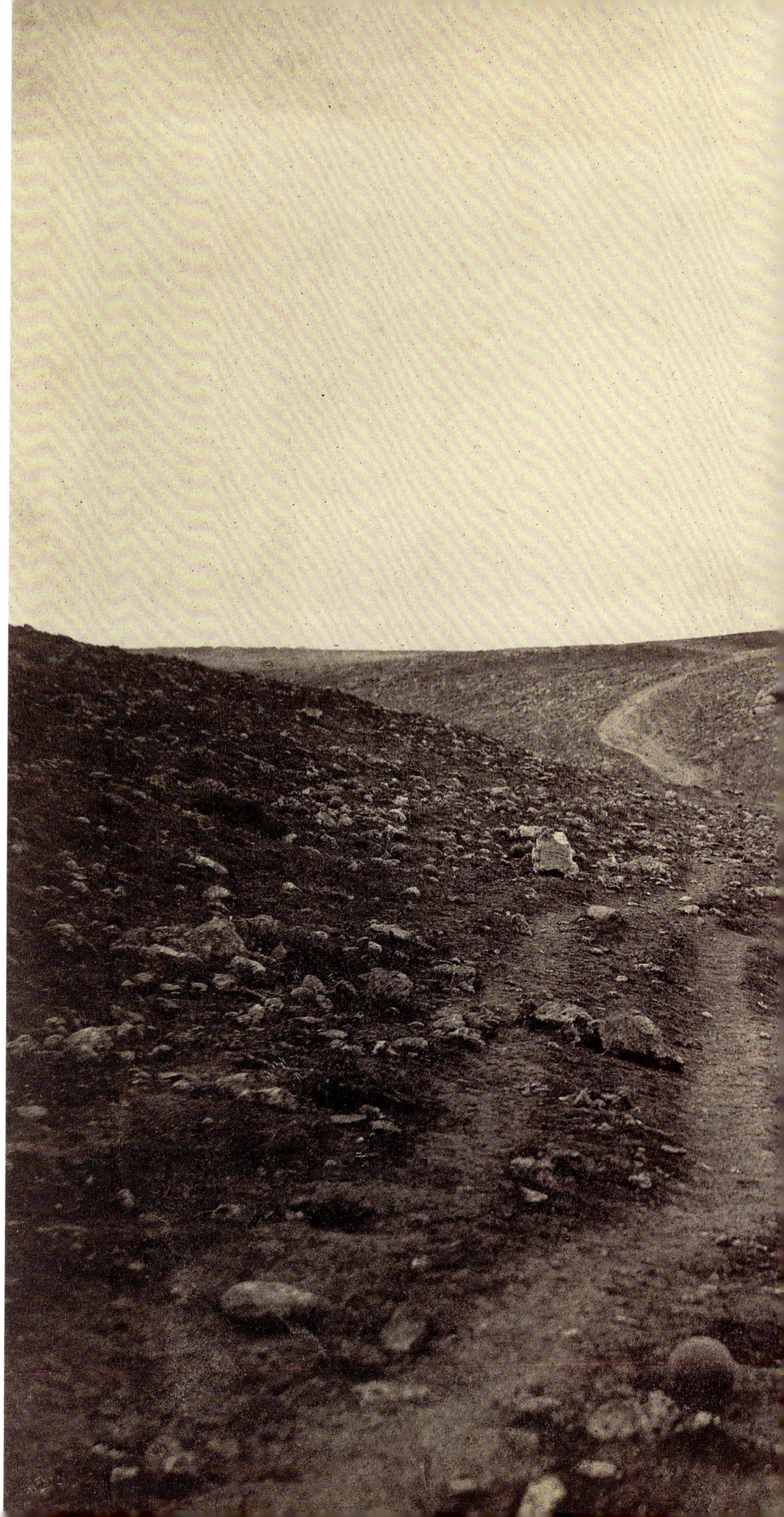

9 Roger Fenton, *Valley of the Shadow of Death*, 1855. Salted paper print, 27.6 × 34.9 cm. Getty Open Content Programme

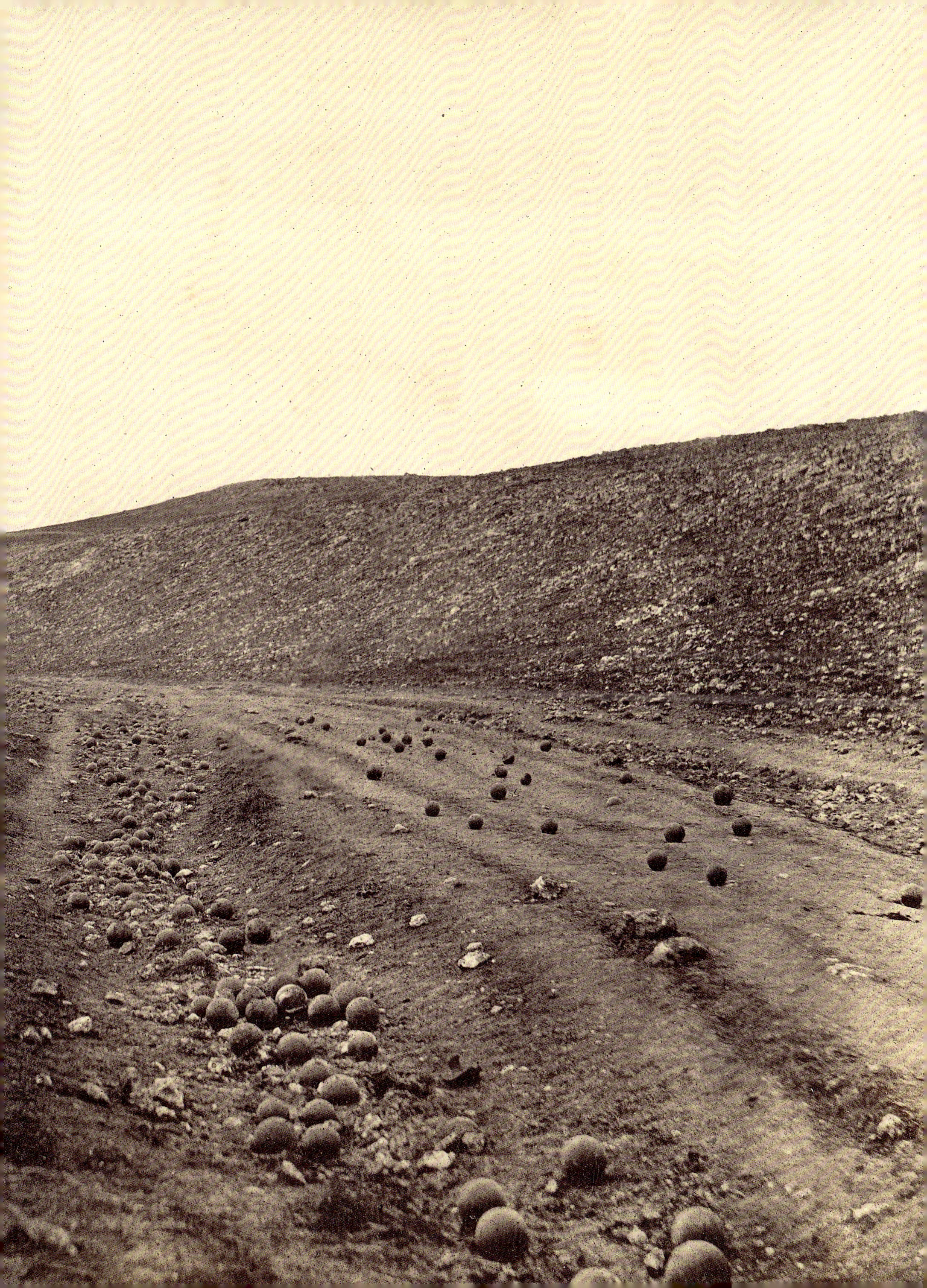

the Shadow of Death (fig. 9), shied away from displaying actual casualties, opting instead to show an empty and barren track littered with deadly projectiles. Yet in spite, or perhaps because, of this departure from the negative account of the war popularised by Russell's reports, Fenton's images met with considerable acclaim when they were exhibited at the Water Colour Society at Pall Mall in September 1855. The photographs, wrote *The Athenaeum*, were 'more interesting than the finest works of imagination, though they had the colour of Titian and the tenderness of Raphael.'[20]

VISUAL EPISTEMOLOGY

The real value of Fenton's photographs of the Crimea lay not in their aesthetic appeal but in their supposedly unparalleled status as historical records: they were 'perceived as independent and unmediated facts'.[21] Faith in photography's value as evidence which 'we cannot doubt' was tied into a broader cultural investment in the notion of visual detail serving as a guarantor of veracity.[22] The 1850s was an important decade in the development of the Victorian culture of realism; it was during these years that the term 'realism' was first used as a descriptor for literature, while the style of war journalism pioneered by Russell in the Crimea 'shared complex representational norms with the realist novel', presuming the same audience 'united by education, reading habits, and a state of technological modernity'.[23] Realist fiction also shared representational norms with photography; as Nancy Armstrong noted, the realist novel was essentially 'photographic' in nature in that it 'equated seeing with knowing and made visual information the basis for the intelligibility of a verbal narrative.'[24] The two media were mutually constitutive.

War photography thus emerged from within a culture that increasingly sought to make detailed seeing a precondition for ascertaining the truth of a situation. Fenton's photographs were said to enable an unprecedentedly accurate understanding of a historical event because of their capacity for revealing detail: 'Fur, leaves, hair, pebbles, miles of stony plain, recesses of mountain slopes, far, near, sky, sea ... history illustrated by the certainty of a reporter who never blunders.'[25] The agency of Fenton as an author of these images was alluded to but mostly in the context of celebrating his ability to work under adverse wartime conditions; as far as the meaning of the photographs went, 'the Victorian audience', wrote Jennifer Green-Lewis, 'did not presume a teller, nor did it feel it was being told something; it supposed itself, rather, to be directly witnessing the action, as though through a window or mirror.'[26] To metropolitan viewers these photographs offered a new phenomenology of war, one in which indexical visual detail conferred a poignant aura of immediacy and intimacy.

What sort of spectator emerged from such visual encounters? Histories of photography and of modern cultures of spectacle more broadly have tended to emphasise their oppressive nature: in a pessimistic Foucauldian vein, such practices have been seen in terms of the constraints they imposed on intellectual and political freedom, with a pervasive specular matrix producing fairly benighted subjects who were entangled in an increasingly complex web of surveillance and reified social hierarchies. Yet photography was not only experienced as repressive; the modern spectator emerging in the Victorian era was not seen as passive in the face of the rising visual onslaught – indeed, their scrutiny of images provided a site for the exercise of critical judgement. In his recent account of early Victorian photography, Jordan Bear has argued that such 'visual discernment' was a 'key mechanism through which the relative agency of individuals in society was negotiated'.[27] Being a spectator was a critical practice. The rest of this chapter considers how visual prostheses such as photography extended the capacities of sight, understanding and agency – and how, under the pressure of geopolitical violence, such capacities were given a military inflection.

THE INDIAN UPRISING

Visual coverage of the Crimean War should be seen in the context of a broader, global surge in illustrated reportage of conflict. The founding of the *Illustrated London News* in 1842 had created an unprecedented demand for representations of warfare. While European war held a particular fascination when it arrived in 1854, British consumers were already familiar with images of conflict through the newspaper coverage of colonial insurgencies such as the Ceylon Insurrection (1848) and the Santhal Hul (1855–6) in north-east India.[28] The Crimean War both broadened and popularised the visual culture of conflict and produced the new point of reference for future visual coverage, so that, when the Indian Uprising erupted in May 1857, it was not only the images of earlier South Asian insurgencies that governed Britain's aesthetic response to the 'mutiny' but also the visual strategies deployed in Crimea. This was the case even at the level of personnel: Felice Beato, who had been a photographic assistant to James Robertson during the Crimean War, made his way independently to India to capitalise on the colonial crisis; the war artist William 'Crimea' Simpson did the same.

The initial rebellion of Indian sepoys (soldiers) which had taken place at Meerut on 10 May was first reported in Britain in *The Times* on 27 June. Even by telegraph – in which detail was necessarily sparse – news took at least six weeks to arrive from India, whereas more lengthy despatches had to be sent by sea and took almost three months.[29] While the technological complex of steamships, railways and telegraphy had meant that the earlier Crimean War appeared to augur a transformed metropolitan experience of international conflict – characterised by a new abundance of up-to-date information – the war in India seemed to revert back to an older experience of distant war, characterised by a lack of detailed reports from the field and a corresponding abundance of rumour. Wild reports of torture, rape and mutilation supplemented verifiable accounts of mass killings, leading the *Illustrated London News* to complain that 'it happens not infrequently that the telegrams tell one story, and the newspapers and private correspondences received a few days afterwards contradict, or put a different interpretation upon it.'[30] The result of the time-lag was 'an almost unbearable anguished aspect of the situation' for the British public which Christopher Herbert has argued led to the extraordinary outpouring of emotional discussion about the revolt, as people sought to overcome the 'maddening remoteness of events.'[31]

One photographer able to take advantage of the desire for reliable information concerning the Uprising was Dr John Murray. Murray had joined the colonial medical service in the 1840s and had subsequently become one of a number of skilled amateur photographers operating on the subcontinent in the early years of the medium. He first started practising photography in 1849, although the first extant images of his are from 1855. It was from this batch that he selected photographs to be displayed in London in 1857, having by chance found himself on furlough in Britain as reports of the Uprising began to arrive.[32]

Murray's photographs – consisting mostly of architectural studies from Agra, where he worked as a surgeon – proved popular.[33] On 1 December 1857 a series of thirty salt-paper prints was published by Joseph Hogarth, who evidently still considered Murray's photographs to be of marketable interest two years later, when he published a further twenty-five of them.[34] Such was the ubiquity of Murray's work during the war and its aftermath that by the time some of his images were shown at the 1861 *Architectural Exhibition* on Conduit Street, the *Saturday Review* wrote that they have 'been so often engraved and described that they cannot lay claim to the same degree of interest' as the other views of India exhibited.[35] Beato's more grisly Indian photographs (which have become well-known to early histories of photography and will be discussed in Chapter Three) were not published in Britain until 1862, four years after the war.[36] Murray's work thus provided the primary means through which photography shaped the public understanding of the Uprising in Britain as the crisis unfurled.

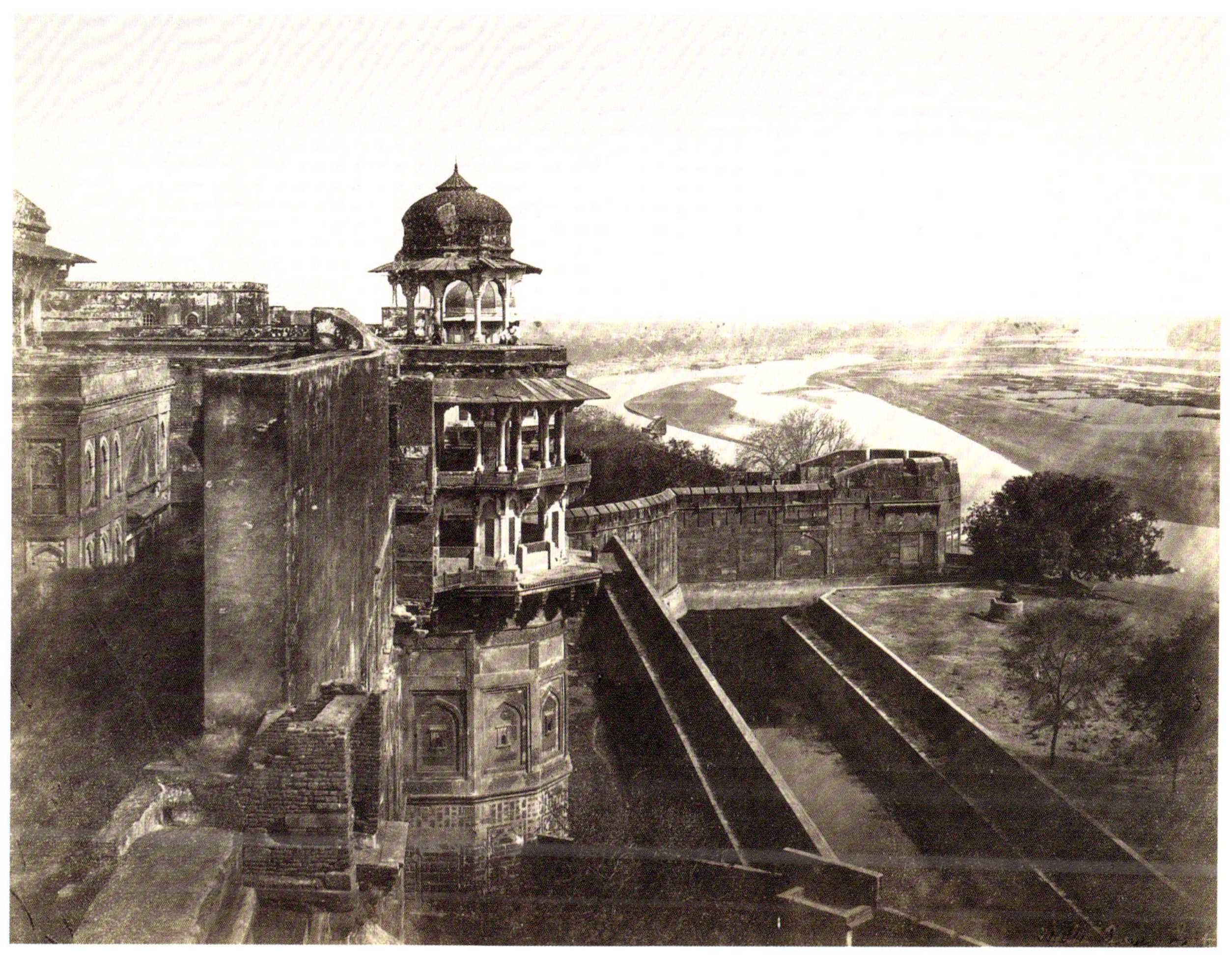

10 Dr John Murray, *The Samman Burj in the Fort-Palace in Agra*, 1855. Salt-paper print, 35.1 × 45.3 cm.

The images were exhibited at Hogarth's Art Rooms, 5 Haymarket, London, in November 1857. While they were not 'war photographs' as such – they were taken prior to the outbreak of hostilities – critics nevertheless invoked Fenton's Crimean photographs as a pertinent lineage for the show. Murray's photographic studies of Indian architecture should be seen in the context of a wider imperial interest in ethnographic surveys, for this was a time when the colonial government was starting to favour the new medium for the work of cataloguing Asian antiquities. Yet photographs such as *The Samman Burj in the Fort-Palace in Agra* (fig. 10), while initially produced as an Orientalist study of architecture, developed some disturbing military resonances for viewers in London. With the depicted Agra Fort now protecting British colonials from attacking Indian armies – six thousand colonial Britons and their servants were reportedly under siege at the time of the show – such a photograph was less significant as an architectural profile of the lavishly ornamented tower in the centre of the scene and more notable for its inclusion of the defensive moat and wall that separates that structure from the surrounding landscape.

So, while Fenton's Crimean images had been received by critics as memorials of a war whose main dramas were already concluded, Murray's photographs entered a public discourse that was racked with anxiety and uncertainty regarding the outcome of conflict. The exhibition space was consequently an emotionally charged environment for metropolitan viewers deeply unsettled by the reports emanating from India; one critic wrote of seeing the photographs 'through a blood-red haze'.[37] Yet such high emotion was mostly subdued by close looking. Noted for their size ('very large, being eighteen by fifteen inches'), the photographs were approached by critics with magnifying glasses in order properly to inspect the details captured by the camera.[38] This ostensibly dispassionate engagement with the visual data worked to ameliorate public anxiety over the viability of the defences of Agra Fort, as the cool, empirical appraisal of detail worked to counteract the 'hallucinatory stylistic register' of public discourse on the Uprising.[39]

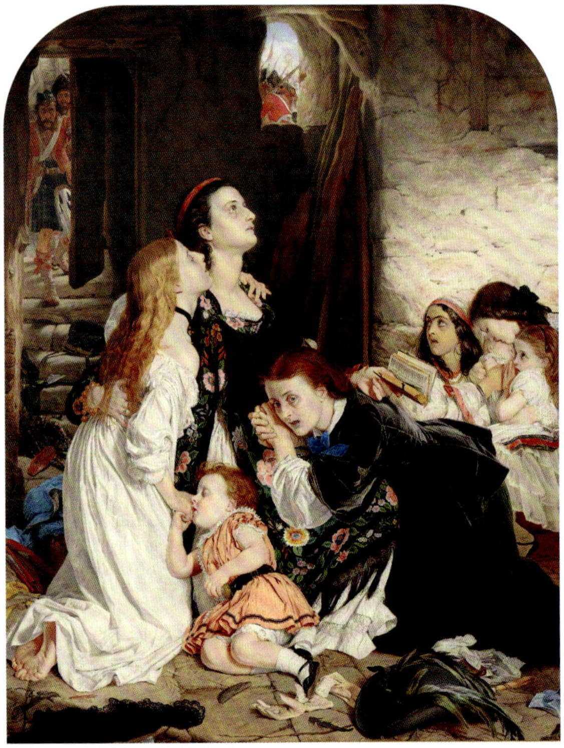

11 Sir Joseph Noel Paton, *In Memoriam*, 1858. Oil on canvas, 123 × 96.5 cm. Private collection

REALISM AND HISTORICITY

Scholarship about images of the Uprising seen in Britain while the war was still raging in India has tended to focus on the controversy surrounding Sir Joseph Noel Paton's entry for the Royal Academy exhibition in London in May 1858.[40] The artist's *In Memoriam* (fig. 11) initially showed a group of Indian sepoys entering a building inside which some distraught and wan-looking British women and children were huddled together in fear, prayer and familial embrace. It thus conjured memories of the slaughter at Cawnpore (Kanpur) the previous summer when, after a gruelling three-week siege, a group of colonials had surrendered to the rebel leader Nana Sahib, after receiving assurances that they would be allowed safe passage up the Ganges to Allahabad. On boarding the boats prepared for them by Nana's men at the Satichaura Ghat, however, the British were massacred. Those who were not killed instantly were captured and the remaining men executed.

It was what happened after this that etched Cawnpore into the memory of the British. The women and children who had been captured following the initial massacre – about two hundred of them – were not executed alongside the men. Instead, they were imprisoned for days in a nearby bungalow, the 'Bibi Ghar' or 'House of the Ladies'. A rescue mission of British troops was soon dispatched to liberate these captives. As it made its desperate and unforgiving way through the Indian countryside – summarily hanging anyone suspected of links with the insurgency as it went – word got back to rebel leaders in Cawnpore. A panicked order was issued to kill the colonial prisoners but, beyond firing a few volleys into the crowded house, the Indian sepoys charged with doing this were too horrified by the task to see it through. In the end, less scrupulous local butchers were brought in to finish the job, hacking hundreds of women and children to death with their meat cleavers. The victims' bodies – both dead and dying – were then thrown into a nearby well.[41]

Against such a traumatic historical backdrop, Paton's decision to deploy detailed realism to bring the catastrophe to the walls of the Royal Academy provoked considerable discomfort. The critic for the *Art Journal* had this to say about commemorating such a troubling and recent event:

> The work presents a concentration of intensity that we rarely witness upon canvas. The appalling details of the murder of our countrymen are yet so fresh in the memory that any mere allusion to these fiendish atrocities cannot be borne without a shudder. What, then, must be the feeling on contemplating a picture like this, representing with all the subtlest cunning of Art, a party of these poor ladies and children awaiting their fateful doom? which appears to be instant, because the sepoys are now rushing into the cell. We are tempted to wish that the picture were less signal in its excellence ... And it is entitled 'In Memoriam' – be it so; it is not painted for the present generation – half a century hence, when the dreadful subject has become a matter of history, it will then more becomingly – though not even then regarded without a shudder – serve the purpose for which it appears to have been painted.[42]

This, then, was a subject still too raw to contemplate. Paton subsequently countered these accusations of insensitivity by repainting an area of the scene, substituting Highlander troops for the Indian figures that had been encroaching ominously on the female sanctuary. This alteration served to transform a historical depiction of impending slaughter at the hands of Indian sepoys into a fantastical one of imminent rescue by colonial soldiers; as a French critic lamented, Paton was 'anxious to spare the nerves of his fair and tender-hearted spectators ... [with] a mere delusion'. 'The painting's photographic realism', writes Julia Thomas, 'ultimately subverts its historical realism'.[43] When depicting warfare, the reality-effect was no slave to factual accuracy; it was a means of navigating volatile wartime sensibilities in a style of objectivity.

Murray's autumn exhibition of photographs, while less sensational than the controversial version of *In Memoriam* which Paton exhibited the following spring, nevertheless had the same grisly massacre as a key point of reference. It consequently provoked a similar ambivalence towards the historicity of events. Reports on the Cawnpore atrocities had dominated coverage of the Uprising through the month of October 1857, demonstrating the potentially disastrous consequences of a broken siege for colonial Britons. Murray's November show did not include photographs of any sites from Cawnpore itself but it offered multiple views of another site of siege. The defences of Agra Fort, which was then protecting colonials from a potential repeat of the Cawnpore calamity, were laid bare before the eyes of gallery-going Londoners. Here, amid all the feverish written reports of the Uprising, was an indexical link to events.

The reviews are curiously summary in their discussion of the Agra siege, however, swinging instead from general statements about the 'important and painful events of the Indian insurrection' to laudatory descriptions of Murray's 'rendering [of] the minute prospects of some of the finest cities.'[44] The *Morning Post*, for instance, after a brief allusion to the photographs representing 'notable scenes of the war', proceeded to catalogue the 'minuteness of architectural detail' in the images: 'the quality and texture of the stone ... the elaborate carvings, the arabesqued ornaments, and the costly inlaid work with which the Eastern architects delight to decorate their buildings.' When the reviewer describes a photograph of Agra Fort it focuses on the architecture in a similar fashion ('the material is sandstone, the prevailing colour being a strong brick red, contrasting harshly with the white marble employed in the construction of some of the buildings') and concludes with a formal description of the photographs ('now golden brown, anon of a rich reddish sepia hue, now grey and lucid, presently almost of a black Indian ink lustre').[45]

Obsession with photographic detail may have served as a distraction from troubling realities. As Steve Edwards has written, the 'sentence that appears utterly dazzled' by the minutiae of a photograph reads 'as if microscopic details exhausted consciousness, filled it to excess, so that no room was left for reflection.'[46] As the most traumatic episode of the war, the Cawnpore massacre constituted a sufficient stimulus for a retreat into minutiae. Yet for these critics, I suggest, visual scrutiny was not a means of avoidance; rather, it enabled them to interpret current events against the historical grain. For this was not the first time the British had been involved in a siege in Agra. As J. Middleton, the Principal of the East India Company's College at Agra, noted in a booklet written to accompany Murray's album (published a few weeks after the opening of the exhibition), the building had been taken 'with little difficulty' by Lord Lake during the Second Anglo-Maratha War (1802–3). Such praise for Britain's past military prowess in India also implied the inadequacy of the very fort that now protected the British, causing Middleton to arrive at an ambivalent conclusion: 'Defended by Englishmen it is perhaps impregnable; though against them of no great strength.'[47]

Visual scrutiny of the photographs, however, yielded a more optimistic assessment than was perhaps justified by the historical record referenced by Middleton. At least some of his scholarship was also used in the November show itself, since the *Morning Post*'s exhibition review repeated verbatim some of the description of Agra Fort later printed in the December booklet; yet if Middleton's captions for the exhibition did mention the ease with which the fortress had once been captured, then the very same paper chose not just to ignore him but flatly to contradict him, stating it 'stood a long siege before it was taken by Lord Lake.'[48] This was a historically dubious assessment. The 1803 Siege of Agra had lasted only two weeks before the British claimed victory, whereas during that same war Lake had also laid siege to Bhurtpore, where he was kept at bay for three months before finally withdrawing altogether. Despite this, however, in every review in which the 1803 siege was mentioned, it was the factually inaccurate but consolatory story of a sturdy fortress withstanding a lengthy assault that was propagated.

How to explain this? The critics, it seems, were making inferences from the evidence of their own eyes. The *Morning Advertiser* advocated the kind of visual epistemology that had also characterised earlier reviews of Fenton's Crimean photographs, asserting that 'a greater amount of knowledge of the actualities of the Indian war can be gained from the study of these views than from any amount of written description';[49] the *Morning Post* provided an inventory of the fort's defences and concluded that it 'is a place of considerable strength';[50] the *Literary Gazette* wrote that 'Within that serried and multiplied rampart of walls, finished at the top with palisading ... our beleaguered countrymen will be quite safe';[51] and the *Art Journal* backed up its questionable military history with visual description: '[it] stood a long siege before it was taken [by Lord Lake]; it is built of red sandstone, occupies a considerable area, and is enclosed by a ditch ... it may readily be believed that it is sufficiently strong to repel a numerous attacking force.'[52]

Vision – at least when aided by photographic evidence – was thus posited as the privileged means of comprehending warfare, even as it entailed a notable disregard for the actual historicity of events. It was claimed that the 'military man' could use Murray's images 'as if he studied reality', making them 'a great service to a party attacking, showing as they do, for instance, in the view of the fort of Agra, the defence within defence which exist.'[53] Through the seemingly unmediated access to the reality of war provided by photography, the spectator could adopt the perspective of 'the military man', making their own assessments of their compatriots' safety via the inspection of visual features from sites of an ongoing conflict. Viewers were thus invited to decipher the evidence of war in relative synchronicity with the war itself. Statements celebrating the photographs' potential value as reconnaissance reveal a desire to use photographic evidence less as a means to understand events that were already past but as a way of furnishing information that could enable interventions into, or forecasts about, current campaigns. The spectator was not a passive witness to an already settled history, then, but an active interpreter of events.

SIGHTS OF WAR

A couple of months after Murray's exhibition – and with reports on the Uprising beginning to bring welcome news of British military success – the influential art critic and social commentator John Ruskin gave a speech at the South Kensington Museum, in which, echoing the reviewers, he asserted the centrality of vision in the epistemology of war. Events in India, he claimed, had revealed a nexus of vision, agency and morality that contained important lessons for institutions like the South Kensington Museum, whose mission it was to educate the public through artistic pedagogy and visual display. Inside the new museum were stored many of the Indian artefacts that had first been displayed at the Great Exhibition; such material formed a key part of the emerging curriculum of art and design here, a curriculum that would be transported to India as teachers from South Kensington took up positions in the colonial art schools on the subcontinent. Ruskin used his lecture as an opportunity to launch a sustained indictment of the type of spectator that he believed was constituted by those collections.

Was it not, after all, Indian modes of vision and visuality that had paved the way for atrocities like Cawnpore? Oriental aesthetics, Ruskin averred, gave rise to 'treachery, cruelty, cowardice, idolatry, bestiality, – whatever else is fruitful in the work of Hell'.[54] His argument was this: Indian art was prey to abstraction and conventionalised forms rather than naturalism, and as such it had turned its back on a God-given reality. Given this unholy retreat from the world, it was liable to corrupt both the sight and the soul of those who were unfortunate enough to become habituated to its aesthetic mores. The presence of Indian objects in the South

Kensington Museum was therefore problematic for the institution's didactic ambitions. His summation of the pernicious effects of India's non-naturalistic aesthetics was damning:

> To all the facts and forms of nature it wilfully and resolutely opposes itself ... the people who practise it are cut off from all possible sources of healthy knowledge ... they have wilfully sealed up and put aside the entire volume of the world, and have got nothing to read, nothing to dwell upon, but the imagination of the thoughts of their hearts, of which we are told that 'it is only evil continually'. Over the whole spectacle of creation they have thrown a veil in which there is no rent. For them no star peeps through the blanket of the dark – for them neither their heaven shines nor their mountains rise – for them the flowers do not blossom ... They lie bound in the dungeon of their own corruption, encompassed only by doleful phantoms, or by spectral vacancy.[55]

Since Indian art had no secure anchoring in the world, its viewers were apparently prey to a malignant solipsism. As Tim Barringer has written, for Ruskin, the 'dissembling conventions of Indian design all-too-easily mutated into the disloyal designs of the mutinous Sepoy.'[56]

In other words, Ruskin was accusing the South Kensington Museum of encouraging a way of seeing that was laced with immorality and violence. The Indian artefacts lurking in British collections were dangerous, threatening to undermine the rationality of vision that was presupposed by the exhibitionary complex, functioning instead 'to summon and send forth, on new and unexpected missions, the demons of luxury, cruelty, and superstition.'[57]

Ruskin was far from disinterested in this assessment. The abstraction of Indian art stood in contrast to the 'go to nature' strictures that he had been preaching in his own writings for more than a decade.[58] The moral challenge that the critic launched against the South Kensington Museum was thereby motivated in part by a desire to position his own work in favourable relation to the war in India, which was being discussed by many commentators in terms of a Manichean battle between Indian savagery and British civilisation. If Indian art had an immoral agency, not only could the South Kensington Museum's exhibition of such art be seen as inviting 'the hasty degradation of our country', it could also be reasonably assumed that other types of art – Ruskin's sort of art – might have a countervailing, moral effect.[59]

Ruskin capitalised on the unseemly associations between Indian aesthetics and violent insurgency by moralising – but in the process effectively militarising – his own advocacy for naturalism. He situated 'naturalistic' ways of seeing at the heart of the counter-insurgency operation in

India. Yet while the critic believed strongly that it was to the Highlander soldiers that Britain owed most for their colonial victories, on his recent trip to Scotland he had been struck by the country's lack of art of any sort. To circumvent this issue, Ruskin attributed to the Scots an intrinsic closeness to nature that supposedly mirrored the kind of communion with the world that was achieved through artistic naturalism: 'You will find that all the highest points of the Scottish character are connected with impressions derived straight from the natural scenery of their country'. This connection is revealed, Ruskin argues, by the rugged cliff in the Highlands that is called 'Craig Ellachie' by the local clan, who supposedly see in its 'scattered pines' and 'flush of heather' a potent symbol 'of the influence of that country upon themselves.' In a military twist, Ruskin claims that this love of nature is 'beautifully indicated in the war-cry of the clan, "Stand fast, Craig Ellachie."' Ruskin even imagines this war cry of naturalism bellowing across Indian fields 'darkened with blood' to give 'strength' and 'indomitable courage' to Scottish soldiers amid 'the hailing of shot and the shriek of battle'.[60]

With some conceptual acrobatics, then, Ruskin aligned his aesthetic theory with the suppression of the insurgency. He believed that his naturalistic ethos had a powerful moral agency that was 'protective and helpful to all that is noblest in humanity.'[61] Yet within this moral vision was an implicit economy of martial utility. The sort of sight that emerged from Indian aesthetics was not just spiritually unsound, it was completely incompetent, involving the '*destruction both of intellectual power* and *moral principle*'. As such it stood in contrast to the perspicacity that supposedly emerged from British aesthetics:

> as the ignoble person, in his dealings with all that occur around him, first sees nothing clearly, – looks nothing fairly in the face, and then allows himself to be swept away by the trampling torrent, and unescapable force, of things that he would not foresee, and could not understand: so the noble person, looking the facts of the world full in the face, and fathoming them with deep faculty, then deals with them in unalarmed intelligence and unhurried strength, and becomes, with his human intellect and will, no unconscious nor insignificant agent, in consummating their good, and restraining their evil.[62]

Abstraction thus leads to a weathervane existence; a person rendered 'ignoble' by their detachment from the world also suffers an erosion of critical faculties and individual agency, becoming a pawn in events that they fail to grasp. Naturalism, by contrast, gives rise to clear seeing and the calm exertion of 'intelligence' and 'strength' amid the 'torrent'. In the context of a speech that sought to reveal the aesthetic underpinnings of 'your victories in the Crimea, and your avenging in the Indies', Ruskin effectively conscripted the virtues of naturalistic vision for military service.[63]

When critics of the Fenton and Murray exhibitions had fixated on photography's visual detail and celebrated its privileged ability to bequeath knowledge of events to the attentive spectator, they were already practising what Ruskin came to preach: a militarised vision that sought to navigate the vagaries of war using the ocular techniques and pictorial technologies of realism. For Ruskin, though, the role of visual practices in times of war went beyond producing detailed and reliable representations of events; aesthetic cultures shaped a person's perceptual abilities, moral proclivities and agential capacities, determining the very parameters of the Victorian subject. Ultimately, for Ruskin, this theory accounted for Britain's global supremacy as a proponent (the South Kensington Museum's curriculum notwithstanding) of a culture of naturalism. While this book does not subscribe to Ruskin's racialised aesthetic framework, it does share with the critic a belief that the Victorian response to crises like the Uprising was shaped profoundly by the surrounding image culture, whose conventions provided the terms in which war and peace were perceived and, for those swept up in events, navigated on ethical, affective and practical levels.

CONCLUSION

As a result of the international crises of the 1850s, the modern bourgeois subject was increasingly positioned in explicit relation to imperial violence. Engagements with distant conflict led to a broader reflection on the utility of vision to the Victorian 'military man'.

This militarisation of vision ultimately had reverberations in the 1862 International Exhibition in London, in which, out of all the countries on display, Britain was 'the only one which has attempted anything approaching a full and complete exhibition of its implements of war.'[64] The 'exhibitionary complex' – whose communal viewing practices had helped to constitute the modern Victorian subject – was invaded by an emerging military complex. It was thus displaying precisely what the Great Exhibition's 'Temple of Peace' had once sought to overcome or at least keep hidden from view: signs of global warfare that revealed the 'dark side' of capitalist modernity's spectacle of progress and prosperity. If the exhibitionary complex was about inculcating a way of seeing and being – teaching visitors a particular geopolitical vision of the world – then the nature of that pedagogy shifted drastically between 1851 and 1862. 'Seriously,' wrote a critic of the latter show, 'there is no avoiding warlike works; and alas for the fact!'[65]

2 · MUTINOUS VISION

Indian Photography, Colonial Insurgency and the 'Civilising Mission', *c.*1857–1859

THE MOOD OF CALCUTTA'S COLONIAL POPULATION DURING THE Indian Uprising was bleak. A mutiny of Indian sepoys against their British officers in Meerut in May 1857 had escalated dramatically into a widespread insurgency against the century-old rule of the East India Company (EIC). Calcutta remained under British control but, as insurrectionary violence spread throughout the northern regions, the European residents of the colonial capital started to see evidence of rebelliousness everywhere they looked. Gripped by paranoia over a murky Islamist threat, the Rev. Alexander Duff wrote in a breathless register of the city's atmosphere of 'a hundred and one rumors':

> rumors of secret night meetings of the Mohammedans – of fanatic devotees rousing the ignorant multitude to rise up and murder the enemies of their faith ... of suspicious-looking characters prowling about the houses of Europeans in the dark ... of intercepted letters said to specify the plan to be adopted, and the very hour when all Europeans were to be swept away in a deluge of blood.[1]

Rumour was a core element of the Uprising. Whispers of an imperial conspiracy to subvert religious caste had fuelled the discontent of the sepoys, while exaggerated tales of Indian atrocities informed the brutality of British reprisals.[2] This chapter investigates a rumour that was doing the rounds in the tense climate of wartime Calcutta. It concerned an amateur photographer from Lucknow, Ahmad Ali Khan, whose facility with the camera had begun to appear sinister to the British in the light of the insurgency. Before the war, the Bengal Directory had listed Khan as one of the 'Respectable Native Inhabitants' of Lucknow, making him a figure that straddled the fraught social divisions of the colonial environment.[3] Well-educated and friendly, Khan was 'a great favourite with

Ahmad Ali Khan, '[Portrait of] Mrs Lewin [and] Lt Lewin, [Lucknow]', in 'The Lucknow Album', *c.*1856 (detail of fig. 16).

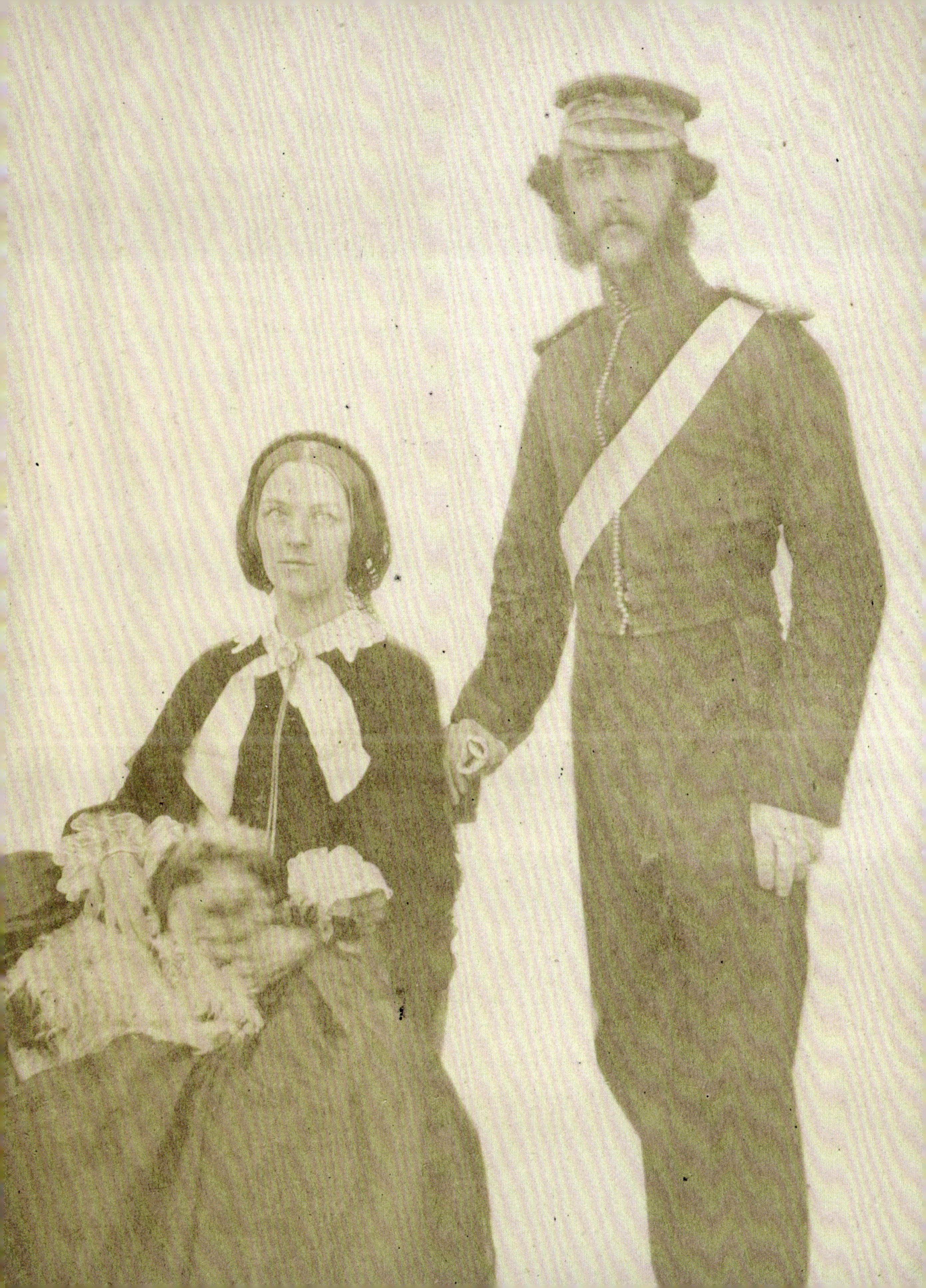

the European residents' in his native city.[4] But when Lucknow revolted, Khan stood with his compatriots against the British, becoming, so a colonial newspaper claimed, one of 'the principal leaders of the Mahomedan section of the rebels.'[5]

Khan's photographs survive primarily in an album of portraits and architectural studies that he produced before the rebellion.[6] The collection was found by the British in the aftermath of the long and destructive battle for the photographer's hometown of Lucknow and was immediately framed by *The Times* journalist William Howard Russell – reporting on the conflict in India after making his name as a special correspondent in the Crimean War – as a 'sad memorial of those who have fallen'.[7] Colonials transformed the album into a mournful palimpsest by the addition of hand-written captions to photographs of people 'killed' and places 'destroyed' in the conflict, thereby situating it within an economy of imperial grief (fig. 12). The evocative surface distortions of Khan's

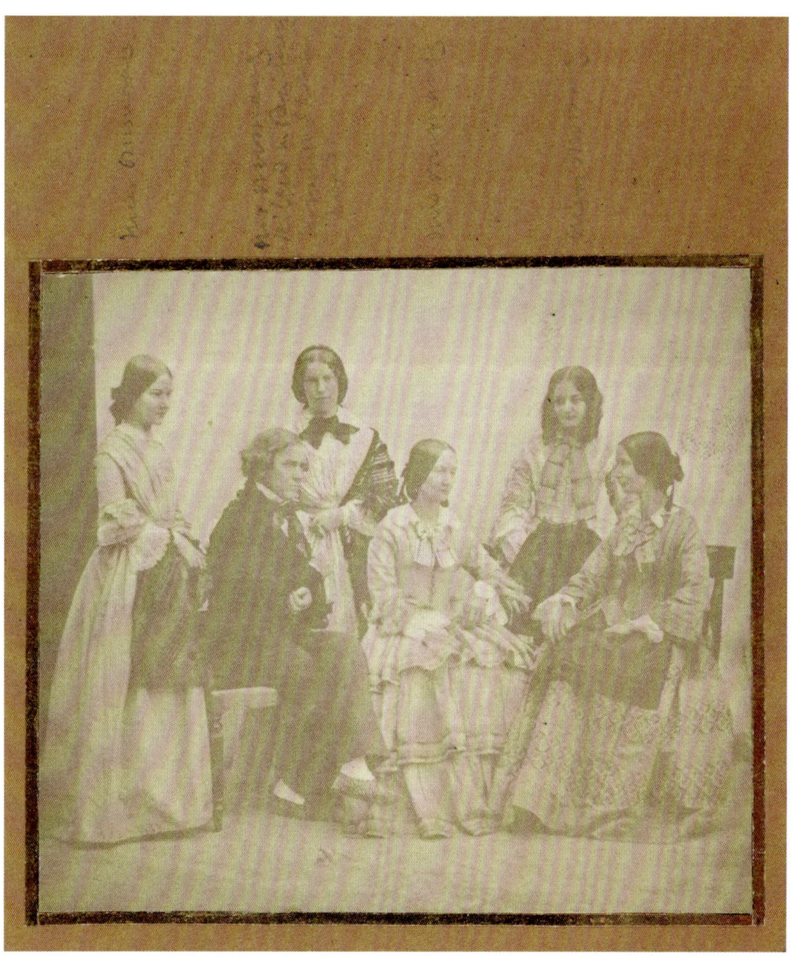

12 Ahmad Ali Khan, '[Group portrait with] Miss Ommaney, Mr Ommaney killed in Residency by round shot in head, [Miss White], Mrs Ommaney, Miss Ommaney [and Mrs Kirk], [Lucknow]', in 'The Lucknow Album', *c.*1856, vol. 1. Salt-paper print. © The British Library Board, Photo 269/1(63)

salt-paper prints and the ghostly, evanescent aura that permeates them are features that lend themselves well to such narratives of bereavement, as Alison Blunt has noted.[8] Yet Khan's photography was not just a spur for imperial meditations on loss.

Khan's decision to join the rebels raised the prospect of an anti-colonial mode of photographic practice. It was said that Khan was putting his proficiency with the medium to 'practical account' by handing over militarily useful pictures to the notorious rebel general behind the Cawnpore massacre, Nana Sahib.[9] It is difficult to know if Khan actually tried to use photography to help the rebels win the war but in some ways this is beside the point, since, as Jonathan Crary has written of the camera obscura, photography is '"simultaneously and inseparably a machinic assemblage and an assemblage of enunciation," an object about which something is said and at the same time an object that is used.'[10] At the level of discourse, if not always at the level of practice, photography became a vehicle for British anxieties about being exposed to the enemy during this time of crisis, as well as for their fantasies of future revenge. When some of Khan's images were shown during a Photographic Society of Bengal meeting in Calcutta in February 1858, for instance, the president of the society 'informed the meeting he hoped to soon exhibit a photograph [of Khan] in another capacity' – meaning, it seems, one of him captured or killed.[11]

British venom for Khan is especially notable because nineteenth-century Indian photographers – who, with the exception of Lala Deen Dayal, have received limited attention in scholarship compared with their European counterparts – have been seen by scholars as relatively unproblematic for the colonial project. An 'identifiable Indian "counter-photography" does not exist in the first few decades of photographic practice', writes Zahid R. Chaudhary in his account of nineteenth-century photography in India.[12] This chapter seeks to complicate such a view, arguing that, during the tumultuous years of the Uprising, an insurgent form of Indian photography called into question the racial and epistemic hierarchies that underpinned colonial rule. Indian photography became a disturbing lens through which the British glimpsed the limits of the colonial state's hegemony, proving especially problematic for the new range of colonial arts institutions that had emerged since the Great Exhibition of 1851 and were seeking to legitimise imperial sovereignty via the rhetoric of the 'civilising mission'.

INSURGENT PHOTOGRAPHY

Photography was first seen in India at a meeting of the Asiatic Society in Calcutta in October 1839, its invention only having been officially announced in Paris by Louis Daguerre on 7 January and – with an independently developed process – in London by Henry Fox Talbot on 25 January.[13] At one of the early meetings of the Photographic Society of Bengal in October 1856, the Rev. Joseph Mullins complained about the lack of a systematic approach to representing the peoples and cultures of India by photographers, a lament echoed by a judge of the society's inaugural exhibition, who noted the lack of 'castes and costumes' on display.[14] The lament indicates a desire that photography shore up a subject–object divide between colonials and Indians, with the former drawing on visual technologies in order to document and classify the latter – an ethnological project that would shortly begin in earnest with the government-led anthropological photography series *The People of India*. Yet Ahmad Ali Khan complicates this story of colonial epistemic privilege; his photography appeared to position the British as the objects of Indian scrutiny. Such 'epistemic disobedience' undermined British intellectual certainties at the same time as it threatened to facilitate anti-colonial violence.[15]

When Indian sepoys had first disobeyed their imperial commanders on a simmering parade ground in Meerut in May 1857, refusing to bite the new greased cartridges for their Enfield rifles, the British interpreted their motivation as fundamentally pre-modern. A rumour had spread that the new cartridges were coated in beef and pork fat, making them religiously offensive to the Hindu and Muslim soldiers expected to handle them – soldiers who, on killing their officers in Meerut, marched on the ancient capital of Delhi to re-establish the power of an aged Mughal emperor lately reduced to puppet status by the British. The wider causes of the Uprising were complex, ranging from cuts to material privileges for sepoys to resentment over unchecked imperial expansion, but it was the supposedly backward-looking agendas of religious superstition and political conservatism that provided colonials with an initial explanation for the violent Indian rejection of 'progressive' imperial rule.[16]

Reports of Khan's 'practical' insurgent deployment of photography therefore launched a challenge against the imperial narratives that positioned Britain at the vanguard of techno-civilisation in South Asia, upsetting the assumptions inherent in the 'endlessly repeated' colonial claim about India's 'pre-scientific theological mentality'.[17] British belief in the resolutely anti-modern mindset of the rebellion was encapsulated by an anecdote about one condemned Indian soldier who, en route to his own execution, pointed at the telegraph system that had been carrying news of military developments to colonial garrisons with unprecedented speed (telegraphy had been introduced to India just a few years earlier) and denounced it as 'the accursed string that strangles us!'[18] The complexities of the war were thus distilled into a simple tale of (Western)

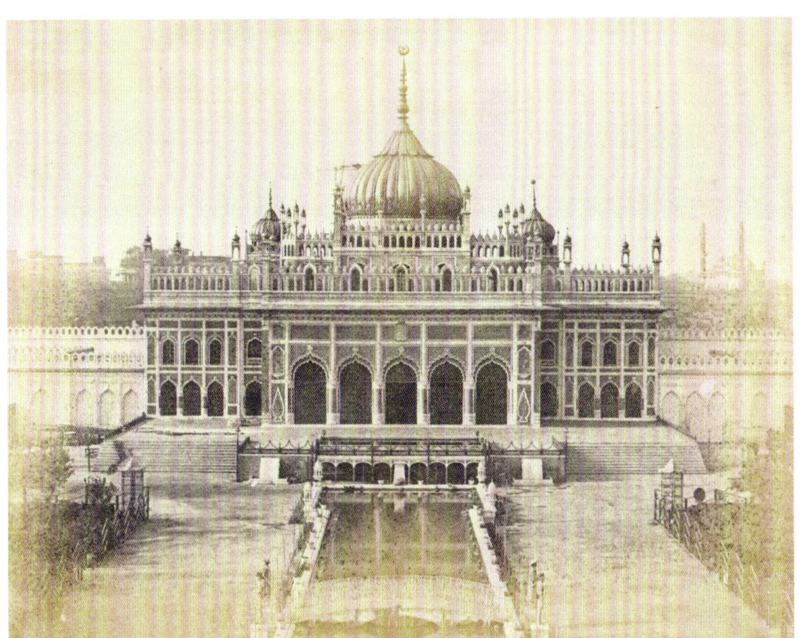

13 Ahmad Ali Khan, 'Husainabad Imambara', in 'The Lucknow Album', *c.*1856, vol. 1. Salt-paper print. © The British Library Board, Photo 269/1(25)

civilisation versus (Eastern) barbarism. By contrast, the insurgency's reported embrace of photography – the most advanced visual technology of the day – prefigures the tension at the heart of recent Anglo-American discourses about Al-Qaeda and the 'Islamic State' (ISIS), which, while cast as medieval throwbacks operating in binary contrast to a progressive Western modernity, utilise cutting-edge visual strategies that severely disrupt the basis for making clear distinctions between the temporalities of religious fundamentalism and secular capitalism.

The camera's strategic role in warfare was still uncertain at the outbreak of the Uprising, defined as much by its perceived potential as by its actual achievements. It had only been placed on the curriculum at the EIC's Military Seminary at Addiscombe, Surrey, in 1855. As Chapter One outlined, the 1850s was a period in which visual technologies like photography underwent a process of militarisation in Victorian thought. During the Crimean War, it was reported that reconnaissance photographs of the contested coastline had been taken from aboard a British ship and that a group of military engineers were 'receiving instructions' in the practice.[19] Yet the ultimate military impact, if any, of such photographic exploits remains unclear. In the Uprising, however, reports emerged that suggested that photography was actively shaping the outcome of the conflict – in favour of the insurgents.

This was most notably the case during the Siege of Lucknow. Home to the court of the Nawab of Oude (Awadh) since the late eighteenth century, Lucknow was an environment that Ahmad Ali Khan had helped

14 Ahmad Ali Khan, 'View of the City of Lucknow taken from the top of the Ferad Bux and looking in a westerly direction', in 'The Lucknow Album', *c.*1856, vol. 1. Salt-paper print. Photo 269/1(31)

15 Ahmad Ali Khan, 'Jama Masjid, Lucknow', in 'The Lucknow Album', *c.*1856, vol. 1. Salt-paper print. Photo 269/1(27)

to nurture: he was credited with the design of the city's Husainabad Imambara (Chota Imambara; fig. 13), under commission from the Nawab of Oude, Muhammad Ali Shah, in the 1830s, and was known locally as the *darogha* (manager or superintendent) of that building. Yet the postwar visual identity of Lucknow became one of rubble and ruin, and Khan was said to have played his part in that as well. It is likely that Khan did not approve of the controversial British decision taken in 1856 to invoke the Doctrine of Lapse, a British decree stating that an Indian ruler forfeited their kingdom if they were 'manifestly incompetent or died without an heir', in order to annex the state of Oude and imprison its allegedly degenerate nawab, Wajid Ali Shah, in Calcutta. Khan had previously been employed as a court photographer for Wajid Ali Shah, producing a series of portraits notable for their combination of Mughal aesthetic traditions and European conventions.[20]

Whatever Khan's personal feeling about the nawab's removal, the EIC's annexation of Oude was a key factor in stoking discontent among the northern ranks of sepoys in the lead-up to the insurrection. Many sepoys hailed from Oude and were aggrieved by its recent treatment. The lavish, courtly city of Lucknow consequently became a central focus of the Indian campaign.

At the start of the war, British soldiers and civilians found themselves besieged inside the Lucknow Residency building. They remained there for a gruelling 148 days, many dying from gun shot and bombardment, others from hunger and disease. This period of grievous hardship quickly became legendary to the Victorians, embodying imperial ideals of fortitude and pluck. By the time the siege was finally relieved by British forces in March 1858 (following an earlier failed attempt), the Residency was a ruin. Reports emerged in Calcutta that Khan had been taking photographs of the makeshift fortress's 'entrenchments and batteries erected for their defence' in order to hand them to insurgent gunners – an action, it was said, that 'fully accounts for the remarkable precision of the enemy's fire, and the partiality with which they singled out apartments into which to pour shot' during the assault.[21] This sophisticated and, reportedly, devastating use of photographs as visual reconnaissance was much more advanced than anything the British appear to have been doing with the camera during this campaign.

No such images of Khan's survive. However, he did have a history of documenting Lucknawi architecture, producing panoramas of prewar cityscapes (fig. 14), as well as studies of individual buildings (fig. 15). The mistiness of these scenes might not appear greatly amenable to the military's demand for clarity and accuracy but such images emerged within an intellectual climate that attributed unparalleled documentary

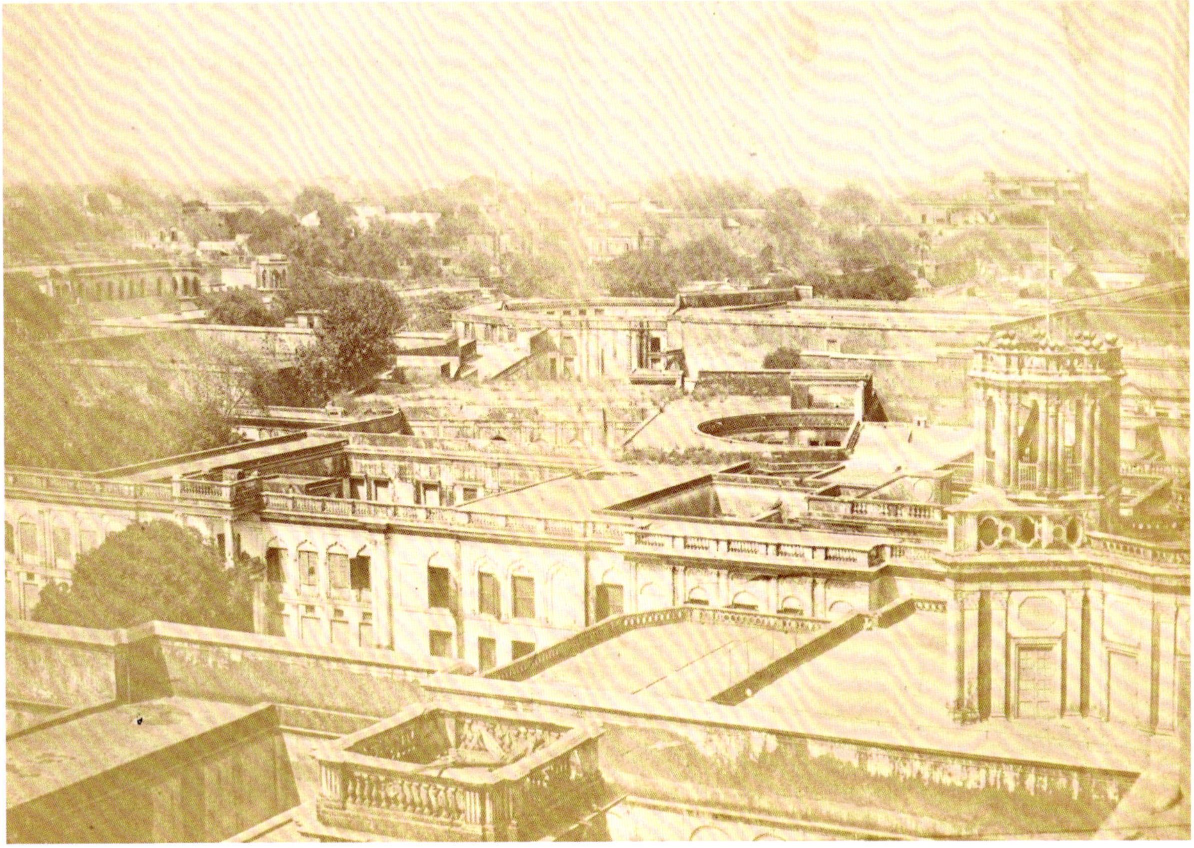

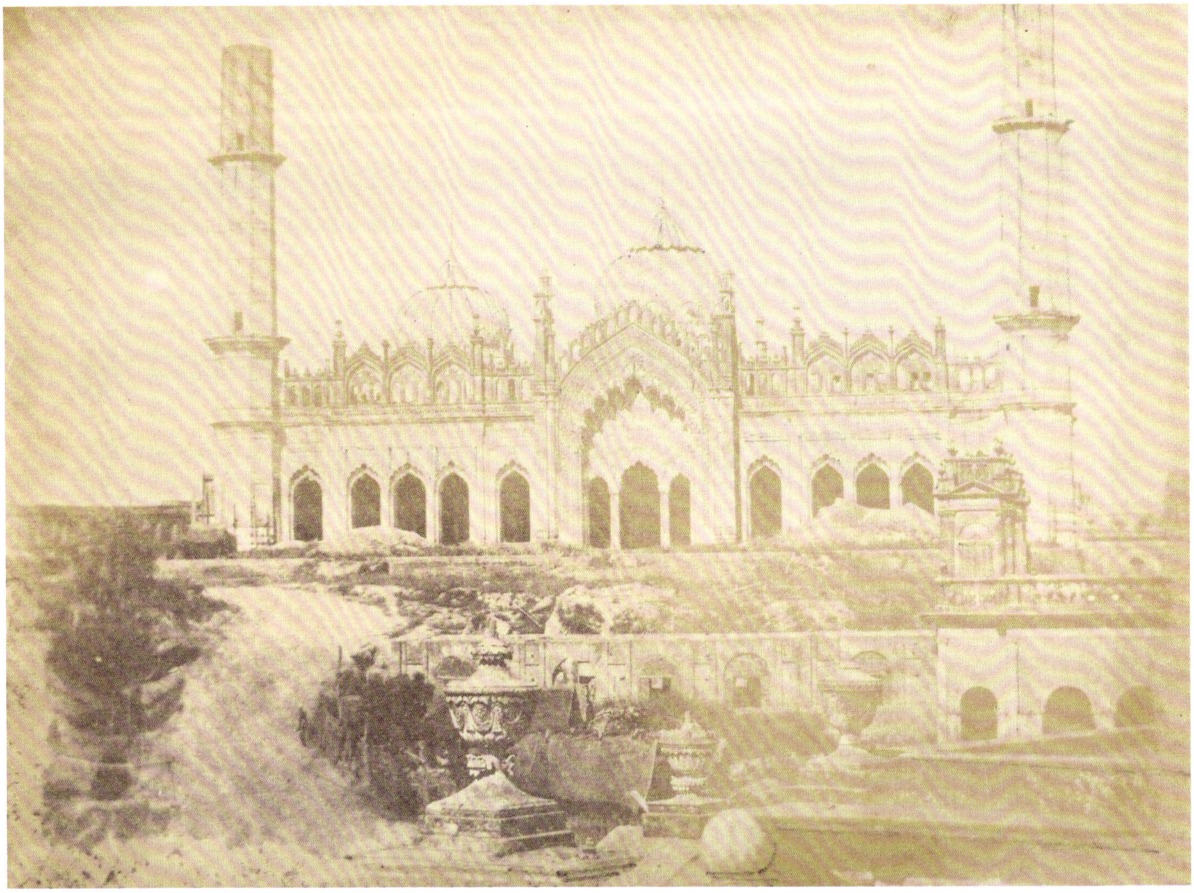

16 Ahmad Ali Khan, '[Portrait of] Mrs Lewin [and] Lt Lewin, [Lucknow]', in 'The Lucknow Album', *c.*1856, vol. 1. Salt-paper print. © The British Library Board, Photo 269/1(69)

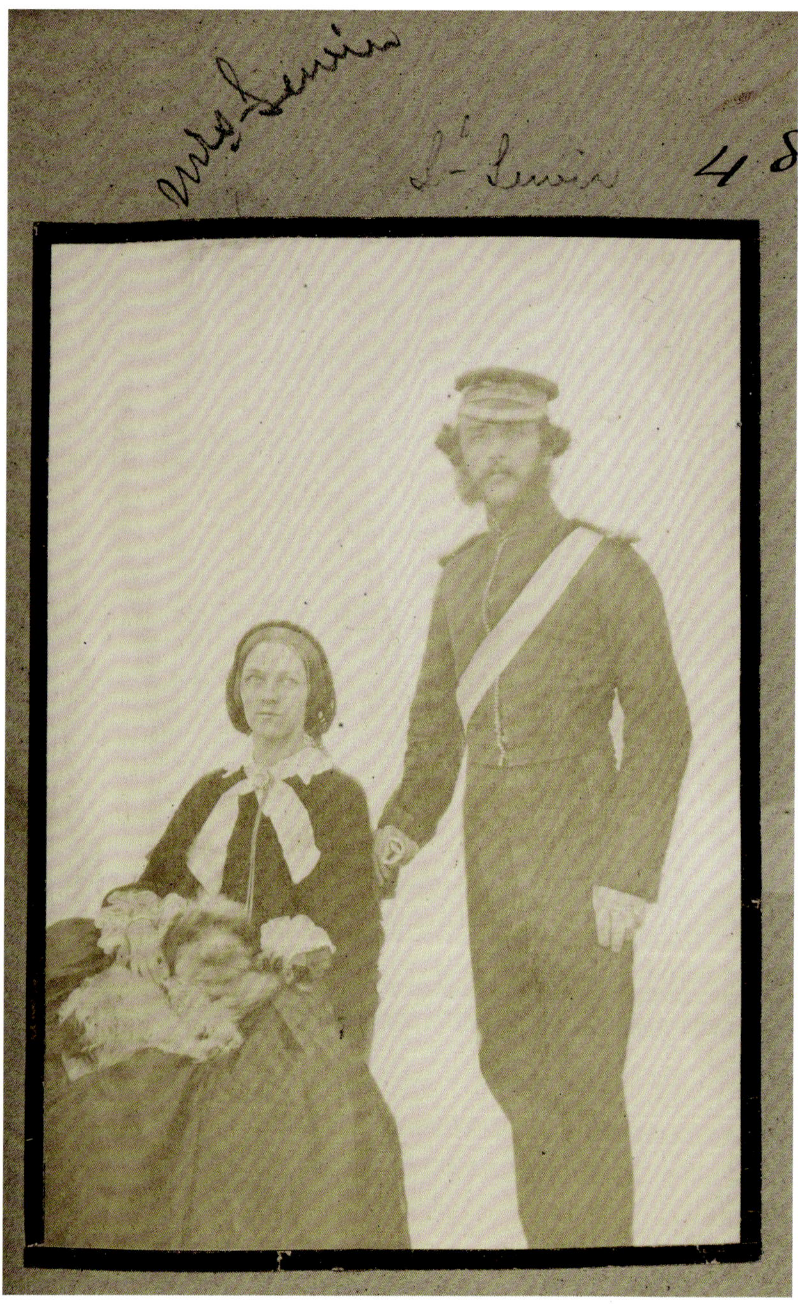

value to the photograph. Khan's activities in this regard mirrored that of contemporary colonial ethnographic photographers documenting similar subjects. In 1857 the Madras Presidency began employing their own official photographer, Captain Linnaeus Tripe, who was charged with the task of delineating sites of historical interest in southern India and who, like Khan, produced salt-paper prints rather than experimenting with the superior clarity of the new and soon dominant wet-collodion process.[22] Khan's photographic endeavours serve to undermine somewhat the rhetoric of imperial rescue that accompanied the activities of photographers like Tripe, since colonial claims to benign cultural paternalism rested on the alleged indifference of Indians to their own material heritage. As Sophie Gordon has written, Khan was committed to a royal vision of Lucknow: his photography 'centres itself on the body of the nawab, sometimes literally through portraits, but more often metaphorically, as represented by [images of] the Chattar Manzil (the seat of royal power) and the Husainabad Imambara (the seat of religious power).'[23] The Uprising thus placed Khan in a peculiar and poignant position: an architect and cultural custodian now helping to wage a destructive war on a city that he had once helped to create and commemorate.

The mere existence of a sophisticated Indian photographer like Khan was disturbing for the British. Even before the war, Khan's photographic practice constituted a fraught imperial 'contact zone' in Lucknow.[24] Khan would have known a good number of the people besieged inside the Residency during the war from his erstwhile practice of offering free portraits to local colonials. Despite his seemingly innocuous, complimentary reproduction of the European-style bourgeois portrait format during these encounters (fig. 16), his photography was still a catalyst for colonial status-anxiety.[25] One British man who died during the Lucknow siege was the city's chaplain, the Rev. Henry Polehampton, who before the war had visited Khan for a portrait and had afterwards complained of how the photographer was 'getting bumptious through having so much notice taken of him. He is the only man in the station who does daguerreotypes, and everyone wants them; so he is becoming an important person.'[26] Polehampton was highly ambivalent: while he saw Khan as 'a very gentlemanly man' who is 'most liberal' and 'takes no end of trouble', the Indian's photographic monopoly at the colonial station was nevertheless a source of troubling social empowerment. '[He] does not take pay', complained the reverend, 'so one has no hold on him'.[27]

Still, while Khan might have been at the forefront of photographic practice in Lucknow, colonials adopted the position of critic. Polehampton believed the portraits 'bad' ('We look like "niggers" don't we?'[28]); Captain John Arthur Bayley claimed Khan 'failed several times' until the colonial sitter had suitably 'explained' things to him;[29] and at a Photographic Society of Bengal meeting during which Khan's images were shown, it was said that they were 'more interesting for the subjects than for the knowledge of the art displayed.'[30] Until the war radically shifted the terms in which the British interpreted Khan's practice, his photography mostly registered as a sign of Indian incompetence or, at worst, impertinence.

To appreciate the significance of the shift that took place here, one needs to understand how thoroughly embedded photography was in what Christopher Pinney has termed the 'colonial habitus'.[31] Pinney's seminal work on photography in nineteenth-century India draws on Derrida's theory of the *pharmakon*,[32] an ancient Greek term denoting a poison and a cure, to highlight the complex and mutable nature of the technology's role in colonial society. Pinney shows how the medium's Janus-faced character was split, roughly, along a temporal axis, so that, from 'the announcement of photography in 1839 until (very roughly) the beginning of the twentieth century, photography was perceived [by colonials] as a cure.'[33] This is because, in its early years, the expensive and cumbersome nature of photography rendered it highly reliant on a diffuse network of colonial permissions, bureaucracy, finance, transport and consumerism, which worked to structure the practice in ways that were foreseeable, 'taken-for-granted' and thus more or less harmonious with the imperial regime. Such a habitus did not explicitly censor Indian photographers so much as compose the social environment in terms of a set of subtle circumscribing mechanisms which, among other things, formed the conditions of possibility for photographic endeavour. Overtly anti-colonial practices were simply impracticable.

The prospect of an Indian counter-photography thus emerged from within the chaos of a rebellion whose upheavals had significantly undermined the standard functioning of the colonial habitus. Insurgent practice constituted what Nicholas Mirzoeff has termed a 'counter-visuality', opening up the possibility of redefining the terms of the Indian engagement with 'the form of the real, the realistic, and realism in all senses'.[34] Subversive photographic activity not only circumvented the institutional and economic structures that had generally worked to prevent the possibility of Indian photographers operating in an anti-colonial manner. It was also disruptive to the intellectual structures of the colonial habitus, whose guiding assumptions should have precluded even the theoretical possibility of such photography.

At stake, specifically, was the validity of a racist hierarchy of vision. The British had an exeedingly dim opinion of the Indian population's ocular abilities. The early 1850s had witnessed an imperial drive to utilise the arts as a 'civilising' interface between coloniser and colonised, with Western models of education being promoted in the art schools that had been established in Madras (Chennai), Calcutta (Kolkata) and Bombay (Mumbai) in 1850, 1854 and 1856 respectively.[35] Such an enterprise was positioned as part of a larger imperial project of making

Indians into 'rational' and 'modern' subjects,[36] echoing the rhetoric of Macaulay's influential 'Minute on Education' (1835), in which the historian had urged the creation of a system that would Anglicise a section of Indian society.[37] A foundational assumption of the art schools was that a pedagogy grounded in European traditions of perspectival naturalism was necessary to enable an optically challenged Indian people 'to rectify some of their mental faults, to intensify their powers of observation, and to make them understand analytically those glories of nature which they love so well.'[38] Without such an education, the Indian people were thought to be incapable of engaging with reality in an empirical manner: they were 'cut off', as Ruskin claimed in his wartime speech at the South Kensington Museum, 'from all possible sources of healthy knowledge.'[39]

The perspectival realism of a photograph was therefore not expected to be properly comprehensible to someone like Khan (at least not without British training), let alone legible as a sophisticated piece of reconnaissance facilitating military assaults. British condescension here was extreme and persistent. In 1855 the Orientalist Sir Henry Yule wrote of a colonial consensus regarding the scopic incompetence of the Indian people: 'all who have lived in India will bear testimony to it, that to natives of India, of whatever class or caste, unless they have had a special training, our European paintings, prints, drawings, and photographs, plain or coloured ... are absolutely unintelligible.'[40] Views such as this meant that when in 1869 a proposal was made to start photographing convicts in India, the plan was rejected by colonial officials on the basis that their native policemen would be incapable of recognising a person from photographic portraits. Even a prominent Indian scholar who utilised photography in his research into South Asian architecture was the subject of a smear campaign by a British historian working in the same field, who claimed that his Indian counterpart's eye was 'uneducated' when it came to the matter of interpreting the medium.[41] As late as 1933, a British psychologist argued that Indians naturally 'see objects in a manner much further from the principles of perspective than do the majority of Europeans.'[42]

Rumours of Khan's sophisticated military mobilisation of photography thus functioned to discredit supremacist narratives at the same time as they suggested an immediate violent threat. Gone were the old certainties about Indian incompetence; all areas of Khan's practice now took on a grisly significance. The portraits of Europeans taken by Khan before the war were said to have been handed over to the nefarious rebel commander Nana Sahib.[43] The exact use to which those portraits could be put was left unspecified; Nana's possession of them was, it seems, self-evidently sinister.

PHOTOGRAPHY WITHOUT HEGEMONY

The British preoccupation with photography's military uses was symptomatic of the more general commitment to a visual epistemology of war outlined in the previous chapter. In its perspectival functioning, photography drew its authority from Cartesian discourses of rationality that had previously found expression in single-point linear perspective and the camera obscura.[44] This rationalised visual order was monocular in nature, privileged sight over the other senses and approached space as an a priori set of geometrical coordinates to be delineated in an objective manner. Such 'Cartesian perspectivalism' was, as Martin Jay wrote, fundamental to the 'scopic regime' of modernity.[45] It constituted a privileged subject 'who, through and by depth, is able to stand aloof from the dramas and intricacies of an objective, grid-like world positioned "beyond" and "outside."'[46] This was an empowering way of seeing that laid claim to visual mastery over the world.

The military implications of this did not go unappreciated. Draughtsmanship was a key component of Britain's martial pedagogy, with linear perspective emphasised: at the Royal Military Academy at Woolwich, perspective was taught 'In theory and practice' in order to qualify students for 'drawing from nature'; while at the EIC's Military Seminary, there was a course teaching 'the Elements of Perspective, Landscape, and Figure Drawing in pencil and brush, and Photography.'[47] Drawing teachers at this latter seminary published educational books on perspective, with one writing that 'to the military man' drawing was something that 'might prove of infinite service' and that 'the study of perspective' was the 'first and most important step towards the attainment of an art of such extensive utility.'[48]

It might then appear strange that the British sought to impart this potentially dangerous skill to a population they had conquered. Yet artistic naturalism was seen to nurture many desirable virtues: moral and intellectual concerns were at stake, making aesthetic education a part of the imperial 'civilising mission'. The particular utility – moral, mental or martial – of the naturalistic practices being taught in India depended on the political context, namely whether imperial rule was seen to be secured by what Ranajit Guha (taking his cue from Antonio Gramsci) has termed 'dominance with hegemony' or by 'dominance without hegemony'.[49] Dominance with hegemony was a form of colonial rule in which direct coercion was unnecessary because Indians, having been successfully interpellated as imperial subjects, exhibited an amount of cooperation and complicity in the imperial project; dominance without hegemony was a form of colonial rule perpetuated against a resistant populace by varying degrees of coercive force. India's ocular abilities could signify in radically different ways according to the presence or absence of colonial hegemony.

'When working with hegemony,' Daniel Rycroft writes, 'the colonized collaborated within the dominant political and cultural systems' of the British, and as such they were 'marked by a subjecthood that was recognized by the colonial administration as loyal, knowable, and useful.' In the early 1850s, amenable Indian subjecthood was communicated to the British public via illustrations like 'Aerolite' (fig. 17), which showed Indian elites participating in the sophisticated spectatorship fostered by the Great Exhibition. For Briton and Indian alike, such viewing practices were coded in terms of edification, signifying 'the acquisition of modern knowledge and rationality.'[50]

Numerous British depictions of the crowds at the Great Exhibition showed South Asian visitors incorporated into these edifying viewing practices (fig. 18), strolling round the display courts alongside British spectators. This harmonious multiculturalism chimed with the lofty claim that the World's Fair was promoting international peace. Peter H. Hoffenberg has argued that the later exhibitions that were held in British colonies over the course of the nineteenth century similarly posited 'the act of seeing' as 'a shared, integrative activity' that functioned as 'a metaphor for [imperial] federation': 'Vision provided an aesthetic

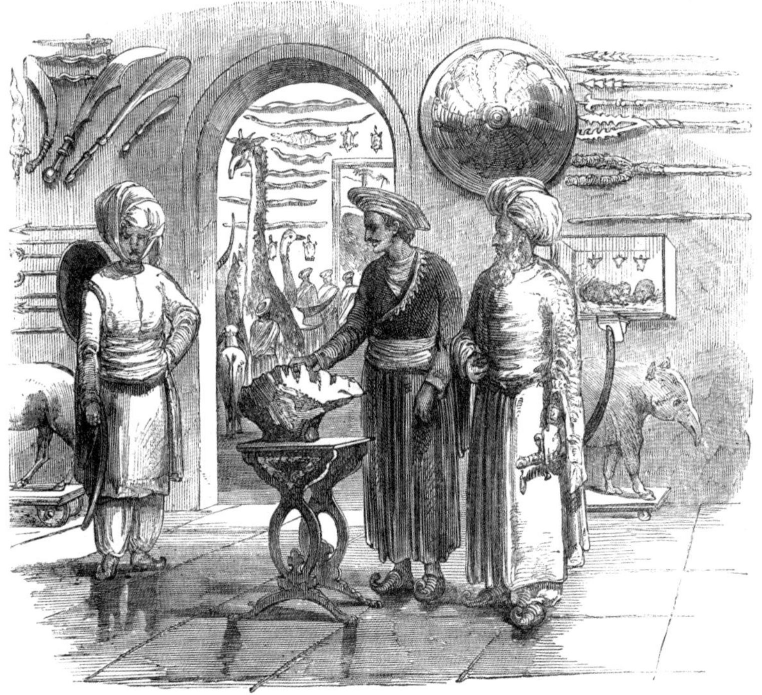

THE GREAT AEROLITE, FROM THE KURRUKPOOR HILLS, NEAR MONGHYR, INDIA.

17 Walter Sherwill, 'Aerolite', *Illustrated London News*, 13 December 1851. Wood engraving. © Mary Evans Picture Library

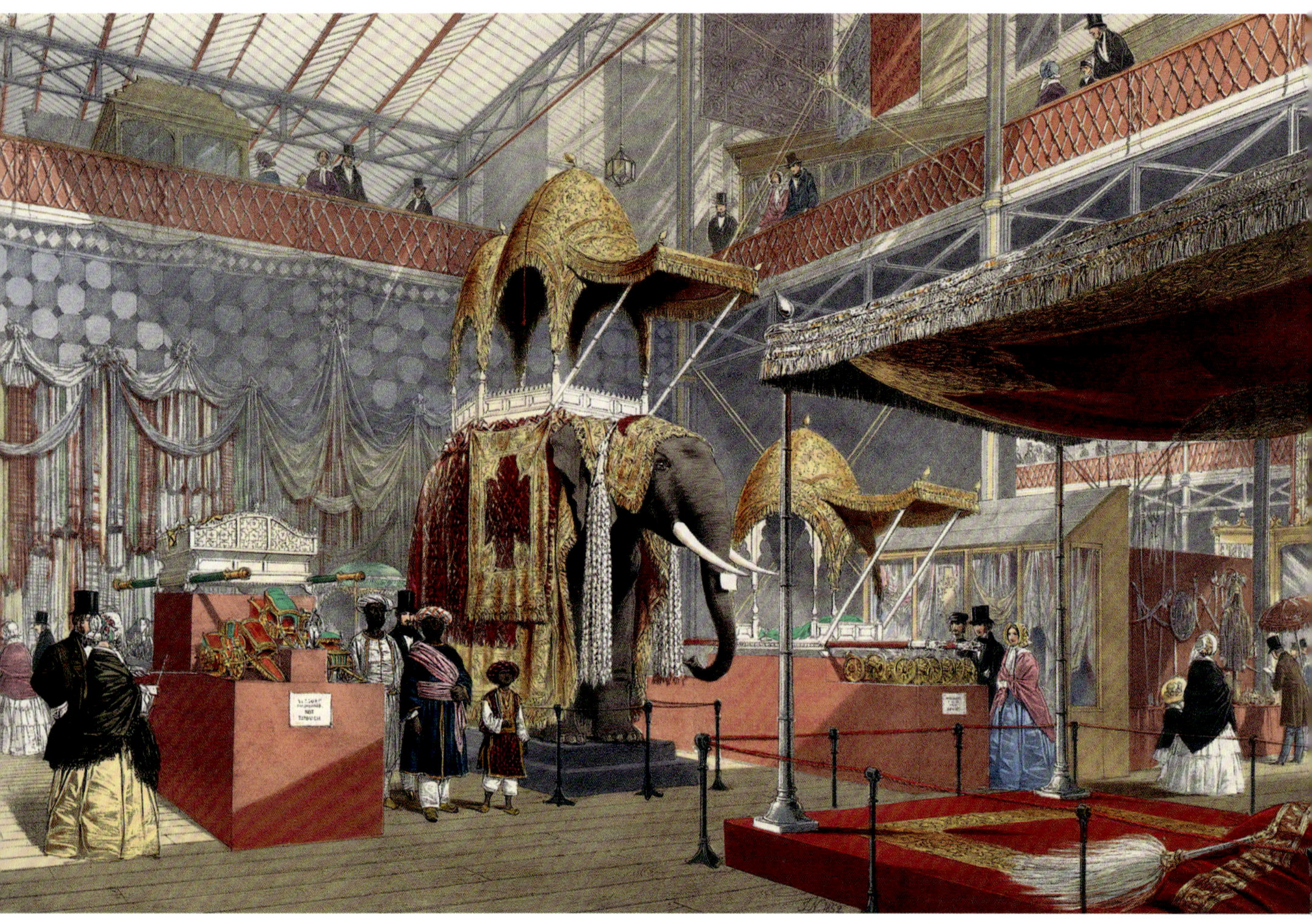

18 Joseph Nash, 'India no. 2', *Dickinson's Comprehensive Pictures of the Great Exhibition of 1851, from the originals painted for H. R. H. Prince Albert by Messrs Nash, Hague, & Roberts*, vol. 2, 1854. British Library Creative Commons

link, but also a synthesized empire and nation; it integrated imperial subjects and national citizens in a shared, simultaneous experience of the shows.'[51] Communal ways of seeing thereby functioned to unify what might otherwise have been antagonistic imperial factions.

The brutal cross-cultural violence of the 1857 Uprising proved to be severely disruptive to such a unifying vision. The British took steps near the start of the war to purge the Photographic Society of Bengal in Calcutta along racial lines. When the society had been instituted in 1856, some of its founding members were Indian. Many more Indians became members within the year, with 348 attending the opening week of the society's first exhibition in March, at which numerous Indian photographers were represented.[52] Such Anglo-Indian cooperation can be seen in the context of what Rycroft, following Tony Bennet's work in *The Birth of the Museum* (1995), has termed the 'colonial exhibitionary complex': an assemblage of aesthetic institutions and practices within British India that worked to secure hegemony by incorporating Indians into European cultures of spectatorship. Yet within months of the eruption of the Uprising, not a single Indian member remained. The British were acting within a new political paradigm – dominance without hegemony, or what Rycroft has called 'the counter-insurgency complex'.[53]

The ostensible reason for the new racial divide within the society was the 'anti-British' speech of one the founding members, the prominent scholar of Indian history, Rajendralal Mitra (*c.*1823–1891).[54] On 6 April 1857, the eve of the Uprising, Mitra had given a speech in which he condemned the rapacious practices of British indigo planters on the subcontinent.[55] At the time these comments appear to have passed with little notice but, following the outbreak of insurgency in May, they became controversial.[56] It was alleged that Mitra's speech was mendacious and indicative of his general hostility to the British community, sentiments which rendered him 'unworthy of continuing to be a member' of the society that he had helped to establish.[57] Mitra was asked to resign, which he refused to do, consequently giving the British portion of the group – by then widely agitating for his removal – a problem, since the rules would not allow for the expulsion of a member.

There was talk of dissolving the society and instituting another one, sans Mitra, but many believed that 'whether specially provided for in the rules or otherwise, every Society possesses an inherent right to expel any member ... who might render himself obnoxious.'[58] This sort of a move towards expulsion was unprecedented; as one man wrote in an impassioned letter to his fellow members, the Asiatic Society had existed 'for seventy-three [years] without finding any necessity for the step which the Photographic Society is now asked to take.'[59] Nevertheless, to the delight of many, a motion for expulsion was carried on 19 August.[60] An arts institution that was supposed to be fostering shared imperial visions thus became a site of rupture. All the remaining Indian members of the society, as well as some renegade Britons, resigned in protest. It was reported that an opposition society had been formed including Mitra as Secretary, Mr James Bruce as President and Major Thullier as Vice President. 'We wish the new Society every success which it is not likely to get', wrote a disdainful local newspaper.[61] Indian members were not brought back into the original society until 1862. Astonishingly, the first to be readmitted appears to have been the one-time insurgent photographer, Ahmad Ali Khan, who was by then working under the alias 'Chota Meah'.[62]

CONCLUSION

Why was Indian membership so distasteful to the British during the Uprising? A possible motive was offered a few months after the expulsion of Mitra, when it was stated in the society's minutes that Ahmad Ali Khan had once been a 'pupil' of the society before he had joined the rebels and began passing his photographs to insurgent forces, a fact that hinted at the potentially damaging consequences of incorporating Indians into the photographic fold.[63]

The threat posed by insurgent photography was ultimately an epistemic one. Michael Taussig argued that if one takes seriously, as the British surely did, the capacity for mimesis to yield knowledge about what it represents, then one cannot merely respond to the Other's mimetic representations of oneself with the classic 'defensive manoeuvre of the powerful in subjecting it to scrutiny as yet another primitive artefact, grist to the analytical machinery' of Enlightenment rationality. The mimetic practices of the Other function to collapse the distance through which '[western] science is nourished', making the coloniser equally the 'object of study'.[64] In the case of British India, such epistemic equality eroded the sort of privileged intellectual detachment that, among other things, sustained the racially supremacist pedagogy of imperial art schools, and the paternalist rhetoric of colonial ethnographers. In making the British the object of study, Indian photography pointed to the menace that Homi K. Bhabha located in colonial mimicry, in which 'the fetishized colonial culture is potentially and strategically an insurgent counter-appeal.'[65]

At stake, therefore, during the wartime furore at the Photographic Society of Bengal was not simply the notion of Indian membership but the desirability of the project of Anglicisation that had informed the imperial civilising mission. This was made clear in a letter of July 1857 to the Calcutta-based newspaper *The Englishman*, where one Briton identifying himself only on racial grounds as an 'ANGLO-SAXON MEMBER' voiced a desire ethnically to cleanse all colonial aesthetic institutions:

> The native must be greatly elevated in the scale of humanity, before he can call upon us to incur the expense and trouble of teaching him either Photography, or any one of the fine arts ... the majority [of members] are Europeans who prefer the society of their fellow countrymen to that of 'Fat Baboos', and who, having neither promotion nor reward to expect from the Government for their labours on behalf [of] the Bengalees, dislike the idea of any portion of their funds being appropriated to such a work, and therefore had better consider before the monthly meeting, whether it would not be advisable to establish a Photographic Society consisting exclusively of European members.[66]

The Uprising thus catalysed a desire in some Britons to arrogate back to themselves the artistic practices that an imperial pedagogy had previously sought to spread. The effects of this mood were limited: imperial art schools remained active following the war. But it shows that, in India as in Britain, the idealistic internationalism associated with the arts during the period following the 1851 Great Exhibition came under significant strain as the violent realities of empire began to bite. The Uprising undermined British confidence in the techniques of colonial hegemony and led to a breakdown in the old racist certainties about British intellectual privilege. It thus opened up a discursive space in which colonials could entertain once impossible notions: that a 'bumptious' Lucknawi Muslim architect was at the vanguard of technological progress in British India; that he had no need of imperial instruction in 'rational' ways of seeing; and that his facility with photography could reduce the British to an object of dangerous Indian study.

3 · 'ADDITIONAL HORRORS'

Photography, Colonial Violence and the Archive

THE PHOTOGRAPHS OF COLONIAL VIOLENCE THAT EMERGED FROM the so-called 'small wars' of the Victorian era are relatively unknown outside the domain of specialists.[1] Popular histories of the British Empire mostly take their cue from the Victorians themselves in favouring the kinetic battle scenes produced by nineteenth-century oil painters and 'special artists' over the comparatively drab and static tableaux of early war photography. There was a sense among the Victorians that the technical limitations of the camera meant it failed to capture the cut and thrust of battle in the same way that an artist could with their pencil or brush; and yet, far from being intrinsically underwhelming, photography was also liable to create documents of violence that were shocking to Victorian sensibilities, and which remain thorny and impactful images from a postcolonial standpoint.

This chapter is concerned with the rare but significant moments when the camera's engagement with colonial violence pushed against the limits of ethical acceptability or even legality. Photographs of colonial brutality were not welcomed into the official annals of the Empire and they are far from being placed centre-stage by the British archives which now hold such material. In an article on the National Army Museum website entitled 'Why Did the Indian Mutiny Happen?', the cartoonish lithographs of George Franklin Atkinson predominate (fig. 19), creating a visual tone for the history of imperial violence which makes it feel more distant and less troubling than would be the case if the curators had chosen to foreground another item from their collection, such as Felice Beato's photograph of the public hanging of two Indian men in 1858 (fig. 20).[2] An Italian-British commercial photographer, Beato had worked in partnership with James Robertson in the Crimean War.[3] He only began producing explicit photographs of death, however, on leaving

Felice Beato, *The Interior of the Secundrabagh after the Slaughter of 2000 Rebels*, negative 1858, print 1862 (detail of fig. 23).

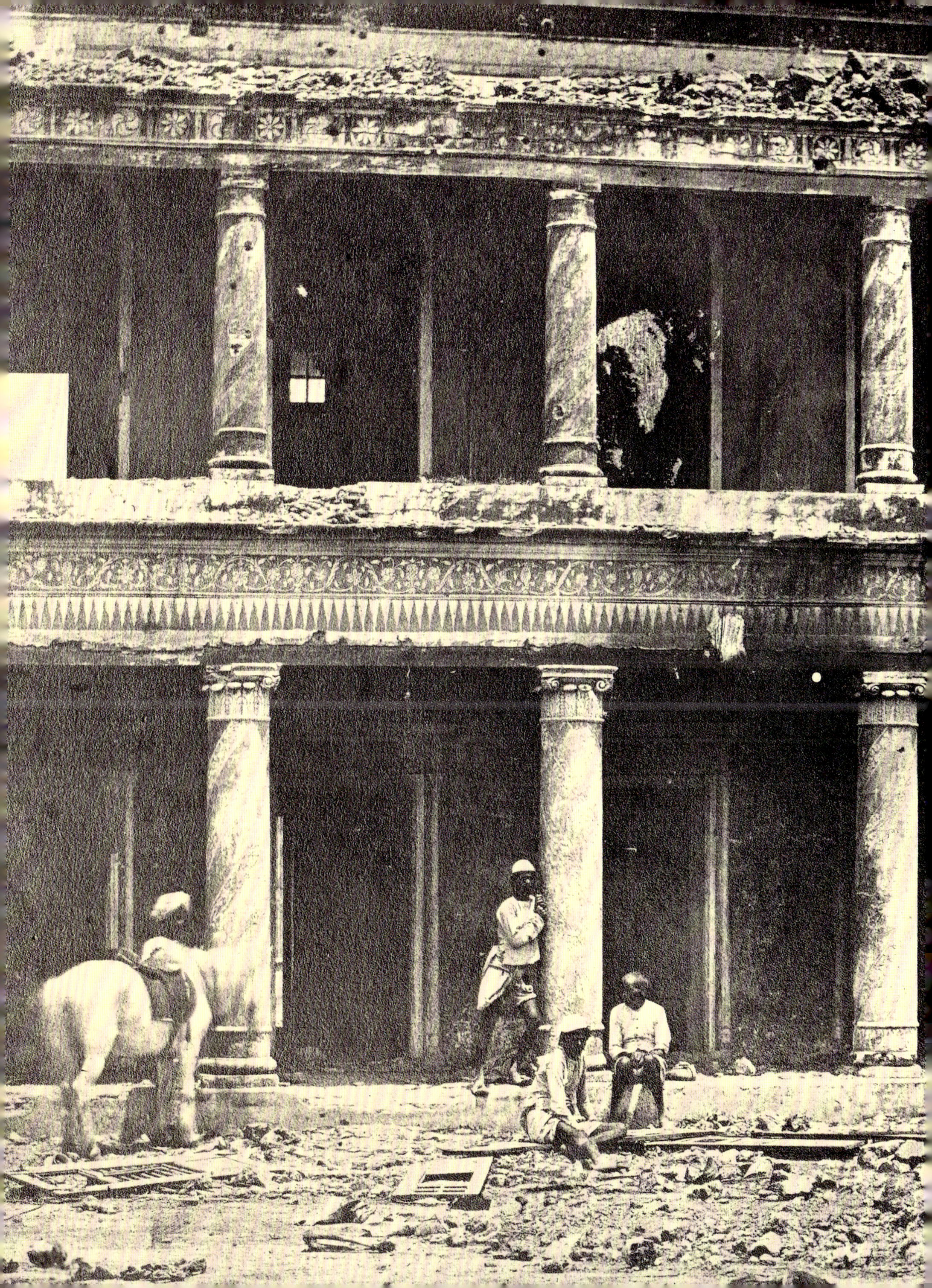

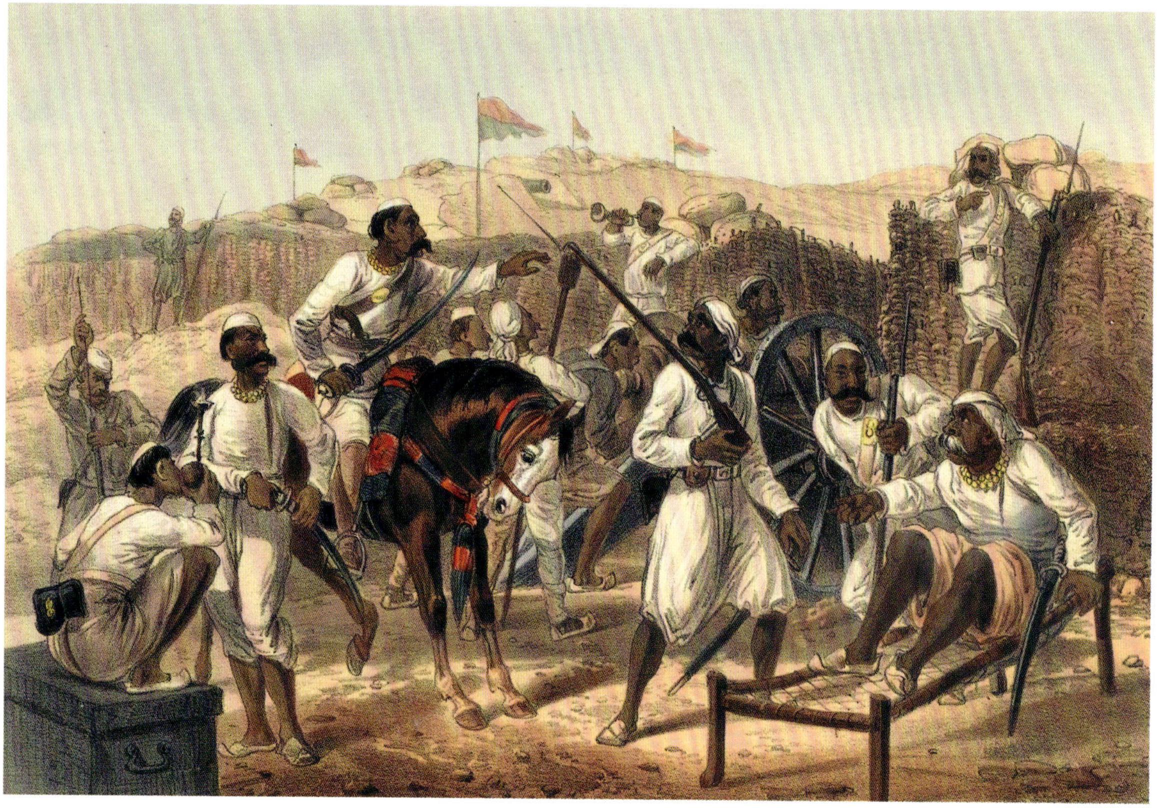

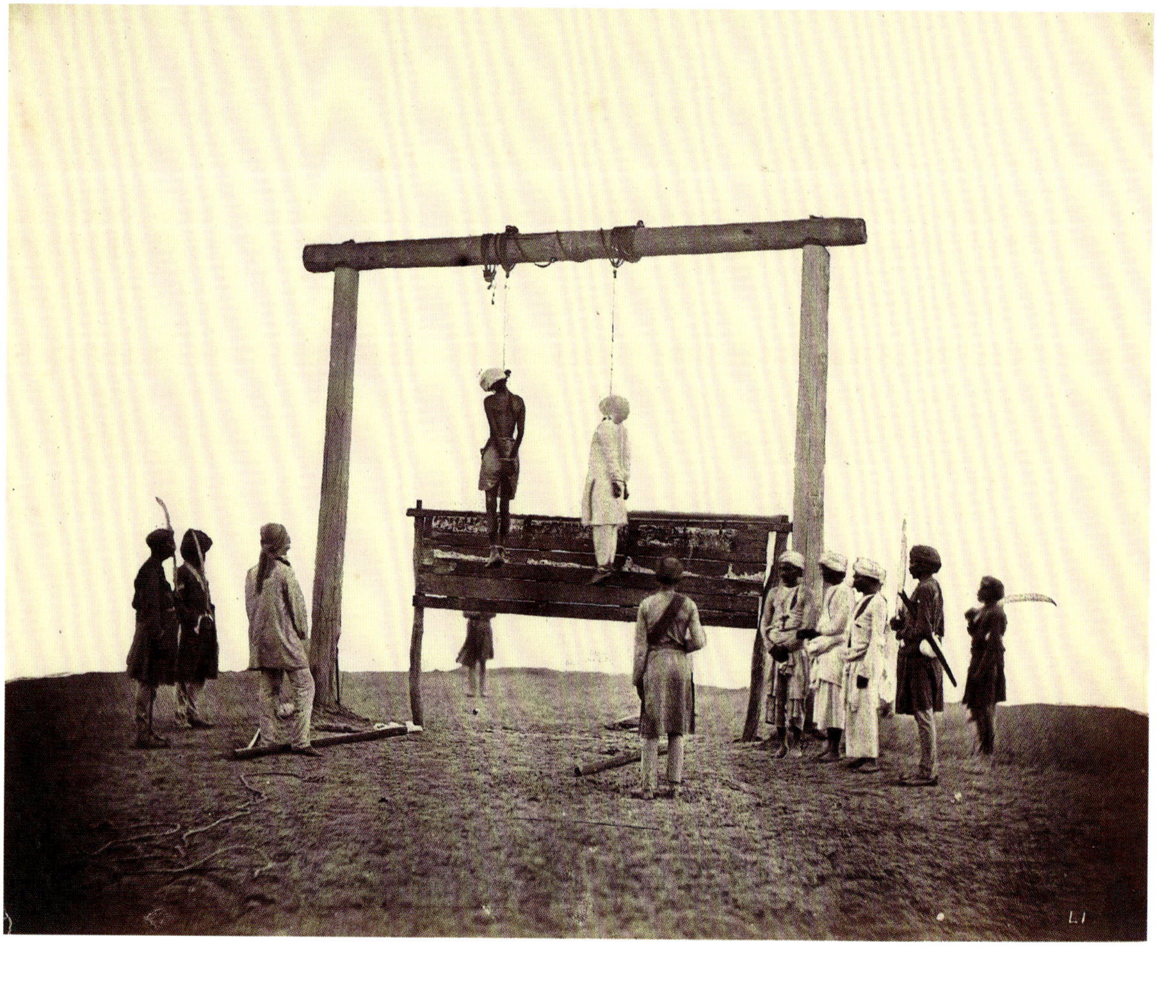

Europe and venturing into the relative anomie of colonial conflict. No photographer had yet produced such a stark vision of violence as this scene of a small Indian crowd gazing at the hanged bodies of 'mutineers'.

Beato's image of the hanging is rarely incorporated into popular histories of the Empire and has been dealt with only summarily in academic accounts. Yet more than any other extant photograph, this grisly execution scene instantiated the logic of 'exemplary violence' that was fundamental to the defence of colonial sovereignty in times of crisis.[4] While the modern British state was starting to eschew punitive spectacles – public executions were banned in 1868 – colonial regimes were becoming increasingly invested in military theories that trumpeted the efficacy of such displays. Kim Wagner's illuminating recent work on the role of violence in the Raj has demonstrated that the British response to the Uprising in the years 1857–9 – in which theatricalised violence was 'both performative and constitutive of colonial power' – formed the template for a counter-insurgency strategy that prevailed in India and its frontier territories throughout the late nineteenth and early twentieth century.[5] The Uprising, which heralded the beginning of a mode of colonial counter-insurgency warfare that was waged as violent spectacle, also marks the juncture at which war photographers started to experiment with visceral and shocking images.[6]

To understand how warfare came to be consumed as a shocking spectacle, however, it is imperative to look beyond photography at wider practices of modern spectatorship. The aestheticisation of suffering and destruction did not emerge as a new problematic for the Victorians with the invention of photography in 1839. Radically new as Beato's photography was, its 'ethics of seeing', to use Susan Sontag's phrase, was rooted in a longstanding, popular and ostensibly unrelated artistic tradition, the picturesque.[7] The picturesque's embrace of rugged and irregular formal qualities had already fostered some morally dubious visual pleasures at the sight of ramshackle dwellings and beggars' rags. This extraction of formal values from social ills provided the perceptual framework in which a budding war photographer like Beato could respond pictorially to violence. A year before Beato's engagement with death and devastation in India, Ruskin had declared that 'the modern feeling of the picturesque, which, so far as it consists in a delight in ruin, is perhaps the most suspicious and questionable of all the characters distinctively belonging to our temper, and art.'[8] Such picturesque visuality – established by theorists like William Gilpin in the eighteenth century and still popular by Ruskin's day – provided the basis on which photography's ethical relationship to the world was negotiated.

19 George Franklin Atkinson, *Mutinous Sepoys*, 1857. Coloured lithograph, 39.6 × 29 cm. © National Army Museum, London

20 Felice Beato, *Two Sepoys of the 31st Infantry, who were hanged at Lucknow*, negative 1858, print 1862. Albumen silver print from wet collodion negative, 23.8 × 30.1 cm. Getty Open Content Programme

Ruskin's critique of the 'lower' picturesque sentiment as 'eminently a *heartless* one' pre-empts more recent scholarship in his suggestion that it was not simply a set of harmless conventions prioritising rough textures, irregularity and ruins.[9] It was, as Malcolm Andrews wrote, a modern way of seeing which, 'with its almost exclusive emphasis on visual appreciation, entailed a suppression of the spectator's moral response.'[10] Photography participated in the 'hardening' of feeling that Ruskin had identified within the modern picturesque temperament.[11] Its technological mediation of vision formed part of a broader shift in the structure of modern perception, a move towards what Zahid R. Chaudhary terms a 'phantasmagoric aesthetic', which desensitised colonials to the sensory shock-effects that Walter Benjamin famously identified as symptomatic of industrial modernity.[12] In Chaudhary's sophisticated reading of photography and perception in nineteenth-century British India, the picturesque is conceived as an instantiation of a modern perceptual 'habitus' that regulated the colonial 'sensorium' by providing 'aesthetic armor' against the shocks of colonial violence.[13]

There was a snag in such armour, however, with photography often serving to problematise the violence it recorded. The 'picturesque' way of seeing, in its very manner of regulating shocking experiences by filtering them through pleasing aesthetic conventions and responding to them in pictorial terms, could confront the British with their dubious capacity to enjoy what Henry A. Giroux terms 'an aesthetics of depravity': human suffering 'subordinated to the formal properties of beauty, design and taste'.[14] At the same time as it enabled modern spectators to respond to poverty, war or ruin with aesthetic satisfaction, then, the modern picturesque disposition was also unsettling. The very fact that such extremities could be perceived 'picturesquely' was itself shocking – hence Ruskin's anxiety. Responding to the horrors of war in the imperial field by making pictures out of those horrors raised troubling questions about the ethical and affective capacities of the colonial spectator. Watching theatrical displays of colonial sovereign violence was one thing; the act of photographing those displays was quite another.

PHOTOGRAPHY AND COUNTER-INSURGENCY

A framework of belatedness and absence has characterised scholars' approaches to photographs from the Indian revolt. Christopher Pinney writes that the 'central technomaterial fact of all photography relating to the 1857 Uprising is that ... [the] photographer only had the scene of an event that has long gone' and of a 'stage, long empty.'[15] While not untrue, the contention that photographers arrived 'too late' (Chaudhary this time) to record the war relies on a narrow understanding of the campaign as a series of famous battles and sieges.[16]

Late Victorian military theorists, looking back over a century of rampant imperial expansion, recognised that traditional set-piece confrontations were only half the story. In his 1896 book *Small Wars: Their Principles and Practice*, Colonel Charles Edward Callwell wrote of how 'campaigns of conquest and annexation' move from formal engagements between armies to 'the war of ambushes and surprises, of murdered stragglers and stern reprisals.' In the 'case of the Indian Mutiny', he wrote, 'as the supremacy of British military power in India became re-established, and as the organized mutineer forces melted away, the campaign degenerated in many localities into purely guerrilla warfare, which took months to bring to a conclusion. As a general rule the quelling of rebellion in distant colonies means protracted, thankless, invertebrate [that is, flexible] war.' In the fluid and indefinite parameters of such a campaign, Callwell asserted, 'fanatics and savages must be thoroughly brought to book and cowed' via dramatic displays of force 'or they will rise again'.[17] While the camera could not capture the movements of a traditional battle, with its cavalry charges and messy close-quarters combat, photography was better situated to document the dramatic public executions constitutive of what came to be known by the Victorians as 'savage warfare'.

Beato's gruesome photograph of a public hanging barely hints at the extent of the retribution that the British visited on India during the convulsive years 1857–9. 'Not one man in ten seems to think that the hanging and shooting of 40 or 50,000 Mutineers beside other rebels, can be otherwise than practicable and right', wrote a distressed Governor-General of Bengal, Lord Charles Canning, to Queen Victoria, admitting that such 'rabid and indiscriminate vindictiveness … is impossible to contemplate without feeling something like shame for one's fellow countrymen.'[18] One British military commander had rendered the Indian countryside quiescent 'by the very simple expedient of burning all the villages in the line of march, and hanging everybody with a black face falling in his way.'[19]

In an attempt to rein in the excesses of colonial violence, Canning issued the so-called 'Clemency Proclamation' in July 1857, which sought to limit the use of the death sentence to those insurgents who had actually harmed British people or property. Yet mass summary executions remained commonplace; the terrorisation of the Indian population via conspicuous acts of violence far outlasted the formal military engagements on which the imperial history books tended to dwell. Photographers whom scholars have noted for their 'belated' documentation of the

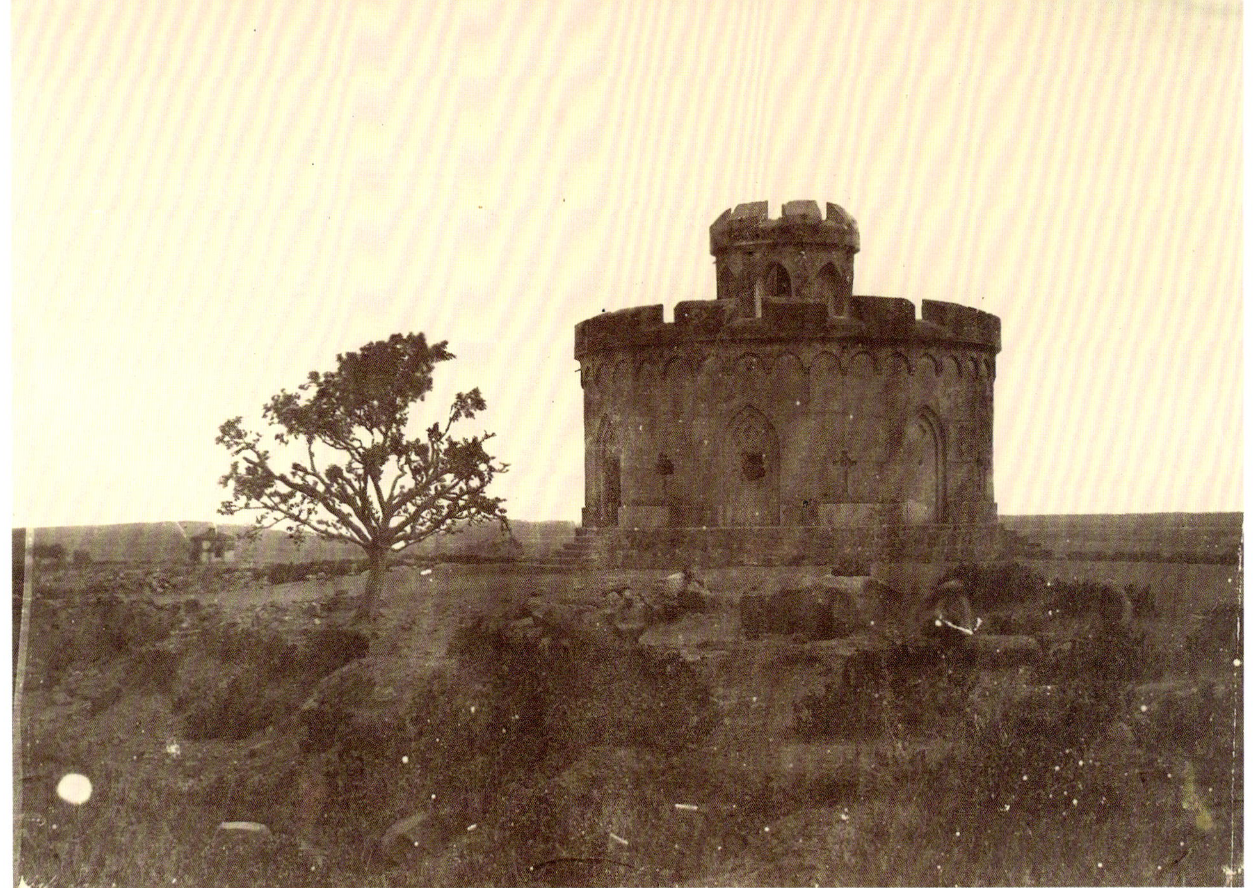

21 Dr John Murray, *Flag Staff Tower, Delhi*, 1858. Albumen silver print, 33 × 42.5 cm. © The British Library Board, Photo 52/(8)

wreckage of past battles were therefore hardly confronting conditions of peace. They were operating in a fierce climate of counter-insurgency.

Such was the state of affairs that the amateur photographer Dr John Murray discovered on arriving back in India on 12 November 1857 following his period of furlough in Britain. Murray missed his own exhibition of Indian photographs in London (see Chapter One) in order to get back to his afflicted colonial hometown of Agra. He found himself detained in Calcutta until January 1858 due to the relevant road 'being in part in possession of the rebels.'[20] While residing in the colonial capital – itself relatively unaffected by the rebellion – Murray received the only official East India Company commission given to a photographer during the Uprising. His imagery has so far received little treatment compared to the more technically accomplished work of Beato but the photographs and diaries that Murray produced during his commission for the colonial government provide us with the fullest account of the experience of a photographer operating during the war.

Murray's imagery from this time has a murky tone which lends a dystopian gloom to the sites of war. Representative here is his scene of the lonely Flagstaff Tower in Delhi (fig. 21), where the British had briefly sought refuge when the city had first become overrun with rebels at the start of the insurrection. Like many of Murray's scenes from this period, the surface of the photograph is distorted by markings which the doctor attributed to 'the imperfect apparatus and inferior quality of some of the paper which I procured at Calcutta, together with the unfavourable state of the weather at Allahabad and Cawnpore.'[21]

Murray's diary adopts a striking equivalence of tone between such technical photographic considerations and the extreme violence of British reprisals occurring around him. Following his arrival in Delhi in February 1858, for instance, he wrote a typically laconic (and ungrammatical) diary entry: 'There were 87 rebels hung this morning', he recorded, '23 by the military at the Kotwalee & 64 at the Jail by the civil authorities – The last batch of [photographic] Plates turned cloudy & bad – from making experiments diminishing the strength of gum & citric acid.'[22] A few days later, he rode across the city towards the famous Qutb Minar with Sir Thomas Metcalf and Mr Layard. This tourist expedition stopped along the way to make some arrests; one Indian *badmash* (rogue or criminal) was 'tried & hanged' immediately, while two more men were condemned to be hanged.[23] Murray's photographs of recent war sites and historic monuments should thus be seen in relation to the summary justice that he (mostly) omitted to show.

VIOLENCE AND THE ARCHIVE

Shortly after he had left Calcutta with his government commission, Murray spent some time in Benares (Varanasi) while on the road to Delhi. He had instructions to produce 'a set of views of the Raj Ghat entrenchment, conveying as clear and complete an impression of the works as possible.'[24] He was also required to depict the parade ground, mosque and Simalah and Bisshesspur temples. Following a public execution there on 18 January, however, Murray went beyond his brief:

> Saw a mutineer blown away from a Gun – *Took a view No. 18 – when they were reading the sentence to him* then got out of the way the pieces of flesh and bone are scattered all round & the head goes bounding in front – the body appears to swell and burst – like a shell – death must be instantaneous The expression of the face was easy *Took some paper views – of the parade ground* & native lines & bells of arms[25]

This entry indicates that Murray documented the last traumatic moments of an Indian man's life by taking a photograph ('No. 18') while the man was strapped to a cannon prior to being 'blown away'. The photograph, now lost, was not included among those Murray sent back to his government employers.

Given that Murray was working for 'Clemency Canning', it is perhaps not surprising that he chose to censor evidence of continuing British

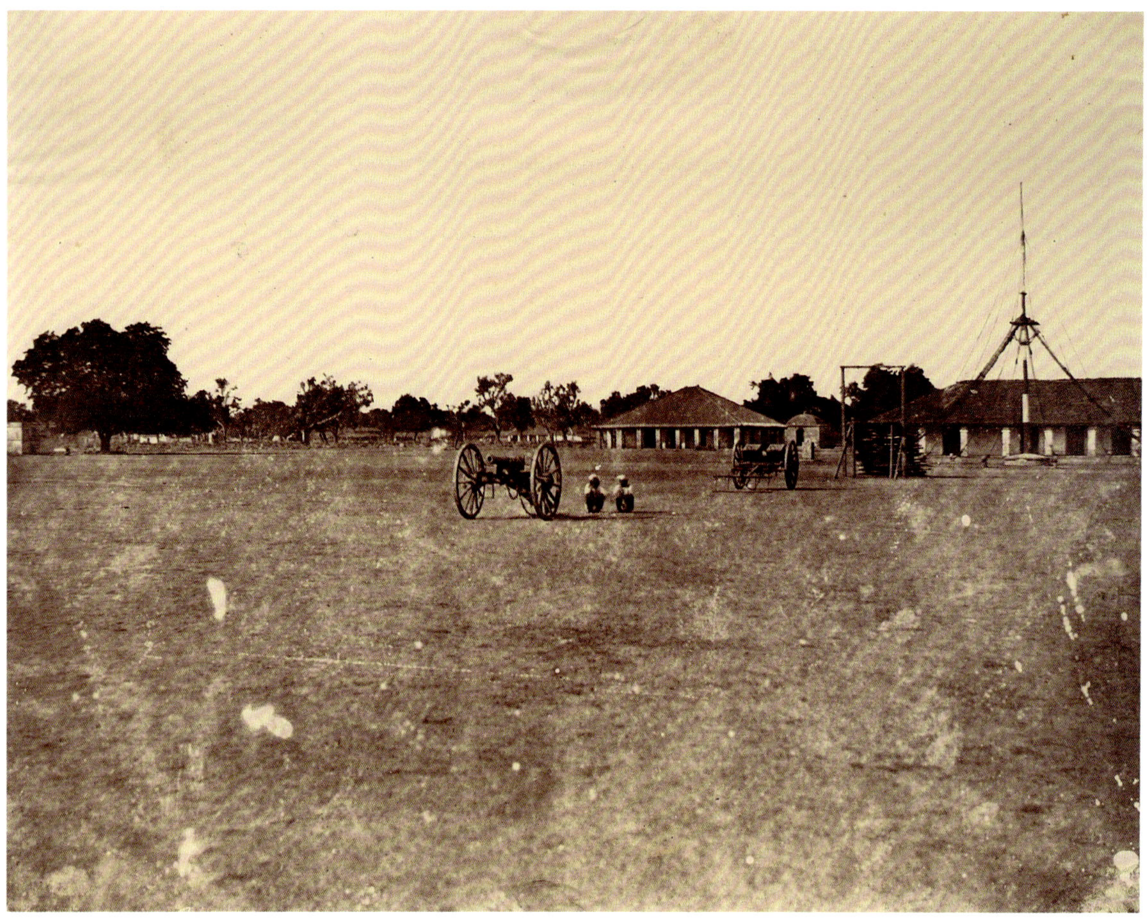

22 Dr John Murray, *Parade Ground, Benares*, 1858. Albumen silver print, 33 × 42.5 cm. © The British Library Board, Photo 52/(39)

brutality. Murray's motivations for taking the photograph of this execution method – which was common practice during the British suppression of the 'mutiny' and represented for the Victorian public in artists' engravings in the *Illustrated London News* – are unclear. He appears to have had a morbid (or, being a doctor, we might say clinical) interest in the physical impact of the explosion on the human body. Yet he does not record taking a photograph of the bloody aftermath which he describes so vividly. The diary entry displays an uncertain negotiation of what was and what was not admissible for a colonial photographer. Just because something fascinated Murray did not mean that he took its photograph; and just because he took a photograph did not mean that he believed the image was suitable for unguarded distribution.

Murray's apparent decision to excise No. 18 suggests that such a photograph was not considered appropriate material for official memory. It embodies Anne McClintock's notion of 'imperial ghosting', in which the imperial archive is structured by 'administered forgettings' that nevertheless leave 'a kind of counterevidence: material and spectral traces' and 'shadowy aftereffects'.[26] One such 'spectral trace' can be detected in a photograph that Murray did send back to the government. In *Parade Ground, Benares* (fig. 22) – one of the sites Murray had been commissioned to document – two anonymous Indian figures are sitting next to a cannon. The diary entry states that this photograph was taken immediately after the cannon-based killing; it functions like a visual echo of that event, in which the viewer and, distressingly, the sitters themselves, who probably witnessed the execution before posing next to such deadly ordnance, are invited to draw their own association between colonial artillery and the bodies of the colonised. The aura of violence becomes palpable when one notices the empty gallows lurking in the background.

Despite seeing other executions, Murray did not record taking any more photographs of such violence. Public executions may have been staged by colonials for maximum visual impact in order to intimidate an unruly population into submission – and we see from Murray's diary entry that such episodes held a visual fascination for colonials – but the dissemination of murderous spectacle as photographs was nevertheless a sensitive issue for the British. It could lead, as this chapter will show, not only to moral disapproval but even to public outcry and official reprimand. The contexts in which extreme images were consumed were therefore different from other types of photographs: they were more informal, more furtive.

'THE HORROR ... '

The British ambivalence regarding the dissemination and presentation of violent photographs can be discerned in their treatment of Beato's *Two Sepoys ... who were hanged at Lucknow* (see fig. 20). Despite occupying a prominent position in Henry Hering's 1862 catalogue, *A Magnificent Collection of Photographic Views and Panoramas taken by Signor Beato during the Indian Mutiny in 1857–58 and the late War in China*, Beato's execution scene was often omitted from the albums and collections that were compiled in commemoration of the Uprising.[27] Thus while the British arranged many of Beato's war photographs sequentially in personal albums in order to be experienced as a visual narrative, *Hanging at Lucknow* – the most direct and unflinching photograph of violence to emerge from war photography's first decades – was mostly left unassimilated. Yet not, it seems, unviewed. The extant copies of the photograph held by the National Army Museum (NAM) and the Victoria and Albert Museum (V&A) are loose items; the NAM's copy is badly faded and torn, while the V&A's is creased where it has been folded into thirds – the battered materiality of the objects testifying to a history of being handled.[28]

The few accounts we have of colonials reacting to Beato's macabre photography run the gamut from malevolent thrill to censorious distaste. At the sadistic end of the spectrum we have Lieutenant Arthur Moffat Lang who, following his role in a victorious British assault on the Sikandar Bagh in Lucknow in November 1857, enthused about how 'It was the first good revenge I have seen!' adding: 'It was a glorious sight to see the mass of bodies, dead and wounded.'[29] Months later, with British reprisals against the Lucknawi population still raging, Lang was riding near the Moti Mahal gateway when he noticed there was 'a crowd about the gallows' and, on getting closer, 'I saw a Sepoy and a Band Nauk of the 48th N.I. just swinging off'.[30] A few yards away, Beato's photographic apparatus was already set up to capture the hanging. Lang watched as the photographer intervened in order to 'steady the bodies, when life was extinct, to be nicely photographed!' The lieutenant's use of an exclamation mark shows his excitement at watching this morbid act of photography, with his punctuation here echoing the exclamatory tone in which he had described the previous massacre. Over the next week, Lang recorded visiting Beato numerous times in Lucknow to buy his photographs.

Note that two of the Indian witnesses stand by the poles that had been supporting the base of the gallows and had therefore probably carried out this execution on behalf of the British before posing as witnesses to it. The photograph thus shows 'implicated witnesses' in the process of 'reading' the execution, a staging of the act of Indians interpreting colonial violence. In his recent analysis of the image, Nathan K. Hensley suggests that such hermeneutic activity 'is the object's defining problematic, what it is "about"', pointing out rightly that 'what the photo depicts is not a hanging but a hanging being watched.'[31] To which I add that, more than this, the photograph depicts a hanging being watched while being photographed. So how did the act of photography affect the hermeneutics of such colonial violence?

Beato's act of photography did not just document or interpret the execution; it intervened in the spectacle and shaped the significance of what was witnessed. 'I should think', wrote Lang, '[that] the Photographing must have impressed additional horrors on the scene to the natives'. In amplifying the horrors of the scene, photography was operating in a feedback loop with the 'exemplary violence' that constituted colonial power. Lang does not specify why the photographic intervention brought 'additional horrors' but the implication is that it was the photographer's cold instrumentalisation of Indian bodies. Lang described how Beato 'ran' up to the gallows the 'minute they were dead', immobilising the swinging corpses for the camera 'by holding their feet!'[32] In the early nineteenth century, the gothic novelist Anne Radcliffe had defined horror as that which 'contracts, freezes and nearly annihilates'.[33] Beato's camera possessed just such a paralysing, nullifying agency. In demanding stasis of the living and the dead at the scene, it instrumentalised all Indians in essentially the same way, formally collapsing the distinctions between the insurgents and the spectators: all are reduced to the status of inert props. A public execution like this was a warning to Indians of the consequences of crossing the British; some of the witnesses are even wearing white *pajamas* like those of one of the hanged men, creating a threatening visual association between the condemned and the crowd. I therefore suggest that the 'additional horrors' arose at least in part from the apprehension that the photographer's manipulation of dead Indian bodies was an extreme, intimidating and possibly prophetic form of the living Indian men's orchestration for the camera.

A similar dynamic is at work between the living and the dead in *The Interior of the Secundrabagh after the Slaughter of 2000 Rebels* (fig. 23). This is Beato's shocking record of the November 1857 massacre in which Lang had participated with glee. Skulls, ribcages, femurs, pelvises: a horrific explosion of bones dominates the foreground of the scene. 'Such a sight of slaughter I never saw', Lang wrote of the original assault, 'Pandies [i.e. Indian rebels] were shot down and bayoneted in heaps, three or four feet deep.'[34] In Beato's photograph the remains of such heaps appear to be scattered in front of an architectural ruin, as if the victors had left the dead to decompose wherever they had fallen. But this was not in fact the case. By the time that Beato arrived at this location in March, the bodies had 'been buried and counted – 1,840.'[35] The photographer arranged for their exhumation in order to make this photograph, creating what Pinney has called 'a complex reanimation of the Uprising as a theatrical spectacle'.[36]

Scholars have primarily discussed Beato's grisly reconstruction in terms of its 'hypermediated' status.[37] Pinney stresses the tension between the camera's fidelity to the scene it documents and 'our doubt about the reliability of what has been recorded' because this is not, in fact, the aftermath of the battle but a restaged version of it. Yet what gets left behind in such epistemological inquiry into the nature of the photographic index vis-à-vis 'truth' or 'accuracy' is the way in which the relationship between the 'micro event' and the 'historical event' – between the mise-en-scène and the massacre to which it gestures – was understood by those participating in the 'stage-management' of the scene.[38]

This theatricalisation of violence should, I think, be seen with Lang's perception of 'horror' in mind. It is unlikely that Beato dug up the bodies himself. In fact, it is probable that the Indian men seen in the photograph had also been required to gather the bones, then to distribute them

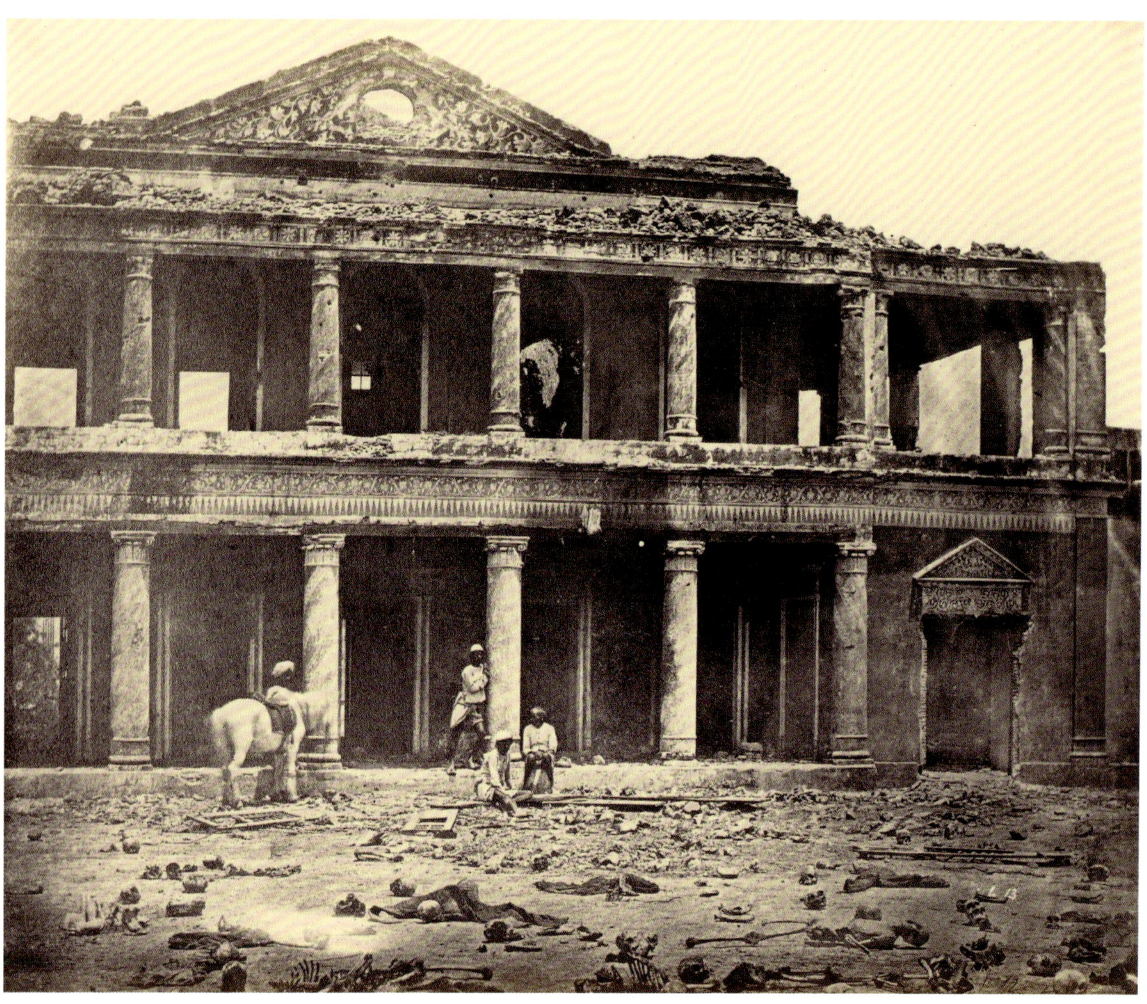

23 Felice Beato, *The Interior of the Secundrabagh after the Slaughter of 2000 Rebels*, negative 1858, print 1862. Albumen silver print from wet collodion negative, 24 × 28.7 cm. Getty Open Content Program

according to the demands of Beato (and if not these particular Indian men, then others standing outside the frame) and finally to pose beside them. Dragging the skeletons of battle back into the light of day for the camera created a sepulchral framework for these men. The figures are arranged like so many more bones, forging a threatening formal equivalence between living staffage and cadaverous props, as each is turned into pictorial fodder.

The necrotic positioning of the Indian figures frames their lives in terms of what Judith Butler has called 'precarity': a 'politically induced condition in which certain populations ... become differentially exposed to injury, violence, and death'.[39] Given the excessive and arbitrary nature of colonial violence during the counter-insurgency campaign, it is unlikely that the pictured Indian figures felt completely exempt from reprisals while their own bodies were being used by colonial photographers like Beato and Murray to document sites of violence. As the Bengali writer Bholanauth Chunder recalled shortly after the war, 'It mattered little who the red-coats killed – the innocent and the guilty, the loyal and the disloyal, the well-wisher and the traitor, were confounded in one promiscuous vengeance'.[40]

Beato's photograph is rare in how explicitly it situates the Indian body in relation to colonial violence. But 'archival anomalies' should be seen 'not as a singularity but relationally, as part of and in relation to a larger set or archive.'[41] The picturesque placement of Indian figures on sites of war is endemic to colonial photographs from this period and remained so throughout the rest of the century. I have argued in greater depth elsewhere that some of these, too, should be seen in terms of a visual rhetoric of intimidation, whereby sitters were invited to consider their status and safety under an imperial regime that had demonstrated its capacity for spectacular violence.[42] Elizabeth Edwards has described photography as a performance in which 'concentration or containment has a heightening effect on the subject matter'.[43] While she is talking about the photograph itself here, the point holds for the tableaux of the photographic event: the intensity of focus on sites of war heightens the significance of the relationships forged therein – in this case, between colonial violence and Indian bodies. The pictorial device of staffage – with its generic, de-individualised approach to the Indian figure, who merely appears as an embodiment of Indianness rather than as a differentiated subject – creates a 'zone of indistinction' between the 'innocent' and the 'guilty'.[44] As Richard Wendorf argued with regard to the theatrical portrait sittings of Joshua Reynolds in the eighteenth century, 'To find oneself posed in a certain way, within a particular setting ... let alone *as* someone else or embodying abstract qualities – is to see oneself anew.'[45] It was to see oneself exposed to the 'promiscuous vengeance' of the colonial regime.

Posing 'generic' Indian figures on sites of war thus worked in concert with the performativity at the heart of counter-insurgency doctrine. As Wagner writes, 'individual guilt' was 'ultimately of no real significance to the logic of colonial violence.'[46] In times of unrest, when the Indian population began to be looked on by colonials as an unruly, racialised mob, the undifferentiated nature of staffage contained a dangerous resonance. It registered the vulnerability of the posing bodies and of Indians more broadly to what Alex Tickell, invoking Agamben's theory of sovereign violence, has described as 'the fearful misrecognitions of a militia-led colonial society ... [which] involve the potential interchangeability of any Indian man with a "mutinous" racial Other who is potentially beyond the law as a racially-coded version of bare life.'[47]

PICTURESQUE VIOLENCE

Unlike Beato's photograph of the hanging, the grisly Sikandar Bagh image was frequently incorporated into the colonial photography albums that narrativised the war.[48] Why this difference in treatment? While both images contain their own kind of horror, the latter scene has pictorial qualities that would have rendered it more widely palatable to Victorian audiences. For instance, the horse softens the violent impact of the scene, with a certain order being re-imposed on the chaos of war through the inclusion of a domesticated animal. Harnessed and docile, the animal's presence recalls the pastoralism common in picturesque aesthetics, whereby elements of wildness are counterbalanced by signs of human habitation and control. The conventional nature of Beato's photograph is evident from an engraving after the eighteenth-century colonial artist William Hodges, whose *A View of the Gate of the Tomb of the Emperor Akbar, at Secundra* also depicts passive Indian staffage congregated round the faded grandeur of architectural ruins (fig. 24).[49] Such picturesque strategies have been seen by scholars as archetypically imperial, domesticating

24 John Browne after William Hodges, *A View of the Gate of the Tomb of the Emperor Akbar, at Secundra*, 1786. Etching, 46.5 × 62.2 cm. © The British Library Board, P2327

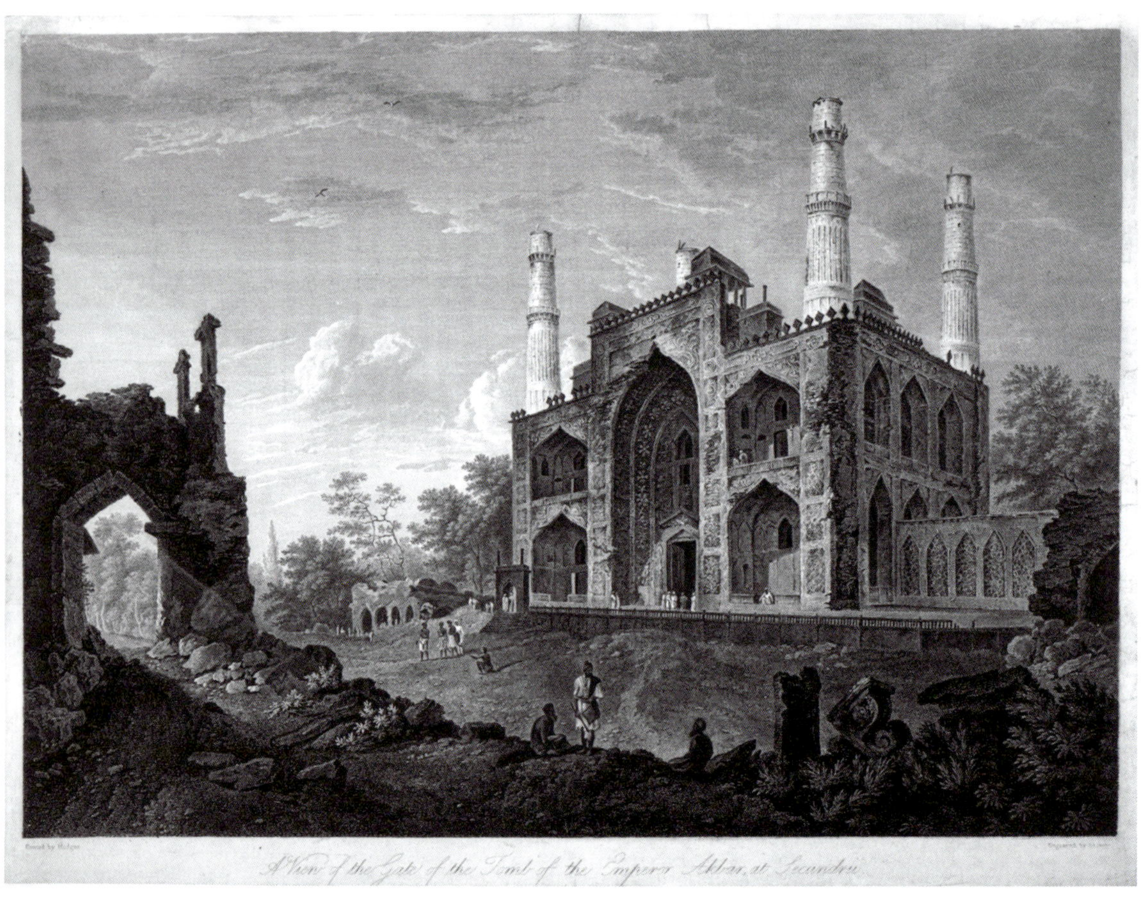

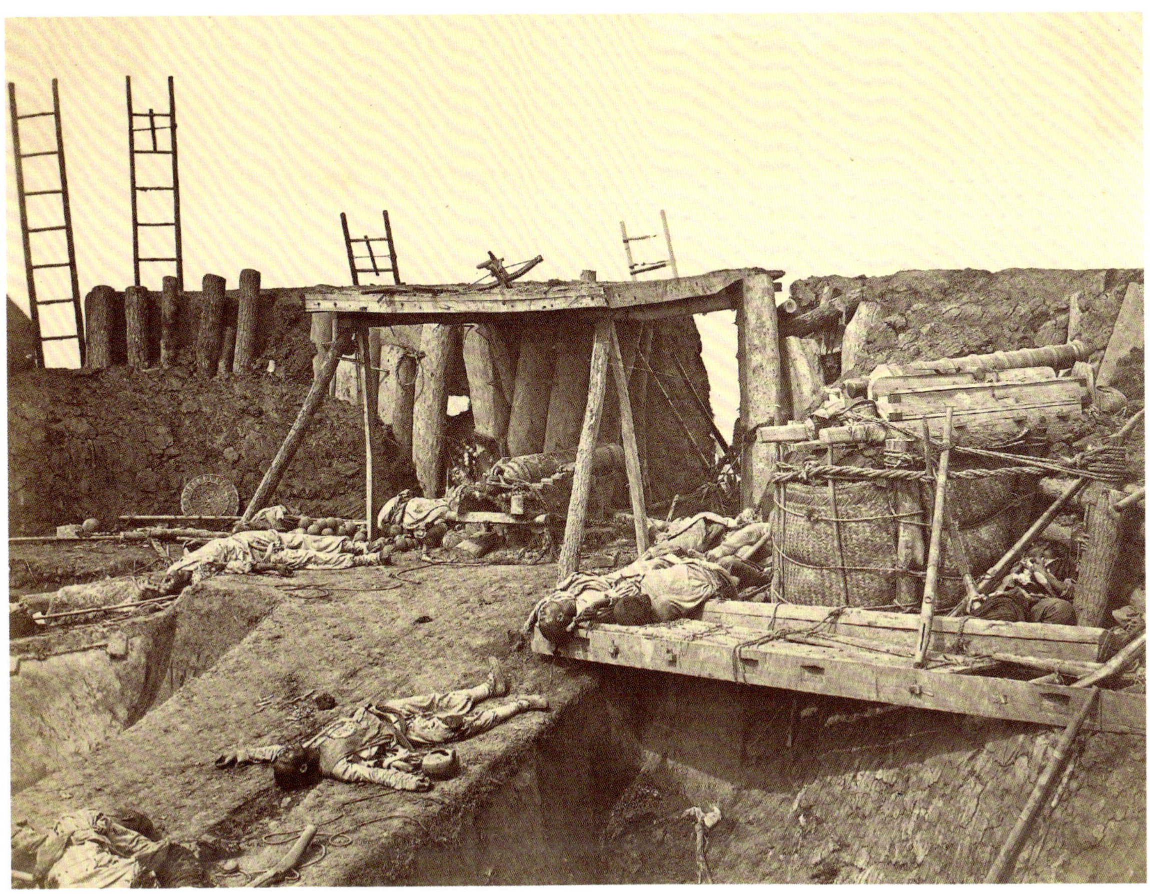

25 Felice Beato, *Angle of North Taku Fort at which the French entered*, negative 1860, print 1862. Albumen silver print from wet collodion negative, 22.3 × 30 cm. Getty Open Content Programme

alien terrains and working to provide a coherent expression of Britain's empire by making diverse landscapes submit to familiar visual schemata.[50]

Beato, a versatile photographer, drew on such longstanding and popular picturesque traditions at the same time as he engaged in more 'documentary' modes of practice.[51] By using classic landscape motifs – equine and human staffage – Beato situated modern war's horrors within a familiar aesthetic register, deploying a partial idiom of picturesqueness to help manage the reception of an imagery for which there was little precedent. It is unsurprising that, on confronting the shocking architectural wreckage created by modern artillery, photographers resorted to a visual style that had always fetishised ruination; as Ruskin wrote, the 'sight of disorder and ruin' could be readily embraced by the picturesque adept: 'Fallen cottage – desolate villa – deserted village – blasted heath – mouldering castle – to him ... they do but show jagged angles of stone and timber, [and] all are sights equally joyful.'[52]

Yet Beato's transformation of 'brutality into beauty' involved more than the straightforward application of picturesque motifs.[53] Two years after

Beato's time in Lucknow, he had moved east to China to chronicle the Second Opium War (1856–60). Following one battle, a British medical surgeon, Dr David Field Rennie, recalled walking past 'distressing' scenes of 'frightful mutilations' and heaps of 'dead and dying', only to find Beato in a state of 'great excitement', standing next to a group of Chinese corpses and 'begging that it might not be interfered with until perpetuated by his photographic apparatus'. Rennie's horror at the sight of 'carnage' contrasts dramatically with Beato's happy photographic engagement: the latter even called the scene 'beautiful'.[54]

The resulting images (fig. 25), while meditating on ruin, do not appear conventionally 'picturesque' in their composition and are not 'beautiful' in the classical sense. Rather, the term appears to borrow clumsily from established artistic discourse in order to articulate the compelling visual interest of carnage from the inchoate perspective of a 'documentary' mode of photography.[55] Beato clearly saw the commercial value in photographic coverage of global events, moving from the Crimean War to the Indian Uprising to the Anglo-Sino conflict in just five years. Yet, at this early stage in photography's history, there was no established photojournalistic framework in which to interpret such exploits. Beato's approach to potentially disturbing subject matter – the way he steadies swinging corpses, exhumes skeletal remains and aestheticises the bodies of the slain – indicates what Chaudhary describes as the 'changing perceptual arrangements of modernity'. Increasingly, the world was transformed into a picture in order to experience it, a reflex instantiated first by the picturesque disposition in the eighteenth century and then by photography in the nineteenth.[56]

The processes of image-making – and the language and conventions of aesthetics – were thus increasingly starting to regulate the affective resonance of even the most extreme experiences. Consuming warfare as a visual spectacle had significant implications for how one felt about it. Dr Rennie, seeing the devastation in China in terms of the suffering of flesh-and-blood bodies, finds the scene 'distressing', while Beato, perceiving the same scene in explicitly pictorial terms, appears in his aesthetic 'excitement' to be devoid of sympathetic response. So, even when Beato did not adopt explicitly picturesque devices, he embodied the ethically stunted way of seeing that Ruskin had identified in those (such as himself) who had inadvertently got 'rid of all claims of … compassion by treating all distress more as picturesque than as real'.[57]

In an 1845 letter to his parents, Ruskin had rehearsed the ethical anxieties that ultimately made their way into his disquisition on the picturesque in *Modern Painters*, confessing that he had a certain artistic investment in suffering:

> Yesterday, I came on a poor little child lying flat on the pavement in Bologna – sleeping like a corpse – possibly from too little food. I pulled up immediately not in pity, but in delight at the folds of its poor little ragged chemise over the thin bosom and gave the mother money not in charity, but to keep the flies off it while I made a sketch.[58]

Ruskin's response to human misery here is startlingly similar to Beato's in China, with a dubious aesthetic pleasure sparking the selfish desire to leave everything in place for the sake of a picture. It anticipates Sontag's concern, more than a hundred years later, that the photographic way of seeing is predicated on a cold abdication of social responsibility, being 'a way of at least tacitly, often explicitly, encouraging whatever is going on to keep on happening ... to be in complicity with whatever makes a subject interesting, worth photographing.'[59] Indeed, Ruskin's unease over the pathologies of the picturesque mindset in the middle of the nineteenth century is strikingly similar to the anxiety that has since motivated a good portion of modern scholarship on photography. It indicates that the new visual technology did not give rise to a novel moral problematic but reiterated the structure of feeling apparent in an earlier artistic disposition (the picturesque), while raising the ethical stakes by introducing an indexical element to the relationship between the image and the (suffering) referent.

What were the consequences of such aestheticised responses to human suffering and death? In Chaudhary's reading, these 'picturesque' reactions were manifestations of a broader shift in the modern sensorium, part of an emerging 'phantasmagoric aesthetic'. This denotes a perceptual mode under which modernity's shocks are dealt with by shielding oneself from stimuli in a process of 'sensory self-alienation', a domination over one's own feelings, which becomes the precondition for dominating others, be that through reducing populations to biopolitical statistical patterns or attempting, like Beato, to transform the chaos of war into 'aesthetically coherent assemblages of a reality placed at a distance and on display.'[60] Such a reading follows Susan Buck-Morss in its conception of aesthetics not simply in terms of pictorial conventions but as a means of shaping one's sensory engagement with the world – a protective filter between inner and outer.[61] Numbing oneself through the 'anaesthetising' qualities of aesthetic mediation was highly useful in political situations that required the maintenance of brutal hierarchies, when excesses of sympathy could threaten the stratified social order – hence Walter Benjamin's famous contention that the 'aestheticisation of politics' was the precondition for fascism.

Yet, as demonstrated by Ruskin's interrogation of his own picturesque inclinations, a certain affective numbness could coexist (even in the same person) with an anxiety about that very numbness; there was, it seems, an ethical undertow to what Ruskin called the 'merciless' picturesque engagement with suffering.[62] As John Macarthur argued in his account of Ruskin's critique of the picturesque, there was a double movement to the aestheticisation of misfortune: 'at the sight of human misery we are jolted, disgusted (at the objects and then at ourselves for aestheticizing them).'[63] Compared to Ruskin, Beato is an inscrutable historical figure, in spite of his commercial success. No writings of his exist to give us a sense of the moral psychology behind his photography but the popularity of his morbid images does not necessarily indicate that colonials were unconflicted about the aestheticisation of violence. One man's 'beauty' could be another's 'carnage' and the aesthetic approach to war, far from mitigating shock, could itself be shocking.

AESTHETICS VS ETHICS

The judicial commissioner of Lucknow, Sir George Campbell, recalled that by the time Beato had arrived in the city many months after the storming of the Sikandar Bagh, 'The great pile of bodies had been *decently* covered before the photographer could take them, but he *insisted* on having them uncovered to be photographed before they were finally disposed of'. Here we get the perspective of a prominent agent of the colonial state: Campbell was responsible for the exercise of judicial functions and the management of jails, as well as having 'all the powers of a High Court'.[64] Given the extent of public hangings in Lucknow in 1858, it is unlikely that Campbell was unused to grisly sights, so his apparent distaste for Beato's actions is perhaps somewhat hypocritical. Still, the fact that Beato was able to 'insist' on exposing corpses that had once been 'decently' covered – note the distinction between an unseemly photographic demand on the one hand and an ethical treatment of the dead on the other – points to a form of authority residing outside the (by implication) 'decent' order of the colonial state.

Such imagery could thus be experienced in terms of transgression: according to Campbell, it was a 'very horrible' photograph that Beato made in Lucknow. Photography was a new medium and as such it was of particular interest to bystanders – and some of its ability to disrupt norms was surely drawn from this novel technological status. Yet Beato's macabre photographic inclinations gained traction in a culture already habituated to the routine picturesque consumption of 'disorder and ruin'. A formalism rooted in eighteenth-century aesthetics had created the conditions in which such a scene could be dealt with as an occasion for a picture; but such a cool manoeuvre could itself be disturbing, even leading, as Ruskin feared and as Campbell's comment implies, to a loss of moral authority. 'Ruskin's disgust at picturesqueness', Macarthur wrote, 'is an exact parallel to the picturesque viewer's having forgotten to be disgusted.'[65] Likewise, Beato, consumed by the pictorial interest of corpses, 'forgets' his moral disgust, an omission that appears unseemly to colonial onlookers.

I do not want to push this point too far. Beato was certainly no pariah, and the shock-value of his photographs was probably an important part of their marketability in colonial circles. But considering Campbell's perception of horrid indecency, and bearing in mind Rennie's exposure of the 'frightful mutilations' that Beato took for 'beauty', it is apparent that the aesthetic mediation – indeed, in the case of Beato's grave-digging, the deliberate intensification – of shocking subjects was experienced as troubling or indecorous, at least at the moment of image-making itself. Even those who approved of Beato's practice, like Lang, appear to have been revelling precisely in the unseemliness of such photography. For Lang the 'horror' of the intervention was a positive thing, since it amplified the psychological intimidation inherent in the initial violence; whereas for Campbell – perhaps more mindful of keeping up appearances on behalf of the colonial state – the term 'horrible' had a more censorious valence.

Such episodes of aestheticised violence can be seen in terms of a conflicted habitus: this is what Pierre Bourdieu called the 'system of internalized structures, schemes of perception, conception, and action' that provides the coordinates for thought and agency within a society.[66] Both Chaudhary and Pinney have drawn on the habitus to theorise colonial photographic culture, the former emphasising its status as a mode of 'aesthetic comportment – the a priori grasping of the world as a picture' (a process which the picturesque 'formalizes'),[67] and the latter stressing its technomaterial and institutional components, in which colonial bureaucracy, transport networks and commerce 'came to define in certain respects the proper use of photography.'[68] Yet, in the face of violence, the perceptual habitus, which regulated experience by digesting it as a picture, was not fully normalised or integrated at an ethical level with the wider social habitus (the 'tacit system of codes which quietly encode a lifeworld'), even as the former sometimes managed to pursue its ends within the latter from both a logistical (Beato was permitted to act like this by the colonial authorities) and commercial (Beato's imagery was popular) perspective.[69] Photographing violence was a complex and conflicted enterprise for the Victorians. The modern, pictorialising disposition could be offensive to British sensibilities, even amid the anomie of bitter imperial warfare.

PHOTOGRAPHY IN EXTREMIS

Following the successful repression of the Uprising, a 'belief in the spectacle of violence took seed' among colonials.[70] Yet, even as the British put their faith in the efficacy of demonstrative brutality, particularly when it came to cowing the 'fanatics' and 'savages' living in the fractious and expanding frontiers of the Raj, explicit photographs of colonial violence are a relative rarity in the archive, in spite of the fact that camera technologies became increasingly affordable and prevalent as the century progressed.

This does not mean that such photographs were not taken. When, in 1903, a colonial soldier involved in the invasion of Tibet sent photographs of enemy corpses back to his family, he was distressed to discover that the images were circulating outside this private network because his mother had sent them to the illustrated magazine, *Black and White*, leading him to urge her to stop 'sending photos of dead people' to the press.[71] The public circulation of violent photographs had the potential to scandalise. In 1886, for example, as John Falconer's research showed, there was a public outcry when *The Times* ran an exposé about a situation in Mandalay in which the public execution of Burmese 'dacoits' (bandits) had been photographed by Colonel Willoughby Wallace Hooper, under whose regime of martial law the men had been summarily condemned.[72] The article that broke the story claimed that Hooper's attempt 'was not an isolated case', a fact backed up by none other than the Viceroy of India, Frederic Hamilton-Temple-Blackwood, 1st Marquess of Dufferin, who admitted in his correspondence with the home government that he had 'heard of prisoners being photographed on such occasions, but I did not see any picture.'[73] Like Murray's elusive 'No. 18', Hooper's practice draws our attention to an intriguing archival absence.

Hooper had joined the 7th Madras Cavalry in 1858, introduced to colonial service during a time of intense counter-insurgent violence. A keen amateur photographer, he contributed, along with many of his photographic peers, to the anthropological project *The People of India* in the aftermath of the Uprising. Yet Hooper's output grew increasingly distinctive over the coming years due to his embrace of morbidity: vultures feasting on carrion; the carcasses of hunted tigers; the haunted, skeletal desolation of Madrassi famine victims; and the corpses of Burmese enemies strewn among the wreckage of a frontier assault. He had a 'passion' for photographing 'any exceptional incident', wrote a contemporary journalist, telling the tale of a disgruntled sepoy who had turned on his British commanders only to have Hooper respond to the mortal threat by fetching his camera and taking a photograph of the sepoy, 'who

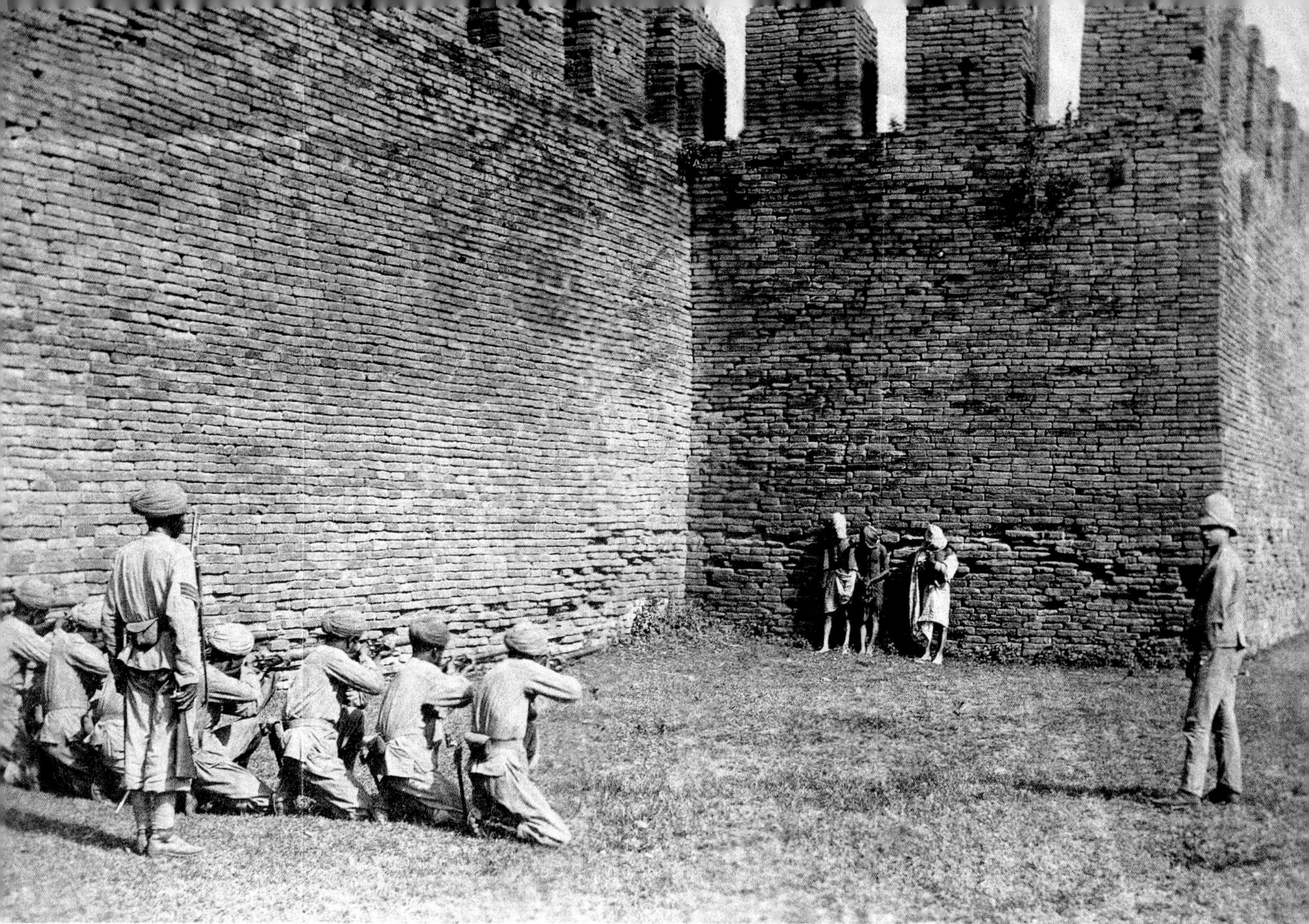

26 Willoughby Wallace Hooper, *Execution of Dacoits at Mandalay*, negative 1885, print 1887. Albumen print 66.5 × 44.7 cm. © Alamy Stock Photo

was in the act of taking aim at him'.[74] This story is unlikely to be true but it positions Hooper as an embodiment of an emerging perceptual disposition that responded to the world primarily as a picture and only secondarily in terms of affects or (as became controversial) ethics. Hooper's 'craze about photography', as the viceroy characterised it, culminated in his desire in 1885 to use the lately much improved shutter speed of the camera to capture the instant the bullet hit the body of the condemned.[75]

Two photographs of the executions survive. In the first (fig. 26), three hooded and manacled Burmese men stand with their backs against a pockmarked wall, facing a firing-squad of anonymous-looking sepoys taking aim. A lone British colonial directs the action. In the second there is a white cloud of smoke billowing from the sepoys' rifles and, looking towards the wall, we can see that one of the Burmese men has collapsed in a heap on the ground, leaving two hooded figures still standing, awaiting bullets of their own.[76] The instantaneity of the snapshot mirrors the instantaneity of death; in Hooper's practice, writes Pinney, we see 'photography's mortiferous *eidos*: the camera as trigger and a ballistic photographic image, hitting the spectator "like a bullet", as Walter Benjamin would later write.'[77]

The episode in Burma provoked a debate in Parliament and an official inquiry in India. It was not the public execution that troubled the authorities so much as the fact that it had been photographed. As Grattan Geary, a journalist for the *Bombay Gazette*, noted acidly in his book about the Burmese campaign (published the same year, 1886), there was a rank hypocrisy to a British sensibility that was revolted at 'photographing a batch of men at the moment of their execution, when their execution in batches is accepted as an ordinary incident in the subjugation of a conquered people.'[78] Indeed, as reported in *The Times*, the executions were part of a wider spectacle of horrors: under Hooper's regime, the bodies of the dead were carried through the streets and 'seen by hundreds' ('entrails were protruding from one body through the wounds made by the bullets').[79] In a counter-insurgency culture in which such atrocities bloomed, what was controversial about an execution being photographed?

Geary believed that such photography was disturbing to the British because it had become 'the custom to close the eyes and ears to the real nature of the "salutary severities" which are sparingly alluded to in the narratives of military operations in a vanquished country.' Hooper's photography risked piercing the veil of ignorance that arose from the British tendency to 'slur over' the violent excesses of conquest: 'It would be a great gain to the course of humanity', wrote Geary, 'if there were more Colonel Hoopers, who would focus and fix and make widely known ... the real nature of the price which subjugated populations pay for the blessings of civilisation.'[80] Photography was indeed becoming increasingly crucial to the emergence of Victorian humanitarian discourses, enabling ethical practices of witnessing.[81] Hooper, of course, did not have humanitarian objectives in mind; it was after all he who was arranging the executions. Yet, while this is an example of perpetrator photography, it did not simply express or consolidate Hooper's own desensitised perspective on colonial violence. It altered the terms in which that violence was seen, shining a critical light back on the colonial culture in which such a photograph could be taken. An execution that would have remained uncontroversial in itself (if reports were to 'slur over' it in the customary manner) came to be problematised because it was photographed.

Why? It was not the graphic nature of Hooper's actual photographs that was troubling so much as what the act of taking such a photograph seemed to suggest about colonial military methods and mindset. Geary wrote, 'there is something unpleasant and almost sinister at the coolness and deliberation with which the action and the tragedy was suspended in order that a scientific record might be taken of the effect, physical and moral, of the shock of bullets on the persons of defenceless and despairing men.' And yet such unpleasantness was perhaps merely the 'inevitable' consequence, he added, of a colonial military culture 'which ordains the practice of cruelty ... dulling the moral sense until it is impossible to draw the line with any precision between what is legitimate and what is not.'[82] For Geary, the taking of the photograph signalled a broader degradation of moral sensibilities under the military doctrines of 'savage warfare'.

For the authorities, though, the extent to which Hooper's actions were problematic seemed to rest on whether or not he had altered military protocol in order to arrange the scene to his liking. The initial article in *The Times* insisted that Hooper's photography had prolonged the execution proceedings:

> The ghastly scenes which constantly recur in executions carried out by the Provost-Marshal constitute grave public scandals ... after the orders 'ready', 'present' have been given to the firing party, the Provost Marshal fixed his camera on the prisoners, who at times are kept waiting several minutes in that position. The officer commanding the firing party is then directed by the Provost Marshal to give the order to fire at the moment when he exposes his plates. So far no satisfactory negative has been obtained, and the experiments are likely to be continued.[83]

This photography-induced time-lag between the words 'present' and 'fire' became the main point of contention. When the viceroy responded to parliamentary questions about Hooper's practice, he insisted that the photographer 'did not arrange details of the execution so as to suit his camera as alleged' and that since the condemned men were blindfolded, 'they were consequently unaware of what was going on, and no delay took place.'[84] In a defensive letter to *The Times*, Hooper similarly asserted that 'no delay of any kind took place' and that the men 'knew nothing of the fact that the camera was there.'[85]

It seems probable that Hooper knew that the camera created a more sensational and distressing spectacle, if not for the blindfolded men about to be shot, then for the crowd of Burmese witnesses to this act of exemplary violence. *The Times* claimed that his photography amounted to a mode of psychological terrorism: 'These proceedings take place before a crowd of mixed nationalities, and cannot fail to have a demoralizing effect.'[86] Recalling Lang's belief that the taking of a photograph heaped 'additional horrors' onto already horrific proceedings, we see that the camera was an intimidating supplement to colonial violence, not a neutral means of documentation. Yet it was a supplement that also raised troubling issues for colonials themselves.

Ultimately, such photography threatened the legitimacy of the colonial violence it commemorated: the viceroy suspended all military executions in Burma as a consequence of the scandal. The camera 'added an unseemly element' to the proceedings.[87] It seems to have exposed what Lee Ann Fujii terms the 'extra-lethal' nature of such killings, a category of violence in which an excessive theatricality transgressed 'shared norms and beliefs about appropriate treatment of the living and the dead'.[88] Hooper's desire to capture the execution as an image compromised the sanitised veneer of military violence, revealing what Slavoj Žižek, in reference to the Abu Ghraib prison photographs of 2003, termed the 'unknown known' of military-imperial culture: its libidinal investment in the violence it enacts, which is not merely professional or strategic in character, but contains an excess of 'obscene enjoyment', a disavowed but constitutive element of the culture.[89]

The execution images were not included among the hundred prints from the Burmese war that Hooper sold as a photographic album published in 1887.[90] Thus, while photography was increasingly shaping Victorian perceptions of global conflict, its most extreme instances (as with Murray and Beato) were not its most prominent. However, when a copy of Hooper's *Burmah* was auctioned at Christie's in 2007, it was marketed as 'rare' because it contained an additional two prints not found in most copies – the execution photographs.[91] What might be termed the 'canonical' photography of imperial warfare, from standardised commercial albums to government records, was thus shadowed by a more controversial imagery of colonial violence, an obscene supplement to the official vision of war.

CONCLUSION

For the Victorians, the most disturbing thing about the photographs of violence examined in this chapter seems not to have been the representational content of the pictures themselves. It was the nature of the image-making encounters from which such photographs emerged. The presence of the camera in the imperial field introduced an 'unseemly' or 'horrible' element into the colonial engagement with violence, prompting interactions in which, as Ruskin had feared, compassion was supplanted by pictorial demands.

The aestheticisation of violence was unpredictable in its effects. Photography entered a culture that had already been primed by picturesque traditions to interact with the world as a picture. This was, as Chaudhary has argued, key to the management of the Victorian sensorium in the face of the ever-increasing visual novelty, fragmentation and shock of modernity. A perceptual habitus helped to orient the Victorians, providing a visual framework in which to apprehend exotic and difficult stimuli; yet these habits of vision and representation also compromised their ability to engage with people and places according to ethical logics – the humane sympathy that Ruskin aspired to in his rejection of the 'lower' picturesque; the decent and seemly treatment of dead enemies; the appropriate management of military executions. The aestheticisation of violence was laced with ethical quandary; embedded within the aesthetic regulation of troubling scenes was the risk of a certain excess of picturesque enjoyment, a spectre of moral indifference or even sadism that rendered this modern coping mechanism a potential disturbance.

4 · SKETCHING 'ON THE SPOT'

Shaping the Victorian Experience of Colonial War, *c.*1854–1900

IN 1901 THE AUSTRALIAN-BORN AND LONDON-TRAINED ARTIST Mortimer Menpes (1855–1938) cast a wry eye on a phenomenon that he believed was endemic to the late Victorian engagement with warfare. He claimed that military campaigns were increasingly mediated affairs within which journalists had conspired to claim a privileged status for themselves: newspaper reporters and war artists 'suited one another to perfection,' for while 'one described his companion in the midst of bursting shells, the other sketched him in that uncomfortable but gloriously conspicuous position.'[1] These adventure-loving journalists were apparently so heroic that by the time Menpes was employed as a 'special artist' for the illustrated magazine *Black and White* during the Second African War (1899–1902), he could speak acerbically of believing that military generals were entirely 'unnecessary' on the battlefield since, 'as anyone knows who has studied the records of recent wars, it is almost invariably a special correspondent who leads the troops to victory, or directs great operations, or comes to the rescue of Field-Marshals.'[2]

The artist's tongue is firmly in cheek here but I nevertheless want to take seriously the wartime agency he describes. How did the conspicuous presence of artists 'on the spot' – to use the parlance of the nineteenth-century press – alter the experience of conflict for combatants? This question remains unaddressed in scholarship, in spite of the period from the 1850s to 1900 constituting a 'golden age' of military correspondence because of its combination of frequent wars, minimal official restrictions on journalists and an expanding popular press.[3] The rise of pictorial news in the Victorian era meant that large sections of the general public were exposed to images of global warfare on a regular basis for the first time. The *Illustrated London News* and *The Graphic* catered to what Rudyard Kipling described in his 1890 story *The Light That Failed* as 'the

William Simpson, *The First Shot*, 1878 (detail of fig. 32).

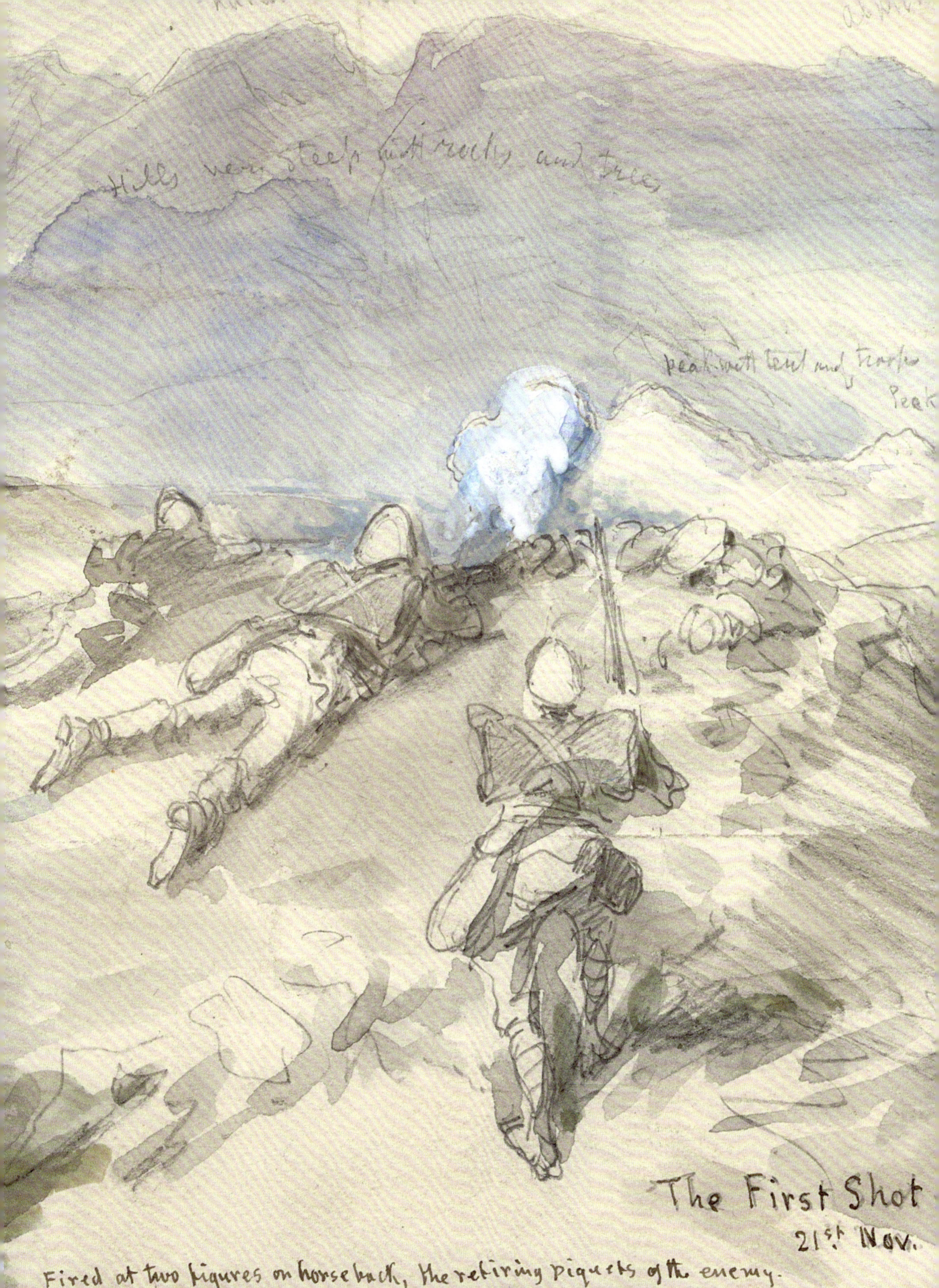
Hills very steep with rocks and trees
Peak
The First Shot
21st Nov.
Fired at two figures on horseback, the retiring piquets of the enemy.

27 'The Afghan War: Special Correspondents Sleeping on the Battlefield, Night Before the Attack on Fort Ali Musjid', *Illustrated London News*, 4 January 1879. © Mary Evans Picture Library

blind, brutal, British public's bestial thirst for blood.' Journalism was to modern society what gladiatorial combat had been to the ancient world: 'They have no arenas now', Kipling wrote, 'but they must have must have special correspondents'.[4]

The phenomenon of the 'special' has lately begun to receive more attention in scholarship but recent accounts have prioritised the text-based reportage of figures like William Howard Russell of *The Times* and Archibald Forbes of the *Daily News*.[5] Special artists, by contrast, have received severely limited treatment, with once popular and prolific artists like William Simpson (1823–1899), Melton Prior (1845–1910) and Frederic Villiers (1851–1922) remaining almost entirely overlooked by art historians.[6] Yet these men's names, images and articles would have been familiar both to the nineteenth-century metropolitan reading public and to the soldiers and colonials involved in the far-flung campaigns being reported. The people involved in imperial military campaigns were doubly exposed to the imagery of the special artist, consuming the engravings ultimately published in the newspapers but also seeing, and posing for, the plein-air sketching practices that were documenting – and constituting – geopolitical events in the first place. While some of the pictures worked up by Richard Caton Woodville (1856–1927) in Britain have been subject to sophisticated analysis, little has been said about the independent significance of the original sketches emanating from 'the field'.[7] Yet it was the sketch that accrued particular value in the Victorian imaginary as a symbol of the new breed of swashbuckling journalist that Menpes came to mock; and it was the sketch that was seen to express the phenomenology of the modern conflict from which it came.

During its coverage of the Second Anglo-Afghan War (1878–80), the *Illustrated London News* ran a front-page visual report from their man on the spot, William Simpson – 'the *doyen* of Special War Artists, as Dr. William Howard Russell is the *doyen* of Special War Correspondents'[8] – in which he advertised his embedded status on the campaign.[9] 'The Afghan War: Special Correspondents Sleeping on the Battlefield, Night Before the Attack on Fort Ali Musjid' (fig. 27) showed three reporters – Phil Robinson of the *Daily Telegraph*, Forbes of the *Daily News* and Simpson himself – sleeping out in the open in an Afghan valley on the eve of a military assault, exposed to the same conditions as the soldiers whose recumbent bodies populate the middle ground of a sublime vista that stretches back into the shadowy mountains of the Khyber Pass. The image embodied the main conceit of the special correspondent, that they were immersed in the events they chronicled. 'He is found risking his life in the passes of Afghanistan, and in Zululand assisting at the defeat and capture of Cetywayo', wrote the picture editor of the *Illustrated*

THE ILLUSTRATED LONDON NEWS

REGISTERED AT THE GENERAL POST-OFFICE FOR TRANSMISSION ABROAD.

No. 2064.—Vol. LXXIV. SATURDAY, JANUARY 4, 1879. WITH TWO SUPPLEMENTS } SIXPENCE. By Post, 6½d.

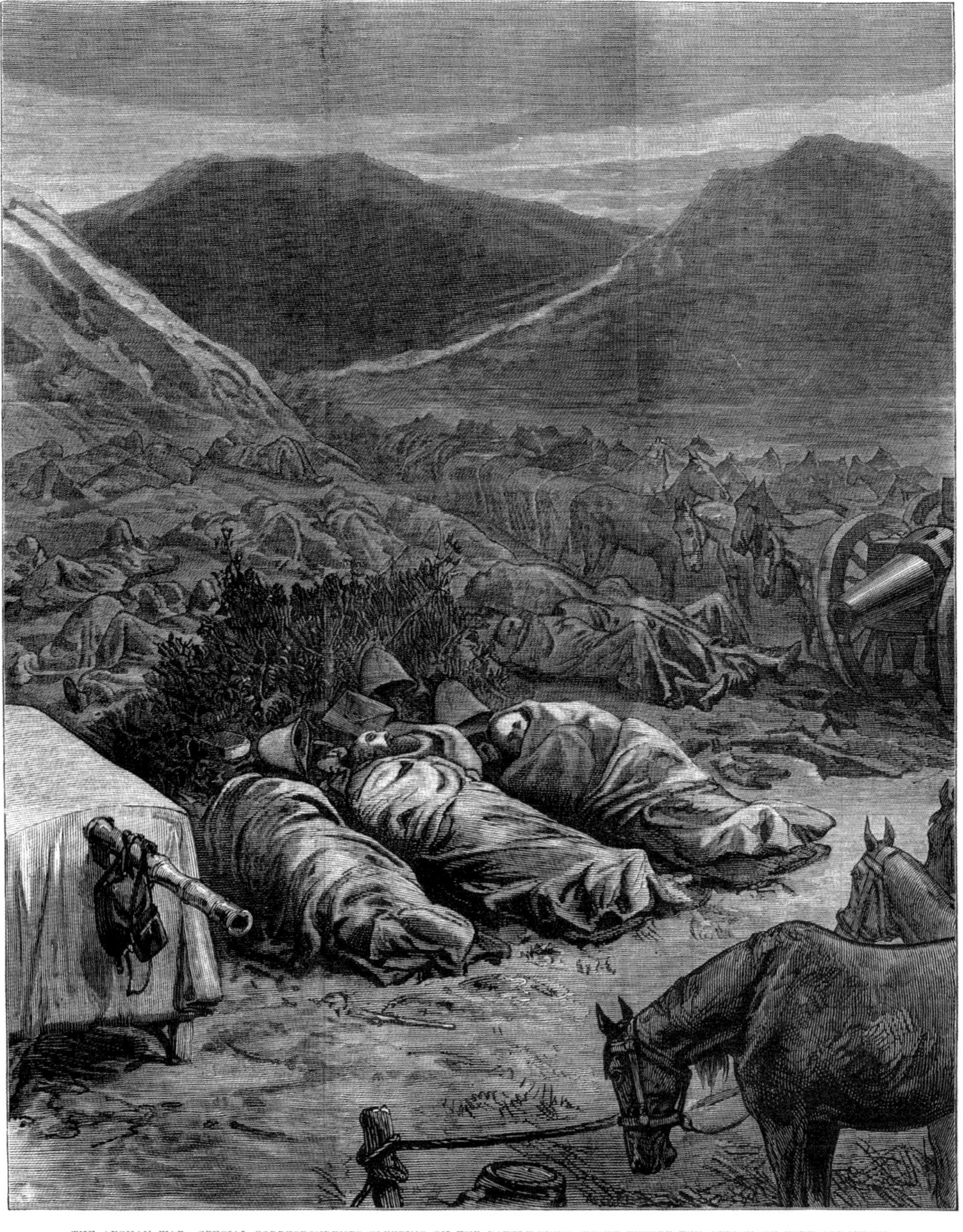

THE AFGHAN WAR: SPECIAL CORRESPONDENTS SLEEPING ON THE BATTLE-FIELD, NIGHT BEFORE THE ATTACK ON FORT ALI MUSJID.
FROM A SKETCH BY MR. WILLIAM SIMPSON, OUR SPECIAL ARTIST.

London News, Mason Jackson, 'the special artist pursues his purpose with stoical self-possession in spite of cold, hunger, and fatigue.'[10] Clearly, this is partly the stuff of masculinist fantasy but it points to the fact that sketching on the spot was not an impassive record of events by an artist standing with Cartesian imperiousness outside the situation they were documenting. It engaged what Christine Ferguson, in her account of nineteenth-century fiction's construction of (non)normative bodies, terms a 'somatic epistemology', in which the narration of mental and physical processes worked to shape Victorian sensory capacities.[11] In the textual and visual narratives of the nineteenth-century press, the correspondent's bodily experience was both productive of knowledge about the hardships of campaigning and performative of a certain normative vision of the Victorian military physique as able, adaptable and tough.

What did soldiers make of their new journalist bedfellows? I argue that the presence of press representatives like Simpson shaped the psychological engagement of combatants with hardship and violence, helping to regulate the affects and stabilise the meanings of volatile and potentially unsettling events by framing them in terms of what Martin Green called 'the energizing myth' of empire – adventure.[12] Both textual and visual journalists tended to this mythology, creating narratives of derring-do that drew on fictional tropes of the *Boys' Own* variety; yet artists also presided over spaces of performance in the field wherein those tropes of masculinity were enacted by the bodies of combatants. The act of sketching on the spot, I suggest, was a nodal event in which multiple logics – artistic, journalistic, literary, military, theatrical and epistemological – converged to manage the perception of colonial violence. With the invention of photography in 1839 there had been much excitement over the new technology's capacity to serve as a reliable 'pencil of nature', yet throughout the nineteenth century the humble pencil of the artist remained dominant in war journalism. The artist, this chapter will show, had some distinct advantages over the photographer when it came to bearing witness. For both colonial combatants and metropolitan consumers of news in the Victorian era, conflict was frequently consumed via the charismatic interventions of the special artist and the expressive capacities of the sketch.

EPISTEMOLOGY OF EXPOSURE

Amid general critical swooning over the unparalleled realism of Fenton's photographs of the Crimean War in 1855, one reviewer had briefly struck a more disappointed note: 'As photographists [sic] grow stronger in nerve and cooler in head, we shall have not merely the bivouac and the foraging party, but the battle itself painted; and while the fate of nations is in the balance we shall hear of the chemist [i.e. photographer] measuring his acids and rubbing his glasses to a polish.'[13] The *Athenaeum* critic did not put the absence of dynamic battle scenes down to the long exposure times of early photography; he attributed it to the camera's lack of immersion in events. The implication here – that Fenton failed to produce scenes of actual combat because he did not have the 'nerve' to get close enough to the action – was a criticism pre-empted by the photographer himself, who told of operating under fire, with his assistant even getting wounded while they worked.[14] Yet this did not stop a similar charge being issued in 1862 when, on seeing photographs from the American Civil War, a writer for *The Times* noted that it was Fenton who first 'pitched his camera stand under fire' before adding, 'but Mr. [William] Simpson was out before him in the Crimea'. The primary meaning of this phrase 'out before him' is chronological – the enterprising Glaswegian artist had arrived in the Crimea in November 1854, many months before Fenton – but it is also suggestive of being closer to the front line, 'in the trenches', where Simpson was able to produce scenes that the critic believed 'were much more interesting than the likenesses or groups or other works of the photographer.'[15]

From the trenches of the Crimea to the passes of Afghanistan, Simpson went out of his way to cultivate an adventurous professional persona that drew its journalistic authority from his experience of being 'out in the thick of it'.[16] Following a stint as an artist for the London print publisher Colnaghi's in the 1850s, he had gone on to cover the Abyssinian Expedition in 1868, the Franco-Prussian War of 1870–71 and numerous other global events as a special for the *Illustrated London News*, all the while making a name for himself among Orientalist circles as an authority on Eastern architecture. More so than photography, it was Simpson's practice of sketching in the field that came to be seen as the ideal means of capturing warfare. Partly this was due to the kinesis of the artist's sketch compared with early photographs which could not yet capture movement; and partly it was simply because newspapers could not easily print photographs until the end of the century. But early photographers were also hampered by their burdensome equipment, which rendered them far less mobile and thus less consistently immersed in the cut and thrust of battle; an 1870 military article about photographic fieldwork called Fenton's wagon-cum-studio in the Crimea 'manifestly useless', since in order to acquire worthwhile reconnaissance a photographer would have to 'accompany our skirmishers, and get well in front'.[17]

As for reconnaissance, so too for reportage: by the late Victorian period, a journalistic ethos had emerged that saw a correspondent's credibility as the product not of their distance, detachment or disinterest but of their being thoroughly enmeshed in the action and prey to the dangers they were documenting. We might call this an 'epistemology of exposure', wherein the observer's authority was attained by opening themselves up to the extreme conditions they were chronicling. In an era characterised by an increasing intellectual wariness regarding the regrettable fallibility of the human senses, it is noteworthy that the illustrated press began investing considerable faith in the authority of the corporeal eye-witness immersed in world events. The Victorians had celebrated photography for its compelling truth-value precisely because the camera appeared to transcend the limitations of subjective vision and the untrustworthy vagaries of creative authorship, providing instead a 'mechanical' and 'non-interventionist' image of reality.[18] Yet even this photographic fantasy of an autogenic and thus objective document – what Jennifer Green-Lewis, writing on Fenton, describes as 'the logically nonsensical disembodied perspective of realist photography [which] was gradually endowed with the badges of disinterest and authority' – was in fact frequently supplemented by an appeal to an alternative authority rooted in the (supposedly transcended) authorial body.[19]

Take, for instance, the highly successful commercial photographer Samuel Bourne. In photographs like *Manirung Pass* (1866; fig. 28), Bourne produced images of India in which a soaring panopticism laid claim to a 'transcendent'[20] viewpoint that was seemingly not prey to the limitations of the body – a manifestation of the 'monarch-of-all-I-survey' perspective which Mary Louise Pratt has identified as key to the aesthetics of empire.[21] But Bourne, like Fenton and many other travelling photographers of the period, went out of his way in his accounts to stress exactly what his images seem to deny: his 'suffering', 'labour' and 'anxiety'.[22] Photographers were keen that audiences knew of their struggles with adverse climatic conditions, volatile photographic chemicals, burdensome equipment, disgruntled servants, recalcitrant sitters, hostile terrain, challenging transport and tropical sicknesses. There was a concern with exactly how photographs came to be made – painfully, laboriously – in the field via corporeal 'privations' and what Pinney terms 'technomaterial complexity'.[23] Such accounts undercut the Victorian fantasy of the autogenic image, emphasising the blood, sweat and tears of the authorial producer. In this respect they are not dissimilar from the narratives of exposure that worked to authorise the special artist.

This insistence on the somatic agency of the observer in the recording process owed much to eighteenth-century Enlightenment methods of science, which had invested the body with considerable authority, providing the senses were appropriately disciplined. An ethos of fieldwork – exemplified most famously by Alexander von Humboldt and his

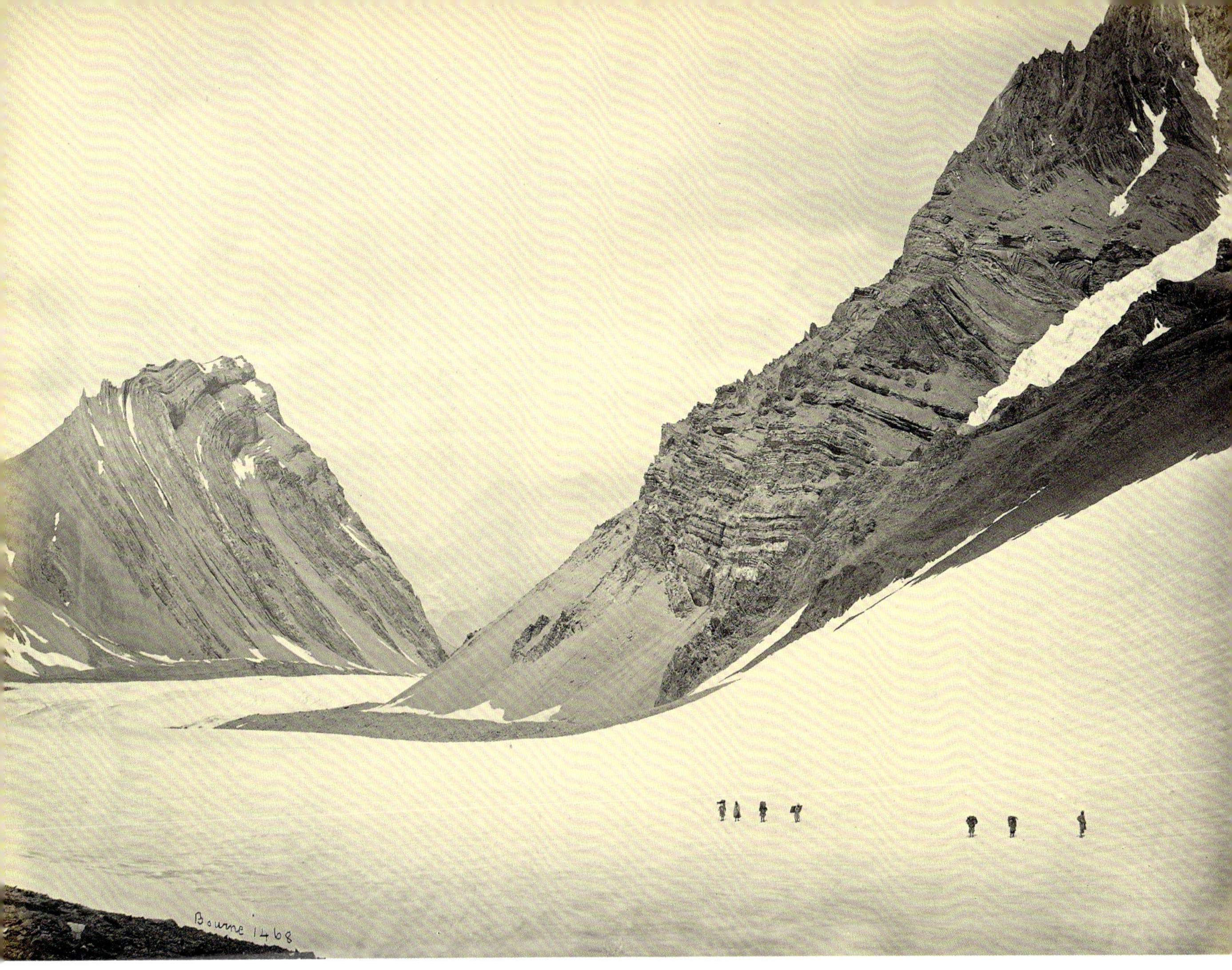

observations of tropical nature in South America – placed particular emphasis on 'an expert type of viewing that involved training and specialized practices of observation and representation – not merely sight but insight.'[24]

28 Samuel Bourne, *The Manirung Pass – Elevation 18,600 Feet*, 1866. Albumen print from wet collodion negative, 23.3 × 29.2 cm. Getty Open Content Program

The Humboldtian intellectual methodology of in situ observation finds echoes in the journalistic ideal of the special correspondent – the newspaper's man on the spot who could distil the complexities of geopolitics and the fog of war into intelligible textual and visual reports. When it came to insight over mere sight, artists enjoyed a privileged position vis-à-vis the camera precisely because their practice was seen to involve an interpretative dimension that enabled them to extract 'an idea of some sort in every incident'. 'If mere facts were all that were required,' wrote Henry V. Barnett in an 1883 article on illustrated war reportage, 'the special [artists] might throw away his pencil and take instantaneous photography.'[25] Journalism was not unusual in its persistent embrace of drawing. Photography struggled completely to supplant draughtsmanship in numerous fields, from archaeology to botany, because the pencil enabled one to exercise judgement in emphasising 'typical' or 'essential' characteristics while disregarding anomalous details.

SKETCHING IN THE FIELD

The epistemological ideal of the artist working in the field had emerged at the intersection of scientific, aesthetic, imperial and even ethical practices of witnessing during the 'Age of Exploration'.[26] The British artist William Hodges (1744–1797) pioneered the practice of plein air painting while accompanying Captain Cook's second voyage to the South Pacific islands in 1772–4, a journey that officially took place for the enlightened pursuit of scientific knowledge (tracking the transit of Venus) but nevertheless saw many territories being claimed for the British Crown along the way. Hodges was part of a new breed of 'travelling artists', from naturalists to abolitionists, working in various degrees of alignment with Humboldtian ideals of observation in the late eighteenth and early nineteenth century.[27] His method of immersive visual engagement, in which he attempted to capture the effects of the scene in front of him, led to a more spontaneous manner of painting that moved away from the rigid classical conventions that were then dominant in the Academy, pioneering a style which came to define the anti-academicism of the Romantic movement.[28] Yet this art historical trajectory – which takes us all the way to the shimmering lily ponds of Claude Monet by way of the evanescent clouds of John Constable – also had its roots in the practical concerns of sailors.

By 1801, the Board of Admiralty was issuing instructions to Captain Matthew Flinders regarding his expedition to Australia, stating that the resident artists be given 'time to finish as many of their works as they possibly can on the spot where they may have been begun.'[29] As Michael Charlesworth has noted, here we have a 'truly extraordinary' occurrence in which 'the Lords of the Admiralty, of all people, should, during the last third of the eighteenth century, be making demands on professional artists ... that anticipate revolutionary nineteenth-century painting practices by the French Impressionists.'[30] The methods of visual fieldwork that developed in the periphery thus rebounded on the metropole in ways that came to define the visual culture of modernity.[31] The experiences of travelling artists in the eighteenth century led to major changes in how European artists tackled their own environment, as a plein air ethos incubated under imperial direction in exotic climes ended up providing the basis for the visual ephemera of the illustrated press and the innovations of European art.

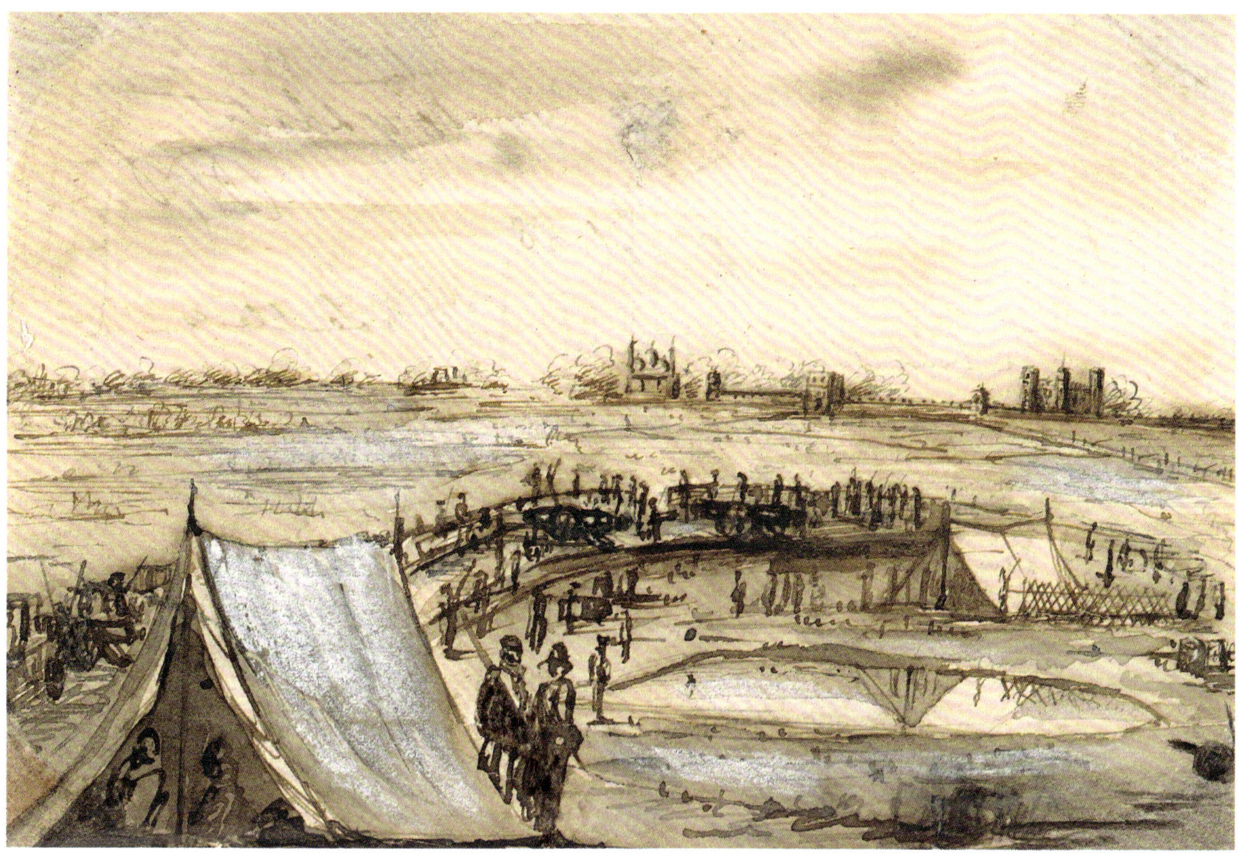

29 Constantin Guys, *War Encampment*, *c.*1854. Pen and brown ink with gouache on paper, 8.5 × 12.7 cm. Morgan Library and Museum, New York

Journalistic and avant-garde vectors of image-making converged in the figure of Constantin Guys, a French artist whose Crimean War drawings (fig. 29), 'hastily sketched on the spot' for the *Illustrated London News*, caught the attention of the prominent French poet and cultural critic Charles Baudelaire. In a foundational text of European modernism, Baudelaire christened Guys the eponymous 'Painter of Modern Life' and urged fellow artists to follow the humble correspondent in his passionate engagement with modernity through the portrayal of 'the ephemeral, the fugitive, the contingent'.[32] Defined by its evanescence, modernity called for a correspondingly dynamic mode of artistic capture – speedy sketching from within the metamorphic spectacle itself. Baudelaire claimed that Guys was the 'perfect *flaneur*' whose genius was 'to become one flesh with the crowd ... to set up house in the heart of the multitude, amid the ebb and flow of movement ... the lover of universal life enters into the crowd as though it were a reservoir of electrical energy'.[33] Again, here is an observer whose artistic authority is seen to be the product of their immersion, their exposure to what they wished to record.

Speed and exposure, then, were the defining characteristics of the special artist's method. Through his 'rapid method of working', wrote Jackson in *The Pictorial Press: Its Origin and Progress* (1885), the special artist 'can, by a few strokes of his pencil, indicate a passing scene by a kind of pictorial shorthand.'[34] 'He must have sound sense and rapid judgement', concurred *Macmillan's Magazine* in 1904, 'a quick observant eye, capable of taking in the ever-shifting scenes and changing incidents of a field of battle, and a capacity to convey his impressions readily and vividly to paper.'[35] The nimble quality of the sketch thematised the fugitive nature of modernity; the artist's minimal tools 'facilitated mobility and restlessness of vision', allowing them, as Romita Ray writes of the picturesque landscape artist, 'to travel and live *within* the experience of producing [images]'.[36] Portable drawing technologies allowed for the sort of inconspicuous mixing in the dynamic crowd that was characteristic of the flaneur's 'emblematically modern mobility of gaze' – a mixing and mobility which photographers did not achieve until the invention of the hand-held Kodak camera in 1888.[37]

Mobility was key to the Victorian conception of white male agency in the world; the popular imperial tales of H. Rider Haggard and Robert Louis Stevenson were predicated on the fantasy of traversing cultures across time and space while maintaining the essential integrity of the self.[38] Special artists aped the style of such imperial romances in their reports, fashioning a journalistic *mythos* of brio and pluck that stressed their versatile yet reliable spectatorship. As Jackson summarised it:

> in addition to undergoing the privations of beleaguered places, they had also to run the risk of shot and shell, and sometimes they were obliged to destroy their sketching materials under fear of arrest. The danger of being seen sketching or found with sketches, in their possession was so great, that on one occasion a special artist ... purchased the largest book of cigarette papers he could obtain, and on them he made little sketches, prepared in case of danger to smoke them in the faces of his enemies.[39]

Artists told of making clandestine sketches on tissue paper rolled up into small balls 'to be chewed up or swallowed if "in extremis"'; surreptitiously drawing lines in the dirt with an umbrella as an aide-mémoire for a later rendering; sketching on the back of a roll of wallpaper in lieu of more traditional materials; and sending multiple photographic copies of sketches by air balloon so as to avoid censors.[40] Such tactics were necessary because the sketchbook was touted as a 'most dangerous article to be found in your possession' during warfare due to the 'spy fever' that could prevail; indeed, the *Illustrated London News*'s best-known special artists, Simpson and Prior, were both apprehended as spies during European

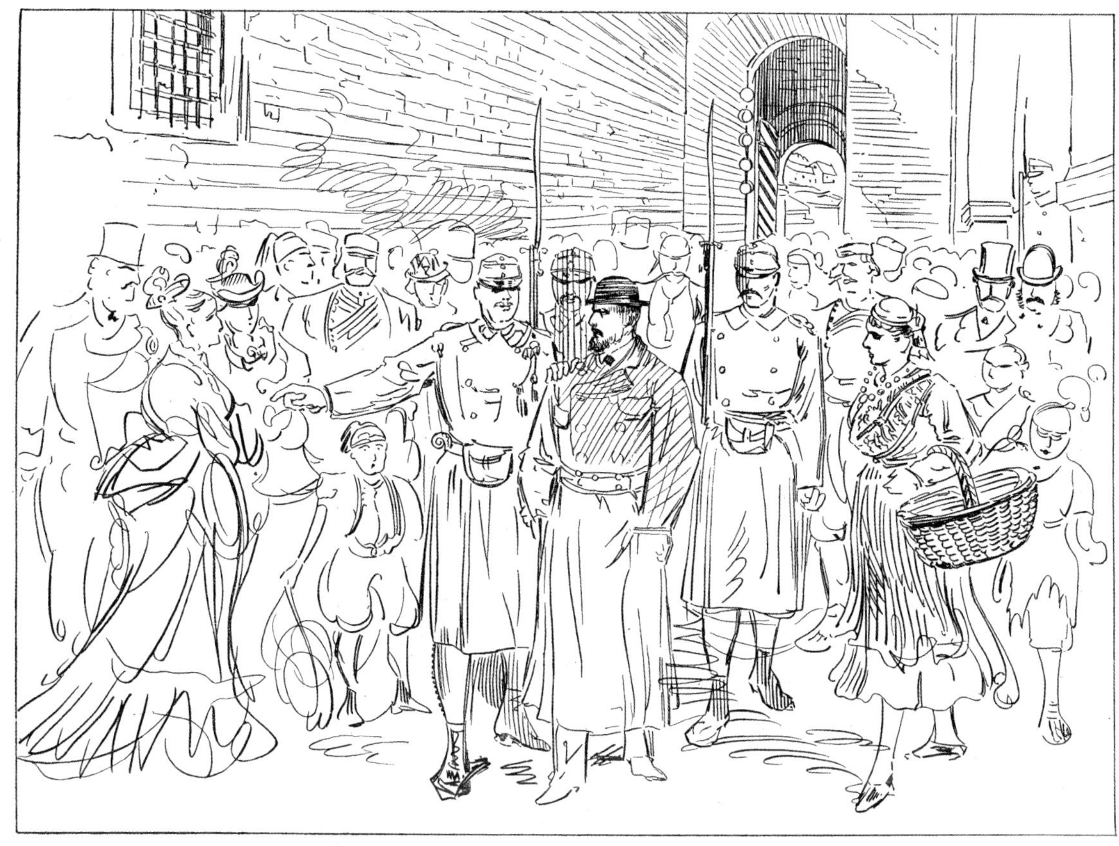

30 Melton Prior, 'Arrest of Our Special Artist at Ragusa [Sicily]: Facsimile of Sketch', *Illustrated London News*, 25 December 1875. © Mary Evans Picture Library

wars, as recorded in the latter's sketch (reproduced in facsimile by the newspaper) of his own arrest (fig. 30).[41] But the adaptable materiality of the medium meant that, with a little ingenuity, artists could theoretically operate even under highly hostile conditions, using subterfuge to keep their sketches – and themselves – moving.

The British followed Baudelaire in seeing something particularly thrilling in these original sketches. Unlike many of the worked-up prints that eventually appeared in the pages of the news, the sketch had an auratic materiality that spoke to the fraught conditions of its own creation. The process of wood engraving, via which a sketch would be re-drawn or traced onto a wooden block in order to undergo mass printing, 'meant that the work of intermediate artists, however good, all too often obliterated the individual style' of the correspondent.[42] Thus, in the autumn of 1870, at the Crystal Palace in Sydenham, there was an exhibition of 140 such sketches by Simpson and others, on loan from the *Illustrated London News* and *The Graphic*, with a catalogue that asserted 'they have far higher interest than many more finished productions, as they were taken on the spot, at the risk of life and limb.'[43] A critic for *The Times* celebrated the ability of the sketches to 'bring us without doubt nearer to the tremendous events they portray.' There was something about the 'rude and hasty scrawl on a crumpled bit of paper', he wrote, 'with its terrible dashes for exploding shells and scratches that do duty for outline, [that] give[s] us a better idea than did the engravings of the confusion and terror.'[44] The medium itself, in its fragile materiality and abbreviated forms, seemed to speak to the vulnerability of the body and mind in conditions of war. Something of this is detectable, I think, in Simpson's Crimean sketchbooks in the Yale Center for British Art, New Haven, Connecticut, which contain meditations on mortality that undercut the devil-may-care persona he cultivated fastidiously in his writings. Graves figure prominently, as do dead bodies that are traced by tremulous pencil lines which, in their very delicacy, seem to embody an anxiety about life's precariousness (fig. 31).

The sketchbooks used by Simpson were often no larger than one's hand, and when viewing them in the archive one gets a palpable sense of this being an apparatus intended for flexible and discreet operations. Their palm-sized smallness indexes the artist's body in a way that speaks to what Nancy Forgione, in reference to the spectatorial practice of the flaneur, calls the 'phenomenological fullness' of 'an activity that coherently intertwines body, mind, and vision.'[45] I want to understand such experiential 'fullness' in terms of what Natasha Eaton, writing on the Belgian painter Balthasar Solvyns and his depictions of caste in eighteenth-century India, has termed 'cyborgian play', a method of investigating the world in which 'the body of the artist is used as an instrument, complete with its inscription devices: hand, brush, sketchbook.'[46] The artist comes to know their subject by turning their own body into an object of experiment, so that his 'subjects were pressed upon him' – a sensory openness that muddies the traditional Enlightenment binary of observer and observed. Like the apocryphal tale of J. M. W. Turner having himself lashed to the mast of a ship in order truly to know the sea-storm he wished to represent, the artist's method is not merely visual but a multi-sensory, immersive experience.

Thus, while it owed its genesis to aggressive eighteenth-century processes of imperial expansion, the special artist's practice of being on the spot was not an uncomplicated enactment of hierarchy and epistemic power, since it also involved being existentially exposed to the geopolitical upheavals one was documenting. Sketching, write Luciana Martins and Felix Driver, was the product of the 'laboriousness' of 'physical labour', its processes of observation existing in 'the tensions between the knowledge of the study and the threat of the field.'[47] The fact that plein

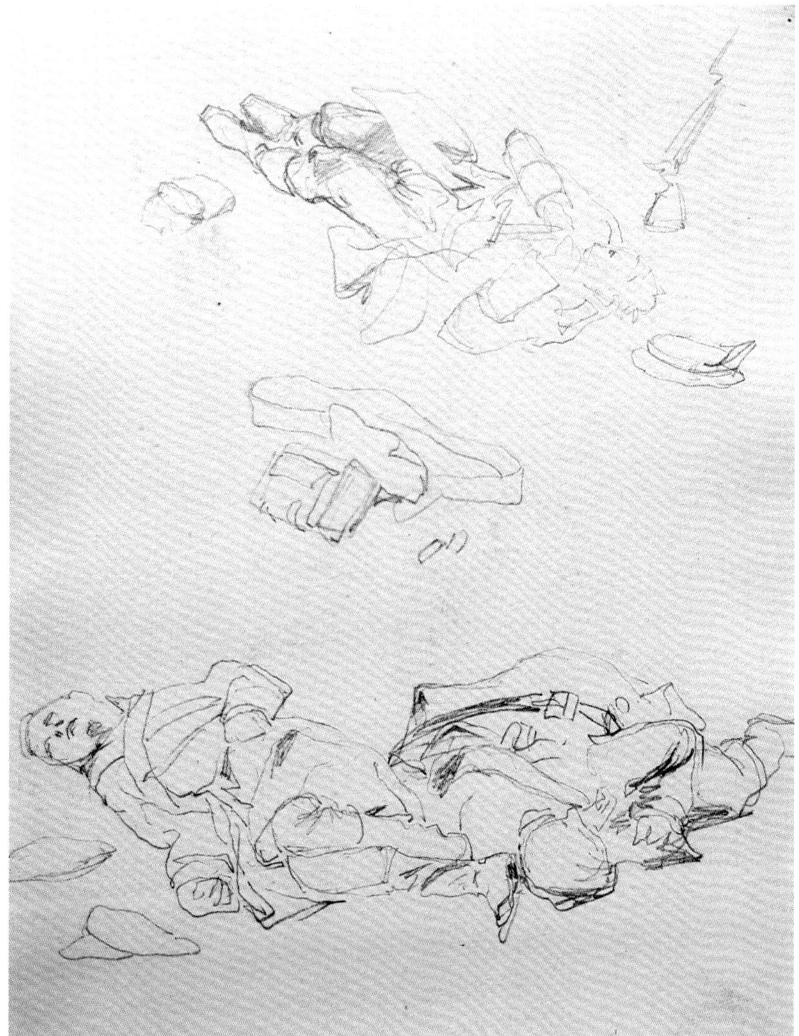

31 William Simpson, page from Balaklava Sketchbook, October to December 1854. Graphite on wove paper, 12.7 × 17.8 cm. Yale Center for British Art, New Haven, Connecticut

air practice was enmeshed in these potentially dangerous interactions of the body with 'the field' lays down a challenge to the sense of imperial mastery contained in the 'monarch-of-all-I-survey' perspective and its Cartesian subject–object distance. A focus on the embodied nature of vision presents the imperial eye 'not as transcendent, all-knowing, global, but instead as situated, partial, local.'[48]

And yet, if such a 'grammar of contingency' did speak to a 'loss of privilege' for the colonial British, one might wonder why artists and photographers went to great lengths to project a public image in which their exposure to peril and uncertainty was emphasised.[49] Taking into account the discursive framework in which colonial admissions of vulnerability occurred, it becomes apparent that a focus on the embodied processes of image-making was not necessarily a disruption of imperial privilege. The epistemological value of being on the spot was contingent on a certain degree of physical exposure; and this somatic epistemology existed in a culture that worked to channel these moments of uncertainty and vulnerability into formulaic narratives of masculinity via the literary conventions of the imperial romance. In other words, as the next section outlines, colonials were incentivised to find themselves in peril, situating the body in relation to violence so as to conform to a swashbuckling ideal of colonial manliness and, in doing so, gain epistemic authority as a witness of events.

THE ART OF SWASHBUCKLING

Special correspondents were adept at channelling the experience of war through heroic narrative frames whose tropes had developed in tandem with the Victorian adventure novel, which by the middle of the nineteenth century had become 'a veritable industry'.[50] As Andrew Griffiths writes, 'New Imperialism, New Journalism and fiction were so closely enmeshed in the writing of (and the responses to) the special correspondents that it is impossible to fully separate them.'[51] Embodying this nexus of literature, empire and reportage was the highly popular author of *Boys' Own* fiction G. A. Henty, who had been a special correspondent for the London *Standard* before he began turning his globe-trotting journalistic exploits into hundreds of formulaic tales of imperial 'pluck' and manly derring-do. His stories were often accompanied by illustrations by artists, such as Frank Feller, Stanley L. Wood and Wal Paget, who had experience of producing battle scenes for the popular press, thus creating a visual traffic between adventure fiction and war art. The 'phallic tropes' of these tales created a blueprint for the real world; Henty fashioned a public image that was 'characterised by a deliberate blurring of the line between author and narrator', personifying the confident and jingoistic adventurers of his stories.[52]

Such performativity was a key aspect of the success of the special correspondent, who maintained their privileged reportorial position – being not only highly paid but also published as named authors in newspapers dominated by anonymous contributions – through the charisma of their journalistic persona both in print and in the flesh. 'The "I" of the special correspondent', wrote the historian Alfred Baker in 1890, 'is a necessary as the "we" of the editor ... facts of no great moment become important, when associated with the personality of the correspondent by the magic of the first person singular.'[53] Special artists thus promoted themselves as bluff, tough and soldierly. *The Graphic*'s Frederic Villiers tended to his own legend by giving speeches while dressed in full campaign uniform and medals; he 'carried into the lecture room that air of the swashbuckler which was at one time considered the correct comportment for the soldiers of the pen.'[54] The better-known correspondent for the *Illustrated London News*, Melton Prior (a friend of Henty's), also cultivated a military air by carrying guns (which he used) and winning, as his own newspaper noted, 'an array of war medals and other decorations which probably even few soldiers could match.'[55]

During campaigns, such popular artists engaged image-making processes that shaped Victorian combatants' perceptions of warfare as it happened. Sketching on the spot, I suggest, functioned as a theatrical event that mediated between the uncertain here and now of the colonial body's exposure to violence and the comforting military motifs that characterised both contemporary adventure fiction and the special artists' own journalism. When Simpson was covering the Second Anglo-Afghan War for the *Illustrated London News*, for example, he had soldiers pose for him while under fire so that he could make a sketch for a scene depicting the 'first shot' of the campaign (fig. 32). The field of battle was thus overlaid with a tableau representing that very field in a slightly earlier – and more newsworthy – state of combat. 'The Afghan War: Attack on the Ali Musjid – The First Shot (About 10am, Nov. 21)' was published on 28 December 1878 (fig. 33) and showed de-individualised soldiers in the bleak vastness of a mountainous landscape on which are marked the positions of the Afghan army. The scene thus coordinated the imperilled pose of these soldiers with many of the keynotes of visual war reportage at this time, abstracting a fairly generalised set of tropes – a shadowy enemy, a forbidding terrain, an energetic body of British troops – from the precarious performances of particular men.

Such a blurring of the distinction between 'authentic' eye-witnessing and the realm of theatrical enactment was not uncommon. In the Crimean War, Simpson once commented to an army captain that he had seen no fighting that day; in response to this, the captain offered to have his men fire a cannon at the Russians so that Simpson could 'have some experience' – but he also warned that a return shot would be the consequence of this aggression. The artist assented to the offer, consequently watching as the British fired at the enemy position only to have a Russian gun promptly 'return the compliment' with a shell 'that struck the outside of the parapet, then burst, throwing up in the air a great quantity of earth and stones, which came down in a shower upon us.'[56] Since some of this debris landed on Simpson's open sketchbook, the artist 'left some of the earth in the right-hand corner, and worked it into the light and shade of a shell.'[57] The sketch itself thus became a symbol of Victorian unflappability.

This cool transubstantiation of the dust from a shell into a depiction of a shell is probably too much of a good story to be true, but the initial manufacturing of peril for the eyes of an artist was a recurring motif of Simpson's narratives. The same man who ordered that the cannon be fired, Captain Peel, also 'stood with half of his body visible above the parapet while I sketched him … as calm and unconcerned as if he had only been sitting in a studio.'[58] Exposure to real violence was staged under theatrical conditions wherein bravado worked to mask the vulnerability that was in reality being increased by such performances. That is to say, the dramatisation of bodily peril 'screened' (simultaneously displayed and occluded) the physical and psychological vulnerabilities intrinsic to warfare.

Given the artist's provocation of such idealised, devil-may-care performances, we might understand their presence on a campaign in terms of the 'I dare you' injunction as it has been theorised by Eve Kosofsky Sedgwick:

> In daring you to perform some foolhardy act (or else expose yourself as, shall we say, a wuss), 'I' (hypothetically singular) necessarily invoke a

32 William Simpson, *The First Shot*, 1878. Pen and ink on paper, 57 × 38 cm. Anne S. K. Brown Military Collection, Brown University, Providence, Rhode Island

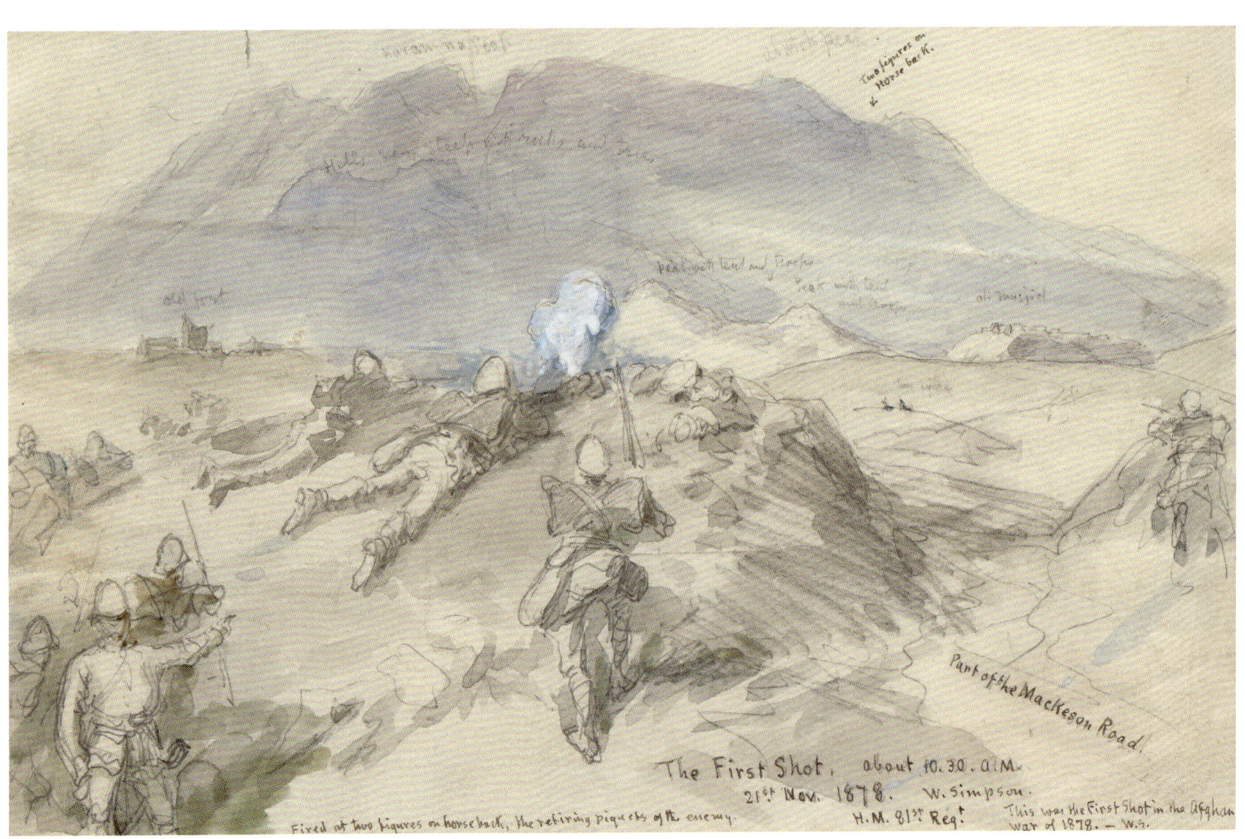

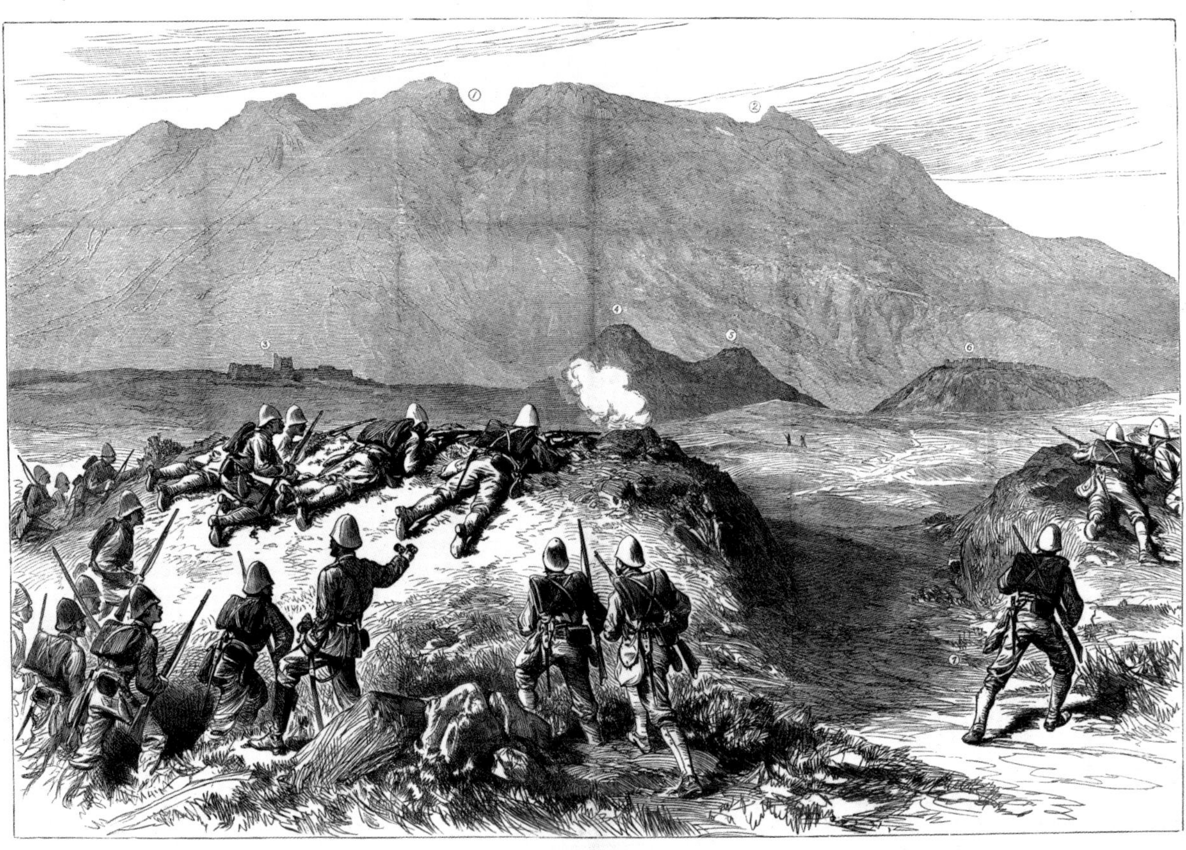

33 William Simpson, 'The Afghan War: Attack on the Ali Musjid – The First Shot (About 10am, Nov. 21)', *Illustrated London News*, 28 December 1878. Wood engraving. © Mary Evans Picture Library

> consensus of the eyes of others. It is these eyes through which you risk being seen as a wuss; by the same token, it is *as* people who share with me a contempt for wussiness that these others are interpellated, with or without their consent, by the act I have performed in daring you.[59]

Similarly, the artistic demand for compelling visual subject matter (cannon fire, the first shot of a campaign, an exposed pose) constituted a gaze contemptuous of 'wussiness': the special stood for the 'consensus of the eyes of others' – the Victorian public – who increasingly consumed warfare as a dramatic and tropological spectacle.

How did such artistic interventions shape the experience of war for the soldiers involved in it? Drawing on Lacan's notion of the *point de capiton*, Slavoj Žižek noted that potentially traumatic features of 'the real' are kept at bay in discourse by semiotic interventions that work to fix an event's symbolism. These serve as a 'quilting point' via which 'the subject' (in this case the posing soldier) was 'fastened, pinned, to a signifier [heroism/manliness] which represents him for the other [the reading public], and through this pinning he is loaded with a symbolic mandate, he is given a place in the intersubjective network'.[60] The image-making event therefore stabilised the meaning of a potentially overwhelming experience of war by hailing the subject as a 'hero' in the vein of popular imagery with which they and the wider Victorian public were familiar. Such a discourse gave positive narrative value to the otherwise disturbing first-order experience of violent exposure. Simpson says as much in his account of posing men during the Afghan battle: 'They were both looking a little scared', claimed the artist of the young soldiers, 'and I asked if this was the first time they had been under fire, and they said yes.' But these men were journalistically literate recruits and they weathered the existential threat 'with the idea that they would appear as heroes in the illustrated [London News].'[61] Simpson's image-making intervention created a space in which negative affect – fear, vulnerability – could be traversed in a spirit of play.

'DANCERS OF ARCHAEOLOGY'

Just one week after he had made sketches under fire while capturing 'the first shot' of the Afghan War, Simpson wrote a letter to a friend, W. Harry Rylands, in which, quoting Hamlet, he complained, 'This place is getting "weary, stale, and unprofitable", they don't shoot at us, at least for two days past no reports of that kind have been heard, and that makes life rather slow – meals are now regular.'[62] The sudden lull in fighting made Simpson's duties as a swashbuckling special artist harder to perform, but imperial conquest offered more than gladiatorial spectacle.

While the Afghan campaign saw Simpson sending home dramatic images of conflict – from chaotic scenes of close combat to the orderly brutality of prisoners getting executed by colonial firing squad – one often gets the sense that this kind of reportage merely served as a pretext for him to pursue his true passion: 'you will find', wrote an interviewer in 1894, 'that it is as an orientalist and archaeologist that he would, by preference, be handed down to posterity, rather than as the pioneer of illustrated war journalism.'[63] Simpson's wartime output was filled with structural plans, architectural details and, when necessary, imagined reconstructions of Afghan antiquities, which he sent to luminaries of the Orientalist scene back in Britain, James Fergusson and Sir Henry Yule.[64] That such an extensive archaeological archive was produced by one of the leading special artists of the period demonstrates the intimate connection between colonial violence and ethnographic fieldwork.

Simpson was no eccentric in seeing warfare as a stepping-stone to architectural appreciation. In addition to his journalistic duties (sending

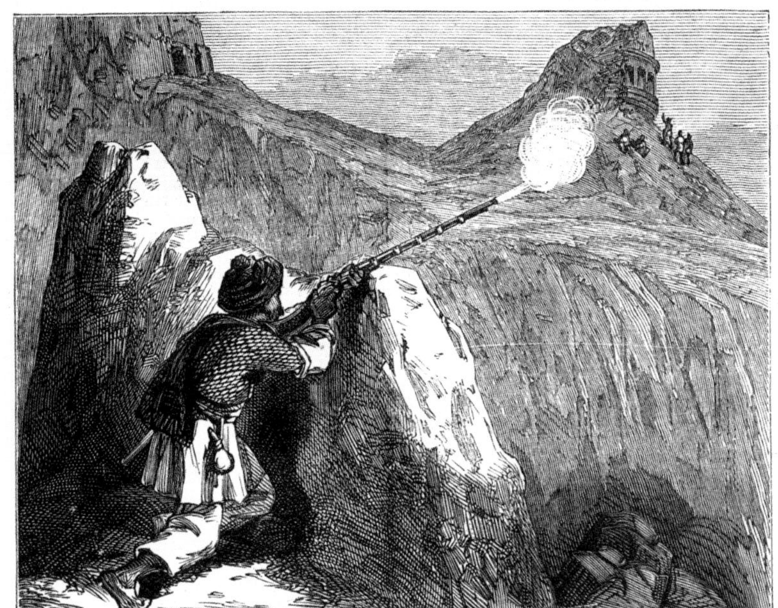

34 William Simpson, 'Dangers of Archaeology at the Pheel Khana Tope', *Illustrated London News*, 19 April 1879. Wood engraving. © Mary Evans Picture Library

written reports to the *Daily News* and sketches to the *Illustrated London News*), he was working in association with the Archaeological Survey of India, an arm of the British Indian government, and had the support of Major Pierre Louis Napoleon Cavagnari, the flamboyant and ill-fated Deputy Commissioner of Peshawar leading the British mission in Afghanistan. Simpson's exploits were aligned with the longstanding aims of the imperial state under such circumstances. In the opening decades of the nineteenth century, following the death of the staunch anti-British ruler Tipu Sultan of Mysore during the Battle of Seringapatam in 1799, the victorious British had conducted the extensive Survey of Mysore, in which Colin Mackenzie and his assistants went into the 'field' not only to map topography (as had been common colonial practice for decades) but also to document material of historical or cultural interest.[65] Such ethnographic surveys remained the modus operandi for absorbing new – or sometimes simply assessing prospective – imperial territories throughout the Victorian era.

What did such fieldwork mean to the invaded culture it sought to represent? I consider this question in more depth in the chapters that follow. Yet Simpson gave one possible answer when he pictured his own ethnographic exploits from the perspective of a combatant defending the territory that the artist was documenting. 'Dangers of Archaeology at the Pheel Khana Tope' (fig. 34) depicts the moment Simpson – shown here in the distance pointing at the Tope – discovers that his artistic attention

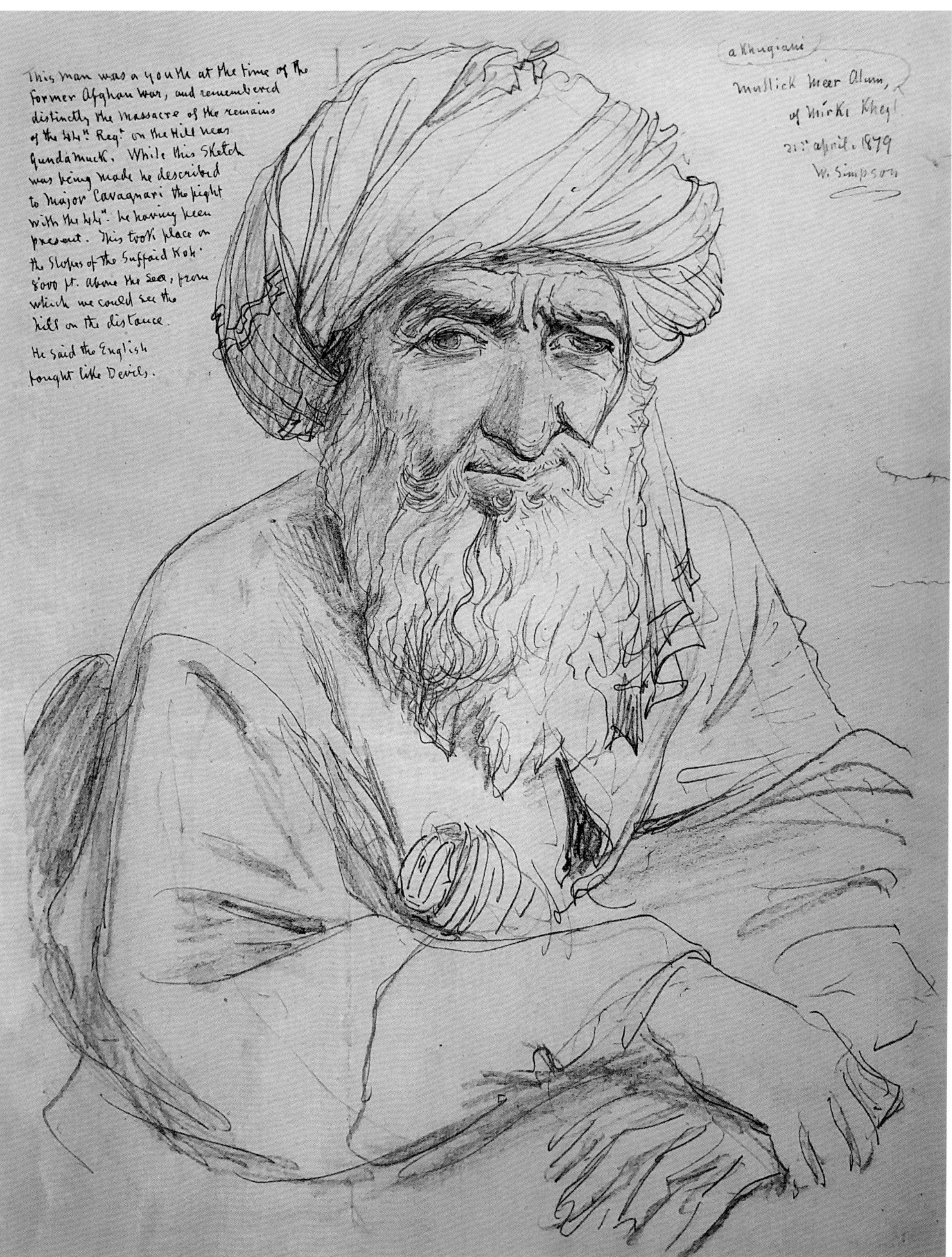
This man was a youth at the time of the
former Afghan War, and remembered
distinctly the massacre of the remains
of the 44th. Regt. on the Hill near
Gundamuck. While this Sketch
was being made he described
to Major Cavagnari the fight
with the 44th. he having been
present. This took place on
the Slopes of the Suffaid Koh.
8000 ft. above the Sea, from
which we could see the
hill on the distance.
He said the English
fought like Devils.
a Khugiani
Mullick Meer Alum,
of Mirki Khel
21st April. 1879
W. Simpson

has registered as hostility; Simpson 'heard the crack of a gun, and the whistle of a bullet went past very close.' The attack is no surprise given the nature of Simpson's escort: the artist boasted of his habit at the start of the war of going out and sketching alone in what the army thought to be 'a reckless manner', and so an order was soon issued 'that a guard was to be given me when I left the camp to sketch.'[66]

35 William Simpson, *Mullick Meer Alum of Murki Kheyl*, 1879. Pencil on paper, 57 × 38 cm. Anne S. K. Brown Military Collection, Brown University, Providence, Rhode Island

Simpson's heroic self-promotion here points to an important reality about the art of the colonial encounter: on the spot image-making was dependent on, and implicated in, a broader imperial-military vanguard. Yet, in being so, such image-making events could serve as an opportunity for members of an invaded population to 'talk back' to their invader. When Simpson was not indulging in 'the dangers of archaeology', for instance, he produced portraits of numerous prisoners of war and tribal elders. Under the watch of Major Cavagnari, one such sitting turned into a case of what Priyamvada Gopal terms 'reverse tutelage', as the elderly subject regaled the colonial pair with his memory of the First Afghan War thirty years earlier (fig. 35).[67] The British, he said, 'fought like devils' back then – but they were massacred nevertheless. Simpson recorded the man's comments on the original sketch, accepting a dialogical process of history-making. He was documenting the war on behalf of Cavagnari and the British press; yet the Afghan elder also displays historiographical agency, his oral testimony serving as a thinly veiled warning to the British. The Afghan people had already once expelled their European invaders from the very hills in which the elder was now posing.

In sitting for Simpson, the Afghan man was not merely turned into an instrument of colonial narrative. He acquired historiographical agency through the sitting, capitalising on the attention paid him by the foreigners to remind them of Afghan fortitude. For Cavagnari – soon to be installed as the first British Resident in Kabul since the 1840s bloodshed – the story turned out to be grimly prophetic, as the next chapter will show.

CONCLUSION

Special artists may not have been 'directing great military operations' and consistently 'coming to the rescue of Field-Marshals', as Mortimer Menpes put it in his waspish satire of the fin-de-siècle correspondent, but the trope of the swashbuckling and interventionist artist was, I think, an exaggerated means of registering something real: that the presence of artists on the spot was an influential component of the phenomenology of conquest, shaping soldiers' manner of engagement with violence and endangerment. Violence increasingly came to be seen in terms of its status as an enjoyable and newsworthy spectacle.

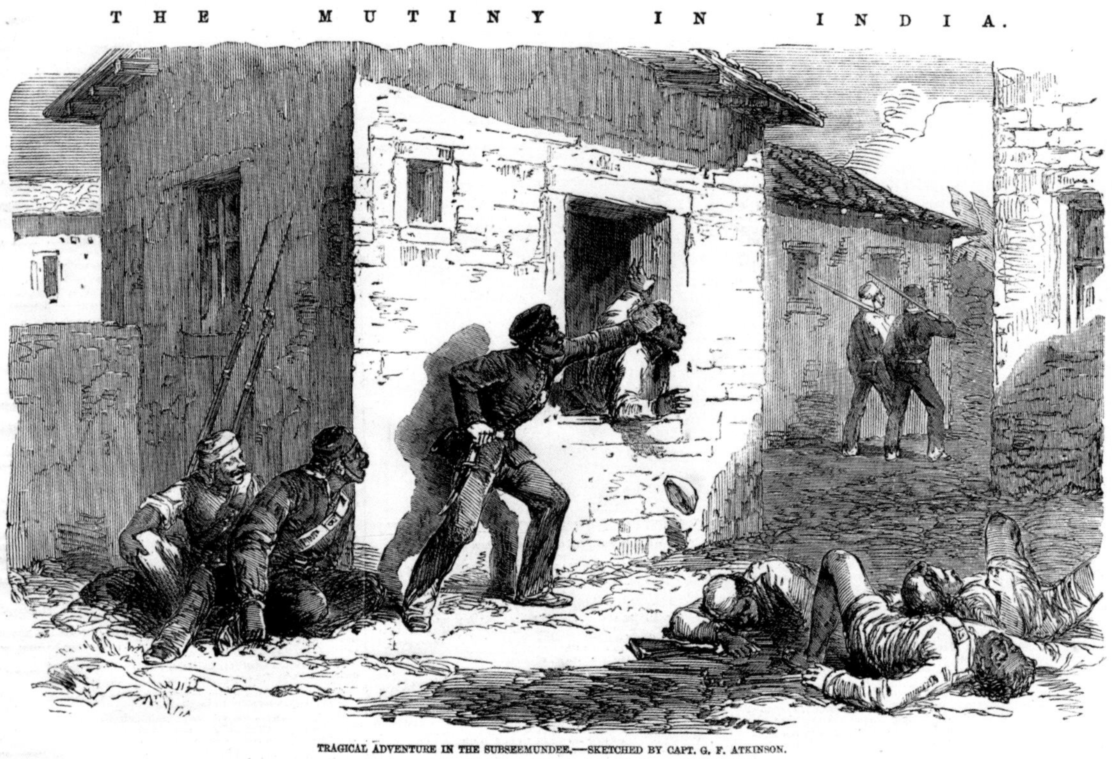

THE MUTINY IN INDIA.

TRAGICAL ADVENTURE IN THE SUBSEEMUNDEE.—SKETCHED BY CAPT. G. F. ATKINSON.

36 George Franklin Atkinson, 'Tragical Adventure in the Subseemundee', *Illustrated London News*, 10 October 1857. Wood engraving. © Mary Evans Picture Library

Yet if, like Walter Benjamin's fascist, the colonial soldier was able to enjoy his own potential destruction as a spectacle of the highest order, then this enjoyment could only emerge, as Zahid Chaudhary suggests, as 'an afterimage of the pleasurable spectacle ... of the native's denigration.'[68] When one British trooper witnessed a Gurkha soldier decapitate an Indian insurgent during the 1857 Uprising, for example, he wrote that 'Atkinson should make a sketch of this for the Illustrated London News.'[69] George Franklin Atkinson was a regular correspondent for that newspaper, which on 10 October 1857 duly published an image by the artist depicting a Gurkha, knife in hand, grabbing hold of an insurgent's head (fig. 36). Beneath the illustration was an article in which the beheading scene was explained.[70] Here we have an early manifestation of what Henry A. Giroux terms the modern 'depravity of aesthetics': 'representations of human suffering, humiliation and death [offered] as part of a wider economy of pleasure that is collectively indulged.'[71] This chapter's account of the aestheticisation of colonial peril is accordingly the 'afterimage' of the previous chapter's consideration of the spectacle of colonised bodies being exposed to imperial violence.

The mediatisation of violence explored here was part of a broader convergence of Victorian art and war. In 1861 William Michael Rossetti could still make the claim that, due to their apparently superior moral sensibility (compared to, say, the French), British painters 'have never fully grappled with military art, they have only hovered around the edges'.[72] Yet the following decade saw an expansion of the market for just this sort of painting. The increasing visibility of warfare in the illustrated weeklies and the growing enthusiasm of the middle classes for the army – as demonstrated by the Volunteer Movement established in 1859 – marked a significant militarisation of bourgeois values that paved the way for the newfound prominence of military subjects at the Royal Academy.[73] The popularisation of such art was spearheaded by the work of Elizabeth Butler, whose breakthrough piece, *The Roll Call* (1874; Royal Collection Trust), struck a sombre and humanitarian tone. But the genre was increasingly dominated by the more triumphal compositions of the male military painters who followed in Butler's wake, such as Richard Caton Woodville, Charles Edwin Fripp and Godfrey Douglas Giles.[74] These men's pictures owed more to the style of the pictorial press and in figures like Woodville, who worked as an engraver for the *Illustrated London News*, the press artist and the battle painter were one and the same.

Such visual narratives were not just subject to passive consumption. For some (male) colonials on military campaigns, they were providing the coordinates for experiencing danger and violence. Neither were the artists passive in their approach: military action was not simply transcribed by a journalist standing somehow 'outside' the situation they were documenting; the very presence of the special correspondent functioned to constitute 'the field' as a stage for conventionalised performances of imperial masculinity and 'adventure'. The Victorian combatant was being interpellated by what Giroux, following Adorno, has described as the 'ideology of hardness' and 'aggressive masculinity' that is incubated in the 'affective economy' of image-regimes in which 'digestible spectacles of violence are endlessly circulated through proliferating media forms.'[75] While not always completely blind to the horrors of war, artists frequently operated in such a way as to regulate affective responses to violence by metabolising the shock of corporeal vulnerability into the familiar spectacle of heroic masculinity. Sketching in the field was therefore a 'performative and normative practice' in which the 'thick' experience of warfare (as an ethically fraught, physically dangerous and psychologically unnerving event) was to some extent dissolved into the 'depthless world' of the imperial romance and its promise of aesthetic gratification.[76]

5 · 'SAVE ME FROM MY FRIENDS!'

The Art of Diplomacy in the Age of its Technological Reproducibility

'SAVE ME FROM MY FRIENDS!' THIS WOEFUL LINE FROM *PUNCH* IN November 1878 – serving as a caption for a Joseph Swain caricature showing the Emir of Afghanistan, Sher Ali, standing with gloomy obstinance between a slathering Russian bear and an expectant British lion (fig. 37) – perfectly encapsulates the perils of imperial geopolitics for countries caught up in the 'Great Game'. The cartoon exposes the aura of threat that lurked behind the imperial hunt for allies. Diplomatic overtures from imperial powers could hardly be accepted naively or rejected lightly by countries like Afghanistan; 'friendship' was a dangerous state of affairs and could appear as little more than imperial predation. The British Empire had been built on the back of a practice of 'gunboat diplomacy' that embodied Carl von Clausewitz famous thesis that warfare is simply 'the continuation of State policy by other means'.[1] If satisfactory relations could not be secured through coercion or threat, the British achieved their aims through conquest, unilaterally sending out emissaries to recalcitrant rulers with a military escort in tow. Sher Ali had just suffered such a fate – 'invade[d]', as the quotation from *The Times* beneath the cartoon had it, 'in pursuance of a policy which in its intention has been uniformly FRIENDLY to Afghanistan'.

This chapter examines imperial diplomacy by considering the grand political missions sent by Britain to territories, like Afghanistan, over which it did not exercise full formal control but with which it sought to come to terms on issues of borders, trade and foreign policy. The apogee of such aggressive diplomacy came in 1904, when the Younghusband Mission marched on the Tibetan capital of Lhasa, and demonstrated the deadly efficacy of the Maxim gun to a local soldiery armed with little more than swords and protective amulets, thus compelling the horrified authorities of the 'holy city' formally to receive the embassy and open up

William Simpson, engraved by Richard Caton Woodville, 'Major Cavagnari arranging with the Shinwarries for the Protection of the Road from Dakka to Lundi Khana' (detail of fig. 47).

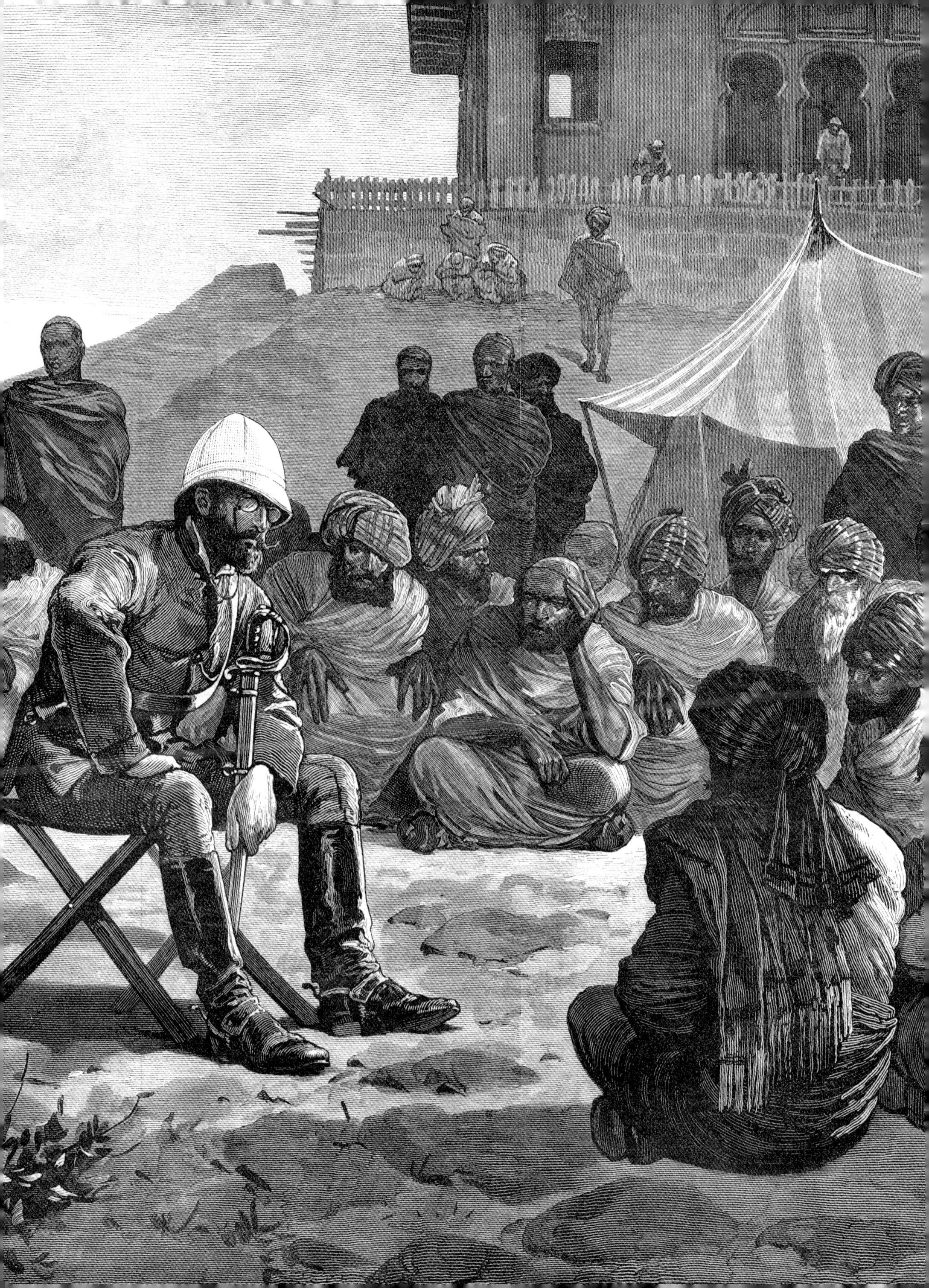

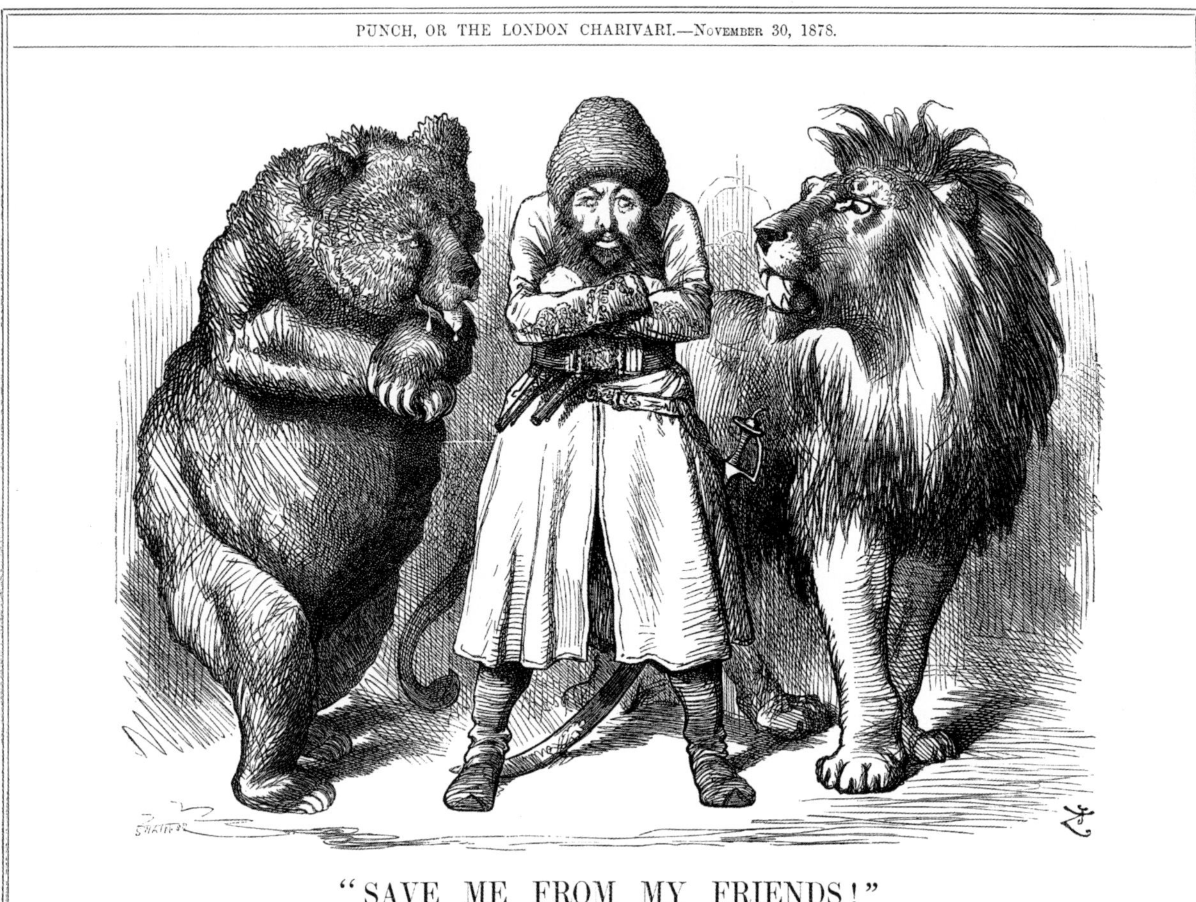

37 Joseph Swain, 'Save me from my Friends!', *Punch*, 30 November 1878. Wood engraving, 41.5 × 32.5 cm. © Alamy Stock Photo

their reclusive regime to British treaties and trade. Such missions were extensively documented episodes in which diplomatic rituals sought to reconstitute regional sovereignty. Diplomacy not only shadowed warfare as a kind of post-conflict balm but also served to realise the conflict's aims, bringing into being, through its ceremonies, rituals and images, the new dynamic of power that colonial violence had made possible. Since such expeditions were in part a means of staging political relations as a spectacle – whereby the choreography of diplomatic ceremony and its inscription by visual media were key to the perceived success or failure of a mission – artists and photographers working on the spot played a key role in shaping the contours of sovereign relations.

The visual culture of nineteenth-century British imperial diplomacy has hitherto received little treatment in scholarship but it offers rich material for exploring how Victorian visions of war and peace were constituted by the tropes and temporalities of modern mass-media networks. Diplomatic expeditions were multifaceted affairs, composed of envoys, soldiers, artists, photographers, cartographers, botanists, capitalists and journalists. These missions' aims were epistemological and commercial as much as they were political: they provided the opportunity for landscapes to be surveyed, flora and fauna to be documented, resources to be appraised. The 'ethnographic surveillance' that was associated with the imperial embassy will be considered in a later chapter.[2] Here I am concerned with the art of diplomacy itself. Walter Bagehot, a Victorian writer attuned to the ways in which aesthetic display incubated sovereign authority, put it like this: 'An ambassador is not simply an agent; he is also a spectacle.'[3] Envoys and sovereigns both paid anxious attention to how they presented themselves to the artists and photographers who were attached to diplomatic missions, with negotiations and agreements about the fate of nations occurring in a feedback loop with commemorative acts of image-making whose products were anticipated for mass international distribution.

First I look at the early modern roots of the visual conventions that shaped diplomacy in colonial art, before moving to consider the role of the portrait sitting – the event of portraiture itself – in mediating imperial relations in places including Burma and Afghanistan. Colonial portraits of foreign rulers were part of a broader 'representational imperialism' that accompanied the performative acts that constituted surrender (and, diplomatic niceties notwithstanding, such occasions were indeed about surrender): treaty signings, oaths, declarations, exchanges, ceremonies.[4] The processes of striking a pose, being directed or compelled to pose, refusing to pose or getting captured in a pose without one's consent all worked to posit new formulations of sovereign power. Portrait sittings were vexed rituals of geopolitical transition, in which the regal body was required to perform both its sovereignty and its subjection to an imperial suzerain.

The work of imperial statecraft in the age of its technological reproducibility was thus geared, in highly self-reflexive terms, towards asserting sovereign agencies through the processes and products of image-making. This chapter concludes with an extended analysis of the imagery produced for the illustrated press by special artists and photographers representing the signing of the Treaty of Gandamak following the 'friendly' British invasion of Afghanistan in 1878. Image-making performances in the field yielded photographic negatives and pencil sketches that were seen at the time by those who were party to the negotiations. However, the significance of those images to those initial viewers was to a large extent merely provisional; the final products

– positive photographic prints, woodcut engravings in the illustrated press and so on – could only be imagined and anticipated. I argue that the image-making event thus served not so much to commemorate an already settled history as to smuggle a sense of contingency and deferral into proceedings, whereby the meaning of the summit (and the reputation of its participants) were increasingly only properly intelligible after the fact. As Eduardo Cadava writes of modernity, events had become meaningful only insofar as they were 'inscribed within the language of communication, representation, and information'.[5]

DIPLOMATIC FETISHISM

The aesthetic conventions used by the Victorians to affirm diplomatic triumphs were inherited from an older 'art of surrender' in the Western canon. Robin Wagner-Pacifici has identified Diego Velázquez's *Surrender at Breda* (1634–5) as emblematic of an artistic strategy stretching from the early modern period to the present day that seeks to resolve conflict by invoking a set of 'archetypal' gentlemanly performances, exchanges and images which rendered triumph and subjection intelligible in 'civilised' terms.[6] This sublimation of geopolitical violence into tropes of genteel resolution was a core element of the visual narratives that developed about the East India Company in the eighteenth century. The visual template for colonial triumph was laid down in the history painting which Francis Hayman (1708–1776) produced in response to Robert Clive's celebrated victory at Plassey in Bengal in 1757; the painting was exhibited in London's Vauxhall Gardens during the early 1760s. While the finished, large-scale version of Hayman's work has since been lost, the National Portrait Gallery holds an oil on canvas design (fig. 38) for the scene that centres on an avuncular-looking 'Clive of India' engaging with the Indian general Mir Jafar in the aftermath of battle. Jafar had agreed in treaty with Clive to betray the Nawab of Bengal, Siraj-ud-daula, by moving troops away from the battlefield in return for the Company anointing him, Jafar, as ruler. The deal placed the British in a position of unprecedented power in northern India, paving the way for the extension of colonial influence across the subcontinent.

For eighteenth-century audiences, Clive's achievement was framed in terms of his diplomatic, rather than military, nous. Warfare is presented here as a pretext for gentlemanly conduct. Hayman adopts a visual scheme that locates a classical pedigree for British power, recalling Charles Le Brun's well-known painting of Alexander the Great displaying post-conflict magnanimity, *Alexander before the Tent of Darius* (1660–61; Versailles).[7] While Hayman alludes to the flesh and blood realities of the

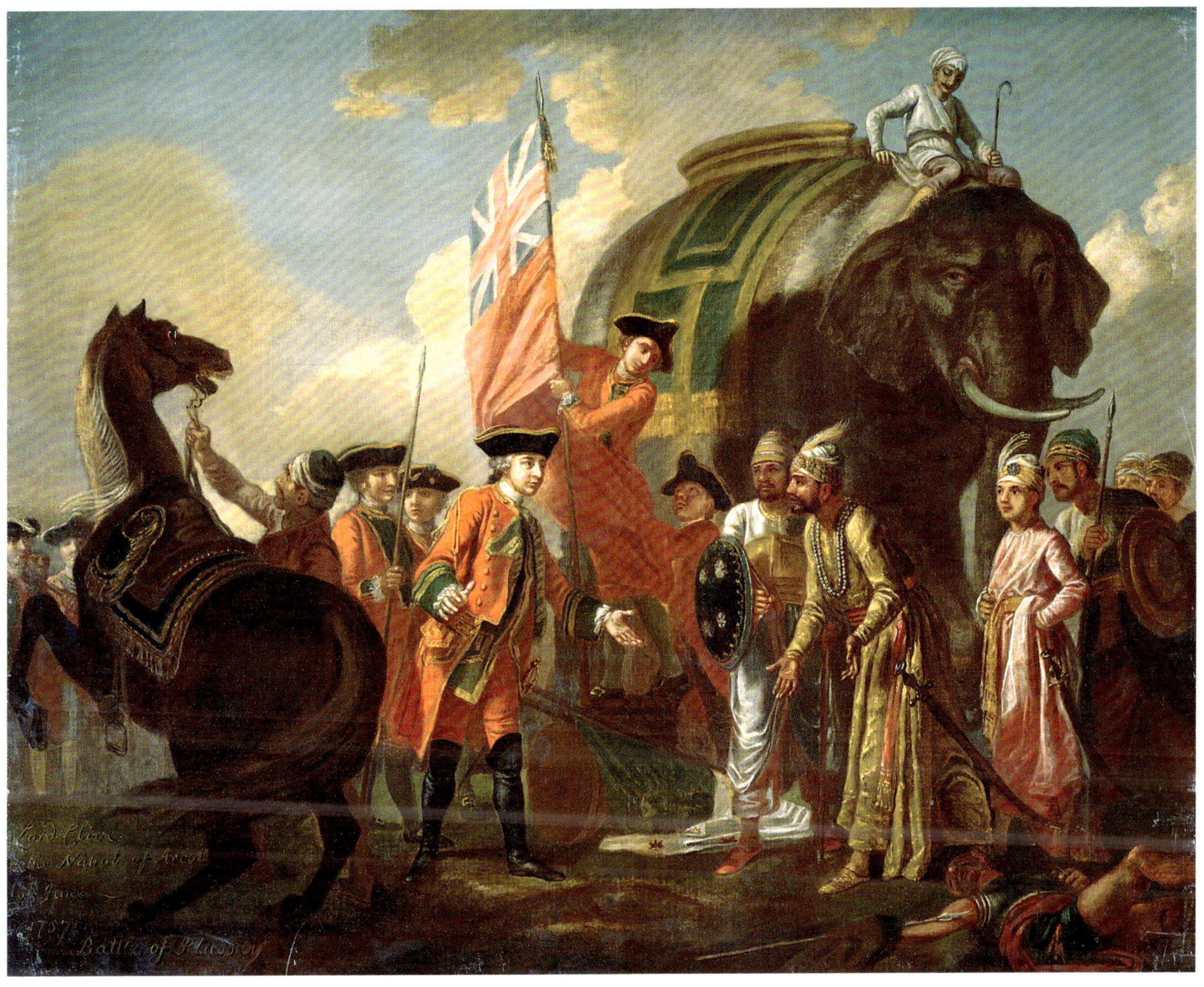

38 Francis Hayman, *Robert Clive and Mir Jafar after the Battle of Plassey, 1757*, c.1760. Oil on canvas, 100 × 127 cm. © National Portrait Gallery, London

Battle of Plassey via the inclusion of the corpse of an Indian soldier in the bottom right-hand corner of the painting, this nod to violence is marginalised by a composition that privileges the civil encounter between Clive and Jafar. The central protagonists mirror one another's open gestures and it is from within this locus of Anglo-Indian accord that the British flag is raised over Indian terrain.

Later artists took their cue from Hayman: the violence of imperialism was repeatedly obscured by artists such as Benjamin Wilson, Benjamin West (fig. 39), Mather Brown (fig. 40) and John Platt (fig. 41) with reference to diplomatic encounters. Treaties and other legal documents feature heavily in this genre of colonial art, first through the history paintings of the eighteenth and early nineteenth century and later through the new media of photography and the illustrated press.

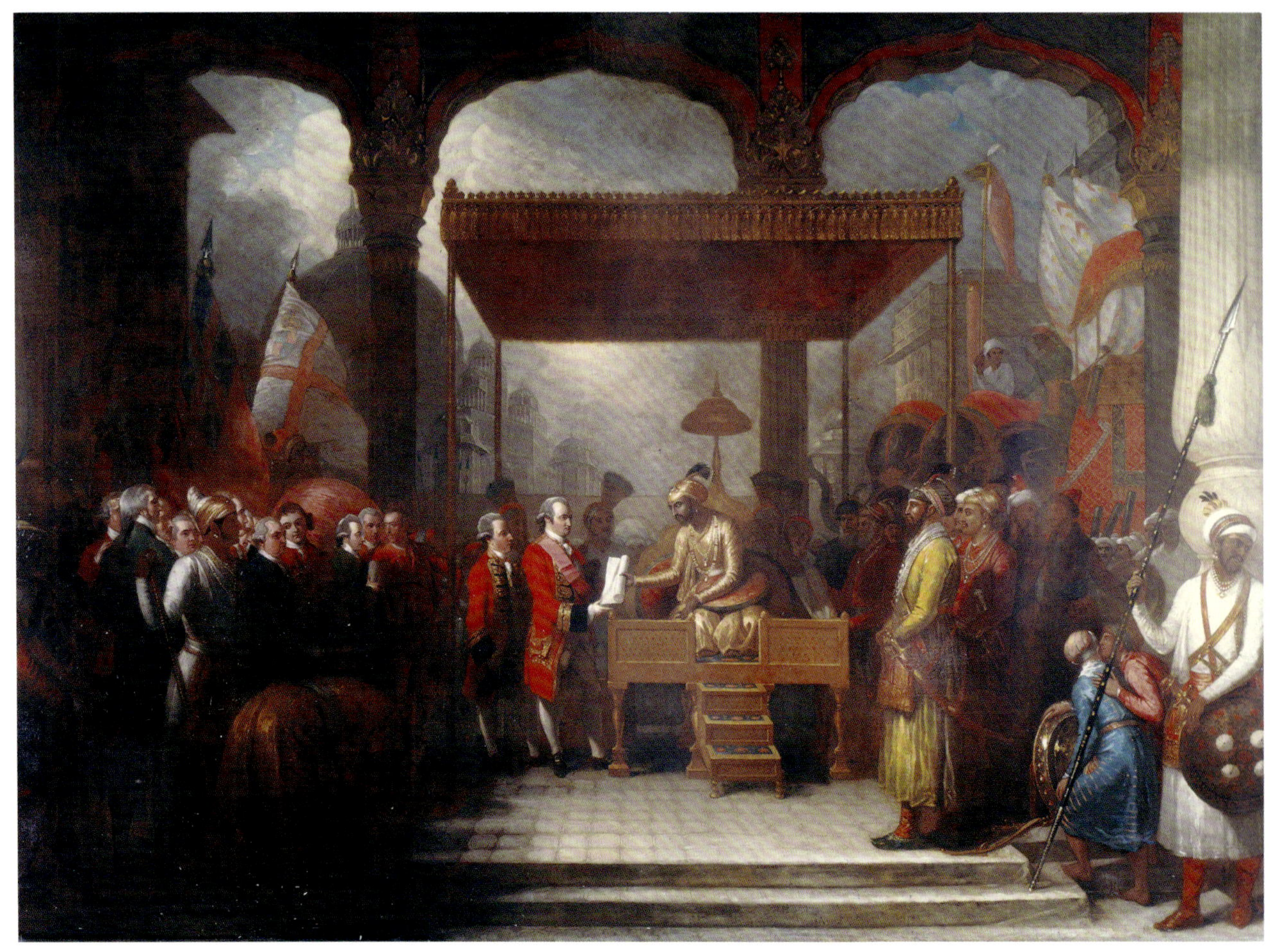

39 Benjamin West, *Shah 'Alam conveying the Grant of the Diwani to Lord Clive*, c.1818; copy of original of 1774. Oil on canvas, 290 × 400 cm.

40 Francesco Bartolozzi after Mather Brown, *The Delivery of the Definitive Treaty by the Hostage Princes*, c.1794. Line and stipple engraving, 51.4 × 64.5 cm. Yale Center for British Art

41 Captain John Platt, *The Signing and Sealing of the Treaty of Nanking*, 1842. Engraving, 47.1 × 87.9 cm.

Treaties provided closure to the geopolitical limbo of military aggression and diplomatic negotiation, replacing conflict – also a popular topic for artists – with a visual grammar of accord.

Such treaties drew states into a Eurocentric framework of international relations.[8] While many Indigenous and African peoples remained outside the scope of international law because they were perceived as lacking civilisation, Asian states often did have legal status; the Treaty of Paris (1856), for example, admitted the Ottoman Empire into the 'family of states' bound by international law.[9] This was commemorated in the group portrait of plenipotentiaries published on the front page of the *Illustrated London News* on 26 April, derived from a photograph produced as part of a commemorative album by the Parisian studio Mayer and Pierson.[10] Images commemorating treaties foregrounded the diplomatic and legalistic aspects of the emerging global order. They therefore enabled Britain to present its imperial conquests as

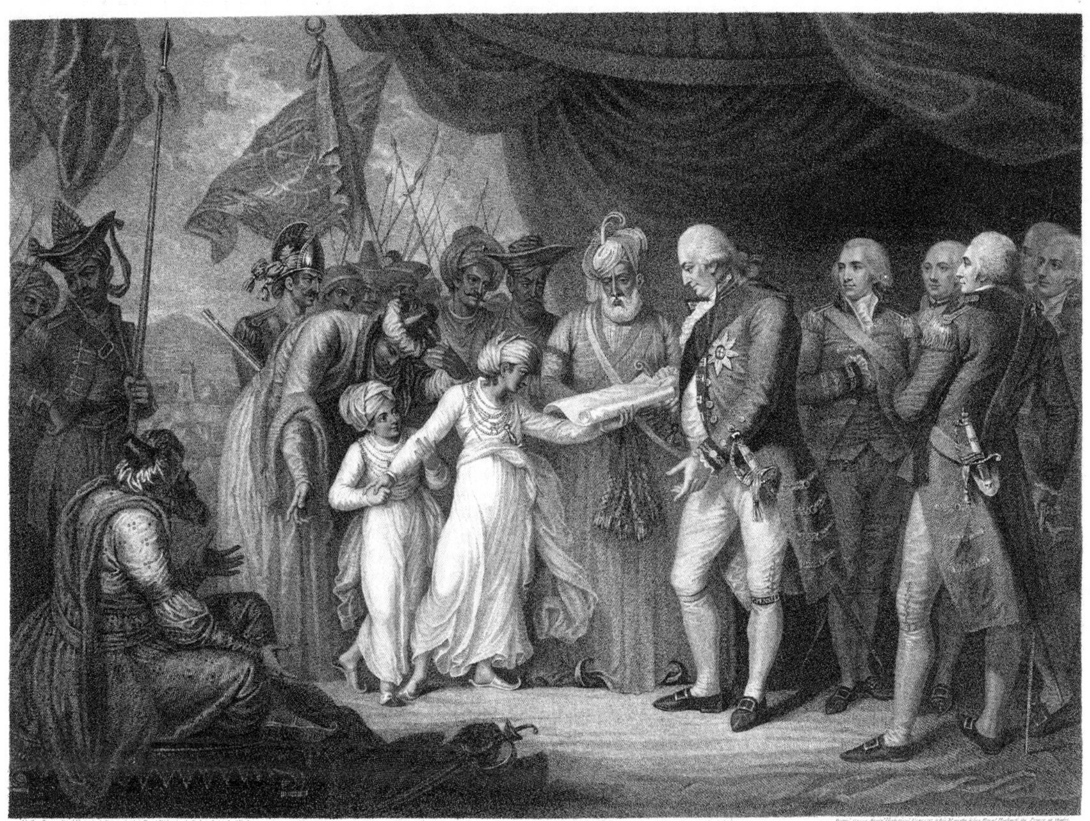
To the Honourable the East India Company
This Plate representing the Delivery of the DEFINITIVE TREATY BY THE HOSTAGE PRINCES
Lord Cornwallis

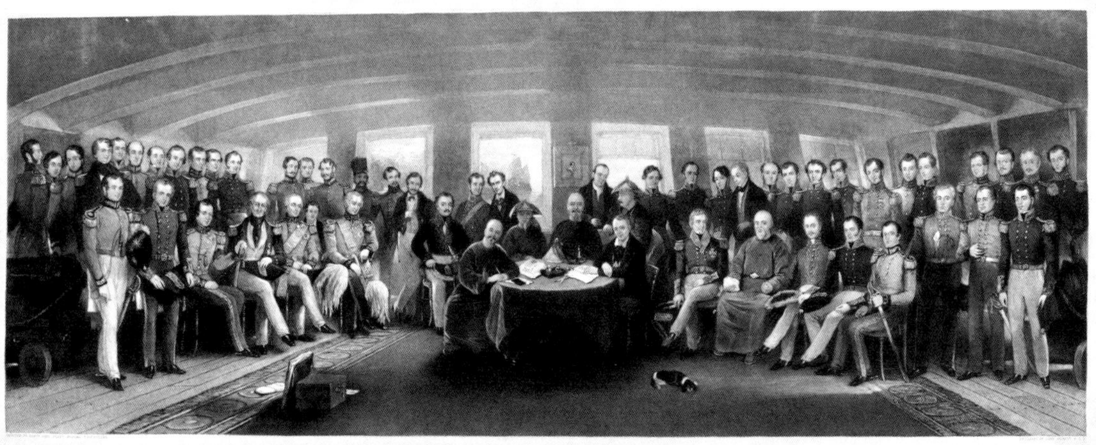
This Print of
THE SIGNING AND SEALING OF THE TREATY OF NANKING.

a 'necessary evil' for ensuring that non-Western states were properly integrated members of international society.[11] The treaty's dry legalism did not detract from its pictorial interest: the dullness, I think, was in many ways precisely the point, a diplomatic salve for the wounds of imperial militarism.

In its mythic guise, then, colonial history was predicated on a sort of diplomatic fetishism, with the architecture of empire seen not as a deadly relationship among warring bodies but as an abstractly legal relationship among treaties – a gentlemanly enterprise. This cannot be attributed wholly to bad faith. In a real sense, Britain's empire was sustained by a complex web of geopolitical treaties, rounds of formal and informal international negotiation and spectacles of diplomatic ceremony. The figure of the envoy was therefore crucial to navigating an international order based on treaties and formal trading arrangements; he negotiated the geopolitical detail and managed the public image of cross-cultural relationships. Envoys were well aware that their mission was in part to curate ceremonies and their associated commemorative images in such a way as to conform to a certain set of aesthetic and cultural conventions, ones that rendered diplomacy – often engaged in matters that were technical or abstruse – immediately legible as a successful expression of imperial sovereign power to both the local population and to metropolitan audiences back home. He was, as Bagehot remarked, 'sent abroad for show as well as for substance.'[12]

'HOW WARS ARE GOT UP IN INDIA'

In 1855 the East India Company dispatched one such envoy, Major Arthur Phayre, to the Burmese Court of Ava. This mission laid the groundwork for future imperial embassies with its multifaceted personnel: as well as 440 soldiers (a fairly modest number – Younghusband's 'diplomatic' mission to Tibet in 1903–4 had 2500), the expedition included Major Allen reporting on future defensive strategy and boundary arrangements; Dr J. Forsyth investigating geography; Mr Oldham producing geological and cartographical surveys; Captain J. Rennie making a survey of the Irrawaddy River; and two unnamed 'gentlemen of mercantile knowledge and experience' recruited in order to assess the current state and future potential of Burmese markets.[13] This was in addition to the artist Colesworthy Grant, drafted as the official artist of the mission; Captain Linneaus Tripe, an amateur photographer charged with documenting Burmese architecture; and Colonel Sir Henry Yule, a keen amateur draughtsman commissioned to compile the data of all these men into the official narrative of the mission (for an account of such ethnography, see the next chapter).[14]

Diplomacy thus provided cover for the assimilation of new lands into the imperial archive, but the primary aim of the British in Burma was to try to convince its new king, Mindon Min, formally to recognise the Company's recent annexation of Pegu (Bago), known as Lower Burma, during the Second Anglo-Burmese War (1852–3). Conflict had exploded abruptly in January 1852, when Commodore George Robert Lambert was sent to extract £1000 in compensation from authorities in Rangoon for what was seen as the unjust fining of some British merchants. After turning up unannounced at the Burmese governor's home – and without conforming to basic Burmese etiquette by removing his shoes – Lambert was told that the Burmese governor was asleep. Taking this as a slight, Lambert commandeered a Burmese ship, fired on Rangoon's port and imposed a blockade. The Governor-General, Lord Dalhousie, while censuring the 'Combustible Commodore' in private, publicly upped the demand for compensation from the Burmese to £100,000. When this was refused, Burma was invaded and its coastal regions subsumed into British India.[15]

Given the inglorious nature of the war's origins, it behoved the Company to settle the matter without courting further accusations of intemperance. Diplomacy allowed for a show of magnanimity to emerge from within this theatre of unchecked aggression. The imperial embassy of 1855 was thus pitched not merely as a means to secure terms of peace with the Burmese (no treaty had been signed at the end of hostilities) but also to defang British critics like Richard Cobden, whose polemic 'How Wars Are Got Up in India' had emphasised the shameful absurdity of the *casus belli*.[16] The spectacle of diplomacy provided a chance to transmute capricious violence into something that had the appearance of legitimacy.

'SEMIOTIC DANCER'

Diplomatic interactions were highly self-conscious and guarded. Major Phayre, on approaching the outer gate to King Mindon Min's palatial grounds in Ameerapura in September 1855, was asked by his Burmese hosts if he would follow them in removing their shoes to 'show respect'. He refused, even reprimanding the Burmese for asking; he wanted 'no more mention in such a way of customs.'[17] Cultural negotiations like this were the stuff of jingoistic newspaper reports back in British India: 'One officer of the mission intends, unless he sees the Governor General's written order to that effects, to resist stoutly taking off his boots before the king of Ava.'[18] There was a belief among the British that the Burmese exaggerated the scope of their shoeless procedures merely to 'throw dust in the eyes of foreigners'. 'It is never done,'

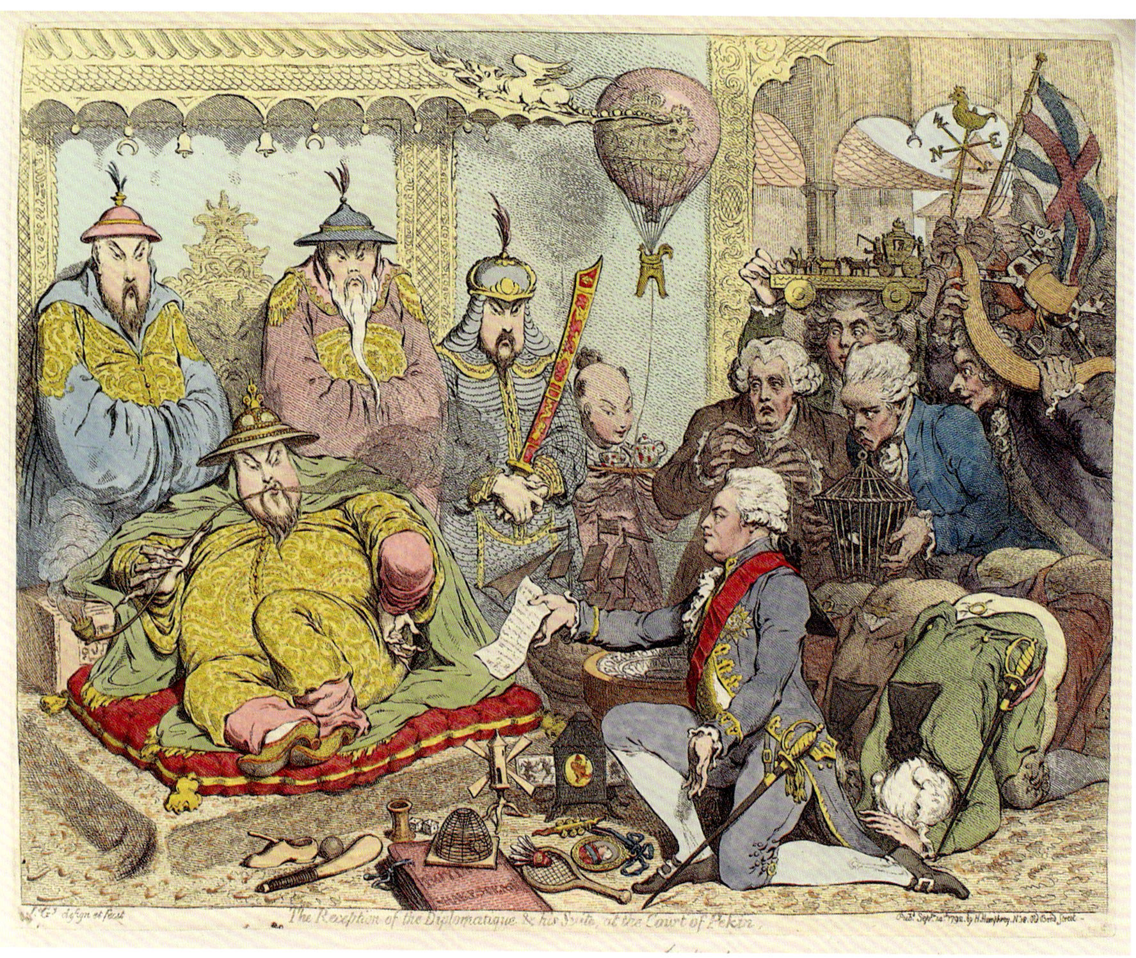

42 James Gilray, *The Reception of the Diplomatique and his Suite at the Court of Pekin*, 14 September 1792. Hand-coloured etching, 32 × 39.9 cm. National Portrait Gallery, London

claimed Yule of the practice of removing shoes at the outer, rather than inner, gate, 'excepting on the occasion of introducing Envoys from other states.'[19]

The British sought to avoid the indignities suffered by past British representatives. In 1795, for example, the diplomat Captain Michael Symes had been 'bullied into taking his hat off to the Palace. So did Captain Hiram Cox two years later, and even dropt [sic] to one knee and bowed his head'.[20] Such episodes formed part of a wider historical narrative of resentment over Oriental sovereigns insulting the dignity of Britain's envoys – and thus Britain – by presuming their inferior status, as captured in Gilray's caustic 1792 caricature of Lord Macartney's embassy to the Chinese Emperor Qianlong, *The Reception of the Diplomatique and his Suite at the Court of Pekin* (fig. 42). In referring to such episodes but refusing to follow suit, Phayre and Yule were exorcising the ghosts of previous national embarrassments.

As much control was exercised over the manner of greeting as was possible, with both sides attempting to choreograph the encounter in accordance with their own custom or political objectives. Envoys were aware of the 'semiotic danger' of ceremonies: their actions had a potent yet unpredictable signifying potential in such moments and small missteps could determine one's place in history.[21] The British thus refused to abide by many local customs not simply out of cultural arrogance but from acute personal nervousness about reputation. And yet, diplomats – even haughty imperial diplomats – had to be somewhat diplomatic. Phayre and Yule thus deigned to remove their shoes

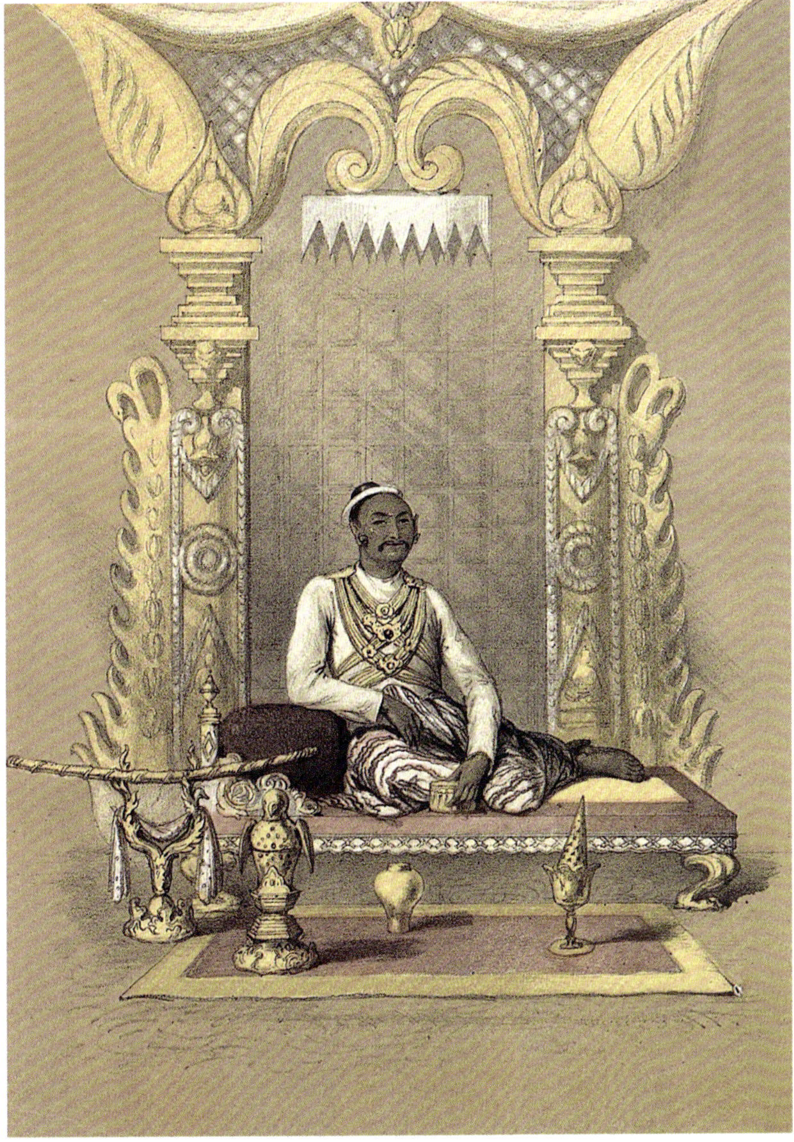

43 Sir Henry Yule, *The King*, 1855. Pencil and watercolour, 30.3 × 22.2 cm. Library of Congress, Washington D.C. Public domain

before entering the Hall of Audience and parleying with King Mindon Min himself; this was 'ludicrous and degrading', Yule admitted, but 'unavoidable'.[22]

These men were not unusual in their sartorial neuroses. The Victorians were obsessive over the proper forms of greeting and dress between colonials and the multitude of Indian maharajas on the subcontinent (see Chapter Eight). To a remarkable extent, imperial relations in South Asia were arranged with an eye to their visual impact. With so much riding on the aesthetics of interaction between different sovereign powers, portraiture came to carry particular weight. The Burmese king, duly protective of his own image, prohibited the official embassy artist from entering his palace along with the British legation: 'the Envoy might bring any gentleman with him, except Mr. [Colesworthy] Grant; for his Majesty objects strongly to sitting for his portrait.'[23] Burmese sovereignty was thereby asserted via the king's control of his own image.

When cooperation and consent were lacking, portraits could still be achieved by coercion or subterfuge. The mission's chronicler, Yule, was allowed to accompany Phayre into the Hall and was thereby given the opportunity to subvert the king's sovereign injunction. Having removed his hat out of courtesy to the monarch, Yule twisted this show of deference into an act of disrespect: 'I made certain notes and sketches inside my cocked hat', he claimed, 'from which I afterwards compiled a rough view of the hall with their Majesties enthroned.' The portrait that emerged from this clandestine operation (fig. 43) is a fairly crude representation that contrasts markedly with the significantly more delicate and humanising sketches of lower-rank Burmese officials produced by Grant in consensual sittings during the mission's time in Ava (see fig. 6). The king was later confronted with his stolen likeness; he complained about the 'crooked eyes'.[24] The final insult came when Yule made the portrait the frontispiece for his book, thus announcing the official historical record with an emblem of slighted Burmese sovereignty.

Such pictures constituted highly ambivalent events in which the lines between the 'honorific' and 'repressive' functions of a portrait were blurred.[25] The intensity of the British desire for an image of foreign rulers was borne of a recognition of their sovereign status; and yet, by the nature of the pursuit, execution and circulation of such portraits, this sovereignty was often diminished or denigrated. Such portraits signified not the autonomous sovereignty of Asian heads of state so much as their incorporation into imperial taxonomies and British-led international structures.

The Burmese king's refusal to sit for a portrait was thus symptomatic of a broader geopolitical impasse regarding the partitioning of Burma; no treaty was signed as a result of the 1855 embassy. As much as Yule's illicit portrait signalled a petty victory over the king, then, it was at the same time an index of the mission's wider failure to create a shared language-game that could formalise conditions of peace. As Wagner-Pacifici has argued in her study of the semiotics of surrender, 'surrenders work only when both the victor and vanquished participate in the same military, legal, and cultural paradigm.'[26] Refusals to sit for a colonial artist or photographer constituted a sovereign act of resistance to imperial paradigms, but it was not framed as such by colonials, often instead being presented as the product of a primitive iconophobia.

Conversely, participating willingly in the cultural paradigm of the portrait-sitting was heralded as a marker of a more advanced civilisational status. Take the frontispiece of the photographer John Thomson's *Illustrations of China and its People* (fig. 44), a commanding portrait from

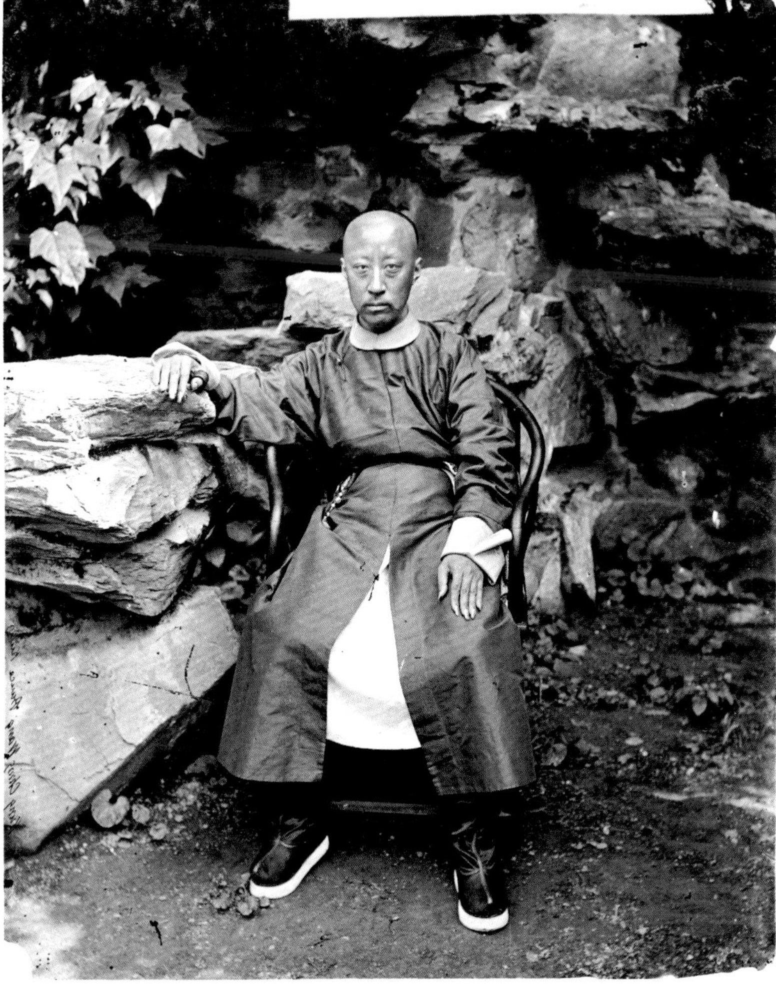

44 John Thomson, *Prince Kung*, 1872. Digital positive of glass-plate negative, 25.5 × 20.5 cm. Wellcome Library, London

1872 of Prince Kung (Gong), an influential Qing Empire statesman known to the British primarily from his earlier role in negotiating and signing the Convention of Beijing in 1860, thereby ending the Second Opium War. At the time of the signing, Felice Beato, who had attached himself to the British military expedition in China following his time in India documenting the Uprising, made the prince's portrait. Back then, it was reported, Kung had a fear of the 'infernal machine' of the camera, 'which really looked like a sort of mortar ready to disgorge its terrible contents into his devoted body'.[27] Such an elision of the camera and the cannon was endemic to contemporary accounts of photography, framing the former in terms of the latter's violent aggression. Yet Thomson's later portrait registered a subtler triumph than the crude technological machismo of the camera/cannon analogy. It had become an emblem of imperial hegemony.

By the time that Thomson arrived in China in 1870, the country was undergoing a process of transformation. Thomson's appraisal of Prince Kung in his written account stresses the sitter's role as a relative moderniser in the Chinese government, one who showed 'considerable interest in the process of taking a [photographic] likeness.'[28] As one critic wrote in the opening to a positive 1873 review of the illustrated book, Thomson's frontispiece portrait of Kung was symbolic of the rapid Westernisation of China in the decade since the last Anglo-Sino war:

> At the moment when Lord Elgin was putting his signature to the last treaty concluded with China [in 1860], a photographer, who had previously been introduced into the Hall, gave great annoyance to the Prince Kung by taking a general view of the 'high contracting parties'. So great has been the advance made since those days even by the Chinese in the knowledge of foreign arts that the same Prince who thirteen years ago attempted to conceal his face from the camera of Signor Beato appears ... seated quite at his ease, and in the attitude of a man as thoroughly inured to the process as any one of our own princes could possibly be. The idea of placing his likeness in the front of the book was a happy one, as he may truly be said to embody the comparatively enlightened policy which has made photography possible in China.[29]

The portrait was thus pressed into the service of an imperial narrative arc in which British intervention spearheaded Chinese modernity. A rhetoric of violence (camera-as-cannon) is replaced by a rhetoric of hegemony, with the consensual portrait standing for Kung's interpellation as a subject of imperial modernity, albeit not a literal subject of the British Crown.

Shared portraiture conventions could thus help to bring a degree of closure to previously conflictual relationships and enable a totalising vision of the world in terms of the imperial progress of modernity. Diplomatic missions to foreign states provided one way in which such a shared horizon could be forged; and while the central aims of such missions were geopolitical and commercial rather than aesthetic, those aims were frequently only fully realisable – and successes only properly perceptible – within the paradigm of the diplomatic spectacle as it had emerged in the history painting traditions of early modern European art. Gentlemanly exchanges, cordial signings, choreographed ceremonies and their visual and textual representations were used to redraw the territorial and conceptual boundaries of space, identity and sovereignty.[30] Realignments of power were formalised through and constituted by such geopolitical theatre.

DIPLOMATIC WARFARE: AFGHANISTAN, 1878

When in 1878 the British invaded Afghanistan 'in pursuance of a policy which in its intention has always been uniformly FRIENDLY', they did so in part because they wished to enforce face to face diplomatic relations. In July of that year, Sher Ali had been compelled to accept a Russian diplomatic mission in Kabul after it had marched to his capital uninvited, thereby compromising the emir's stance of non-alignment and dragging him into the geopolitical contest for influence that was being played out between Britain and Russia in Central Asia – the so-called 'Great Game'. Lord Lytton, Viceroy of India, was disturbed by this Russian overture, seeing it as confirmation of the warnings of the 'forward school' of political thought that the integrity of the British Empire depended on a more hawkish approach to securing its spheres of influence.

The first Earl of Lytton was new to the viceregal role but he was an experienced diplomat, having been posted all over Europe, and it was his desire that Kabul would accept a permanent British resident – something that it had lacked since the humiliating British retreat from Kabul during the First Anglo-Afghan War (1839–42), when colonials were massacred almost to a man (and woman). Given this history of violent antipathy towards a British presence in the capital, Lytton's proposal had proved unacceptable to Sher Ali, especially since he was attempting to steer a course between the bear to his north and the lion to his south. Yet now that the Russians had forced the issue in Afghanistan, the viceroy saw no excuse for further protestations by the emir about a British Resident.

Lytton dispatched an embassy of his own to Kabul. Led by General Sir Neville Chamberlain – a veteran of the First Afghan War – the British diplomatic mission only got as far as the Khyber Pass before it was turned

45 Frederic Villiers, 'Mr Burke Posing the Ameer' and '"Fixing" the Negative', *The Graphic*, 12 July 1879, cover. © Mary Evans Picture Library

back at the command of Sher Ali, who pointed out that the Russians had not come by invitation. Thus rebuffed, the British – or, at least, Lytton, who was acting beyond the bounds of the Prime Minister Disraeli's line on the issue – declared war on Afghanistan. The Russians promptly abandoned the ally they had recently courted so forcefully. Despondent, the emir fled Kabul and died shortly afterwards, his delicate strategy of neutrality in tatters. His son, Yaqub Khan, claimed power and soon endeavoured to come to terms with the British forces that then occupied large parts of his country. Under intense pressure, the new emir agreed to allow a British Resident in Kabul, while also ceding the Khyber Pass and numerous border districts to the Raj, all while giving up Afghan control of foreign policy. The head British negotiator – Major Pierre Louis Napoleon Cavagnari – was knighted for his efforts.

Portrait practices were organised to commemorate the peace. One year after the Russian diplomatic mission had arrived at Kabul and precipitated the ruin of Sher Ali, *The Graphic*'s front page reported the new geopolitical settlement (fig. 45) with two illustrations by their special artist, Frederic Villiers, portraying the triumphant photographic capture of the new emir. This reformulated the visual coverage of the campaign, which heretofore had been characterised by scenes of combat, military encampments, executions and captured weaponry. The war had been illustrated extensively from the start by special artists as well as the photographer represented here, John Burke (1843–1900). Having failed to secure official patronage from the colonial Indian government, Burke had decided to accompany the invading force anyway as a freelance operator.[31] While neither he nor the special artists were on the payroll of the military or Indian government, their activities nevertheless came to be interlaced with the official processes of imperial diplomacy.

THE EVENT OF PHOTOGRAPHY

Villiers's depiction of Burke's photographic process – the photographer standing tall with an arm gesturing over the head of the seated emir – imbues the Anglo-Afghan settlement with a dramatic aura of baptism. The photographer is positioned as a commanding representative of imperial power; Khan is anointed as ruler in a sort of coronation by camera. It was not uncommon for visual journalists to portray on the spot image-making practices but it was usually a form of self-advertising, dramatising their own exploits in the field, as the previous chapter showed. Villiers was far from shy when it came to self-promotion ('a terrible poseur who did much to perpetuate his own legend', as John O. Springall put it[32]), yet he diverts attention away from himself here in order to highlight the diplomatic agency of photography.

THE GRAPHIC

AN ILLUSTRATED WEEKLY NEWSPAPER

VOL. XX.—No. 502
Regd. at General Post Office as a Newspaper

SATURDAY, JULY 12, 1879

WITH EXTRA SUPPLEMENT

PRICE SIXPENCE
Or by Post Sixpence Halfpenny

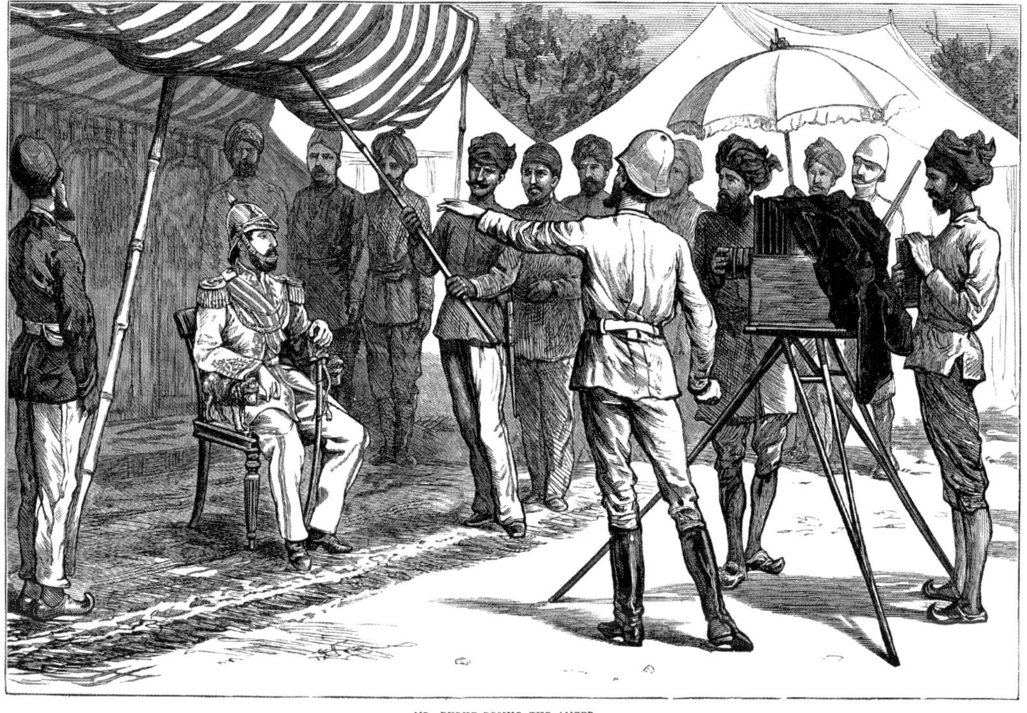

MR. BURKE POSING THE AMEER

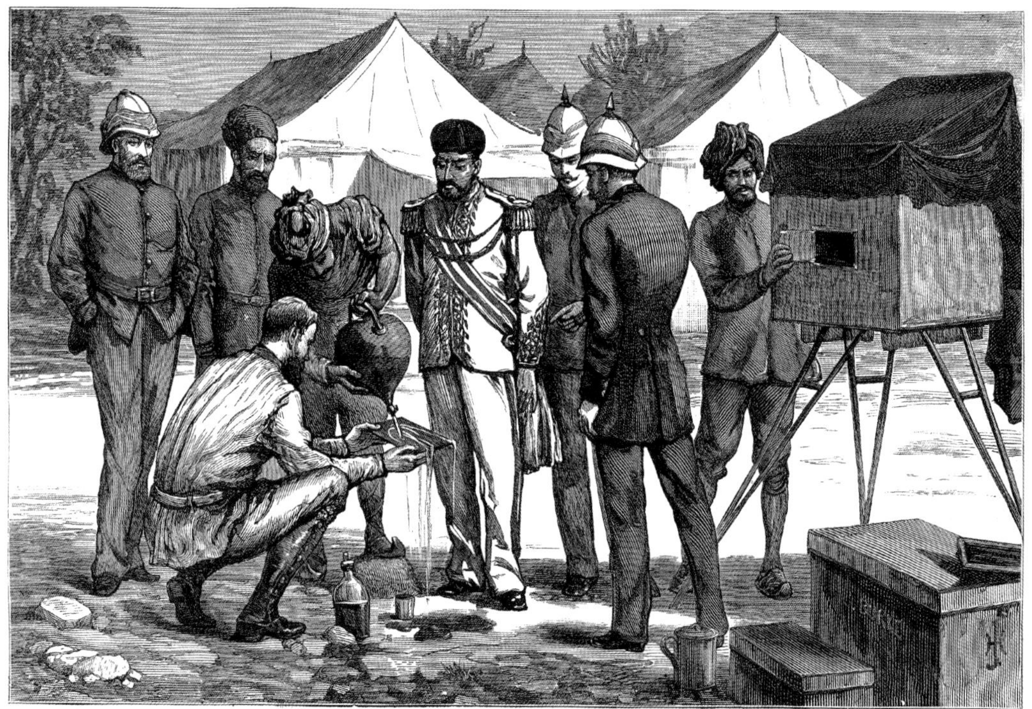

"FIXING" THE NEGATIVE

THE END OF THE AFGHAN WAR—PHOTOGRAPHING THE AMEER YAKOOB KHAN AT GANDAMAK

46 *below* Frederic Villiers, 'Major Cavagnari sealing the Treaty of Peace at Gandamak', *The Graphic*, 12 July 1879. © Mary Evans Picture Library

opposite, top row

47 William Simpson, engraved by Richard Caton Woodville, 'Major Cavagnari arranging with the Shinwarries for the Protection of the Road from Dakka to Lundi Khana', *Illustrated London News*, 20 January 1879. © Mary Evans Picture Library

48 William Simpson, 'Negotiating Peace with Yakoob Khan at Hashim Kheyl', *Illustrated London News*, 27 September 1879. © Mary Evans Picture Library

This was a neat solution to the problem of locating imperial sovereignty, which was highly diffuse in its operations. Another of Villiers's scenes, included in the same issue of *The Graphic*, captured the decentred nature of imperial power when it showed the head British negotiator, Major Cavagnari, carefully wrapping the treaty 'before sending it to Simla for the Viceroy's ratification' (fig. 46). The son of a Napoleonic French officer and an Irish mother, Cavagnari had cut his military teeth as an East India Company cadet during the Indian Uprising, before transferring to the political service in the 1860s and developing a reputation for himself along the North-West Frontier. He was well-liked by Simpson, who represented him for the *Illustrated London News* as a confident and attentive diplomat in drawings which emphasised the dialogical and procedural aspects of imperial relations: 'Major Cavagnari arranging with the Shinwarries for the Protection of the Road from Dakka to Lundi Khana' (fig. 47); 'The Negotiations for the Treaty of Peace' (fig. 48), 'Writing out the Treaty of Peace' (fig. 49), and 'Signing the Treaty of Peace' (fig. 50), among others.

It was thus not only the visual impact of military conquest or grand diplomatic ceremony that interested the British. The more mundane intersubjective elements of geopolitical administration were advertised. Power and legitimacy were not shown to emanate from a single figure; they emerged from the interactions of numerous loci of authority and from within the legal process itself. Khan negotiates with Cavagnari but, as 'Cavagnari sealing the Treaty of Peace' shows, the deal must be ratified

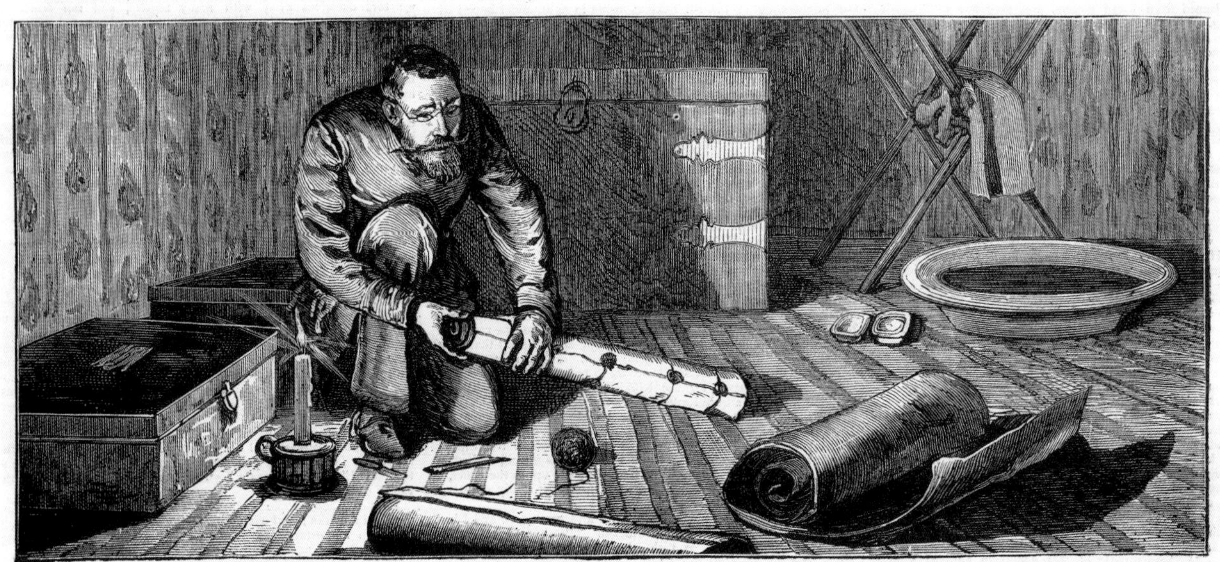

MAJOR CAVAGNARI SEALING THE TREATY OF PEACE AT GANDAMAK, MAY 26TH, 1879

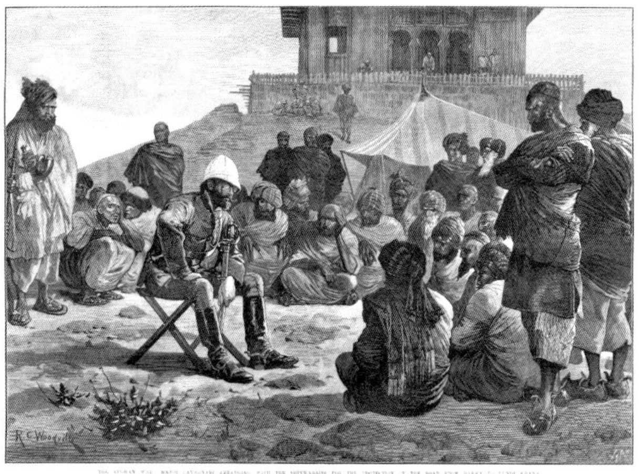

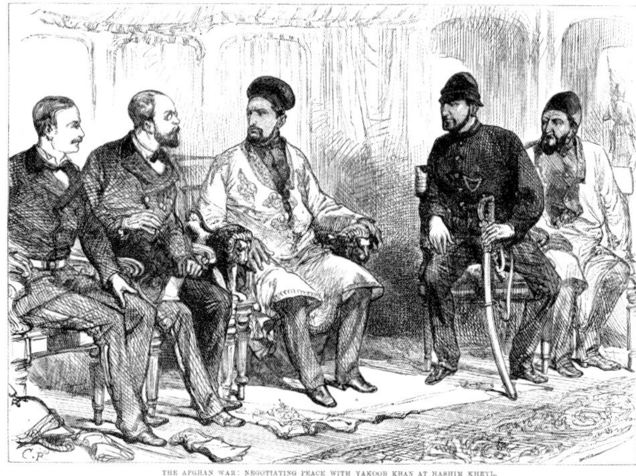

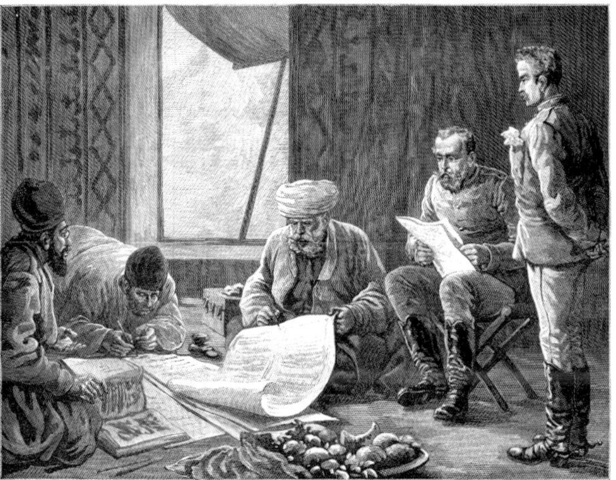

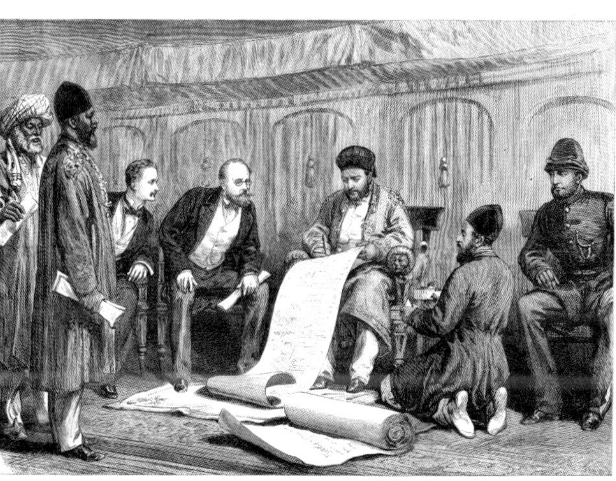

bottom row

49 William Simpson, 'Writing Out the Treaty of Peace at Gundamuk', *Illustrated London News*, 27 September 1879. © Mary Evans Picture Library

50 William Simpson, 'The Ameer Yakoob Khan and Major Cavagnari signing the Treaty of Gundamuk', *Illustrated London News*, 27 September 1879. © Mary Evans Picture Library

by the viceroy, who was himself a representative of Queen Victoria and answerable to the British government. Add to this the fact that the Treaty of Gandamak invoked a form of relations in which Afghan sovereignty was not entirely dissolved but was subjected to imperial suzerainty, with control of foreign policy ceded to the Raj, and we see that it was not a simple thing to distil such complex geopolitical dynamics into an intelligible visual report. The hailing of Khan as ruler was paradoxical, his regal status invoked to dilute Afghan sovereignty; following the traditional European 'art of surrender', the diplomatic portrait-sitting was 'an ironic exercise of power that erases its source of authority in the very moment of its utterance.'[33]

Given these complex sovereign dialectics, Villiers's decision to depict not the finished portrait but the portrait sitting – with its interplay of authorial and regal authorities – is deft journalistic shorthand for the

51 Mayer and Pierson, *Napoleon III and the Prince Imperial*, c.1859. Albumen silver print from glass-plate wet-collodion negative, 21 × 16 cm. Getty Open Content Program

new composition of regional power. In choosing to depict the photographic sitting rather than his own artistic medium, he additionally reveals a particular colonial interest in the poetics of the photographic act (an issue I continue to explore in the next chapter). His privileging of the photographic process over its finished products – Villiers shows not only the drama of posing but also the subsequent theatre of technical procedures – speaks to the recent turn in scholarship towards thinking about photography not merely as image but as an intersubjective 'event'. In Ariella Azoulay's influential reading, the camera institutes a 'dynamic field of power relations' that is not organised under the sign of a single, unified 'sovereignty'.[34] Indeed, Villiers's visual narrative is reminiscent of the mise-en-scène that Azoulay draws on to make her argument. In an 1859 photograph of Napoleon III's young son (fig. 51), the prince can be seen in a Parisian photographic studio seated on a horse in front of a formal backdrop. To the side of the backdrop stands an attendant, while on the opposite edge is Napoleon III himself watching the proceeding. The photograph by Mayer and Pierson is not a straightforward portrait of the imperial prince but 'attests to the ritual [of photography] itself' and in doing so, Azoulay suggests, it demonstrates how the camera participates in 'the erosion of sovereign authority'.[35]

For who has power in this scene? Is it the emperor, who rules France but is here relegated to the sidelines as a passive spectator? Is it the prince, who is completely dependent on the adults but is also the centre around which the event is organised? Or is it the photographer, who, in widening their focus to include not just the prince but the emperor, has 'pilfered' the image of the sovereign to whom they are subject? The scene discloses the complex game of negotiation and subversion intrinsic to the act of taking a photograph, in which authority is compromised or transgressed as power is distributed in unpredictable ways among photographer, sitter, apparatus and viewer(s). The photograph 'escapes the authority of anyone who might claim to be its author, refuting anyone's claim to sovereignty.'[36] Something similar occurs in the diplomatic ritual recorded by Villiers: the emir's regal status marks him as the esteemed centre of the scene, but in being such a focal point he is simultaneously subject to orchestration by the colonial photographer; and this oscillation between having authority and taking direction dramatises Afghanistan's new status as a semi-autonomous entity.

'Sovereignty has always been regarded as divisible', wrote the legal scholar Sir Henry Maine in 1862: 'there is not, nor has there ever been, anything in international law to prevent some of those rights [of sovereignty] being lodged with one possessor and some with another.'[37] In Azoulay's theory photography functions to disrupt claims to sovereign

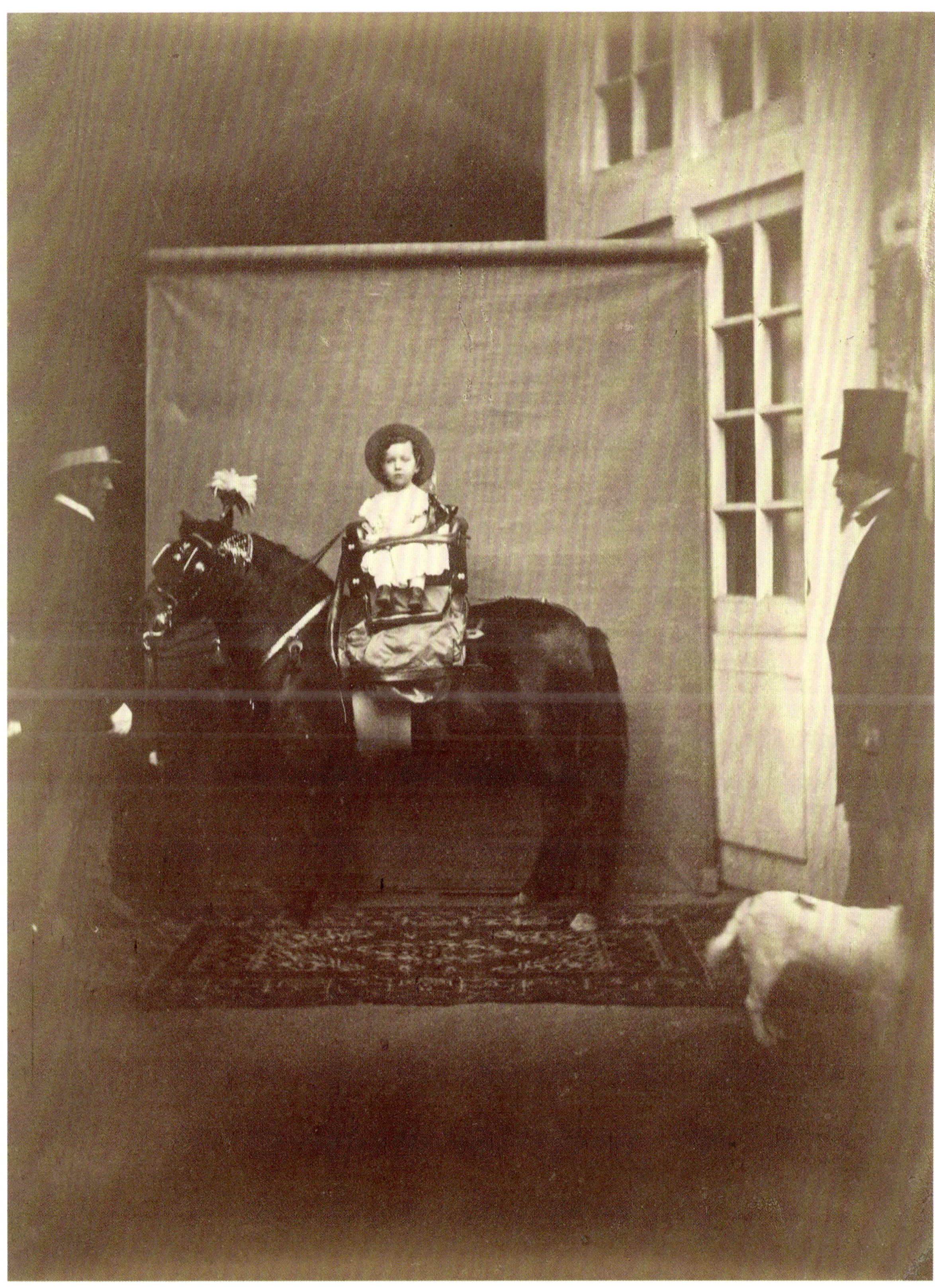

mastery, but the British Empire was pragmatic and adaptable in its approach to such matters. A complex and protean network of treaties and power-sharing arrangements amplified Britain's global influence. Imperial sovereignty was not necessarily ineffectual for being partial; the decentring of power was essential to the maintenance of the Empire.[38]

Still, the portrait event did open up a space for Khan to assert his own vision of Afghan sovereignty. In an incisive recent engagement with Azoulay's work, which I have found useful for thinking through issues of agency and subjection, Simeon Koole has argued for an increased sensitivity to the ways in which the event of photography can open up new horizons of political possibility for its participants. The image-making event does not simply 'reflect' pre-existing power structures but is generative of agency: power is not something 'brought to' the event and put to work in the act of photography but, rather, is something 'received' from the event. The camera is thus not a mere instrument of an a priori colonial agency but can foment conditions in which – as with Azoulay's reading of the regal portrait – agency is 'distributed across' the event of photography in ways that are not neatly reflective of the external political structures. Photography scholarship, Koole contends, has too often involved a crude 'hermeneutic of suspicion' that views agency as something 'behind' the camera rather than as something at stake within the event of photography itself – 'across its surface'.[39]

This recasting of agency as something that emerges from within, rather than lurking behind, the event of photography enables a better understanding of Yaqub Khan's performances during his sittings. Artists and photographers had initially been told by the British officials at Gandamak to keep away from the emir, 'who does not care to allow himself to be sketched'.[40] But, following the treaty negotiations with Cavagnari, these 'most important organs of the British press' were introduced to Khan – who, it transpired, was already familiar with the *Illustrated London News*. Khan's awareness of that paper means that his portrait should be seen in terms of his response to the 'global scrutiny' inaugurated by the illustrated press's 'regime of visibility'.[41] In agreeing to post-negotiation portrait-sittings with Simpson, Villiers and Burke, the new emir was well aware that he was being assimilated into a global network of news reportage and that he was therefore in a position to project his kingship beyond the bounds of the immediate political context.

Such knowledge makes Khan's outfit worthy of note. When he arrived at the camp for the negotiations, he was wearing an Afghan *choga*. For his formal portrait, though, he chose to change into a costume 'perfectly European in all its details' but by no means British (fig. 52). In an article for the *Daily News*, entitled 'Photographing the Ameer', Simpson took

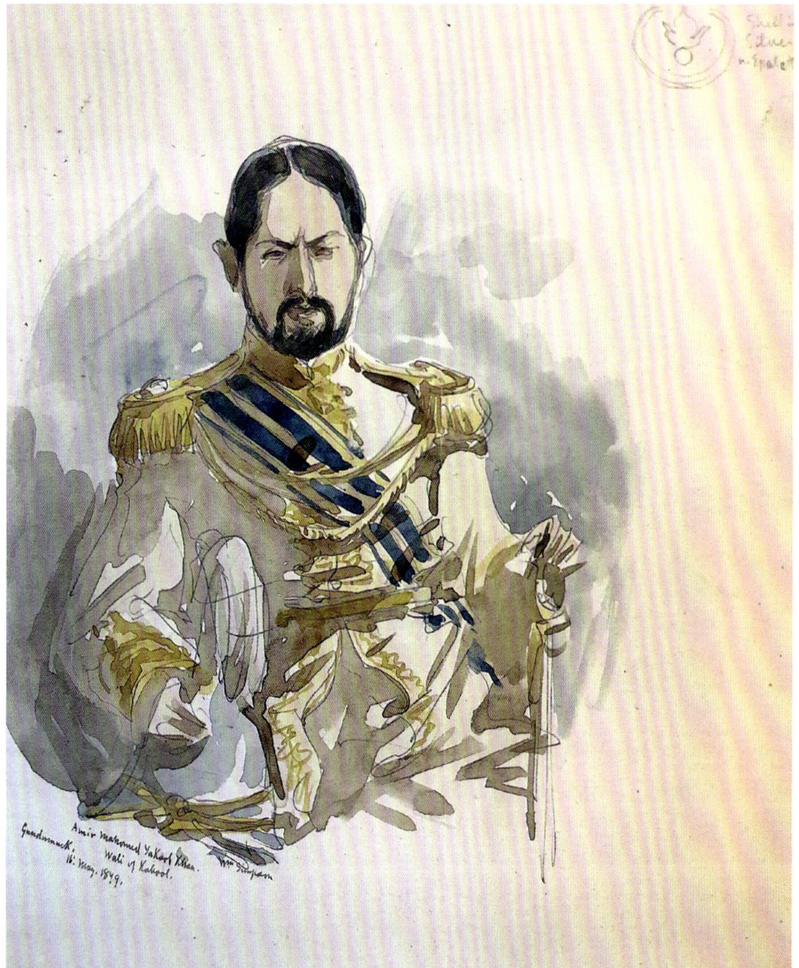

52 William Simpson, *Amir Yakoob Khan*, 1879. Watercolour, 57 × 38 cm. Author's photograph, with permission of the Anne S. K. Brown Military Collection, Brown University, Providence, Rhode Island

particular notice of Khan's attire: 'The style was evidently formed after the model of a dress worn by the German, or most probably, a Russian Kaiser; certainly it was not copied from the Prince of Wales, the Viceroys of India, or from any of our officials, civil or military.'[42] In a cultural mimicry that was not uncommon among Eastern rulers in the late nineteenth century, Khan appropriated signifiers of Western modernity as part of his own kingly self-fashioning – but he rejected its specifically British manifestation. The costume change indicates that the image-making event opened up new horizons for Khan who, in self-consciously orienting himself towards an international audience beyond Central Asia, opted for a mode of dress that refused Orientalist cultural binaries and laid claim to a parity between European and Asian sovereignty. Khan's self-assertion as a modern monarch may explain why Villiers chose to depict Burke actively 'posing' the emir; Khan's modernity thus

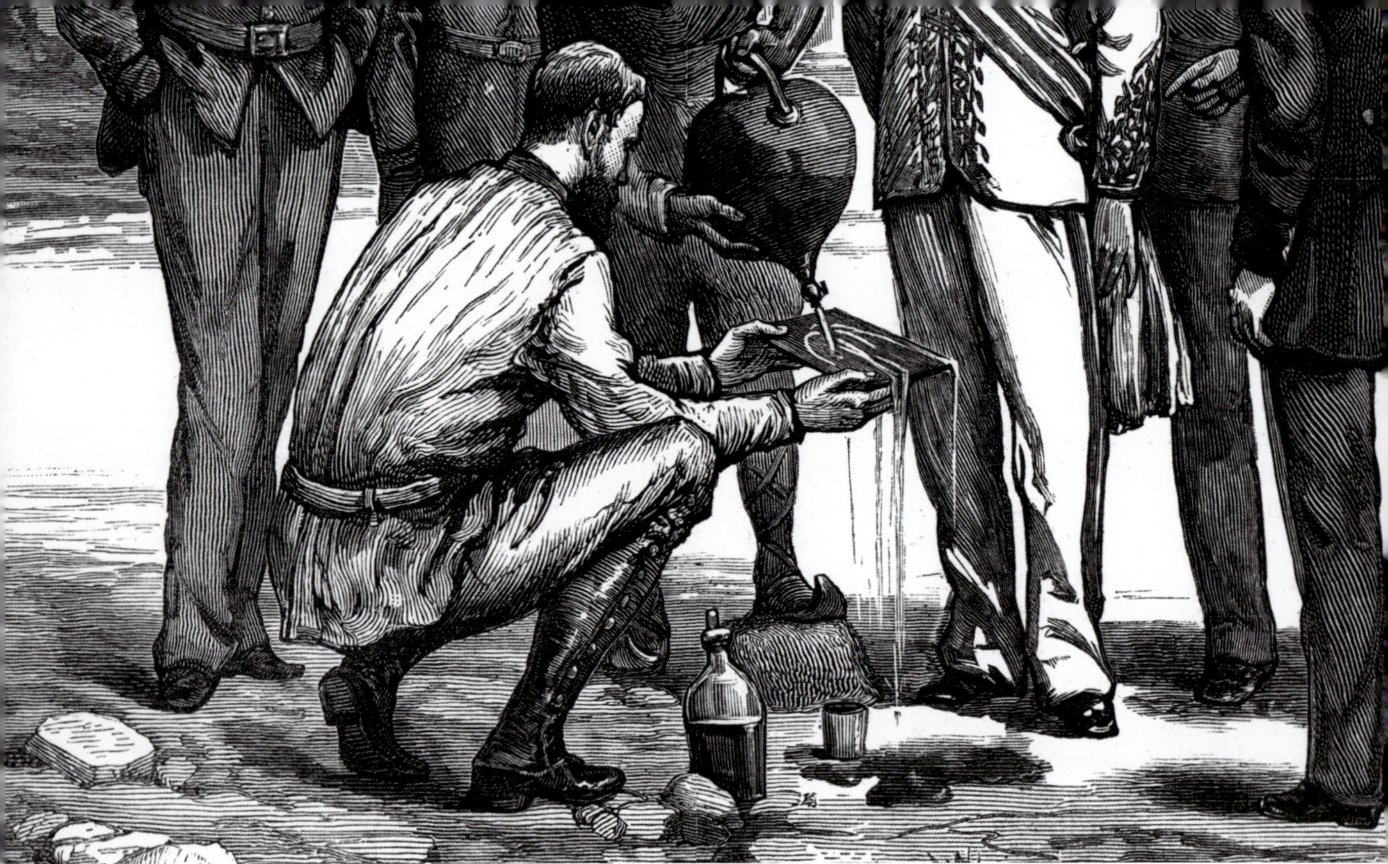

53 *The Graphic*, 12 July 1879, cover with Frederic Villiers, '"Fixing" the Negative' (detail of fig. 45).

appears as part of the imperial script, rather than as a sign of his own self-fashioning.

The event of portraiture was not merely an expression of the anterior power relations that gave rise to it (that is, Britain subjugates Afghanistan), then, but marked an opening within the proceedings which enabled Khan to project another geopolitical story: that of the rise of an internationally minded modern ruler in Asia. A portrait intended to bring closure to a historical episode thus created the 'points of fracture, an opening out' which Elizabeth Edwards has identified as fundamental to the 'raw' nature of photography, a medium which 'registers the possibility of a history that is no longer founded on traditional models of experience and reference.'[43]

SOVEREIGNTY IN THE AGE OF ITS TECHNOLOGICAL REPRODUCIBILITY

An important aspect of the 'new models of experience and reference' introduced by photography was an awareness of becoming an object of the camera's gaze, a self-consciousness about becoming an image and therefore being made available for the scrutiny of unknown future others. This sense of 'becoming-image' is made plain in the second part of Villiers's front-page spread in 1879, '"Fixing" the Negative' (fig. 53), in which he shows the process of treating the collodion glass plate once it had been removed from Burke's portable darkroom (the tripod structure seen on the right). John Thomson described a lengthy and recursive method in the field that involved moving in and out of a portable dark-room tent, developing in the tent before venturing 'into the light' where he preferred to conduct the majority of his operations, washing, fixing, re-washing, drying, storing and eventually re-development 'in broad daylight ... carefully watch[ing] the process of intensifying until it has reached the stage desired, when the picture may be washed, dried, and varnished.'[44] Khan's photographic portrait is shown in the middle of such a process and is therefore inchoate, anticipated and uncertain. As had been described by Oliver Wendell Holmes in his 1863 essay 'Doings of the Sunbeam', such suspense was a key feature of the poetics of the wet-collodion process used by photographers like Burke:

> a ghost we hold imprisoned in the shield we have just brought from the camera. We open it and find our milky-surfaced glass plate looking exactly as it did when we placed it in the shield. No eye, no microscope, can detect a trace of change in the white film that is spread over it. And yet there is a potential image in it, – a latent soul, which we will presently appear before its judge ... We pour on the solution. There is no change at first; the fluid flows over the whole surface as harmless and useless as if it were water. What if there were no picture there? Stop! What is that change of color beginning at the edge, and spreading as a blush spreads over a girl's cheek? It is a border, like that round the picture and then dawns the outline of a head, and now the eyes come out from the blank as stars from the empty sky ... This is a negative, – not a true picture, but a reversed picture, which puts darkness for light and light for darkness.[45]

Once a person had sat for a photographer using the wet-collodion process, they could watch themselves emerge, via numerous chemical interventions, as shimmering forms on the glass. Significantly, then, Khan and the British do not encounter finished prints in this scene but only shifting and spectral negatives that refuse closure because they are defined in terms of potentiality; a degree of inconclusiveness and contingency is thus inserted at the moment of supposed geopolitical resolution at Gandamak. Sovereignties constitute themselves through self-reflexive performances and their anticipated, but unknown, visual afterlives.

The sense of deferral baked into this scene is apt given that photography has what Ulrich Baer terms an intrinsically 'traumatic' temporality, whereby the full meaning of a photographed event cannot be fully processed at the moment of its occurrence but emerges through the future repetitions of the event as an image: 'The photograph's deferral of an experience from the occasion of its registration may affect not only the viewer but also the photographed subject, who is preserved undergoing an event to which he or she can only later attach a meaning.'[46] Such a temporality is thematised, I think, by the turbaned assistant placing the cap back over the portable darkroom, whose gaze addresses the audience of *The Graphic* directly, bridging between the time of the image-making event and the time of the metropolitan consumer who is viewing its products in the pages of the press. Villiers thus represents the 'event of photography' in its most expansive sense; in Azoulay's schema, Burke's act of photography, its representation by Villiers and the subsequent dissemination of such imagery all form part of the unfolding 'event of photography' – the continuous development of the photographed event's significance as it is reframed and re-viewed by different audiences who 'legislate' on its political meaning.

The rise of the illustrated press and photographic means of mechanical reproduction therefore imbued diplomatic events with what might be termed a temporality of abeyance. I use the term 'abeyance' not only to indicate deferral but also for its etymological links to a state of expectancy for the reception of titles, office or property. British and Afghan relations had already been agreed in treaty but the prospect of mass international audiences 'legislating' on the meaning of their respective sovereignties – how their titles and office and property signified – remained. While Burke's photography sought to help 'fix' the geopolitical relationship – reifying with bodies what the treaty had ratified in words – the photographic image, as Baer notes, is always 'radically exposed to a future unknown to its subjects.'[47] As Walter Benjamin wrote of the 'screen actor' in his essay 'The Work of Art in the Age of Its Technological Reproducibility', 'While he stands before the apparatus, he knows that in the end he is confronting the masses. It is they who will control him. Those who are not visible, not present while he executes his performance, are precisely the ones who will control it. This invisibility heightens the authority of their control.'[48]

A final word, then, on how the mass Victorian audience eventually read such photography, which they only saw after a brutal historical twist. In one of Burke's photographs (fig. 54), that went on to be engraved in *The Graphic*, Cavagnari and Khan are seated together, along with the former's secretary, Mr Jenkyns, and, accompanying the latter, General Daod Shah and the political adviser and finance minister Habeebula Moustafi. The British envoy and the emir adopt similar postures to one another and both stare into the distance. Cavagnari, as in many of his portraits, has an aristocratic hauteur to his appearance befitting his high-born Italian ancestry, his bearing simultaneously languid and imperious. There is a sense here of the swagger that so impressed Lytton that he was moved to appoint Cavagnari as the permanent British Resident in Kabul. This new office, created by the Anglo-Afghan agreement in Gandamak, represented a diplomatic coup for the British, who had been denied official access to the emir's court since the infamous 1841 attack on the British mission and the subsequent massacre of the retreating imperial forces. In Cavagnari, Lytton saw a man who was undeterred by the bloody historical precedent for a Kabul embassy. 'If my death sets the red line on the Hindu Kush,' Cavagnari proclaimed, 'I don't care.'[49]

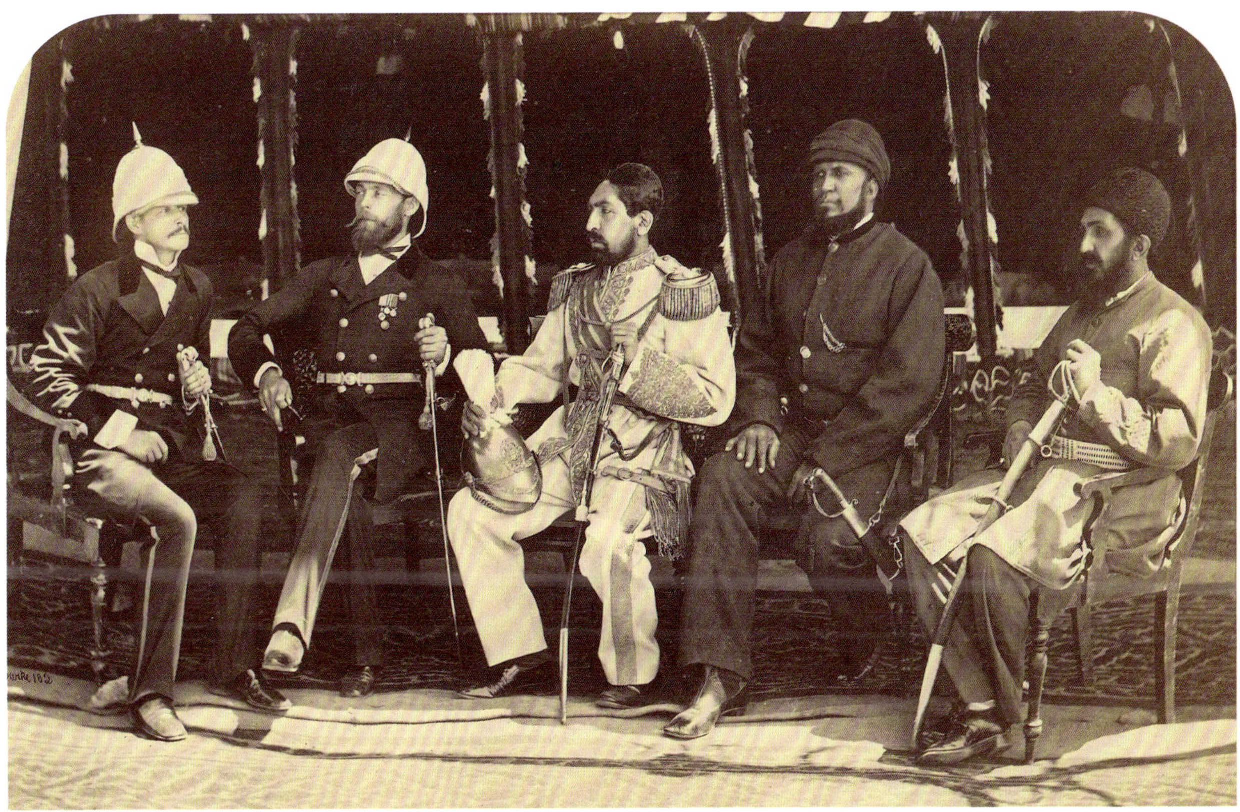

54 John Burke, *The Amir Yakub Khan, General Daod Shah, Habeebula Moustafi, with Major Cavagnari C.S.I. & Mr Jenkyns*, 1879. Albumen silver print from glass-plate collodion negative, 16.3 × 25.8 cm. Getty Open Content Program

Khan, resplendent in his European military attire, looks less at ease by comparison but he gazes fiercely and resolutely in the same direction as Cavagnari. The latter was optimistic about Anglo-Afghan relations, believing Khan would 'turn out to be a very good ally', albeit he was 'not to be thoroughly trusted any more than any other Oriental.'[50] This group portrait thus speaks to the men's shared vision for their countries' future relationship; it an image of imperial triumph in the vein of the diplomatic tradition of history painting outlined at the beginning of this chapter, sublimating colonial violence into a vision of gentlemanly accord.

Yet the collegial mirroring of postures here was ultimately not enough to stop *The Graphic* from speculating that the emir's 'loyalty and friendliness towards us are now, to say the least, extremely doubtful' on first publishing this photograph on 13 September, just four months after it was taken.[51] By then, the resonance of Cavagnari's poise, and the entire tenor of the summit in Gandamak, had shifted from triumphal to tragic. As the caption noted, this was 'The Last Photograph of Major Cavagnari'. An image designed to foreshadow a bright future had unexpectedly become a memento mori, perhaps even a morality tale about imperial hubris.

Left out of this story so far is the Afghan population for whom Yaqub Khan was claiming to speak. Yet it was the Afghan people – who in all likelihood never saw any of Burke's photographs – who ultimately determined the meaning of the photographer's images for future viewers. They played a decisive, albeit invisible, role in the 'event of photography'. On 2 September 1879, having not long established his diplomatic mission in a walled courtyard near the emir's court, Cavagnari sent a sanguine telegram to the colonial government in Peshawar: 'All well in the Cabul Embassy'.[52] By the following evening, however, he was dead, an early casualty of a day-long assault on the British Residency led by Herati soldiers who appeared to be acting against their new emir's wishes; he had not paid them their wages and Cavagnari had also chosen to ignore their appeals. In a grisly echo of the 1840s, all British residents were massacred. 'I have lost my friend the Envoy', telegrammed Khan to the British shortly afterwards, 'and also my kingdom.'[53]

By the time that Burke's photograph of geopolitical resolution in the 'periphery' was seen in the imperial centre of London, therefore, the entire Gandamak settlement had unravelled. Britain was once again at war with Afghanistan. The temporal structure of the Victorian media – whereby telegrams bearing news of global developments arrived relatively quickly but the sketches and photographs of such events arrived only many weeks later via steamship – meant that illustrations could, in their belatedness, undermine teleological narratives by exposing the essential contingency of imperial history. In heralding an abortive peace, Burke's photographs in *The Graphic* showed that 'the present contains the seeds of diverse and mutually exclusive possible futures.'[54]

The confident Anglo-Afghan concord expressed by the image had become an ironic sign of diplomatic overreach. 'It may not be flattering to our *amour propre*,' wrote General Roberts in 1880 following his military victory in the unexpected second stage of the war, 'but I feel sure I am right when I say that the less the Afghans see of us, the less they will dislike us ... we should have a better chance of attaching the Afghans to our interests if we avoid all interference with them'.[55] Given that the longstanding diplomatic tradition of history painting espoused by Burke,

Villiers and Simpson was invested in the notion that Britain's envoys possessed a certain charisma or authoritative aura – as if the British Empire had been negotiated into existence by means of nous and charm – this was not an inconsequential admission.

CONCLUSION

This chapter has argued that imperial diplomacy in the Victorian era was entangled with the processes and products of mass-media networks of image-making. The Victorians wished not merely to be militarily dominant (although of course this was key to the development of – and part of the libidinal thrill of – empire) but also to transmute that violent conquest into a mode of victory that appeared to be rooted in gentlemanly ethics and international law. Tropes rooted in early modern European art and, more immediately, in the history painting of eighteenth-century Britain provided the terms under which the imperial project could be presented as a rational, peace-oriented and at least minimally consensual 'civilising mission'. By the mid-nineteenth century, however, such images were not merely commemorative; they did not only offer an idealised, revisionist account of past events. The processes of picturing the event had become part of the event itself: acts of image-making and diplomatic interactions unfurled in a feedback loop with one another. Portrait-sittings in particular were fraught 'public relations' exercises for both the envoy and the sovereign; they introduced what I have termed a temporality of abeyance into such diplomatic theatre because participants knew that their status was in part contingent on the subsequent interpretation of these images in the illustrated press. In the age of mechanical reproduction, international relations became a hypermediated, self-reflexive and anxious affair.

6 · NEGATIVE HISTORIES

Encountering Colonial Photography 'in the Field' in Burma, China and Tibet, 1855–1904

A PHOTOGRAPH TAKEN BY JOHN CLAUDE WHITE (1853–1918) IN Tibet in the summer of 1904 shows the triumphant Younghusband Mission marching through the streets of Lhasa (fig. 55). 'Every detail both for effect and for defence were regarded', wrote Colonel Francis Younghusband of his long-awaited entry into the 'forbidden city'.[1] The grave significance of this imperial parade to the denizens of Lhasa can be gauged by the fact that Tibetan emissaries had earlier pleaded with the encroaching British embassy to turn back, claiming that their presence in the capital would 'spoil their religion and that the Dalai Lama might die'.[2] Lhasa was marched on nevertheless, 'unveiled' for the colonial camera on 3 August, much to the excitement of the metropolitan public.[3] White, the official photographer of the mission, brought with him six cameras and 'innumerable plates' that required three mules and a team of 'coolies' who were 'experts in the art of carrying and setting up this cumbersome equipment.'[4] He used his large and heavy panoramic camera with glass-plate negatives to capture this scene, an eye-catching apparatus positioned to document the imperial parade from the perspective of the Tibetans. Yet those spectators appear less struck by the procession than by this act of photography. The harsh stares of the local congregation make for a tense scene in which the viewer is positioned as one among many in a crowd but without enjoying the anonymity that a crowd usually provides. There is a palpable sense here of the conspicuousness of colonial photography 'in the field' and its role as a fraught space of political encounter.

The camera and its procedures were just as much a part of such invasive spectacles as the parading soldiers and envoys. It had a clear imperial symbolism in the minds of the British. The popular commercial photographer Samuel Bourne was emphatic about the camera's techno-material impact:

John Claude White, *The Younghusband Mission entering Lhasa*, 1904 (detail of fig. 55).

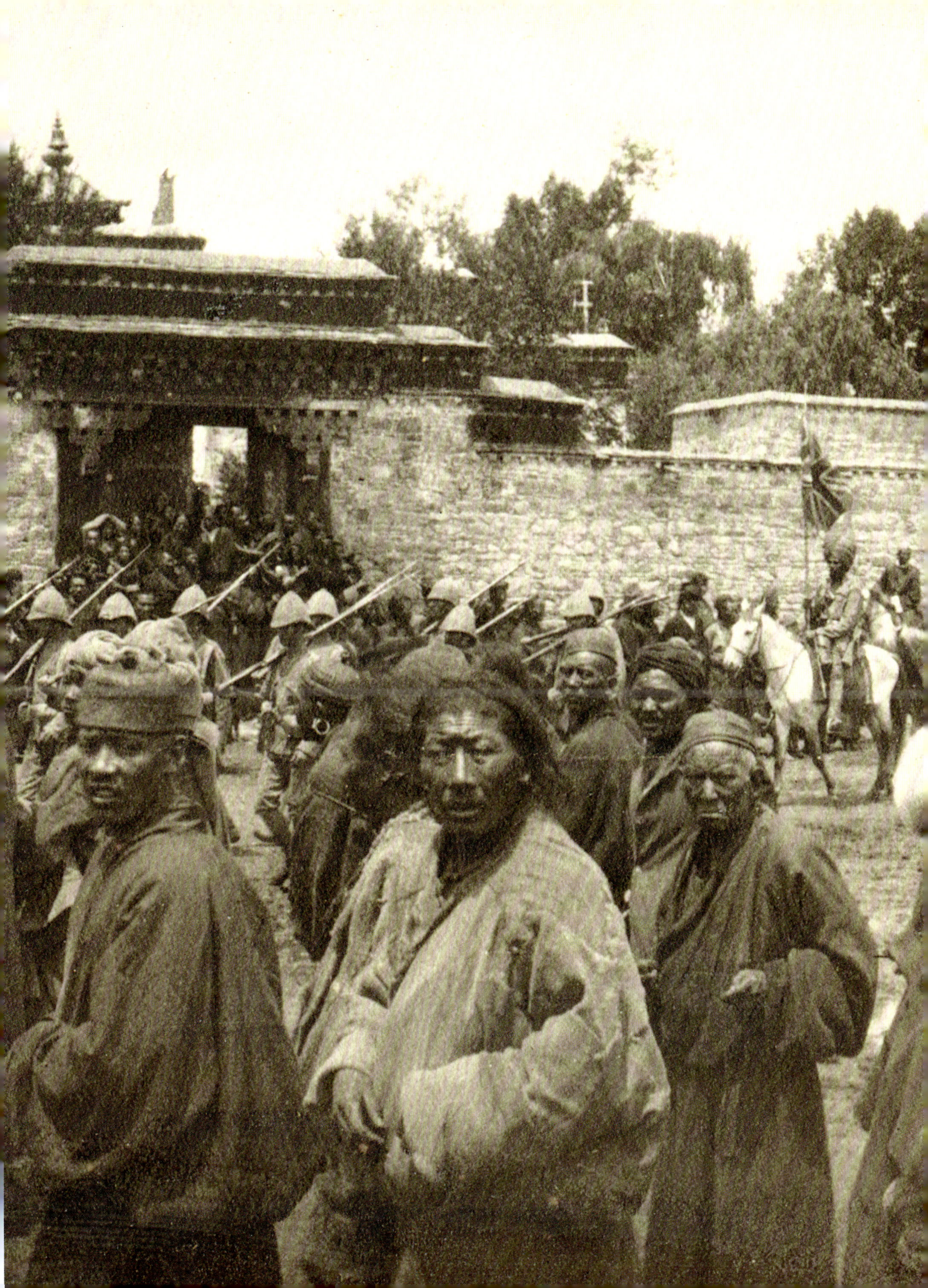

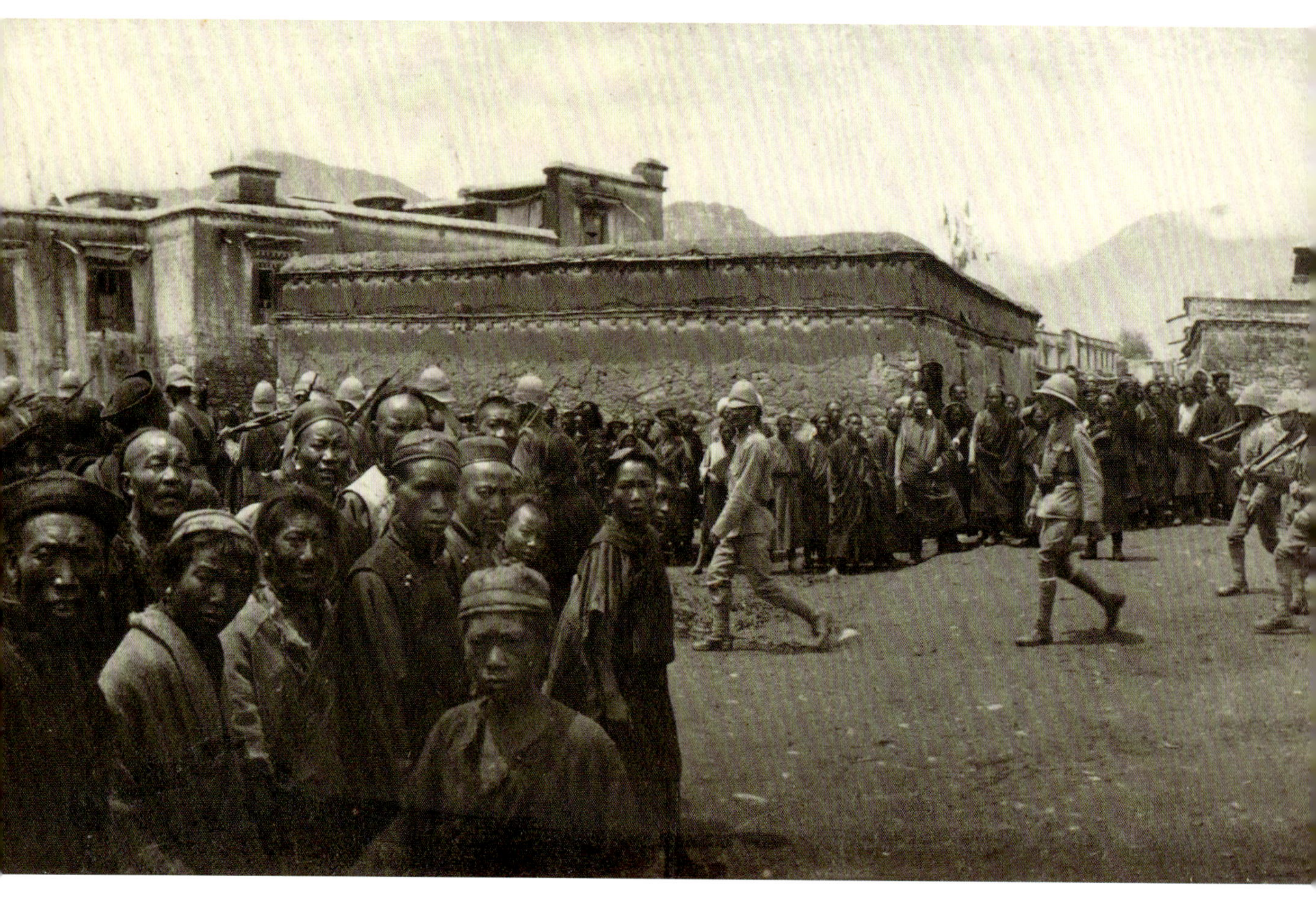

55 John Claude White, *The Younghusband Mission entering Lhasa*, 1904. Albumen silver print from glass negative, 5.1 × 17.1 cm. © Royal Geographical Society, London

> As there is now scarcely a nook or corner, a glen, a valley, or mountain, much less a country, on the face of the globe which the penetrating eye of the camera has not searched, or where the perfumes of poor Archer's collodion have not risen through the hot or freezing atmosphere, photography in India is, least of all, a new thing. From the earliest days of the calotype, the curious tripod, with its mysterious chamber and mouth of brass, taught the natives of this country that their conquerors were the inventors of other instruments beside the formidable guns of their artillery, which, though as suspicious perhaps in appearance, attained their object with less noise and smoke.[5]

Drawing on the commonplace Victorian equation of the camera with the cannon, Bourne posits the photographic apparatus as a form of imperial pedagogy, demonstrating the broader military-technological complex that underpinned British sovereignty in India.[6] The intended audience of such photographic theatre was not merely the British consumers who might buy Bourne's prints but the native inhabitants of

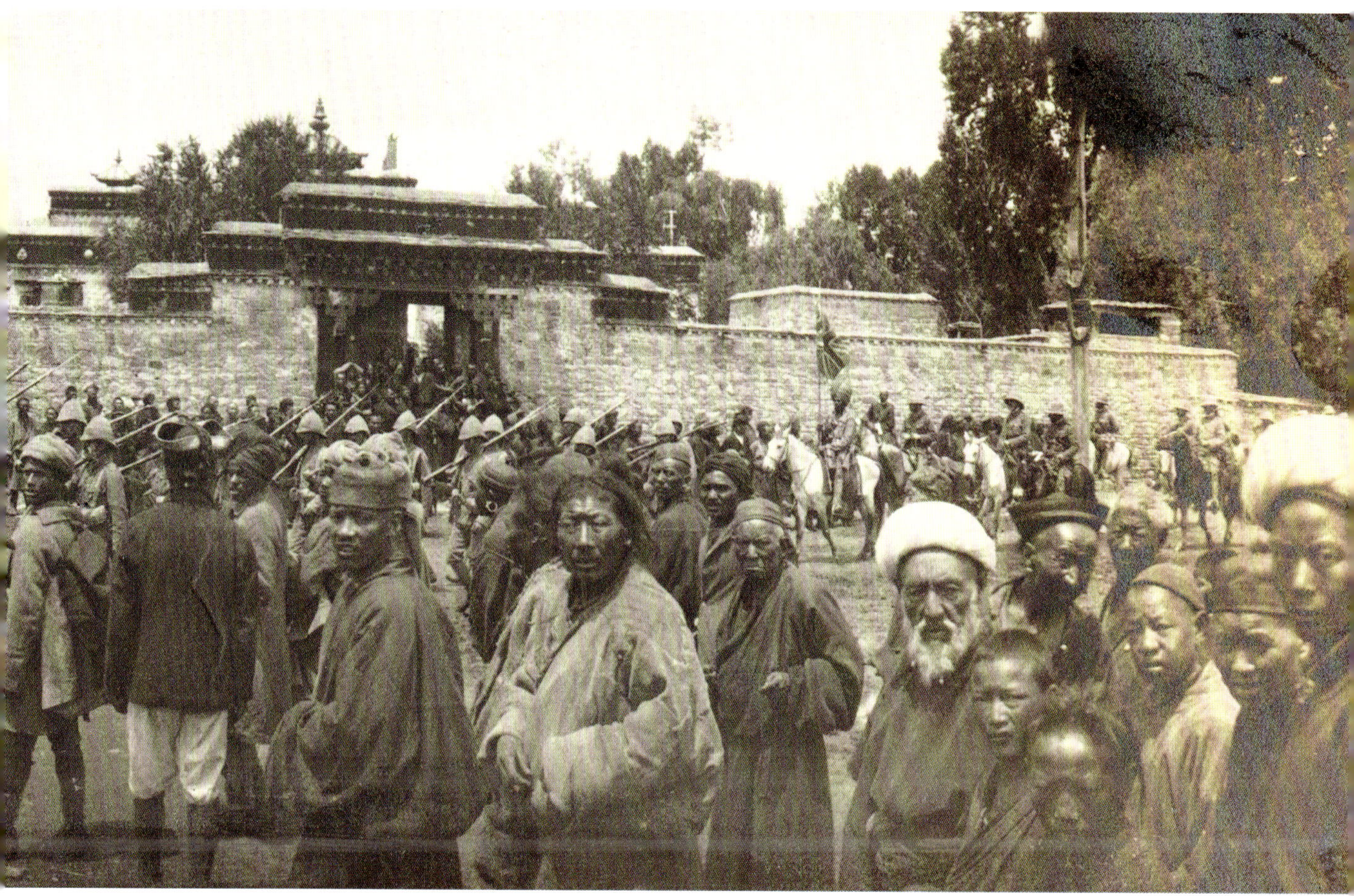

the 'glens' and 'valleys' who would probably never see such photographs yet who were nevertheless exposed to the camera and its chemical mists.

Exactly what this meant to those spectators would depend on the local politics, epistemologies and histories of those regions. There are significant problems with recuperating such perspectives at all, due to the silencing effects of the imperial archive. Such issues notwithstanding, in what follows I draw on examples of cross-cultural encounters in nineteenth-century Burma, China and Tibet, in order to speculate on what colonial photography meant to those who encountered its 'curious tripods' and collodion 'perfumes' – not to mention the glass plates, dark-room tents and bottles of chemicals – and who, under varying conditions of consent and duress, participated in the 'event of photography' as spectators, sitters and protesters.

The photographs that were produced in the field were ultimately circulated as positive prints in museums, archives and publications – contexts that have been subject to important and influential studies in the historiography of photography.[7] Yet the 'negative' history of colonial photography – how it signified before development, printing and circulation – has received comparatively limited attention. In her contribution to an edited collection of essays accompanying the 2003 exhibition *Seeing Lhasa: British Depictions of the Tibetan Capital, 1936–1947*, Elizabeth Edwards writes of the negative as 'perhaps the primary document' of photography, for it is 'the negative which captures the light reflected off an object, passing through the aperture of a camera to be held and stilled on light sensitive chemicals spread across a support of glass or film.' Yet ultimately this primary document is afforded little aesthetic resonance or semantic substance: 'While the moment of inscription or exposure on the negative carries with it the authenticity of the moment, the sense of meaning created through the use of photographs emerges from the moment those negatives are first printed.'[8]

Negatives, then, are what Geoffrey Batchen has recently termed the 'repressed' side of photography's history.[9] The only extended study of Victorian negatives has focused on their representation and metaphorical status in literary fiction and deals only summarily with the defining photographic form of the era, the collodion glass-plate.[10] Yet the negative has its own history of spectatorship in the field that is separate from the positive. John Thomson claimed he had to lock his box of negatives to stop curious locals sneaking a peek and leaving their smudged fingerprints on the glass, which would then come out in his prints; yet other colonials made a point of showing off their negatives to the peoples whose lands were being surveyed, seeing the practice as a kind of litmus test of a population's visual literacy.

The phenomenology of colonial photography was thus not all about indexical clarity and albumen sheen. Recall, for instance, 'Fixing the Negative', the front-page illustration run by *The Graphic* in 1879, considered in the previous chapter, showing the Emir of Afghanistan watching as liquid washed over his collodion-glass portrait (see fig. 53). This chapter continues to explore some of the concerns raised in that discussion, considering the meanings attached to the laborious procedures of producing – and being seen to produce – photographic images in the field. This, I suggest, was how Victorian Orientalist photography was often witnessed by those Others who found themselves sitting for, or witness to, the imperial lens: as a spectacle of image-making, a series of technical, chemical and corporeal processes whose intended final product – the stable and captioned positive print – remained absent.

I consider the negative here as a visually distinctive material artefact but also as a metaphor for how the political significance of the colonial encounter – its conditions of sovereignty and subjecthood – was by no means 'fixed', much less overdetermined, at the moment of image-making, even if subsequent photographic prints were indeed submitted to what Ali Behdad describes as the 'excessive textual anchorage' of Orientalist discourse.[11] The significance of the image-making encounter was instead fluid, underdeveloped and contingent. 'Photography' here is encountered not in terms of the detail which the Victorians prized about the medium but through the haziness of latency; not in terms of the various discursive and archival contexts that comprise the 'social biography' of the print but via the singular materiality of a negative encountered at the time of its own making;[12] and not in terms of the stasis and instantaneity often associated with photography but through the 'durations' that inhered in the contingent processes of preparing, loading, exposing, 'fixing' and rinsing negatives.[13]

THE WAXED PAPER NEGATIVE: LINNAEUS TRIPE IN BURMA, 1855

The satisfaction of Orientalist curiosity was a crucial aspect of the spoils of war for the British. Since the eighteenth century, 'curiosity' had been a central justification for imperialism, presented as a refined enterprise characterised by intellectual and aesthetic interest.[14] Rudyard Kipling hinted at the avarice underlying such refinement when one of his characters posited the 'golden mystery' and 'winking wonder' of Burma as something that 'explained in the first place why we took Rangoon, and in the second why we pushed on to see what more rich or rare the land held' ('Under what new god, thought I, are we irrepressible English sitting now?').[15] So it was that after the British had invaded Burma in 1852 and carved it into 'Upper' (independent) and 'Lower' (British) territories, the embassy sent to the Court of Ava to ratify the annexation included not only diplomats and soldiers but also a photographer from the Madras army, Captain Linnaeus Tripe, charged with documenting the architecture of the region; a professional artist from Calcutta, Colesworthy Grant (recruited initially under the mistaken apprehension that he was also a photographer), with a broad remit to represent the 'natural features' of Burma along with its 'people, cities and palaces'; and Sir Henry Yule of the Bengal Engineers, the official chronicler of the mission, who as an amateur draughtsman and aspiring Orientalist went on to create many ethnographic studies of his own.[16]

Tripe's camera was therefore just one part of a broader colonial ethnographic complex. An epistemology of 'on the spot' observation – photographing, sketching, painting, measuring, mapping – was fundamental to the colonial encounter in general and was especially pronounced during moments of conflict and imperial expansion. Whether it be in the service of journalistic reportage, military reconnaissance, topographical survey

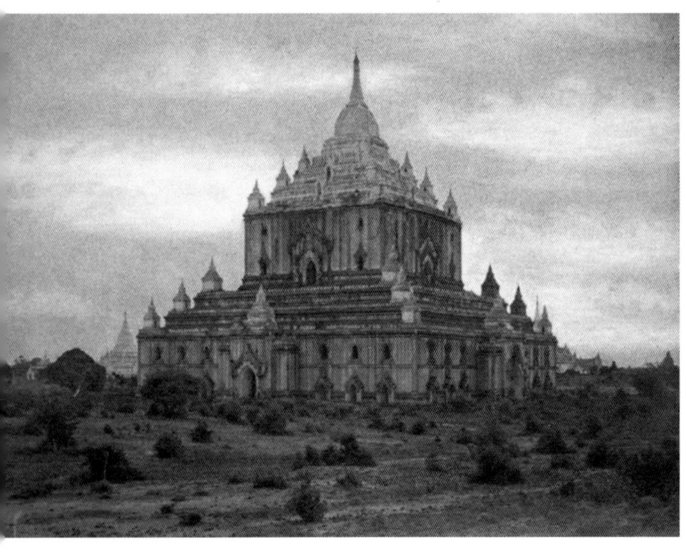

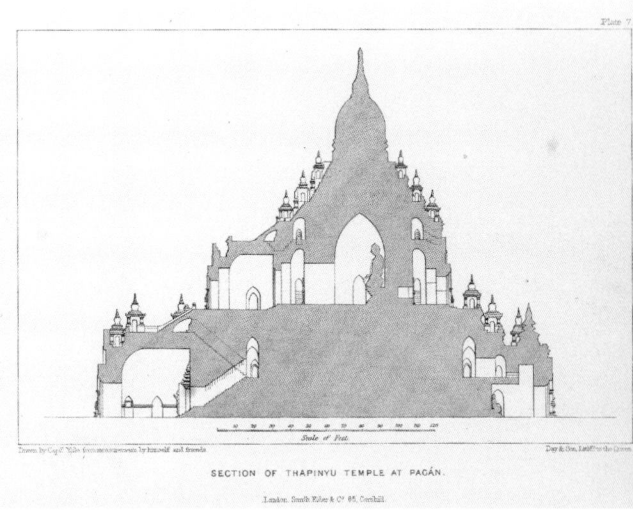

56 Linnaeus Tripe, *The Thapinyu Pagoda, Pagan, Burma*, 1855. Albumen print. © The British Library Board, London, Photo 61/1(15)

57 Sir Henry Yule, 'Section of Thapinyu Temple at Pagán', in Sir Henry Yule, *A Narrative of the Mission sent by the Governor-General of India to the Court of Ava in 1855* (London: Smith, Elder, and Co., 1858), pl. 7. Lithographic print. Library of Congress, Washington D.C. Public domain

or scholarly ethnography (and the lines between these domains were often extremely porous, especially during times of war and its immediate aftermath), British techniques of observation came to shape 'the field' as a colonial or proto-colonial space. The ideal of in situ study was not an ideologically neutral method of knowledge-production but contained an implicit hierarchy: it involved, as Johannes Fabian puts it, 'the enactment of power relations between societies that send out fieldworkers and societies that are the field.'[17] Such practices fed the exhibitionary complex of the ethnographic museum, wherein 'ideas of race science were explored through the military spoils of extractive colonialism.'[18] What I am interested in here is what such 'ethnographic surveillance' may have intimated to recently invaded populations about what it meant, beyond the immediate violence and shock of a military defeat, to exist in political relation to an imperial power like Britain.[19]

Previous studies have tended to consider Tripe's photographs separately from the broader pictorial archive (map-making, sketching, watercolour studies and so on) of the mission but colonials at the time were clear about the interconnected nature of their visual practices.[20] On docking at Pagan along the Irrawaddy River, the British had been surrounded by 'war boats', 'shouting oarsmen' and 'dancing demons gesticulating wildly on narrow canoes'. To the sound of 'deafening music', colonial officials were greeted by the Governor of Pagan and his retinue – 'the largest and best we had yet met with'.[21] Spectacular as the Burmese diplomatic reception was, however, it was the 'marvels of the ancient city' that 'had long been the subject of conversation and anxious curiosity to the members of the Mission'.[22] So, while Tripe quickly got to work producing calotypes of the famed architecture (fig. 56) and Yule honed a diagrammatic approach to the esteemed structures (fig. 57), Grant began a panoramic painting of the temple complex (fig. 58), 'from which the niceties of detail were necessarily excluded … [but] amply provided in the descriptions and sketches by the Secretary Captain Yule, Capt. Tripe's photographs, and Lieutenant Heathcote's measurements'.[23] Different visual fields thus created a self-reinforcing ethnographic discourse via an 'inter-ocular' process of cross-reference, emulation and citation.[24] These men's approaches worked in concert – although not without elements of competition – to produce an extensive visual survey of the Burmese landscape.

Yet there was something going on here beyond a crude imposition of a subject–object dichotomy between the British and the Burmese. As Grant wrote, 'The Mission was more spectacle than spectators.'[25] Yule agreed, telling of being 'immediately surrounded by a mob of monks and their pupils' when making his architectural studies. The Burmese 'took much interest in the pictures which Capt. Tripe, Mr. Grant, and the

58 Colesworthy Grant, *Panoramic View of Pagan, looking S.W. by S.*, 1855. Watercolour, 33 × 47 cm. © The British Library Board, London, WD 540(23)

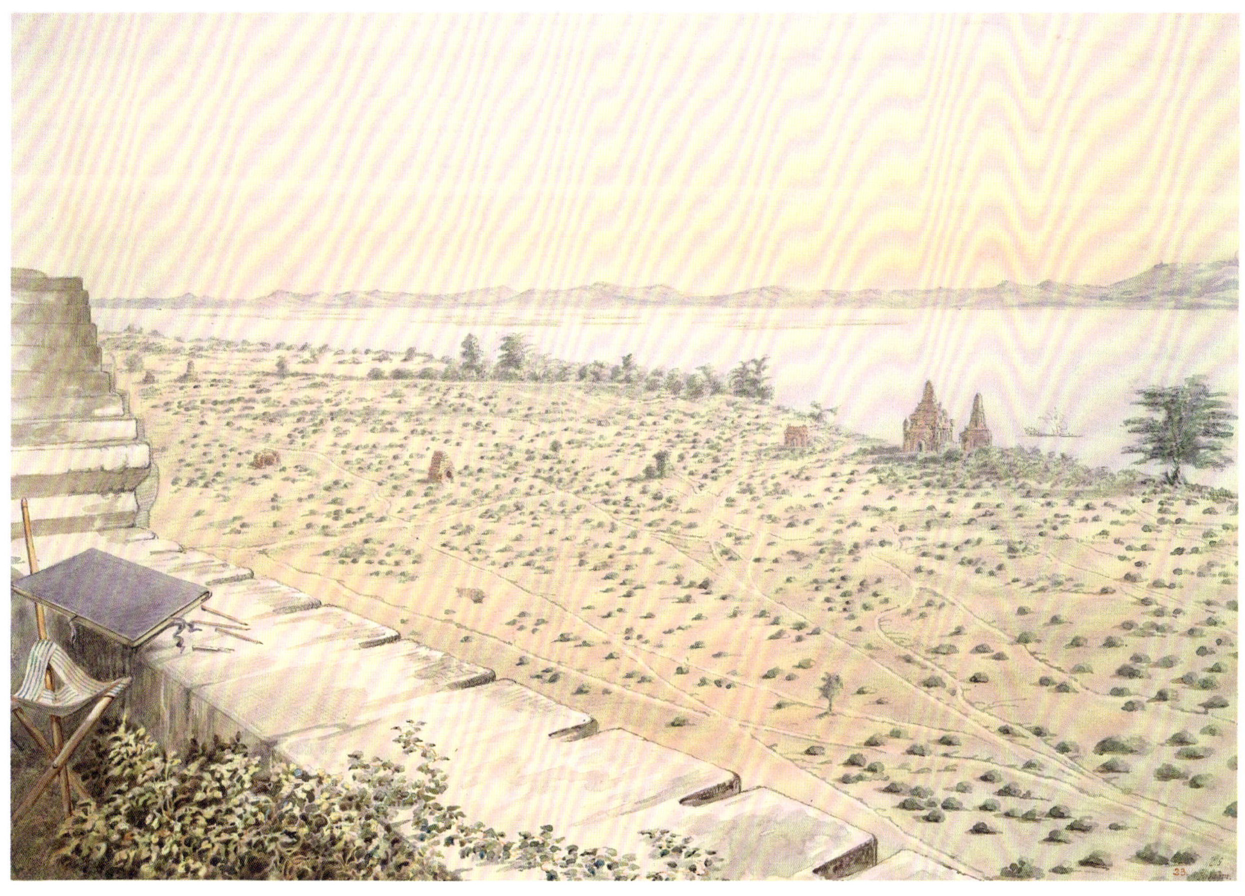

59 Linnaeus Tripe, *Amerapoora, Mohdee Kyoung*, 1855. Waxed-paper negative. © Victorian and Albert Museum, London, RPS.2721–2017

60 Thomas Ruff after Linnaeus Tripe, *Amerapoora, Mohdee Kyoung*, 2018. C-type print. Victoria and Albert Museum, London

sketching members of the Mission produced; and even the photographs, though all remaining in the negative stage, appeared to be understood.'[26]

Photography was encountered here as waxed paper negatives used in the calotype process that had been invented by Henry Fox Talbot in the 1830s. Tripe coated his negatives in an emulsion of silver iodide, placed these into his camera for a lengthy exposure time of up to nine minutes and then bathed the latent image in a solution of sodium thiosulphate. The 'unfavourable weather' of Burma – its heat and humidity – presented particular difficulties for the paper process and led to what Tripe termed 'defective photographs ... he was working against time, and frequently with no opportunity of replacing poor proofs by better.'[27] Nevertheless, he produced more than two hundred studies, with Burmese architecture becoming the subject of prolonged and conspicuous colonial observation; photography, like sketching, was a durational rather than an instantaneous process.

The negatives seen by curious Burmese onlookers would have shown buildings as though wreathed in a thick mist and scattered blemishes across the surface that refer to nothing in the architectural environment but are indexes of photographic production itself (fig. 59). The sky in such scenes was necessarily overexposed and Tripe had to retouch the negative to add effects like clouds. The negative indicates the epistemic limits of photography: what seems transparently clear in a print is revealed by a negative to be what Tina M. Campt describes as 'the creation of technical, material, and cultural processes of conjuring and fixing'.[28] There is little here of the apparently unmediated, window-onto-the-world type of realism that the Victorians prized about photographic prints. As Susan E. Cook puts it, 'The negative promises presence but then negates that presence.'[29]

In 2018 the photographer Thomas Ruff came across four boxes of Tripe's negatives in the Victoria and Albert Museum and was 'utterly captivated' by the 'haunting yet beautiful quality' of the images. Ruff was struck by how Tripe's negatives had aged during their time in storage, many of them showing 'traces of mold, water damage, and even chemical mutation.'[30] He enlarged the negatives (fig. 60) to emphasise these blemishes, thus presenting the artefacts as what Serpil Oppermann terms 'storied matter'.[31] Tuning in to processes of decay calls for an eco-critical perspective on photography as an ongoing interaction of image, object and environment: fading from continuous chemical reactions to light; foxing caused by fungal growth; curling from moisture in the air. As Caitlin DeSilvey has written, 'decay reveals itself not (only) as erasure [of information] but as a process that can be generative of a different kind of knowledge'.[32] The vibrant materiality of the paper negative

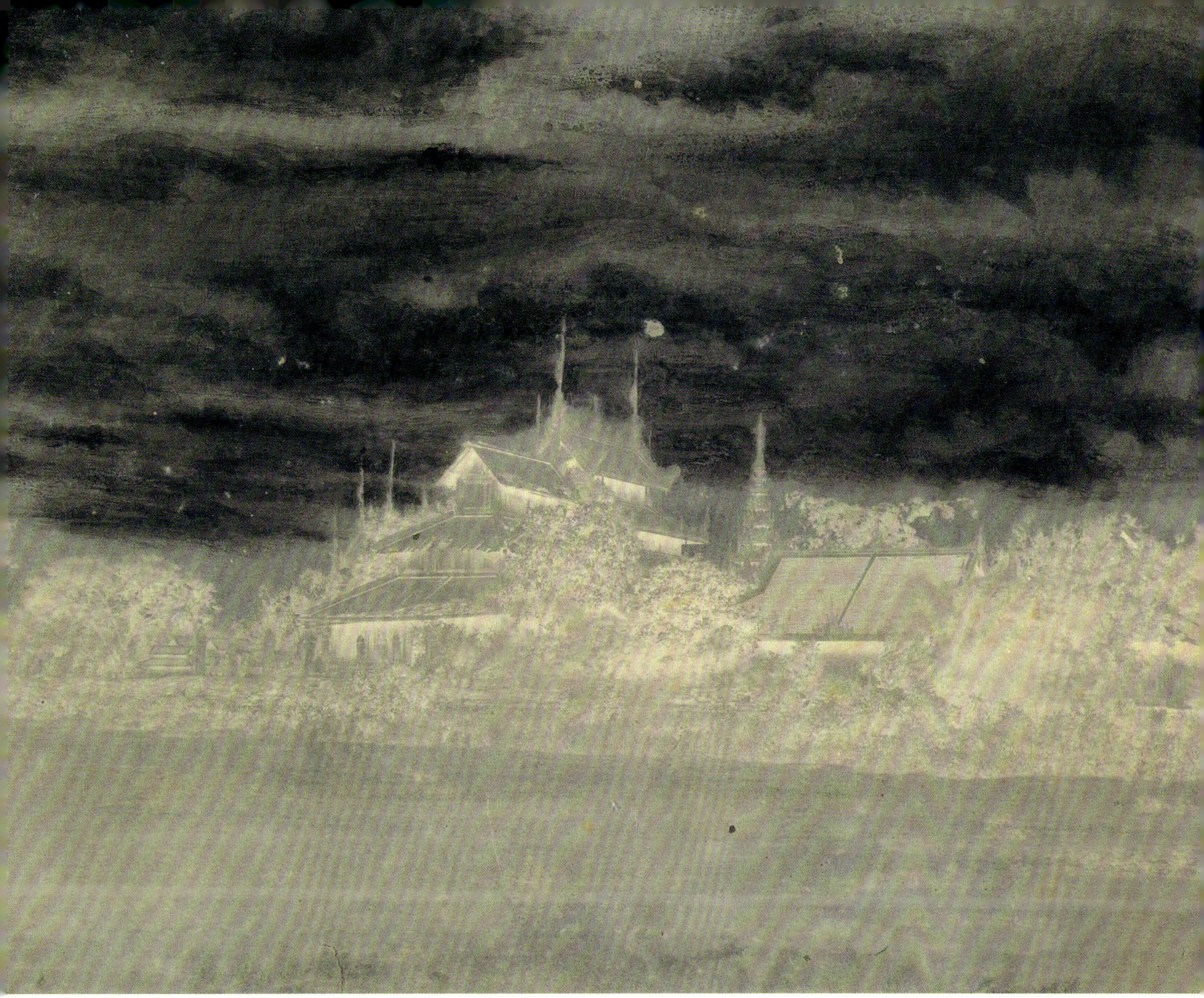

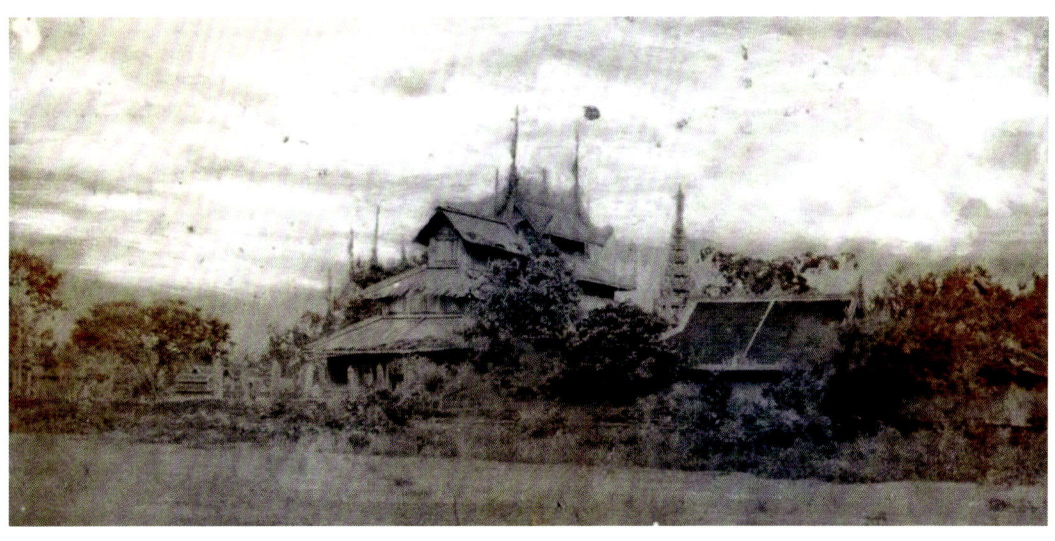

speaks to a form of historic evidence in which 'the materials of remembrance are living, dying, and being devoured'.[33] Colonial photographers experimenting with various early photographic methods in tropical climates were acutely aware that their negatives were not stable and timeless historic records but were instead frustratingly susceptible to material and pictorial transformations, with harsh travelling conditions, climatic factors and experimental concoctions of photographic chemicals meaning that images not infrequently continued to develop or degrade in unpredictable ways. The negative thus indexes the environment in myriad ways, not merely through its intended photo-sensitivity. It was not an inert tool tethered to the colonial will but registered the unpredictable agencies of chemicals and climate in a manner that jeopardised the representational integrity of the document.

What did the Burmese make of Tripe's photography? King Mindon and his ministers seem to have understood something of the science of photosensitivity on which the process was based; a camera was among the diplomatic gifts given to the king by the British envoy, Major Phayre, chiefly because Mindon had earlier expressed 'great curiosity on the subject of the "sun pictures" of which he had heard.'[34] A Burmese man was consequently apprenticed to Tripe during the mission's time in Ava, although it was claimed by Yule that he was unable to master a process 'so involved in niceties and technicalities'. The expedition was nevertheless a 'contact zone' in which both the British and the Burmese staged performances of their own artistic traditions, from photographic image-making to the marionette puppetry, *yoke thé,* put on for the mission.

The significance of the British presence – and thus also of Burma's recent dispossession – emerged in a feedback loop with these multiple forms of image-making. Mindon, for instance, while steadfastly refusing to sit for an official portrait with Grant, nevertheless arranged for a competition between him and a local artist to paint the kingdom's famous white elephant. Such image-making events formed, as Linda Tuhiwai Smith writes of colonial fieldwork more broadly, 'a significant site of struggle between the interests and ways of knowing of the West and the interests and ways of resisting of the Other.'[35]

In order to appreciate what Tripe's lens may have signified to the Burmese people who witnessed its interactions with their architecture, it is also necessary to take into account their responses to the wider constellation of visual technologies that comprised colonial fieldwork. The Burmese crowded round the colonials doing such work, asserting themselves as critical spectators by demonstrating a 'capacity for the appreciation of [photographic] views and sketches'.[36] (This may not sound like much but the fact that they displayed such obvious comprehension of

Western-style images marked them out in the British mind from, say, Indian peoples, who were considered to be incapable of such recognition without imperial tuition.) Colonials were not just surveilling subalterns who did not meaningfully return their gaze; they felt themselves to be scrutinised and appraised during the very act of ethnographic scrutiny. In his official narrative of the mission, Yule claimed that the Burmese 'were gratified at the interest and admiration expressed by us for many of the buildings which formed the subjects of pictorial representation, especially the highly carved monasteries.'[37] It is unlikely, however, that the Burmese audience viewed the colonial observations of their sacred structures as a matter of architectural appreciation conducted in good faith. Nor, I think, were they supposed to.

Consider Grant's *Panoramic View of Pagan, looking S. W. by S.* (see fig. 58), a 'master-of-all-I-survey' view from the upper terrace of the Gawdawpalin Temple in Pagan. This is one of 106 watercolours that Grant produced for the East India Company during the mission, mounted in a large leather-bound album now housed in the India Office Collection of the British Library. Part of a six-segment panoramic survey of the Pagan temple complex, Grant's scene of scattered buildings and winding lanes along the bank of the Irrawaddy seems to speak to the peaceful nature of the mission. Like Tripe, Grant worked in a notably 'picturesque' style that framed the exotic in familiar terms, presenting a tranquil vision of Burma that belied the uneasy conditions in which he was operating.[38] Pillars demarcating the newly imposed frontier separating 'Upper' from 'Lower' Burma had been pulled down by rebels ('a declaration of war', according to one colonial newspaper in July 1855[39]); villages in recently occupied territories were being hit by repeated Burmese raids from across the border;[40] and a British captain had been killed while installing telegraph cables in the region.[41]

Tripe and Grant's picturesque survey of Burma admits little of such political turbulence. Yet I want to read the latter's invocation of his own leisurely presence, achieved through the inclusion of his sketchbook and chair in the scene, as a sign of colonial violence – a violence that was implicit within the very fact of these two men's visual practice in the field. The implications of Grant's emphasis on his image-making materials become clear when it is viewed in the light of the artist's previous trip to Burma a decade earlier, in 1846, when Grant had found himself severely limited in what he could draw. Officials would not sit for portraits and his access to temples was often blocked. It was not simply religiosity that made the Burmese protective of their temples: the British had form for using these structures as military forts. When one British member of the 1855 mission encountered the Grand Pagoda in Rangoon, he noted,

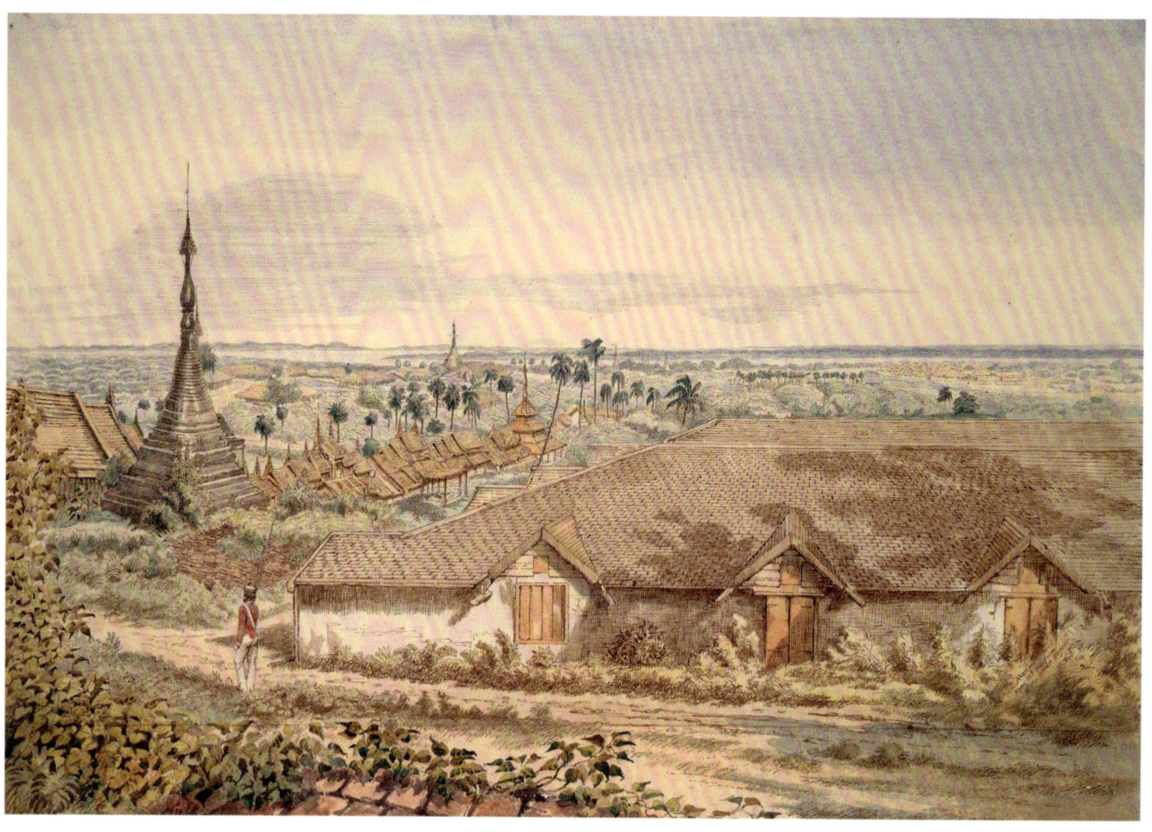

61 Colesworthy Grant, *Rangoon – from the Platform of the Great Pagoda*, 1855. Watercolour, 33 × 47 cm. © The British Library Board, WD540(1)

'I should think two Regiments of European soldiers might live in it.'[42] On the entrance to the building could be seen the graffitied initials of a British soldier from the First Anglo-Burmese War.

The line between architectural study and military reconnaissance was therefore blurred. Indeed, during his 1846 trip, Grant had been arrested as a spy while sketching 'Sale's Pagoda' (Alanpya Pagoda), so named by the British because it had been held by Major General Sir Robert Sale, or 'Fighting Bob', in the 1820s. Grant's documentation of the site led to 'grave charges' being made against him by Burmese authorities speaking 'the ominous words "stranger" – "foreign country" – "war between the nations" – "examining – making writings of Forts."' For the Burmese, then, Grant's fieldwork registered as a form of military intelligence; and, as much as the artist sought to characterise the affair as a comedic instance of Burmese over-reaction, he himself emphasised the utility of the structure ('commands an open and extensive range').[43] This was a kingdom that manifested its sovereignty by imposing tight restrictions on foreign artists, whose architectural studies were viewed in terms of their potential military value.

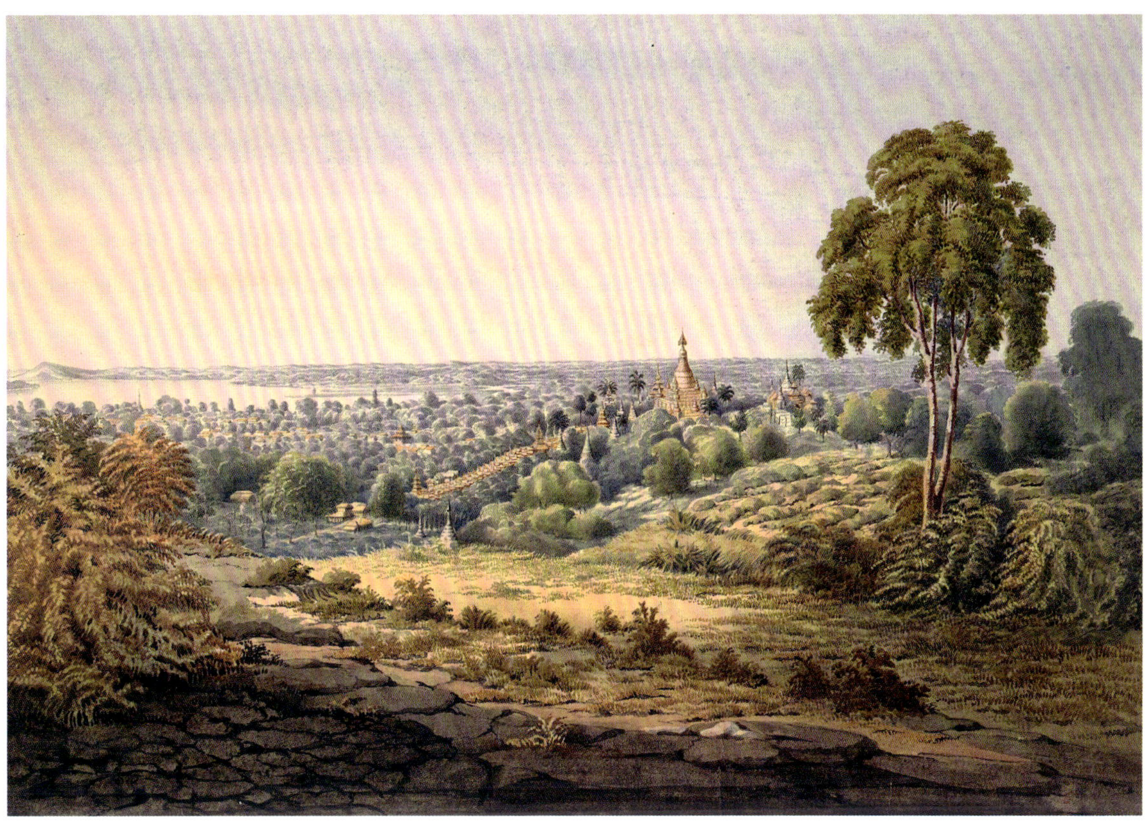

62 Colesworthy Grant, *Prome, from the Southern Heights*, 1855. Watercolour, 33 × 47 cm. © The British Library Board, WD540(6)

All of which is to say that Grant and his fellow image-makers, Tripe and Yule, would probably have been well aware of the anxieties that their architectural fieldwork could spark in the Burmese authorities. In 1855, however, colonial photographers and artists seemed to enjoy more or less unimpeded access to sites that were once off limits. Grant's inclusion of his chair and sketchpad conjure a conspicuous and prolonged observational presence. Consider the difference between the temporality of sketching implied here – slow, open, methodical (he writes in detail about how he painstakingly ensured the alignment of the panoramic segments) – to the rapidity, mobility and anonymity of the special artist celebrated by the likes of Baudelaire and Mason Jackson (see Chapter Four). To sketch in leisurely fashion, without being apprehended by the authorities, was to advertise the diminishment of Burmese sovereignty, while also carrying within itself the implicit threat of a future invasion carried out using such a topographical survey. Grant stressed the military slant to his practice when he produced two views, *Rangoon – from the Platform of the Great Pagoda* (fig. 61), and *Prome, from the Southern Heights* (fig. 62), both sketched from positions once occupied by British soldiers

– a fact he highlighted for his East India Company employers in the notes he submitted to accompany the drawings.

Tripe, an army officer, did the same. Following in the footsteps of his Madras Army colleagues, the photographer positioned his camera on military sites and depicted them via the delicate, volatile and laborious procedures of preparing, exposing and treating the paper negatives in challenging humid conditions. In Rangoon, he produced a study of the Shwe Dagon Pagoda which he subsequently captioned 'From H. M. 84th Barracks', thus 'situating himself in relation to the conflict, temporally, as well as the pagoda, spatially.'[44] There was a fundamental haziness concerning the nature of such image-making: visual fieldwork could simultaneously function as an ethnographic record, military reconnaissance and diplomatic reportage. Such ambiguity was, I suggest, a core part of the significance of such practices to local onlookers. Field observation heralded what Walter Mignolo terms a 'colonial semiosis' in which 'the meaning of a sign no longer depends on its original cultural context (for instance, Castilian, or Amerindian, or Chinese), but on the new set of relations generated by communicative interactions across cultural boundaries.'[45] Meaning was not transparent or fixed; fieldwork was polysemous, staging an imperial gaze that variously aestheticised, militarised, desacralised or ethnographised its subject. Tim Barringer's summation of Lisa Reihana's 2016 panorama showing epistemic encounters in colonial-era Oceania, *In Pursuit of Venus [Infected]*, is apt: 'It is a landscape of misunderstanding, a contact zone of misconception, which is both a landscape of possibility, a space of resistance, and potentially the terrain of terrible violence.'[46]

For the Burmese, Tripe's photographic apparatus was also probably reminiscent of other colonial technologies that had recently begun to upturn their lives. Artillery attacks, the laying down of telegraph cables and the arrival of photography all occurred within months of one another in 1850s Burma;[47] and considering the 'death by assassination' of a colonial engineer constructing the telegraphy system, it seems evident that British technology was perceived in terms of imperial aggression.[48] Yet the 'technomaterial complexity' of early photography meant that it was a far cry from the ballistic photographic capture of the world that the technology was coming to represent in the fevered camera/cannon analogies of the colonial imaginary.[49] To paraphrase Kaja Silverman, it was not so much the world that needed protecting from the camera at this point in history, as the camera that needed protecting from the world.[50] It was a process defined by sensitivity, vulnerability and the ongoing reactivity of its images; it underpins 'the durational, and thus transformational, qualities of images and objects, as distinct from the dogma of representational

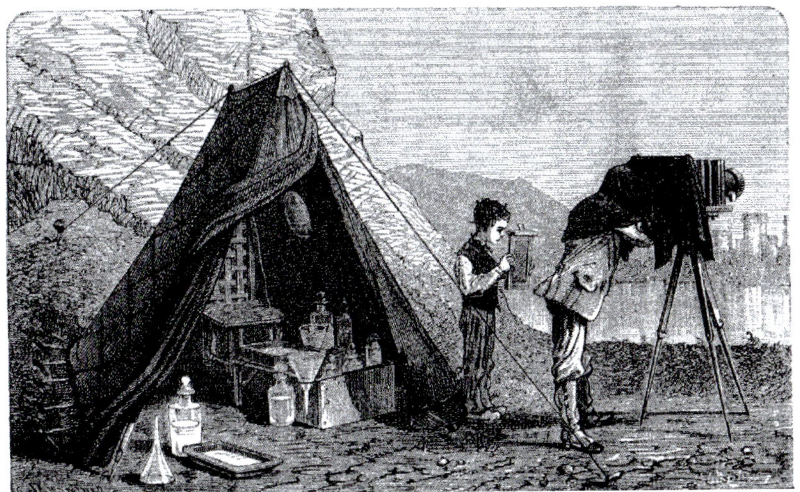

63 Gaston Tissandier, 'Photography and Exploration', *History and Handbook of Photography*, 1876. Wood engraving. © National Library of Scotland, Edinburgh

(instantaneous) accounts that are hooked on the rhetoric of the snapshot and the freeze-frame.'[51]

Thinking with the negatives is not a means of recovering the original moment of exposure, then, but of emphasising photography's status as an unfinished event – an ongoing reaction in an 'open ecology',[52] not just a closed object circulating in the 'visual economy'.[53]

THE GLASS-PLATE COLLODION NEGATIVE: JOHN THOMSON IN CHINA, 1871–1872

The paper negative process was already in decline by the time Tripe brought his camera to Burma. In 1851 Frederick Scott Archer had invented the wet collodion process, a technique that yielded much clearer and more finely detailed photographs. In spite of its reliance on fragile glass plates and temperamental chemical procedures, the method was highly popular with photographers working in the field. This was the technique for which Fenton needed his 'photographic van' in the Crimean War but the more common practice was to use a travelling tent, as seen in an illustration of fieldwork from a manual that John Thomson translated into English, Gaston Tissandier's *A History and Handbook of Photography* (fig. 63). 'Tent work', wrote Thomson, 'I consider to be the most unhealthy part of the photographer's operation in India. You may work with your tent in the shade of the tree, and take every precaution you may for ventilating the interior, and yet, after ten minutes' work, the rapid evaporation of your chemicals renders the air noxious.'[54]

Thomson's account of photography is fairly typical in its emphasis on the physical hardships and technical difficulties of working in the tropics. In a series of papers published in 1866 by the *British Journal of Photography*, entitled 'Practical Photography in Tropical Regions', he nevertheless insisted on the viability of the collodion process in such climes 'providing the chemicals are modified',[55] and went on to express his hope that he had 'done something toward "laying the rails" for the future progress of photography in the far East.'[56] The metaphor of transport and the theme of progress point to recurring concerns in the photographer's writings: he was preoccupied with the technologies that linked international zones, from the emergent steamship routes of empire to the growing 'network of telegraphic nerves'.[57] The photographic volumes published by Thomson over subsequent years – covering his travels in South-East Asia and China – emerged at a time of heightened public interest in the logistics of travel and the new forms of fieldwork that it enabled. The Royal Geographical Society had begun to codify its methods in *Hints for Travellers* (with the 1865 edition containing the first advice on travel photography), while narratives of exploration were beginning to foster popular Victorian notions of intrepid heroes spearheading scientific discovery, civilisational advancement and moral instruction in uncharted territories.[58]

Photography both advertised and instantiated such Western-led 'progress'. James R. Ryan showed how Thomson's photographs helped construct a 'scale of civilisation' which contrasted Chinese barbarism – epitomised for Thomson by punishments such as the *cangue* (a wooden collar used for public humiliation) and practices like female foot-binding – unfavourably with 'Western enlightenment'.[59] Photography stood for an ever expanding communications network which, in its embodiment of the ideals of intrepid exploration and technological advancement, sustained the temporal logic of what Johannes Fabian in *Time and the Other* calls 'one-way history: progress, development, modernity (and their negative mirror images: stagnation, underdevelopment, tradition)'.[60] Christopher Pinney, following Virilio, has shown that the 'colonial dromosphere' of telegraphy, railways and photography kindled considerable excitement among colonials regarding the potential for technology to control crime and wage war; and it duly provoked a countervailing anxiety among, for instance, nineteenth-century Indian intellectuals, who rightly viewed it as an apparatus of imperial repression.[61]

Key to such repression was photography's role in reifying colonial taxonomies, interpellating the Other as a knowable anthropological type. Photographic 'fieldwork' was becoming increasingly crucial to the imperial science of anthropology, as numerous studies have shown.[62] For those 'specimens' who were drafted to pose for the colonial camera, though, photography was mostly encountered not via positive prints captioned according to ethnological categories but as a series of technical procedures whose performances yielded delicate and shadowy negatives (fig. 64). Thomson, for example, published his anthropological

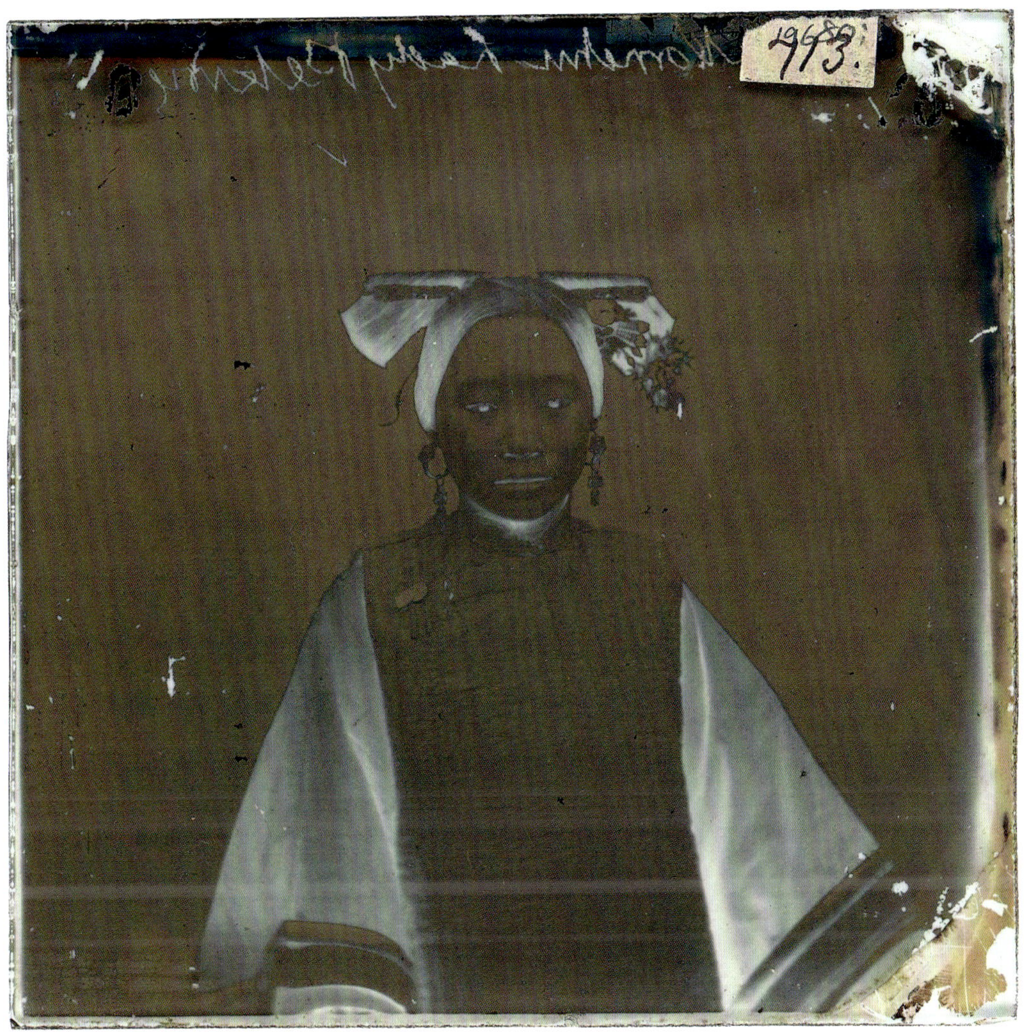

64 John Thomson, *Manchu Female Coiffure*, 1869. Glass-plate negative, 12.1 × 16.5 cm. Wellcome Collection, London

photographs in a variety of forms in Britain, Singapore and Hong Kong as cartes-de-visite, engraved illustrations and autotype reproductions. Yet the significance of such published output only comes into proper focus when it is seen in terms of his archive of glass-plate negatives.

Acquired by Henry Wellcome in 1921, Thomson's glass negatives were recently digitised by the Wellcome Collection (figs 65a and b) in scans of 'such size and quality that in some cases, viewers are able to see more in the photographs today than Thomson himself would have seen through his wooden box camera.'[63] Life-size prints of such scans formed the basis for a popular exhibition, 'Through the Lens of John Thomson'. Touring twenty museums from 2009 to the present across Asia, Europe and America, the exhibition displayed collodion scenes produced by Thomson throughout Singapore, Malaysia, Siam (Thailand), Cambodia,

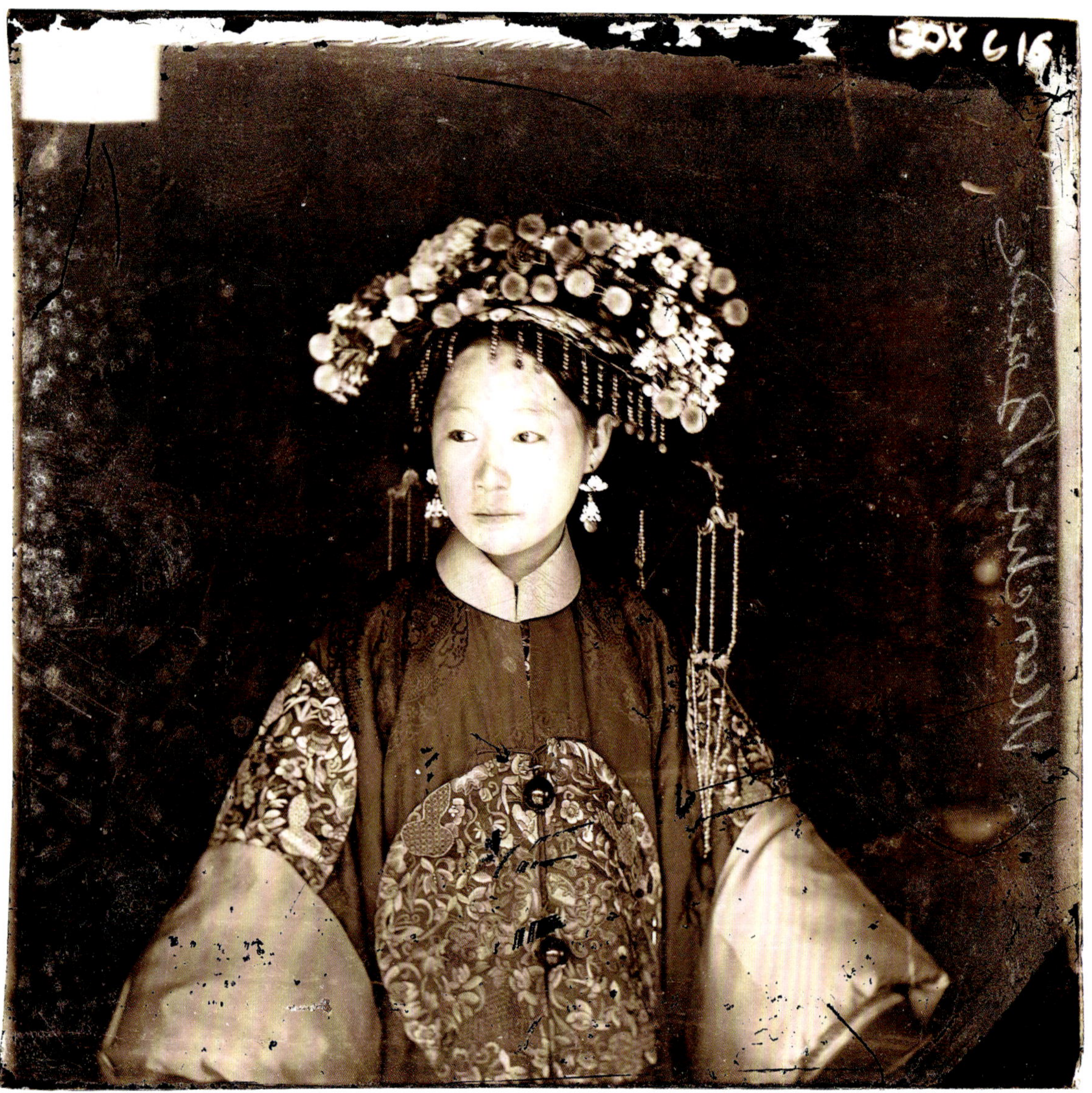

65a and b John Thomson, *A Manchu Bride*, 1871. Digital positive (left) of original glass-plate negative (right), 12.1 × 16.5 cm. Wellcome Collection, London

Hong Kong and China between 1862 and 1872.[64] The particular emphasis of each iteration has shifted according to venue, with different host-countries opting for specific packages of the imagery; so, for instance, there are separate catalogues dedicated to Thomson's work in China and Siam.[65] On the road for more than ten years across twenty-six museums, this popular exhibition has been seen by almost a million visitors.

The captivatingly detailed digital scans of Thomson's plates – each one encompassing the entire negative, replete with signed and inscribed borders, accidental markings on the emulsion and fractures to the glass – invite a gaze which, like Ruff's magnification of Tripe's paper negatives,

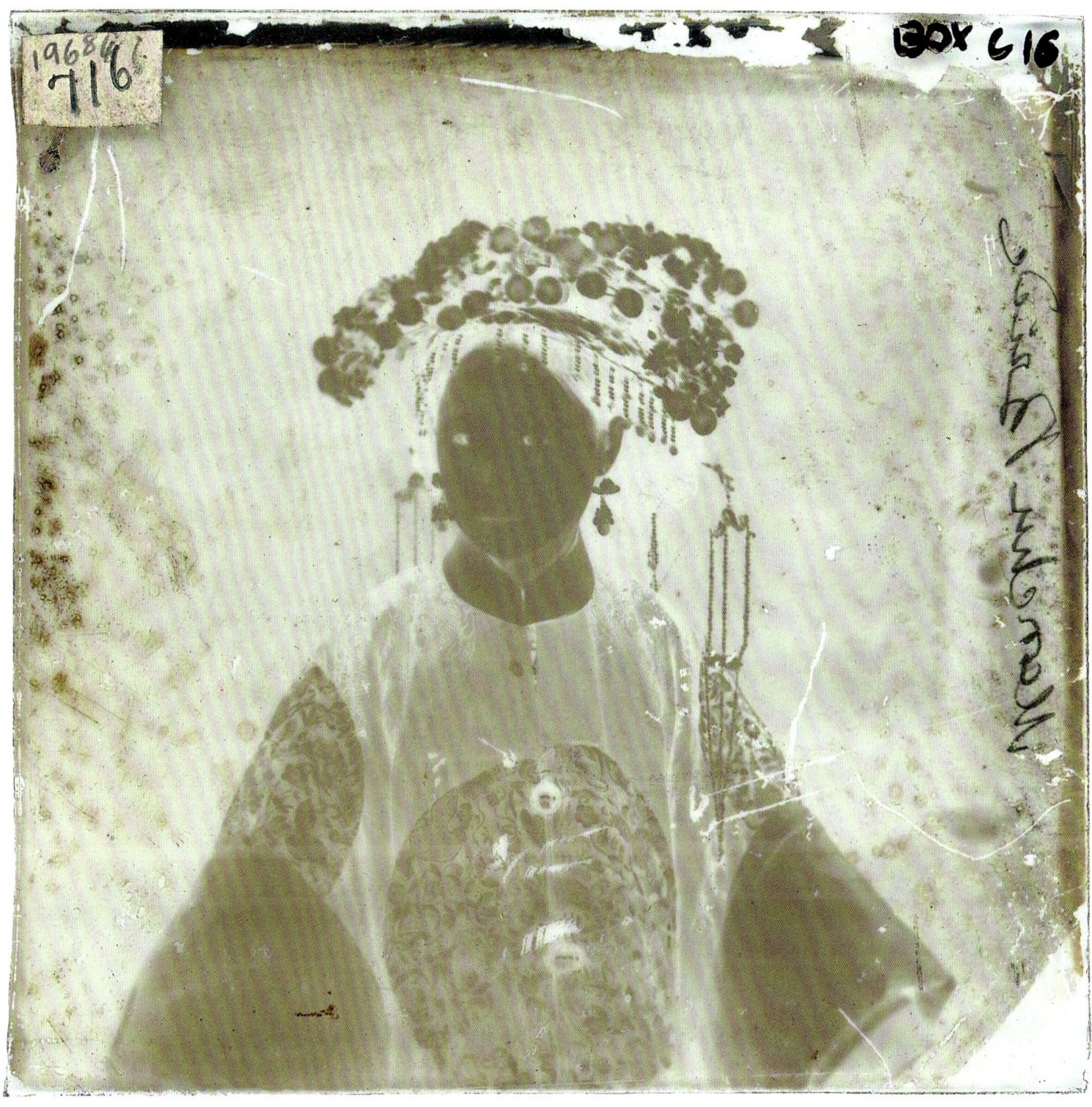

foregrounds, even fetishises, the materiality and contingency of early photographic processes. Appreciating the aesthetic qualities of photographic imperfections has a long history, beginning in the Victorian era with Julia Margaret Cameron (1815–1879) and her manipulation of the visual effects of imprecise focus, as well as her embrace of certain indexes of production like dirt, fingerprints and hair adulterating the photographic surface.[66] Cameron's subsequent canonisation in the history of photography – attested by her prominence in academic surveys of the medium and the increasing number of exhibitions and conferences dedicated to her work – has primed modern-day audiences for the visual pleasures of the blemish. Yet, while contemporaneous with Cameron, Thomson's imagery was always retouched before publication, removing evidence of the collodion process, such as lines resulting from cracked plates or discolouration from smudged emulsion, and instead cultivating a smooth veneer that stressed the documentary transparency of the medium.

The sense of beauty and authenticity – even aura – which curators and viewers may now derive from the fractured materiality of Victorian negatives is to a considerable extent an inheritance of modernism, with its self-reflexive celebration of a medium's material specificity and representational limits. In other words, modern audiences view the aesthetics of the negative somewhat differently from Thomson, for whom marred materials were not so much qualities to be cherished as flaws to be fixed during the development process.

There are shades in the recent Thomson exhibition of the Museum of Modern Art's famous *Family of Man* show in New York from the 1950s (which also toured internationally), with large portraits encouraging an engagement predicated on the universal recognition of subjectivity among culturally diverse sitters – a show with a politically liberal charge. Thomson, as a video on the exhibition website tells us, 'humanised otherwise "exotic creatures" for these westerners.'[67] Yet the humanist reading of his portraiture relies more on the latent qualities of such negatives than it does on Thomson's developed corpus. It is not that Thomson was anti-humanist. In his rhetoric about an 'enlightened', technologically mediated global progress towards a 'universal kinsmanship', he was in many ways your typical nineteenth-century liberal imperial humanist. But his publications frequently shift the register of his portrait studies from an 'honorific' humanising portrayal of subjects to a 'repressive' anthropological mode, thereby lending credence to Allan Sekula's scornful distrust of the humanist gaze, encapsulated by the dictum that 'every proper portrait ... has its counterpart in a mug shot'.[68]

Thomson's photographic practice in China in the early 1870s navigated a complex geopolitical climate in which Qing dynasty sovereignty persisted in the face of British imperial encroachments. The Chinese imperial court was the same that had come to terms with the British a decade earlier following the latter's intervention in an internecine civil war between the established Qing order and a revolutionary messianic uprising known as the Taiping Rebellion. After the punitive looting and burning of the Summer Palace in Peking over three days in October 1860, the British oversaw the ratification of what came to be known as one of the 'unequal treaties'. When Thomson arrived in 1871, he made portraits of some of the Chinese government officials involved in the

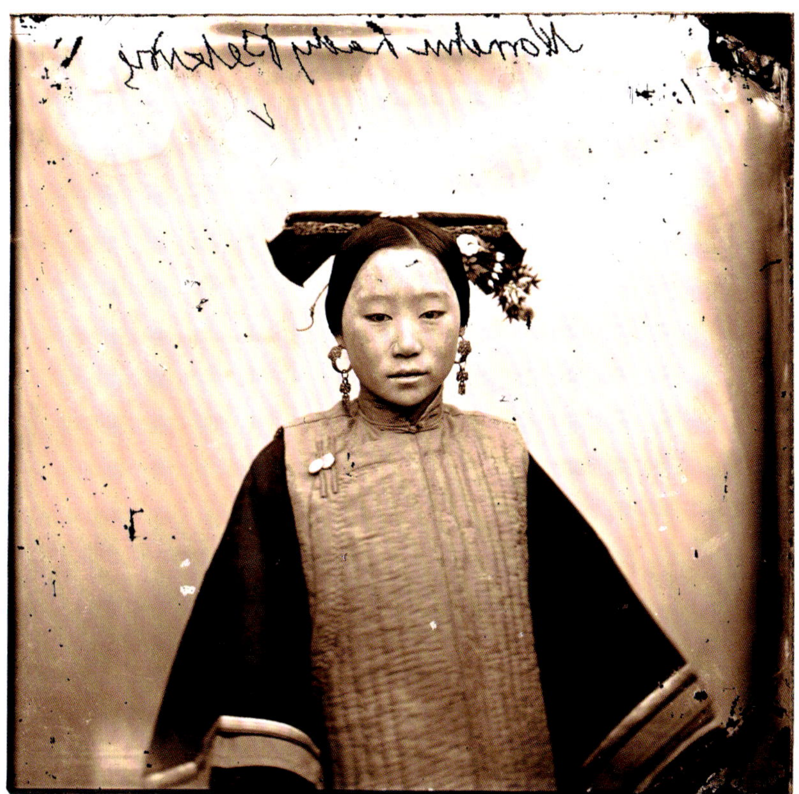

66 John Thomson, *Manchu Female Coiffure*, 1872. Digital scan of glass-plate wet collodion negative, 12.1 × 16.5 cm. Wellcome Collection, London

war's conclusion and in the current Qing administration. These political portraits – instantiations of the diplomatic complex examined earlier in the book – contrast with the typological framing of the majority of his Chinese sitters, who were not named. Yet ultimately the boundaries between such proper portraits and the surrounding format of 'types' was highly fluid.

Take *Manchu Female Coiffure* (fig. 66) for example. Viewed as a digital reproduction of the negative, this portrait has many formal qualities of the sort prized by the recent exhibition: there are aesthetically pleasing marks and inscriptions on the collodion, foregrounding the delicate materiality of the medium; there is the soulful quality to the sitter's gaze, which gives a humanising sense of interiority; and there is the pyramidal construction of the sitter, recalling classic compositional techniques and thereby figuring her within recognisable European aesthetic schema rather than emphasising racial otherness. Yet in Thomson's *The Straits of Malacca, Indo-China and China; or Ten Years' Travels, Adventures and Residence Abroad* (1875), this portrait is reproduced as an engraved vignette captioned simply as 'Tartar' (that is, Manchu), as a representative of an ethnic group, and placed alongside other such Chinese 'types':

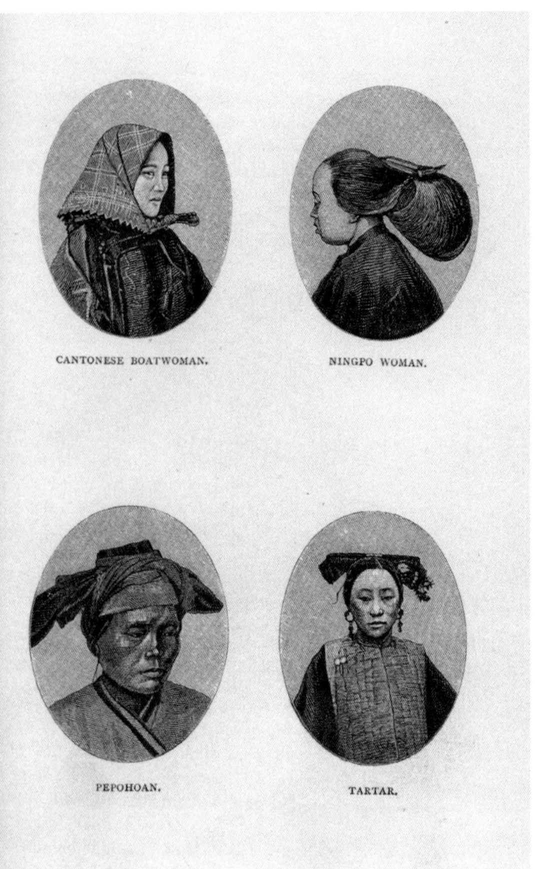

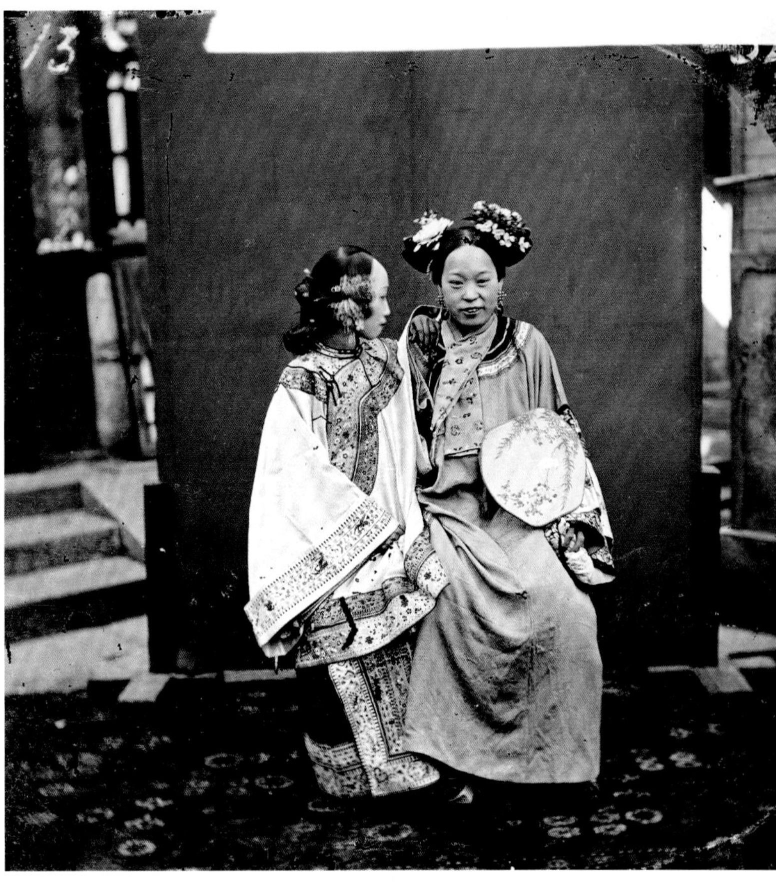

67 John Thomson, 'Chinese Portraits', *The Straits of Malacca, Indo-China and China; or Ten Years' Travels, Adventures and Residence Abroad*, 1875. Engraving after photograph. Cornell University Library, New York

68 John Thomson, *Manchu Bride in her Wedding Clothes, Peking, Pechili Province, China*, 1871–2. Digital positive from glass-plate wet-collodion negative, 12.1 × 16.5 cm. Wellcome Collection, London

'Cantonese Boatwoman'; 'Ningpo Woman'; 'Pepohoan' (fig. 67). Such captioning was commonplace in Thomson's publications: 'Four Heads of the Labouring Class', 'Types of the Pepohoan', 'Male Heads, Chinese and Mongolian', 'Chinese Female Coiffure': the list goes on.[69]

To look at these digital scans of Thomson's glass plates is therefore to see engagements with otherness that appear considerably more sympathetic in their tone than do many nineteenth-century Orientalist photographs. Yet, once we see how such negatives were actually processed for publication, the sense of subjectivity is often lost and instead we see the emergence of an ethnographic visual grammar. This was no accident: Thomson was a proud member of the Royal Ethnological Society. It was, as Geoffrey Belknap has shown, the ideals of Victorian science – in particular its investment in racial taxonomy – that ultimately structured Thomson's photographic output.[70] This anthropological genre came with its own set of what Edwards has termed 'patterns of expectancy', which tended to reduce portraits of the Other 'to a type event obscuring or effacing an earlier political and particular reading.'[71]

It does not follow, however, that the sitters felt themselves to be interpellated as racialised subalterns during these encounters. Thinking about the processes involved in preparing, exposing and handling negatives enables a richer picture of Anglo-Sino relations to develop. In *Manchu Bride in her Wedding Clothes* (fig. 68), two women stand in front of a studio backdrop. The screen is portable and can be seen in numerous other Thomson negatives, its presence highlighting the theatricality and ephemerality of the event. Unfocused glimpses of stairs, pillars and the view from this private Chinese domestic space impinge on the formally framed area of the portrait. Pinney has coined the term 'visual noise' to refer to such peripheral details, arguing that incidental data of this sort points to the contingency of the 'pro-filmic' photographic event: 'no matter how carefully the photographer tries to arrange things otherwise, the pro-filmic always intrudes.'[72] The subsequent cropping of such 'visual

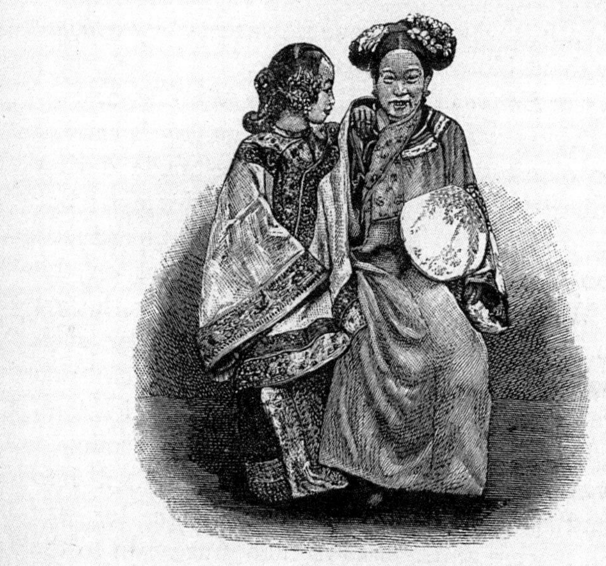

EVENING AMUSEMENTS. 523

tion—there are, alas! but a few—occasionally hire educated widows in needy circumstances to read novels or plays to them. Women capable of reading in this way can make a very comfortable living. Story-tellers and ballad-singers are also employed to entertain them in the courts of their houses.

The evenings they generally spend in their court-yards, smoking and watching the amusements of the

TARTAR LADIES.

69 John Thomson, 'Tartar Ladies', *The Straits of Malacca, Indo-China and China; or Ten Years' Travels, Adventures and Residence Abroad*, 1875, page 523. Engraving after photograph. Cornell University Library, New York

noise' (fig. 69) was an assertion of colonial authorship that worked in concert with anthropological captioning ('Tartar Ladies') to position the Chinese women as static types rather than as named individuals who, ensconced in their own private domestic realm, participate in a dynamic performance with a foreign guest.

Racial typologies notwithstanding, the collodion process could catalyse interactions that trouble notions of photography as the imperious capture of docile bodies. The complexity, delicacy and time-intensive nature of the process often required an amount of complicity on the part of the sitters – perhaps through payment, as Ryan suggests, or, not infrequently in Thomson's case, by ingratiating himself with his sitters. The *Manchu Bride* was taken inside the home of Yang Fang, a wealthy and urbane mandarin who, as an amateur photographer himself, was interested in Thomson's work and may have been able to develop the Scot's negatives in his own 'laboratory fitted up in the ladies quarter' of his estate. At the very least he was involved with preparing the negatives; Thomson wrote of 'teaching my friend how to concoct nitrate of silver and other photographic chemicals.'[73] As Oliver Wendell Holmes wrote for *The Atlantic* in 1863, such concoctions were part of a complicated yet exciting process:

> The syrupy fluid was iodized collodion ... We have plunged this into the bath, which contains chiefly nitrate of silver [which] is eminently sensitive to light. The use of the collodion is to furnish a delicate, homogeneous, adhesive, colorless layer in which the iodide may be deposited ...
>
> While we have been talking and waiting, the process just described has been going on, and we are now ready to take the glass plate out of the nitrate-of-silver bath. It is wholly changed in aspect. The film has become in appearance like a boiled white of egg, so that the glass produces rather the effect of porcelain, as we look at it. Open no door now! Let in no glimpse of day, or the charm is broken in an instant! No Sultana was ever veiled from the light of heaven as this milky tablet we hold must be. But we must carry it to the camera which stands waiting for it in the blaze of high noon. To do this, we first carefully place it in this narrow case, called a shield, where it lies safe in utter darkness. We now carry it to the camera, and, having removed the ground glass on which the camera-picture had been brought to an exact focus, we drop the shield containing the sensitive plate into the groove the glass occupied. Then we pull out a slide, as the blanket is taken from a horse before he starts. There is nothing now but to remove the brass cap from the lens. That is giving the word Go! It is a tremulous moment for the beginner.[74]

Mixing, coating, talking, waiting, looking, veiling, shielding, carrying, walking from darkness into daylight and then the 'tremulous moment' of exposure: Holmes's description gives a sense of the mystery, 'charm' and drama of working with the wet-plate negative. Photography at this time had a 'liquid intelligence', writes Kaja Silverman, borrowing from Jeff Wall's phrase, that made it fluid and 'unpredictable'.[75] The thrill of such image-making lay not so much in the static and captioned positive print, in which many of the contingencies of production were no longer apparent, but in the delicate theatre of a process that was messy, laborious and evanescent.

Such labile processes are a long way off from the camera as cannon conception of photography as an intrinsically explosive and domineering force. In an interesting reading, Silverman suggests that explicitly gun-shaped cameras like Thomas Skaife's Pistolgraph (1858) and Thompson's Revolver Camera (designed by the French company A. Briois in 1862) ultimately stimulated little consumer interest 'because other aspects of chemical photography were still so "wet" – literally as well as metaphorically.'[76] 'Wetness' here means an immersion in the world, a fluid interactivity rather than the 'dry' Cartesian separation that is often attributed to the photographic gaze.

Something of this 'wetness' is still detectable in the blemished surfaces of Thomson's glass plates or Tripe's paper negatives. The negatives thus enable latent photographic histories to develop, in which the camera is not only a crude symbol of imperial violence and ethnographic mastery but also a catalyst for 'liquid' interactions between the collaborative agencies of photographer, sitters, overseers such as Yang Fang and the volatile chemicals themselves. In the *Manchu Bride* scene, sovereignty (in Azoulay's sense of the word, control over the political meaning of the photograph) is split among the unnamed Chinese woman who commands the attention of both the camera and her affectionate servant; the visually absent male head of the household, Yang Fang, whom Thomson had befriended; and Thomson himself, an imperial Briton who wields the photographic apparatus. Thomson's portable backdrop is an ephemeral supplement to a Chinese domesticity governed by those he is photographing, who appear to be enjoying the encounter.

Away from the 'dry' visual style of Thomson's publications, wherein the protean power dynamics he actually encountered 'in the field' are mostly flattened by an imperious ethnological grammar, it is easier to perceive aspects of fluid, participatory and often congenial-seeming image-making encounters, not mere submissions to anthropological categorisation. Smiles, intimacy and an apparent ease before the lens are not uncommon in Thomson's archive of Chinese portraits. One of the most striking of such portraits to be included in the recent exhibition is *Canton Boatwoman* (figs 70a and b). Situated in a three-quarter pose reminiscent of European portraiture conventions, this woman from Canton (Guangzhou) in southern China is a lively and engaging figure. Yet when Thomson came to illustrate a 'boatwoman' in his books, he did not choose this example but opted for a more passive-looking figure (see the top-left portrait of fig. 67), whose downcast and submissive posture better maintains the subject–object split that upholds the epistemic authority of the ethnographic gaze. Not only did Thomson crop and caption portraits in a manner that ethnicised his sitters, then, but he also tended to choose for publication those images in which Chinese agency and individuality were less plainly visible in the first place.

The unchosen and uncropped negatives might therefore be considered as resources for what Azoulay terms 'potential history', recuperating discarded agencies and political relationships.[77] It allows for what could be considered a sort of 'reparative' (to switch now to Sedgwick's terminology) approach to the material, in which elements of this Orientalist oeuvre are read in terms of options that were nullified by the imperial ideologies and anthropological conventions of the Victorian era.

The digitised negatives that predominate in the recent exhibition recuperate engaging Others who maintain a sense of subjectivity, hence the pithy description of Thomson in the video on the exhibition website as the 'Annie Leibovitz of Victorian times'.[78] Yet Thomson's 'humanising' lens was always already compromised by his ethnographic aspirations and the wider imperial culture that fostered them; his 'honorific' portraits contained within them the shadow of the 'repressive' mug-shot, to put it in Sekula's terms. As an exhibition, however, 'Through the Lens' ultimately left one with the impression that Thomson did actively intend and nurture the humanising aesthetic on display. This perhaps explains why the exhibition adopts a fairly lionising tone with regard to him, something that reaches its apogee with their hagiographic funding campaign to restore the photographer's London gravestone to 'provide a lasting legacy'.[79] In fact, though, the Wellcome Trust's digital scans of Thomson's glass plates and the exhibition's framing of them are interventions in the negative archive that provide a way of 'unlearning' the imperial language of Victorian photography, recuperating a more nuanced picture of 'fieldwork' than Thomson, as an ambitious ethnographer, consciously sought to promote.

DRY-PLATE PHOTOGRAPHY: KODAK IN TIBET

An 1887 photography manual for practice 'in the studio and in the field' welcomed with relief the end of the era of wet-collodion photography.[80] Writing of the 'difficulties' and 'trials' of the wet-plate process ('the stains on the hands and clothing incidental to the use of nitrate of silver and

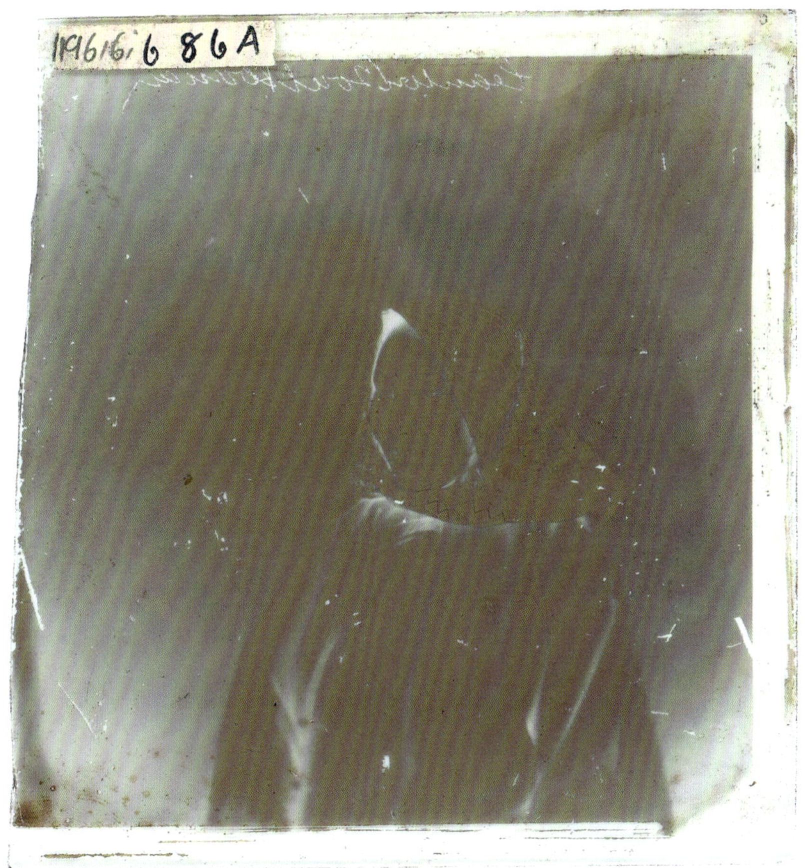

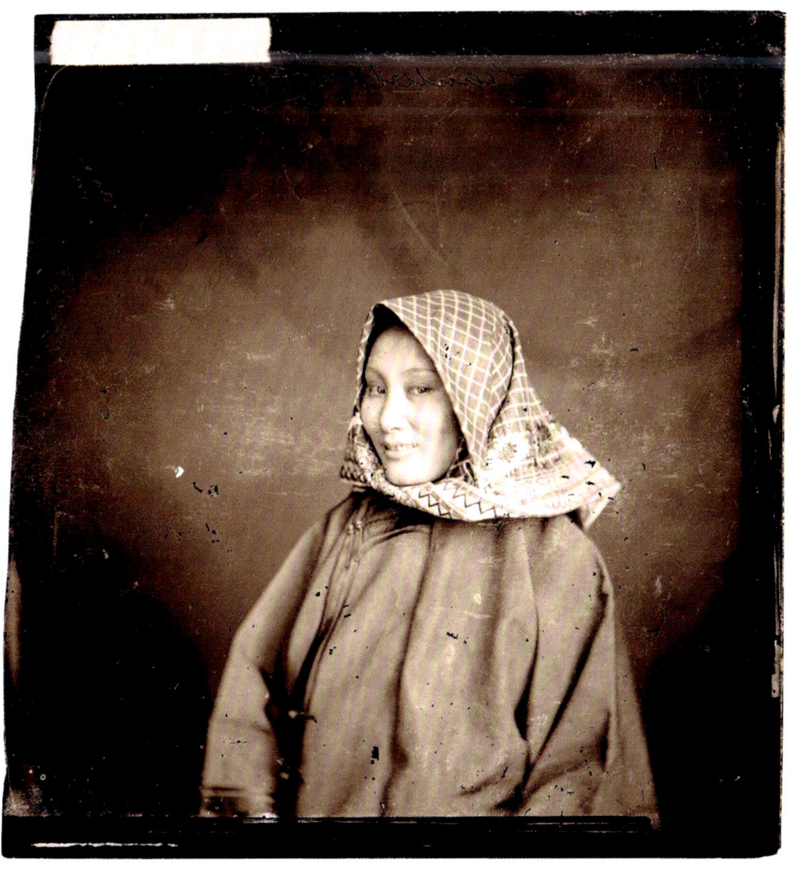

70a and b John Thomson, *Canton Boatwoman*, *c.*1870. Glass-plate wet collodion negative (top) and digital positive (bottom), 12.1 × 16.5 cm. Wellcome Collection, London

the solution of iron, and the heavy and bulky nature of the apparatus'), the author celebrated the newer and more convenient dry-plate methods that had emerged, in which 'all that was disagreeable has been done away with'. Such methods transformed the possibilities of photography, for it no longer required the operator to work with messy chemicals, a convenience encapsulated by the marketing slogan coined for the Eastman Dry Plate and Film Company's new handheld camera in 1888: 'You press the button, we do the rest.'

The success of the Eastman Kodak radically altered the spread of photographic technologies in society. By the early twentieth century, a colonial campaign like the Younghusband Mission could be covered extensively not only through the work of an official photographer – in this case John Claude White and his array of cameras, including the large Thornton-Packard Ruby for panoramic scenes – but by the many Folding Pocket Kodaks, a model introduced in 1895, that had become popular with British colonial soldiers.[81]

As a form of militarised diplomacy and as a spectacle, the Younghusband Mission marked the aggressive culmination of the Victorian-style imperial expedition. In the mythos of empire, Younghusband is 'the last great imperial adventurer'.[82] Indeed, as Clare Harris writes, his leadership oversaw what was 'probably the last British military campaign of the imperial era that can be characterized as a major looting expedition.'[83] Just as in Burma in 1855, photographs were a crucial part of war's spoils. The journalist Perceval Landon wrote of a sense of loss of meaning that came with the photographic capture of Lhasa: 'the world, the richer by the knowledge that has displaced conjecture and uncertainty, will forever be poorer by what may be worth many Tibetan photographs and facts – the last of the great loadstones of man's romance and mystery.'[84] Photography figures here as an instrument of disenchantment for colonials at the same time as it becomes an agent of dispossession to the Tibetans. In spite of objections from the Tibetan authorities and a specific ban on entering monasteries, the British persisted in taking photographs of sacred sites and objects, sometimes even in the face of crowds protesting against their presence.[85]

The process of taking photographs in the colonial 'field' had become in some respects more mysterious to such onlookers even as it became more widespread among the troops. Unlike the earlier photographic methods considered above, in which the negative had to be prepared and stabilised on the spot, the Kodak process was opaque. The negatives were no longer a visible element of the photographic performance; they were hidden in a roll of film that needed to be sent off to the company to be processed and then returned to the customer as positive prints. With the act of taking photographs thus alienated from its complicated chemical procedures, the Kodak system, writes Silverman, 'sealed off photography's liquid intelligence'.[86]

The Kodak could nevertheless generate an awareness that the surveilled action was being turned into a sort of 'text' available for interpretation. In his reading of the role of the Kodak during the Younghusband Mission, Simeon Koole argues that such encounters 'entailed Tibetans receiving from the camera's intervention a 'proposal' to understand themselves and their relation to Tibet differently.'[87] It occasioned a 'hermeneutics of the self' (Koole borrows from Ricoeur here), causing Tibetans to think about themselves from the perspective of the imperial Other and thus to reinterpret and re-present themselves in the light of that perspective. Colonials sometimes made a point (and a joke) of providing some cultural context for their cameras by introducing locals to British newspapers, having them pose with the periodicals, thus drawing attention to issues of reproducibility and dissemination in a manner that pointed to a more expansive matrix of pictures and technologies beyond the immediate image-making event in which the Tibetans were participating.[88] But such demonstrations were not necessary in order for Tibetans to intuit that the camera was something that 'textualised' such encounters, even as the precise nature of photographic imagery – and any particular 'material afterlife' of the photographic encounter – remained elusive.[89]

Yet not all the 'texts' that emerged from such encounters were so elusive. White's panoramic texts were still inscribed in the delicate materiality of the glass plate. With this in mind, I return to his photograph of Younghusband's triumphal entry into Lhasa, with which this chapter began (see fig. 55). A Tibetan crowd faces the camera while an imperial army, having recently subjected other settlements to slaughter and looting, violates the sovereignty and sanctity of the capital. In using his panoramic lens, White opted to frame the imperial parade in the same visual terms he had used to capture the 'Tibetan sublime' of the Himalayan landscape – an aesthetic suggestive of overwhelming forces.[90] The act of photography constituted an 'imperial scripting' of Tibet's geopolitical status, a scripting carried out not just by international treaties but by the actions of imperial bodies across Tibetan space and the representations thereof.[91] Such actions meant that the crowd could no longer sustain what Dawa Norbu describes as Tibet's traditional 'moral refusal to interact with new forces that violated the customary norms of a lamaist conception of inter-state relations.'[92] The camera captures a tense moment in which those traditional moral codes – the refusal of the ruling elite to countenance receiving the British in their 'holy city'

– were shown, spectacularly, to have failed. The camera was an agent of that failure, performing – or rather, to use Koole's more measured terminology, 'proposing' – the very dispossession it was depicting.

What did the Tibetan members of this crowd make of White's glass-plate process? In other instances such negatives became the explicit focus of attention. White demonstrated his large camera to 'an interested and amused' Tibetan monk inside a Lhasa monastery; 'it was an unfailing source of mystification to the Tibetans to be allowed to look at the reversed picture in the ground glass under the black velvet.' Landon claimed that the Tibetans did not comprehend these negatives, 'It was for them merely a beautiful pattern of varying colors seen in a singularly effective manner'.[93] Such assignations of photographic illiteracy were common in colonial discourse and should be treated with caution. Yet it is worth remaining open, I think, to the under-determined nature of photographic imagery and the particular visual strangeness of negatives. What, after all, was one to make of the shimmering, spectral figures that could be seen in the glass plate when it was held at the right angle to catch the light, elusive images that emerged from the unfamiliar instruments and materials of an invader?

Photography in such instances may have registered less in terms of its particular representational content – less as images – than as strange processes and performances of colonial observation which trafficked in fragile aesthetic materials passed with great care between a white colonial and his trained 'coolies'. 'There's a "thingyness" to an image,' notes the photographer Ingrid Pollard, speaking to Tina M. Campt, 'a thingyness that you feel incredibly strongly when you work with negatives.'[94] The theatre of the glass-plate process was entirely different from the Kodak's and it is questionable whether they would have been conceptualised in the same terms by onlookers. One was a durational, delicate and 'thingy' process, while the other was more fugitive, mobile and as far as its products were concerned, virtual.

None of White's Tibetan negatives appear to have survived. Sold to the photography firm Johnston and Hoffman in Calcutta to make prints, they are now lost.[95] Such a loss is not unusual for Victorian glass plates but it constitutes a significant archival absence. Recent scholarship on photography has become increasingly attuned to the medium's status not merely as image but as an event or process that brings into being a series of relations. The dynamics of that event – its contingencies, temporalities and the very (in)visibility of any image at the time of making – were shaped by the chemistry and materiality of the negative. There is no abstract 'photography' or 'event of photography' but only particular negative processes, whether 'wet' or 'dry'. I have thus read photography here in terms of a negative archive – literally in relation to surviving negatives but also in terms of that which has been negated, through selection and cropping and through the archival absence of lost, destroyed and degraded materials. Such a reading is sensitive to the processes of silencing in the production of the visual archive of empire; it helps to make 'visible the logic that structures the archive and authorises its validity as a source of historical knowledge, meaning, and veracity.'[96]

CONCLUSION

'When is a photograph made?' asks Geoffrey Batchen. 'Is it when the photographer depresses the camera shutter ...? Is it when the photographer singles out this exposure for printing, thereby investing a latent image with the personal significance of selection, labour, and, most crucial of all, visibility?'[97] Yet 'visibility' is not, as this chapter has sought to show, the preserve of the print; the negative image has its own histories of spectatorship that are separate from its subsequent positives. Engagement with the negative – with the damaged, the untreated and unchosen, the undeveloped – enable histories to emerge which complicate traditional notions of authorship, subalternity and spectatorship. More so even than the positive prints that form the core of her analysis, I think that it is the negative which bears witness to Elizabeth Edwards's 'raw histories' of photography, 'the unprocessed and the painful'. Yet it is not the originary moment or authentic artefact that I am seeking in the marred materials of the negative but a reading of photography as 'duration': 'a relationship of transmission [that was] always a transformation: preimage to image, latency to bleaching, "processing", translations and inversions, flips and expansions, rinsing and fixing, printings and distributions'.[98] For sitters and onlookers in the field, the transformations of the negative were experienced less as distinct and stable images than as elusive processes, something hovering between the raw and the cooked.

7 · SPECIMENS, SUSPECTS, CITIZENS

Photographing an Imperial Polity in Cawnpore, *c.*1857–1860

THE PERCEIVED LEGITIMACY OF THE BRITISH EMPIRE WAS NOT merely a function of constructing divisive racial hierarchies. It also relied on imagining shared professional and political horizons. Forging a common civil framework was a key theme of Queen Victoria's Proclamation to India, issued on 1 November 1858, in response to the extreme inter-racial violence of the Indian Uprising: 'We hold ourselves bound to the Natives of Our Indian Territories by the same obligations of Duty which bind Us to all Our other Subjects ... all shall alike enjoy the equal and impartial protection of the Law.'[1] Britain's vision of peace was thus explicitly tied to a notion of multiracial imperial belonging. This chapter explores how photography's unique formal features enabled nineteenth-century colonials to picture such belonging, rehabilitating an embattled imperial sovereignty as a viable mode of peacetime administration. The levelling effect of the medium – its capacity to draw heterogeneous peoples into what Christopher Pinney has termed a 'common epistemological space' – meant that it could serve as a visual register for the elusive connective tissue of imperial subjecthood, effectively reifying a useful political abstraction during a time of great crisis.[2]

This chapter is thus situated within a growing body of literature on the relationship of photography, race and citizenship.[3] Recent scholars have begun to see in photography 'the possibilities for counter-narratives and alternative subjectivities' that complicate notions of colonial subalternity.[4] I explore such possibilities in the context of the visual approaches used by colonials to classify the Indian population in the years following the Uprising, outlining the three main categories into which the British sorted their conquered subjects: anthropological specimens; suspected insurgents; potential imperial citizens. Photography held out the promise of indexing these categories and therefore making India appear

Dr John Nicholas Tresidder, 'Cawnpore', in 'The Tresidder Album', *c.*1858–64 (detail of fig. 74).

Cawnpore P.24

113

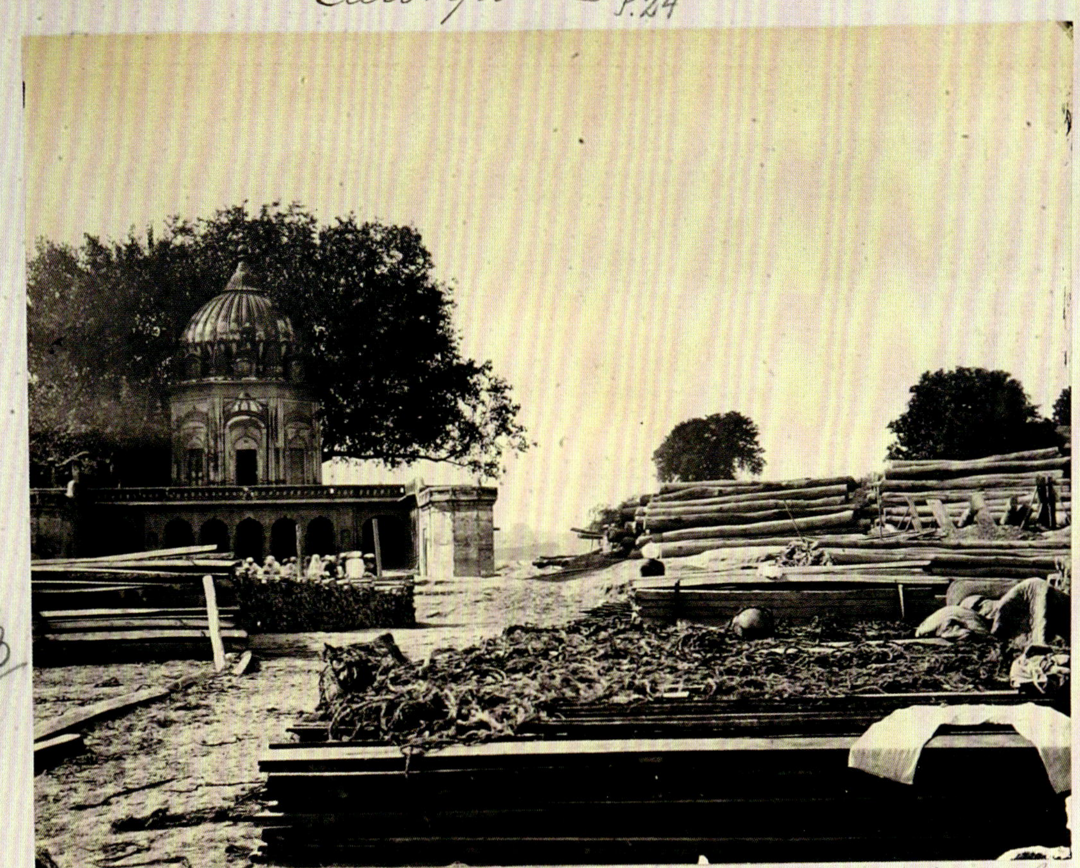

Coela Ghât – Cawnpore – Where Wheelers Garrison were entrapped in the boats by the treachery of the Nana – This shews the Gorge down which they walked to the boats.

44

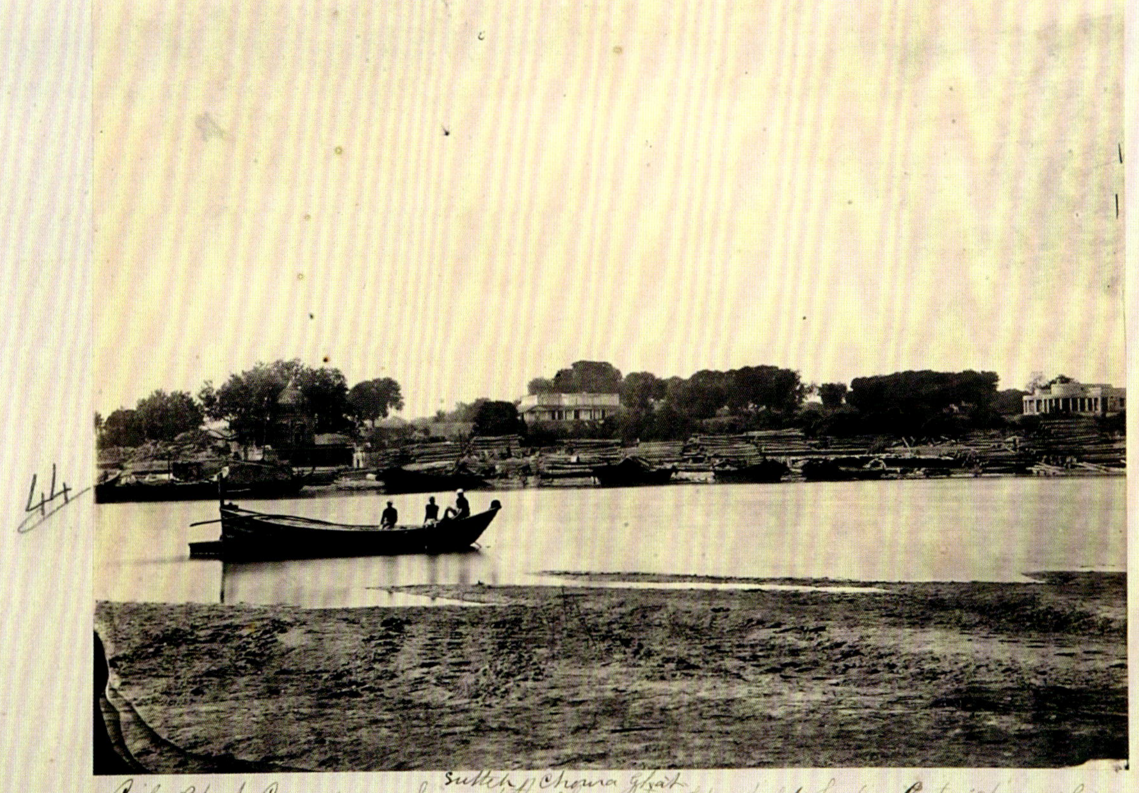

Suttee Chowra Ghat
+ Coela Ghat – Cawnpore – Scene of the slaughter of part of Wheelers Garrison when in the boats provided by the Nana's treachery.

as a knowable and manageable political space; yet so too did the formal properties of the medium threaten to collapse the very distinctions the British were keen to make, revealing an underlying anxiety about the unknowability and thus ungovernability of the colony.

Rather than giving an account of how the imperial state commissioned photography (although such projects will be touched on at various points), my primary focus here is on how the political and epistemic problems of colonial governance – ensuring the legibility and loyalty of a subject population – were also manifested in the visual management of everyday colonial life. I examine Dr John Nicholas Tresidder's (1819–1889) extraordinary private album, which chronicles the doctor's time in Cawnpore and Agra in the late 1850s and early 1860s, some time spent on sick-leave in England around 1863 and his subsequent retirement in Falmouth, Cornwall.[5] Nearly two hundred pages host careful arrangements of albumen and salt-paper prints with handwritten captions that cover everything from picnic parties to atrocity sites. As Rashmi Viswanathan notes in her 2016 article on Tresidder, the album is remarkable for the way in which images of Indian insurgents inflect the photographic construction of self and home.[6] In between this fraught polarity of Indian criminality and British domesticity, however, a third way emerged: the prospect of imperial citizenship. Ultimately, I argue, Tresidder's post-1857 investigation of the formal possibilities of photography as a medium of portraiture – its grammar of seriality (the arrangement of individual portraits) on the one hand and its capacity to embody collectivity (the combination printing of multiple portraits) on the other – doubled as a kind of political thought experiment, one in which he probed the very limits of social cohesion under the Raj.

PHOTOGRAPHY IN THE SHADOW OF ATROCITY

When Indians rose in revolt against a century-old British rule in 1857, they brought the fight to longstanding colonial settlements, threatening the domestic and civic structures of imperial life. This generated an important but hitherto overlooked development in the history of war photography. For the first time, landscapes of violence began to be documented by photographers who were civilian residents of the affected regions, with the camera serving as a means of coming to terms with the dizzying impact of warfare on familiar and familial environments.

A number of colonials turned to photography during and following the insurgency to chronicle what was, for them, not some distant geopolitical convulsion to be read about in the newspapers or viewed in metropolitan galleries, but a local war with serious implications for their way of life. For Dr John Murray from Agra, Harriet Tytler from Delhi and – the focus of this chapter – Dr Tresidder from Cawnpore, amateur picture-making formed part of a rooted and multi-layered – albeit violently contested – relationship to place that was different from the commercial practice of their better-known contemporary, the globe-trotting practitioner Felice Beato. Their photography grappled with warfare's transformative effects on the political, civic and domestic realms of the colonial society in which they lived. Indeed, for Tresidder, I argue, the new forms of visual praxis opened up by photography helped to re-weave the complex social fabric of a settlement that had become a byword for cross-cultural slaughter.[7]

In July 1857, following a period of siege, Cawnpore witnessed the brutal massacre of colonial men, women and children by insurgents. Afterwards, when the town had been reconquered and the British had discovered the bodies of their compatriots (many stuffed down a nearby well), a punitive wartime regime was installed. Indian men suspected of having associated with the rebels were summarily hanged. Those believed to have been ringleaders were confronted with a more inventive vengeance. Prior to execution, they were brought to the dreaded 'house of horrors', within which rebels armed with meat cleavers had hacked to death hundreds of colonial civilians. They were then forced, under the threat of the lash, to lick clean a portion of the blood that still swamped the floor, something that was anathema to high-caste Indians and had been devised to make them believe 'they doom their souls to perdition.'[8] The animus that motivated this grisly episode was persistent. One tourist, writing more than thirty years later, noted that the massacre 'seems to hang over Cawnpore like a cloud even to this day, and to cause bitterness in the minds of Englishmen'.[9] Cawnpore stood for violent Anglo-Indian division, a racial binarism underscored by the fact that no 'native' was ordinarily permitted to set foot in the famous memorial gardens erected during the grief-stricken aftermath of the war.[10]

The disturbing resonance of commemorated violence raised urgent questions about how civil society could be reconstructed in the wake of internecine conflict, or a peaceable community imagined in places defined by crisis and rupture. Cawnpore was just one of numerous famous conflict sites that sustained popular practices of war tourism in British India. The geographical and ideological lineaments of these 'mutiny tours' have been tracked by Manu Goswami and Ian Baucom; post-rebellion travel routes functioned as educational acts of 'pilgrimage' for colonials, cementing divisive narratives of colonial bravery and native treachery and ingraining a sense of hard-won British belonging to the Indian landscape.[11] Photography played a key role here, with amateur and commercial practitioners both producing highly conventionalised images that filtered potentially traumatic locales through the soothingly

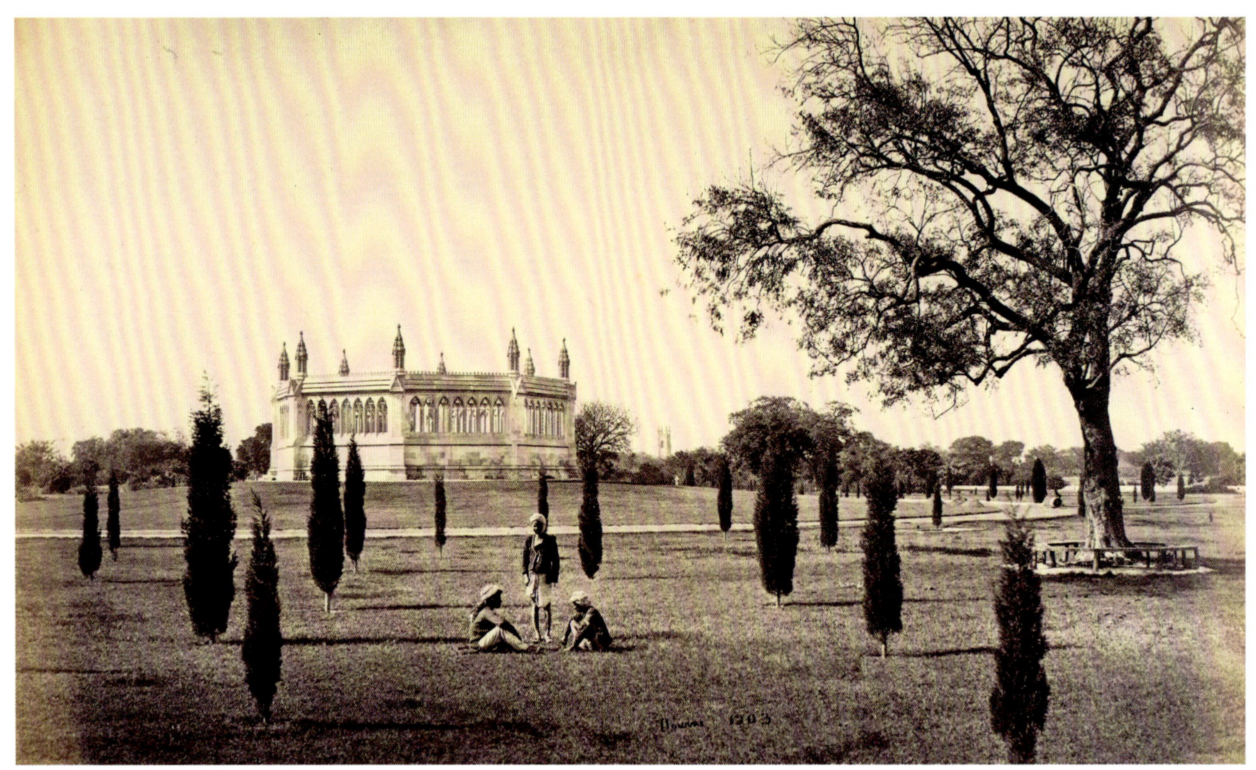

71 Bourne & Shepherd, *The Memorial Well, Cawnpore*, *c.*1865. Albumen silver print from glass-plate wet-collodion negative, 18.7 × 31.6 cm. © The British Library Board, Photo 11/(45)

72 Dr John Nicholas Tresidder, 'Personal', The Tresidder Album, *c.*1858–64, page 7. Albumen and salt-paper prints. Alkazi Collection of Photography, New Delhi

placid aesthetics of the picturesque, as seen in Samuel Bourne's treatment of the Cawnpore memorial (fig. 71).[12] Yet the stress that scholars have placed on the touristic dimension to these sites has meant that each has been situated in an itinerary of shrines encountered transiently across northern India, as opposed to being theorised as multi-dimensional social environments. For all its grisly wartime baggage, Cawnpore persisted as a colonial settlement, wherein a multiracial society was painfully reconstructed in the shadow of atrocity and its memorialisation. But there is little sense of this in existing accounts.

Nowhere does the complexly multilayered nature of post-conflict British India appear more vivid than in the imagery of the Cawnpore resident Tresidder, whose portrait of his colonial home consists of domestic, professional and martial strands of Anglo-Indian society (fig. 72).[13] Composed of photographs taken by Tresidder himself as well as scenes by contemporary colonial photographers like Murray and Beato (none attributed to their makers), the album is a record of photographic consumption as well as production. It affords a uniquely detailed insight into the way that photographs were collected, produced and compiled in ways that formed multiple – and not always harmonious – narratives about loss, revenge and rapprochement in a settlement traumatised by violence.

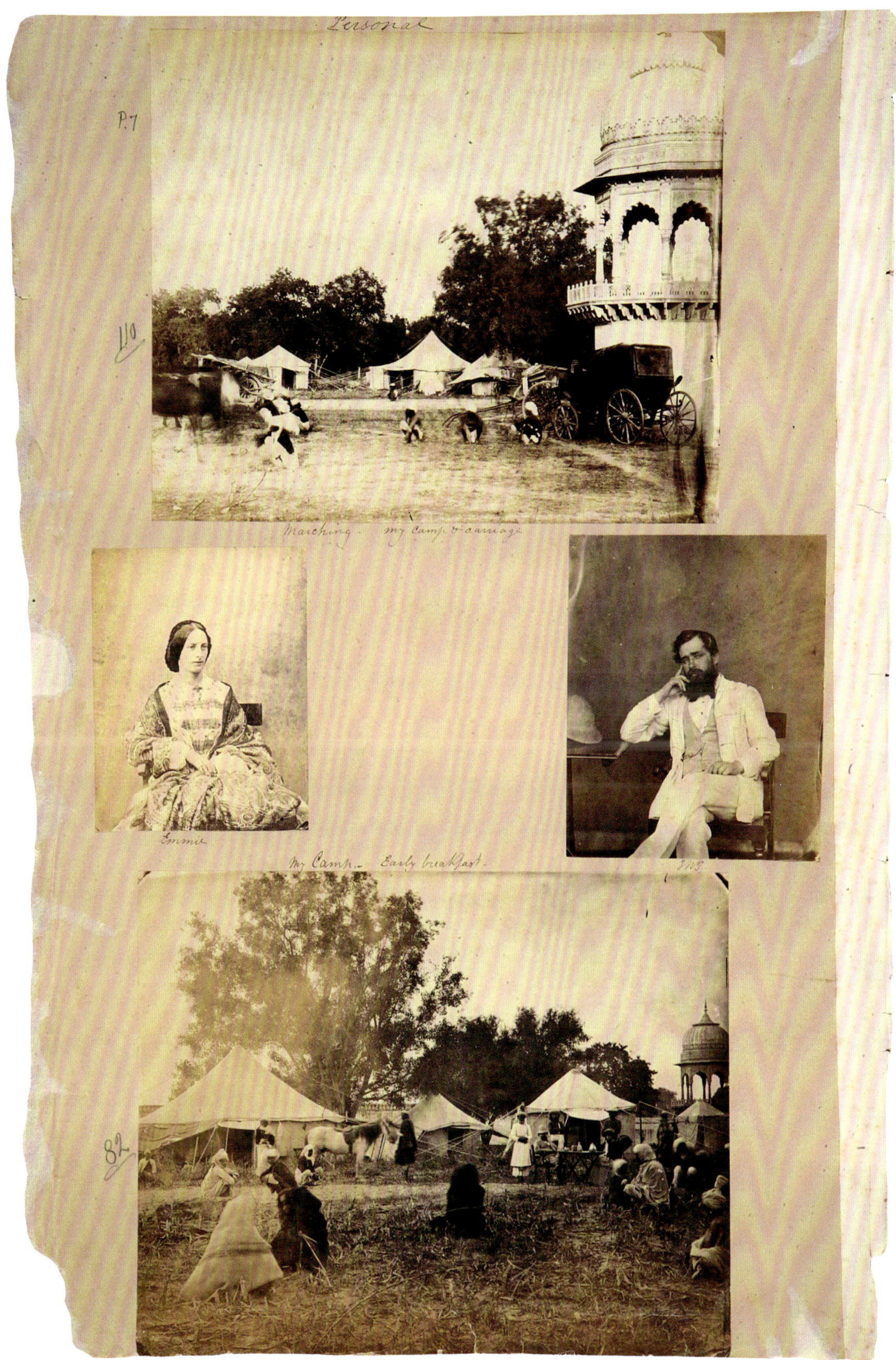
Personal
P.7
110
Marching – my camp & carriage
Emmie
My Camp – Early breakfast –
82

ETHNOGRAPHY OF GUILT

Who exactly were the Indian people? And how did they fit into imperial society? These, ultimately, were the questions posed to colonials like Tresidder by the staggering insurrection of 1857. In the build-up to the Uprising, the British had failed to gauge properly the depth and breadth of Indian discontent over myriad issues. The initial rebellion of a regiment of sepoys in Meerut was one thing; the fact that they soon garnered significant support throughout the northern ranks of the Company army and among Indian civilians was quite another. Evidently, far too little was actually known about the religious, cultural and political sensitivities of the Indian people.[14] The British simply had not seen the unrest coming.

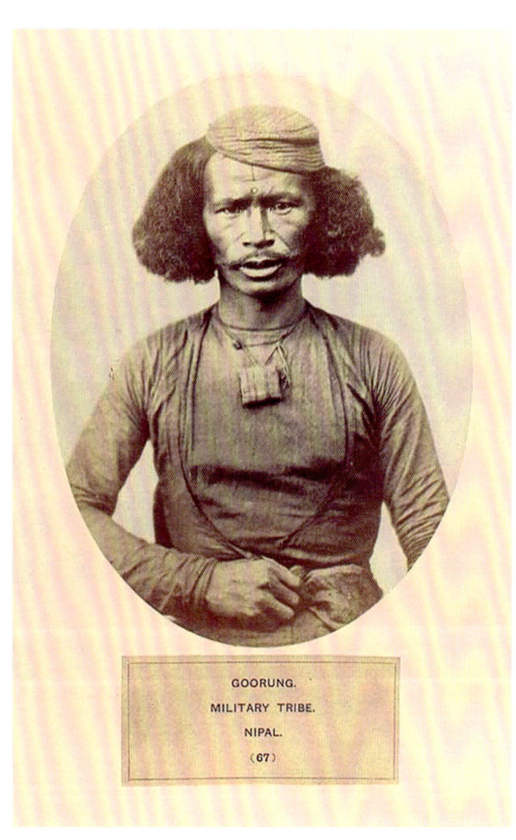

73 Sir Benjamin Simpson, 'Goorung, Military Tribe, Nipal', in Sir John William Kaye and John Forbes Watson, *The People of India: A Series of Photographic Illustrations, with Descriptive Letterpress, of the Races and Tribes of Hindustan*, 8 volumes (London: India Museum, 1868–75), vol. 2, plate 67. Alamy Stock Photo

Photographic practices were thus strategically deployed in the aftermath of the war to garner useful intelligence. Photography's value to the knowledge–power nexus of empire was especially great because its indexicality lent empirical legitimacy to the anthropological projects that sought to collate valuable information on colonised peoples (fig. 73); as Pinney writes, photography and colonial anthropology have a 'doubled history'.[15] The photographing of Indian castes and tribes was officially encouraged by Canning, with the diverse imagery received in response to his call being coordinated into an eight-volume collection of 468 albumen prints, *The People of India: A Series of Photographic Illustrations, with Descriptive Letterpress, of the Races and Tribes of Hindustan* (1868–75).[16] While this was ostensibly a scientific project, any preoccupations with Indian ethnicity nevertheless took a back seat to pragmatic political concerns; there was a strong desire, writes Pinney, 'to provide practical clues to the identification of groups which had so recently had the opportunity to demonstrate either their fierce hatred of British rule or their acquiescence'.[17] Such photographic production – structured, ultimately, by military exigencies – was symptomatic of an imperial mindset that viewed Britain's Indian territories as things that were kept by force.

There were more idealistic perspectives on Britain's power than this, however. When news of the Indian insurgency had first reached Britain in the summer of 1857, *The Economist* outlined a choice as to whether India was to be treated as '*a Conquest*', in which the British were simply the 'natural and indefeasible superiors' of their 'Asiatic subjects', or ‘whether we are to regard the Hindoos and the Mahomedans as our equal fellow citizens ... ripe (or to be ripened) for British institutions’.[18] *The Economist*’s alternative to the colonialism-as-conquest narrative was grounded in a liberal conception of universality, an equality of citizenship that could be ‘ripened’ into being via the implementation of progressive reforms and increasingly inclusive modes of Anglo-Indian political organisation.[19] The ‘citizenship’ that *The Economist* alludes to was not a firm legal category (the category of the citizen was not codified in British law until the twentieth century) but stood instead for a more nebulous liberal aspiration for imperial unity.[20] When I discuss here how colonial photography worked to nourish Indian claims to citizenship, I am not speaking in strict statutory terms but am engaging a tradition of thought that has viewed the category of the citizen with some elasticity. Indian citizenship emerged in the Victorian era as a product of intersecting representational regimes – literary, legal, aesthetic and so on – that together registered a liberal political desire for imperial citizenship through their attempts to portray an Anglo-Indian civic identity.

Liberal ideals exerted considerable pressure on governmental thinking in India after the quelling of the Uprising. Overall, however, the postwar decades saw more insistence placed on Indians’ fundamental difference from the British.[21] The fixity of such difference – determined as it supposedly was by the timeless categories of race and caste – worked to undermine liberalism’s progressive rhetoric. Repeatedly, Indians emerged in colonial photography as anthropological specimens, not imperial citizens. And yet, while it is undoubtedly true that the camera lent significant support to ethnological projects, like Sir John William Kaye and John Forbes Watson’s *The People of India* (1868–75), which sought to portray Indians in terms of their racial difference, the formal properties inherent to photography as a medium – in particular the ‘serial dynamic of photographic likeness’ – also functioned to elide racial distinctions in powerful ways.[22] The rest of this chapter is primarily concerned with how photography’s levelling visual grammar was mobilised by Tresidder in Cawnpore to forge a civil aesthetic that could bridge the Anglo-Indian divide, an effort informed at least in part by a politically liberal impulse towards postwar reconciliation.

By surveying the British and Indian personnel of the Cawnpore civil establishment – those ‘Offices in Our Service’ which the Queen’s Proclamation had declared ‘freely and impartially’ open to all colonial subjects ‘qualified by their education, ability, and integrity’ – Tresidder located imperial institutions as privileged sites for rehabilitating racial relations. Yet this liberal project was embarked on at the very moment when ideals about Anglo-Indian political harmony had never appeared more drastically divorced from the vicious realities on the ground. I read the album as a schizophrenic experiment with photographic form in which images are cut, captioned and arranged in ways that forge multiple political narratives. I illustrate the images here as part of the pages they occupy rather than in isolation; the photographs were clearly not conceived of as discrete items but as a photographic mapping of the familial, social, and political networks of a post-conflict colonial environment – a visual mapping that sometimes channels, and sometimes challenges, the notion of Indian citizenship.

IDENTITY AND WAR

Who exactly was Dr John Nicholas Tresidder? And how did he fit into imperial society? These, too, were the questions posed by the upheavals of 1857. Before I prioritise his album's dealings with the mixed-race civil establishment in Cawnpore, it is worth sketching the particular position from which Tresidder and his lens confronted the issue of Indian citizenship.

Tresidder had been the civil surgeon in Cawnpore before the Uprising. Following the death of his first wife there in December 1856, however, he had taken furlough from the following March and travelled to England, leaving behind him a seemingly tranquil India.[23] He married his second wife, Emily Hooton, in Camberwell, London, on 15 August 1857, just as news of a 'mutiny' was filling British newspapers.[24] The doctor who was chosen to replace Tresidder during his absence was Assistant Surgeon H. P. Harris.[25] Along with his wife, child and just about every other colonial in Cawnpore, Harris was killed during the siege and subsequent massacres of July.[26] Tresidder and his new wife returned to Cawnpore while war was still raging. By the time they arrived, the British were once more in control of the station but fighting continued to plague the area, and there is a record of Tresidder treating a soldier, Mowbray Thomson, for a bullet wound to the thigh in February 1858.[27] This patient was one of the only British survivors of the summertime atrocities.

The backdrop to the construction of the album was therefore the near-total annihilation of everyone Tresidder had known before the war. The doctor had even once treated the rebel commander responsible for leading the assault on Cawnpore, the infamous Nana Sahib. Tresidder's postwar imagery, in combination with some purchased photographs by Beato, grappled with the devastation by surveying key sites from the conflict. Page 24 of the album, for example, displays two photographs of the riverside known by colonials as the 'Slaughter Ghat', where the British had been massacred while they were boarding the boats that Nana Sahib had supposedly prepared for their safe passage up the Ganges to

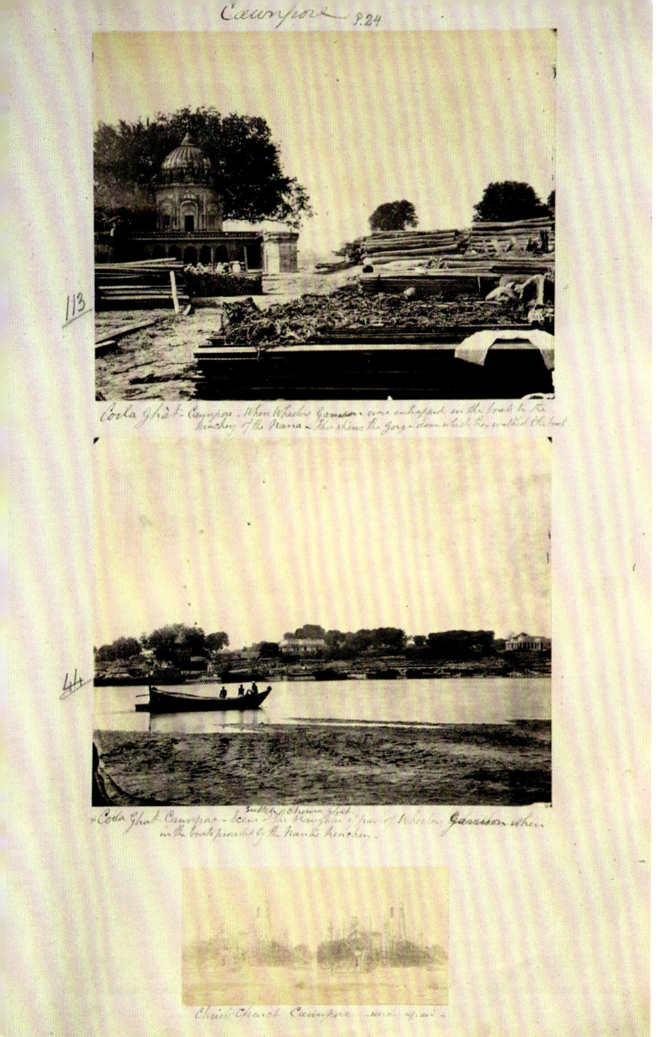

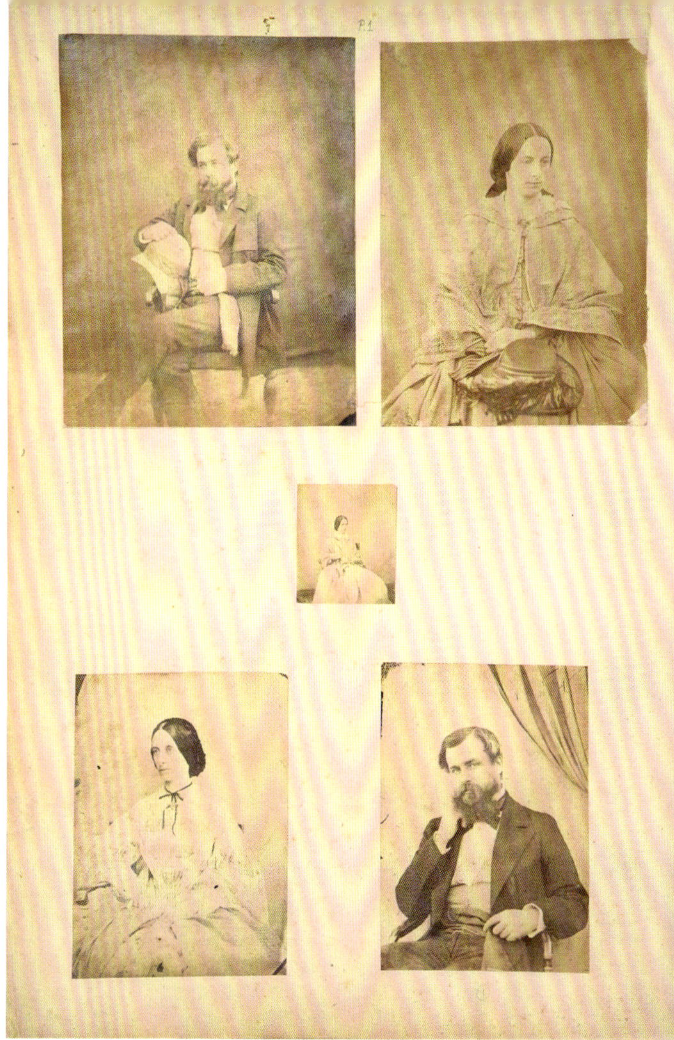

Allahabad (fig. 74). Such scenes' meditation on 'empty' spaces where significant events had occurred is typical of the 'absence' that scholars have noted in war photography from India at this time (although in fact colonial photographers more often than not posed Indians on such sites).[28] Tresidder's desperation to make his photographs bear adequate witness is made plain by the lengthy description given to his 'Slaughter Ghat' scene: 'Where [General] Wheeler's Garrison were entrapped in the boats by the treachery of the Nana – This shows the Gorge down which they walked to the boats.' His engagement with Cawnpore's war sites signalled a 'deep exploration of photography as a history machine, a technology for the deposition and traces of what has been lost'.[29]

Yet the album's spectres of violence are balanced by another form of imagery, one that re-stabilises Tresidder's presence in India by anchoring it in the reassuring features of colonial peacetime. The entire album is framed in personal terms: opening with portraits of Tresidder and both his late and current wife (fig. 75), it goes on to include items of the colonial everyday such as 'My favourite trotting cart', a scene in the top centre

74 Dr John Nicholas Tresidder, 'Cawnpore', in 'The Tresidder Album', *c.*1858–64, page 24. Albumen and salt-paper prints. Alkazi Collection of Photography, New Delhi

75 John Nicholas Tresidder et al., 'The Tresidder Album', *c.*1858–64, page 1. Albumen and salt-paper prints. Alkazi Collection of Photography, New Delhi

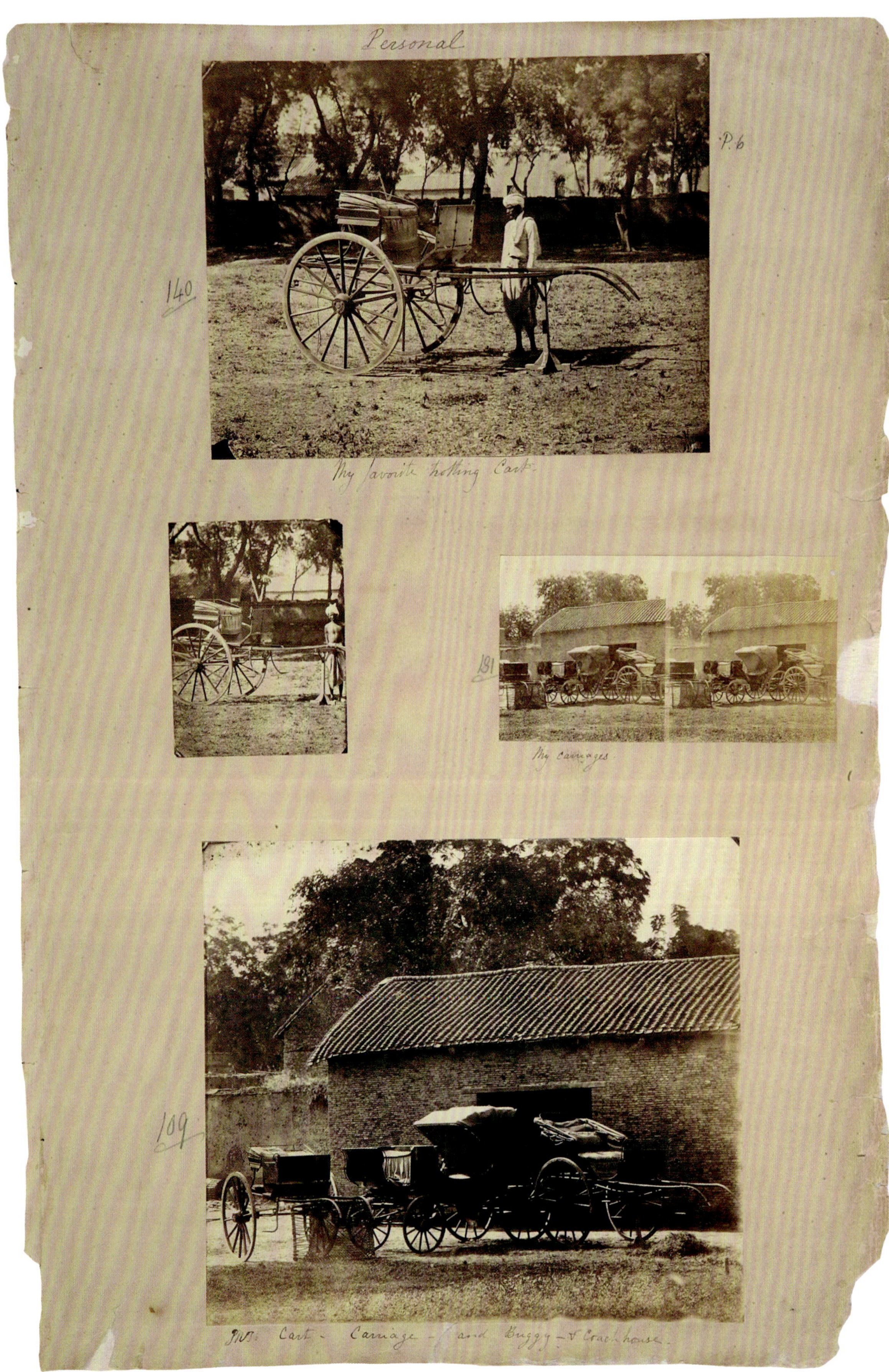
Personal
P. 6
140
My favorite trotting Cart
181
My carriages
109
Cart – Carriage – and Buggy – & Coachhouse

of page 6 replete with the eponymous cart and an anonymous Indian attendant (fig. 76). Insistently intimate in tone – his wife is referred to informally as 'Emmie' – the album constitutes a defiant reassertion of colonial domesticity on the very site that had become infamous for the violation of the colonial home when Indian men had entered Cawnpore's Bibi Ghar, 'The House of the Ladies', and slaughtered the women and children imprisoned inside.[30] The extent to which these events continued to haunt Tresidder's own domestic environment can be gauged by the fact that he gave the name 'Cawnpore' to his retirement home in England.[31] The album's size is such that it could easily have served as a point of focus for more than one person at a time, enabling group viewings among family and friends in which the imagery's broader political narratives could unfurl in relation to the personal identifications among particular persons, places and things.

However, the rehabilitation of British domesticity is just one element of a much more ambitious photographic project: the virtual reconstruction

76 Dr John Nicholas Tresidder, 'Personal', in 'The Tresidder Album', *c.*1858–64, page 6. Albumen and salt-paper prints. Alkazi Collection of Photography, New Delhi

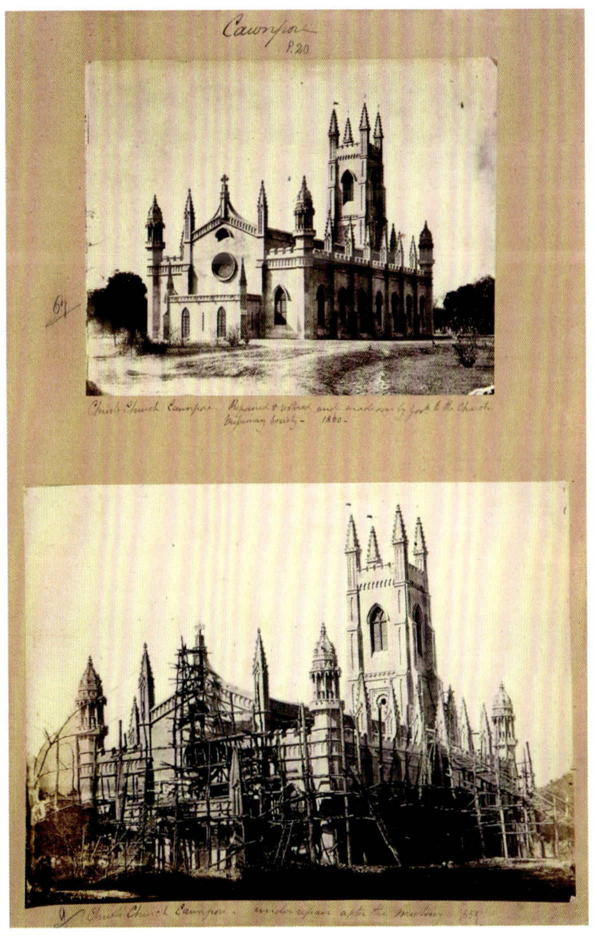

77 Dr John Nicholas Tresidder, 'Cawnpore', in 'The Tresidder Album', *c.*1858–64, page 20. Albumen and salt-paper prints. Alkazi Collection of Photography, New Delhi

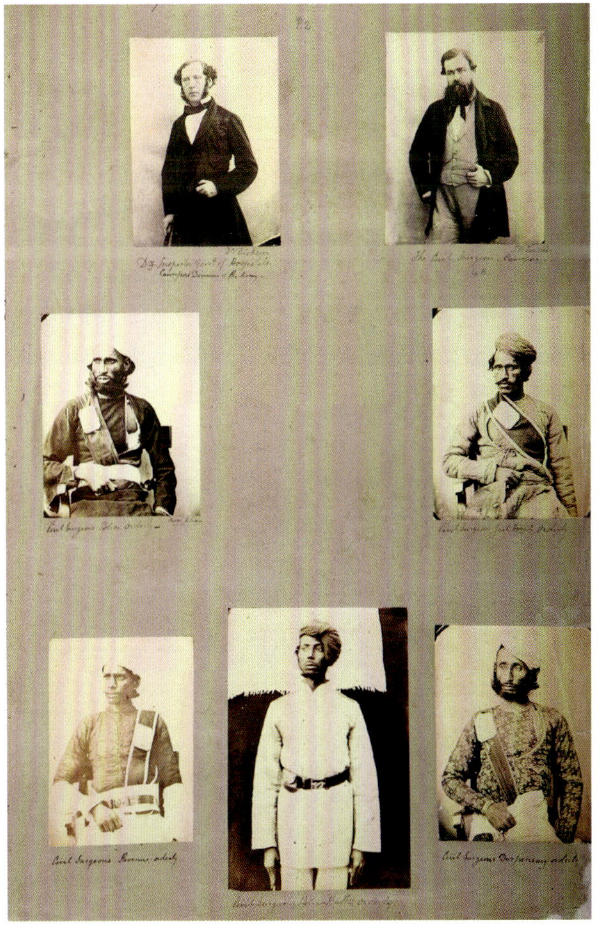

78 Dr John Nicholas Tresidder, 'Cawnpore Civil Establishment', in 'The Tresidder Album', *c.*1858–64, page 2. Albumen and salt-paper prints. Alkazi Collection of Photography, New Delhi

79 Dr John Nicolas Tresidder, 'JNT's Family', in 'The Tresidder Album', *c.*1858–64, page 5. Albumen and salt-paper prints. Alkazi Collection of Photography, New Delhi

of Anglo-Indian society. This project is made particularly explicit in the paired scenes of the war-ravaged Cawnpore church undergoing reconstruction (fig. 77) but it also weaves its way through the assemblages of portraits that work to flesh out the local operations of a colonial state that had so recently been confronted with dissolution. The second page of the album (fig. 78) supplements Tresidder's initial identification of himself as a husband with a portrait of him at the top right-hand side that is captioned according to his public role, 'J. N. Tresidder The Civil Surgeon – Cawnpore'. This professional persona is situated in a series of similar portraits that constitute the district's medical network, most notably the Deputy Inspector General of Hospitals, Dr Dickson (whose pose is identical to Tresidder's), as well as numerous Indian medical staff, including civil surgeon orderlies for the police and the hospital on the same page as Tresidder and assistant surgeons and doctors on the following page.

By and large, Tresidder's imagery is unconcerned with formulating India in terms of difference via a fixation on religion, race or caste. Instead, its treatment of Indians can be placed in a bourgeois framework for conceptualising the colonial state. Tresidder and his British colleague both stand in their portraits, while all but one of the Indian men sit, thereby establishing a precedence that is underpinned by the higher placement of the British on the page. Ultimately, though, Tresidder's engagement with hierarchy and race is considerably more nuanced than this initial differentiation suggests. Europeans do not always enjoy compositional prominence in the album, nor do they often distinguish themselves from Indians through pose.

True, the album's engagement with private life does tend to uphold Anglo-Indian distinctions. On page 5, titled 'JNT's Family' (fig. 79), there is a collage produced from the individual portraits of Tresidder's servants, combined to form a mass of Indian difference against which imperial whiteness (personified here by the individual portraits of Tresidder's children) can be established. But the album's dealings with the public sphere eschew such racial segregations, with Cawnpore society emerging as a network of imperial institutions that find expression in the fairly undifferentiated individual portraits of the British and Indian personnel of the medical establishment, the judiciary and the police.

CITIZENSHIP

In Cawnpore at this time, Tresidder may well have been alone in possessing both the knowledge and the materials needed to produce photographs, meaning that his portrait sittings would probably have been memorable experiences for both their British and Indian participants. All

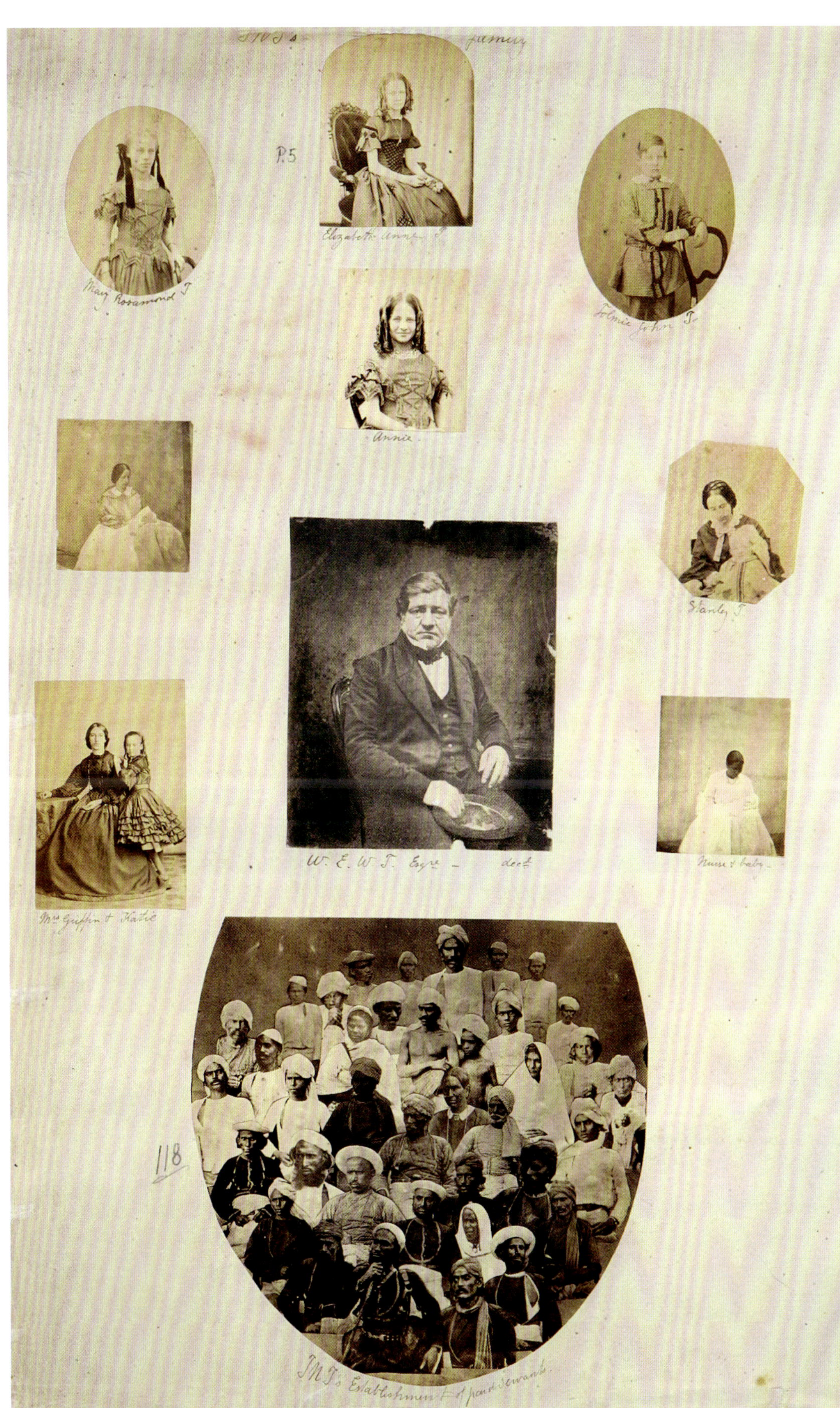
P.5
Elizabeth Anne T
Mary Rosamond T
Tolmie John T
Annie
Stanley T
W. E. W. T. Esqre — decd
Nurse & baby
Mrs Griffin & Katie
118
JNT's Establishment of paid Servants

Cawnpore Civil Establishment

P. 11

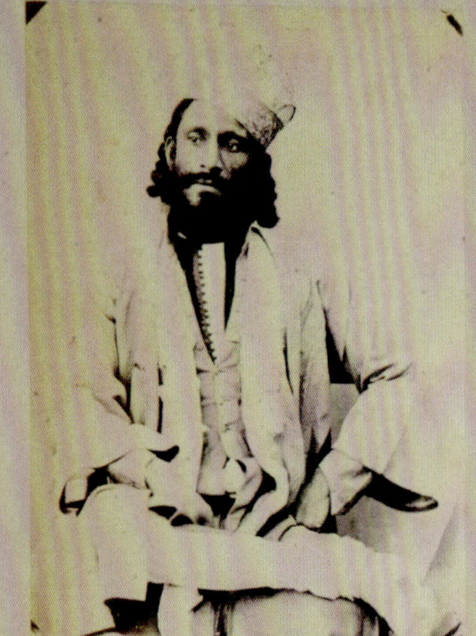

1st Native Judge Cawnpore

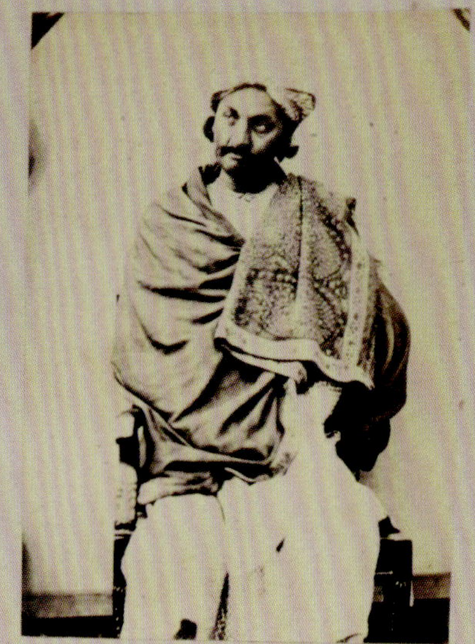

2nd Native Judge Cawnpore -

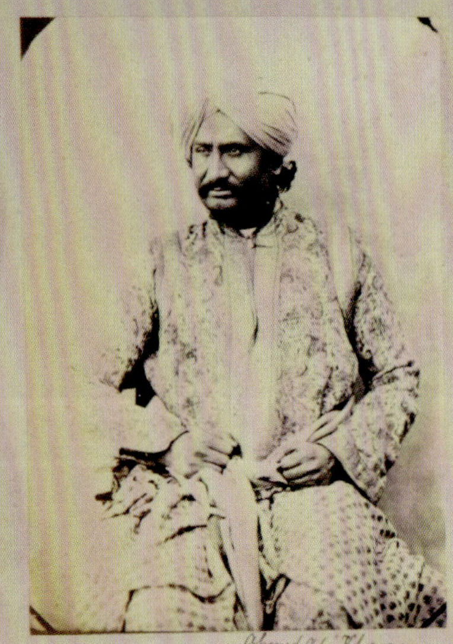

Ahmed Ali Khan -
Govt. Pleader - (Barrister) Cawnpore

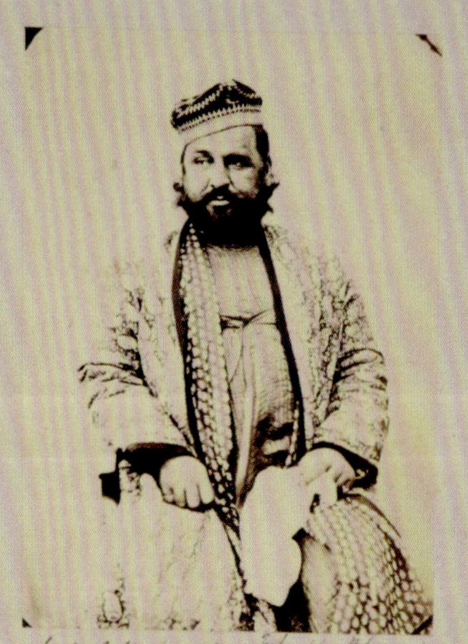

Subreddar Bhogneepore -
Sub-Collector - Cawnpore -

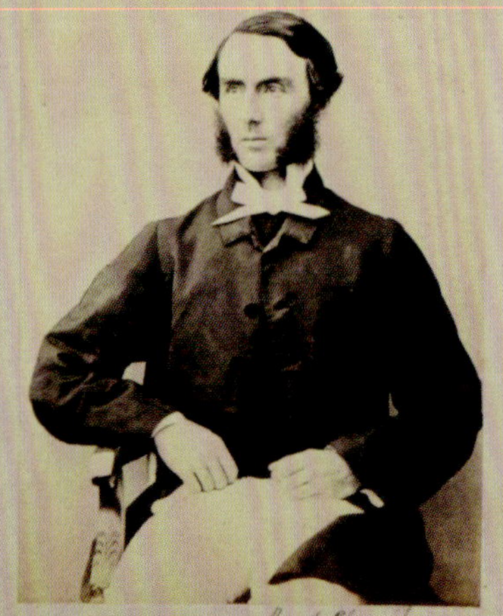

Revd. Thos Shaw -
The Chaplain Cawnpore

those photographed by Tresidder are placed in the same studio environment: they sit in the same chair (on which, in some images, can be seen his initials 'JNT' carved into the arm), against the same white backdrop and all adopt similar poses.[32] Each is defined in terms of their role within a professional matrix, as for example 'Ahmad Ali Khan. Govt Pleader (Barrister) Cawnpore' on the middle left-hand side of page 11 (fig. 80). The sittings were a means of becoming situated in the imperial order.

80 John Nicholas Tresidder, 'Cawnpore Civil Establishment', in 'The Tresidder Album', *c.*1858–64, page 11. Albumen and salt-paper prints. Alkazi Collection of Photography, New Delhi

The standardisation of setting and pose in Tresidder's portraits recalls the bourgeois conventions of the carte-de-visite. Such was the homogeneity of these relatively cheap and small commercial photographic portraits that, as Lara Perry has written, 'Virtually the entire class of objects, estimated in the tens of millions per year at its peak, can be described in a few sentences.' Poses included sitting or standing, often by a table or chair and with props such as books, pillars and curtains. Their interchangeability has been theorised by scholars in terms of offering an index of 'emerging notions of equality in citizenship for the bourgeois body politic that emerged in the nineteenth century'.[33] Accordingly, by the 1870s, the carte-de-visite had become a popular format with the Indian elite, who used the portraits as symbols of their social mobility and status (fig. 81).[34]

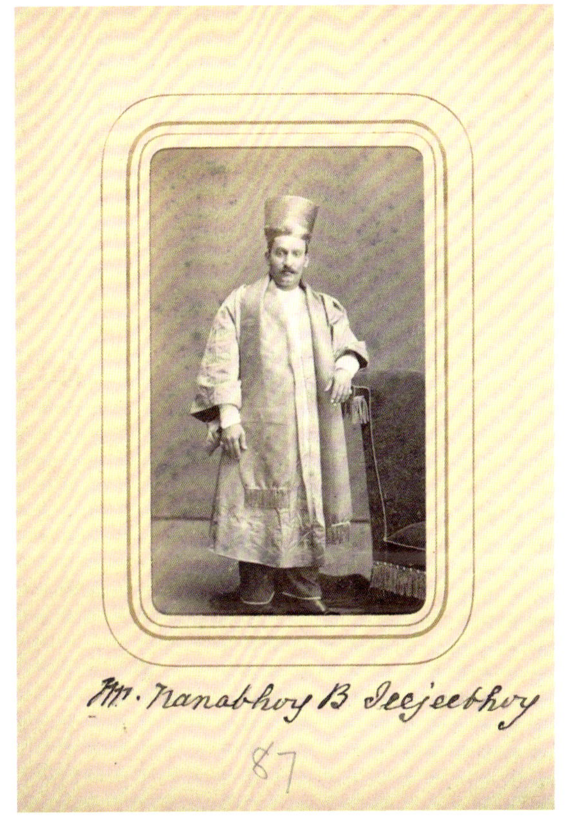

81 Bourne & Shepherd, *Mr Nanabhoy B. Jeejeebhoy*, 1870. Albumen print, 16.8 × 23.5 cm. © The British Library Board, Photo 127/(87)

In her account of such photography and the Bengali middle classes, Malavika Karlekar has pointed out that, while some Indian patrons would have been self-consciously fashioning themselves in accordance with colonial poses, many were simply being 'directed by an authoritarian photographic establishment used to peddling stereotypical models of "the professional"'.[35] This, though, would have been the case with some British patrons as well; and indeed, whether or not the carte-de-visite constituted authentic acts of Indian self-expression, its democratic visual grammar still provided a counterweight to the aesthetics of difference that tended to characterise British imperialism, incorporating diverse racial groups under a common horizon.

Portraits thus allowed Indians to emerge into what Judith Butler has termed the 'realm of appearance' that was the precondition for making any proper claims to citizenship status:

> there are extra-legal conditions for becoming a citizen, indeed, for even becoming a subject who can and does appear before the law. To appear before the law means that one has entered into the realm of appearance or that one is positioned to be entered there, which mean that there are norms that condition and orchestrate the subject who can and does appear.[36]

Citizenship is therefore not simply contingent on the narrow, albeit significant, attainment of specific legal rights. It is the product of diffuse symbolic processes that function to represent a person or group as having a recognisable (and respectable) mode of political agency within society. The diverse '"languages" of citizenship' operative in nineteenth-century India have been explored by Sukanya Banerjee in *Becoming Imperial Citizens: Indians in the Late-Victorian Empire* (2010), a study that 'situates citizenship not so much in the realm of statutory enactment as in cultural, imaginative, and affective fields that both engender it and are constituted by it'.[37] Citizenship was registered by rhetorical as well as legal means, with imperial belonging secured through an engagement with and appearance in certain types of literary genres, images, monuments and spaces. Photographic portraits, with their connotations of bourgeois respectability and professionalism, could thus foreshadow and feed into more wide-ranging liberal agendas.

The capacity for photographic portraiture to harmonise Anglo-Indian relations through a civil aesthetic was articulated more or less explicitly by George Birdwood, the keeper of the Indian Museum at South Kensington, in his introduction to Sorabji Jehangir's collection of photographs of British and Indian men, *Representative Men of India: A Collection of Memoirs, with Portraits, of Indian Princes, Nobles, Statesmen, Philanthropists, Officials, and Eminent Citizens* (1889). The book contained a mixture of prominent British colonials, Indian royals and their ministers, a group of men who, as Birdwood claimed, 'however else they may be otherwise discriminated, are all connected together by the honour they share in common, of having, in their various spheres of Imperial and Civic duty, won the confidence and affection of the people of India.'[38] The photographs provide an alternative to the anthropological mode of representing Indian figures, instead conjuring what Pinney has described as 'a de-ethnicized elite at ease with itself'.[39] Their publication in 1889 can be seen as symptomatic of the increasing currency that had been gained by the notion of a formally equal status for peoples across the empire by the late nineteenth century, even if the British continued to display ambivalence towards the extension of this imperial equality to non-white subjects.[40]

Tresidder's album is thus remarkable for positing a similarly liberal visual argument three decades before Jehangir's photographic intervention in such debates. Indeed, the uniformity of portraits is considerably more striking in Tresidder's work than in Jehangir's. Geoffrey Batchen has argued that the carte-de-visite's interchangeability signalled to consumers that 'class is a look that can be codified and imitated – it's a mode of performance rather than an inherent quality.'[41] Thus while some Indians look ill at ease in Tresidder's studio (just as some Europeans do), the fact that others appear to adapt to the demands of the bourgeois portrait with impeccable confidence (see the '1st native judge Cawnpore' in the top left-hand side of page 11; fig. 80) forges a shared aesthetics of citizenship in the colonial system. It presents an image of Indian men not as conquered enemies who are irredeemably different from the British but, to use *The Economist*'s words, as 'equal fellow citizens' that are 'ripe (or to be ripened) for British institutions'.

An aesthetics of imperial citizenship thus emerged across multiple forms of photographic practice throughout the history of the Raj, from British-led visions to Indian-led visions and from the vernacular to the official. In her recent book *Projecting Citizenship: Photography and Belonging in the British Empire* (2019), Gabrielle Moser argues that, by the early twentieth century, 'it was photography, not cartography' that was most helpful to the imperial state as it attempted to envision its territories as a viable transnational polity. Moser's illuminating study tracks the endeavours of the Colonial Office Visual Instruction Committee (COVIC), a government-backed group of volunteers which ran an international series of lantern-slide lectures between 1902 and 1945 wherein photographic portraits of colonial peoples were used to render imperial 'citizenship' recognisable throughout the Empire. COVIC placed photography at the centre of a liberal imperial pedagogy, using lantern shows 'not just to picture imperial citizens but to teach a particular kind of spectatorship as central to the practices of citizenship.'[42] The scale of this project was unprecedented but in other ways, as James Ryan noted, 'it was simply an amalgam of established ideas, practices and techniques' that had mobilised photography – in particular lantern-slides – as part of an imperial apparatus of visual instruction.[43]

Yet such instruction did not always have to come 'from above' in grand projects of imperial propaganda; it emerged independently, if modestly, out of colonial vernacular traditions. Indeed, arguably, such imperial visions of citizenship emerged, at least to a degree, from the visual logic of photography itself – its 'aesthetics of the same', as Pinney writes.[44] The standardised poses common to photographic portraiture destabilised ideas about essential differences between Britons and

Indians; and for Tresidder, it did so at a historical moment in which Anglo-Indian communities had never been more violently alienated from one another. Against a background of intense racial strife, Tresidder's studio harboured a liberal cosmopolitanism that went against the ethos of exclusion that the war had instilled in colonial India generally and, through the ban on 'natives' entering the cherished local memorial garden, in Cawnpore specifically.

Tresidder's photography can thus be conceptualised as a healing agent in a fragile peace process: the men who visited the studio would probably have been aware that both their British and Indian colleagues were sitting in equivalent circumstances, meaning that the space was one in which social antagonisms were temporarily suspended in favour of what Pinney terms a 'Photographic Civil Society'.[45] The doctor's inclusive practice can be seen as a palliative photographic treatment of the community, working to soothe the wounds of a ruptured imperial body politic and serving as a prophylaxis against future outbreaks by identifying a certain bourgeois professionalism as the cooperative endeavour of multiracial imperial citizens.

THE LIMITS OF COHESION

Tresidder's efforts to document a collegial Anglo-Indian society took place under the shadow of counter-insurgency. Even as the photographer's studio was envisioning peace by staging a parity of professionalism between British and Indian civil servants, Cawnpore itself was in the throes of a vicious political purge.

One man invited to sit for Tresidder was Mowbray Thomson (whose bullet wound to the thigh the doctor had previously treated). Having survived the horrors of the siege and wartime massacres, Thomson took up the post of Superintendent of Police in Cawnpore following the recapture of the garrison. He can be seen in both European and Oriental garb in his portraits at the top of page 13 of the album, situated above his Indian sergeants (fig. 82). According to Thomson's 1859 account of the war, his duties as a police officer 'involved secret service, executions, raising native police, and the sale of plunder'.[46] Policing doubled as counter-insurgency. In a favourable official report, it was noted that Thomson's 'Police have distinguished themselves during the year, by eradicating a gang of dacoits, and by the apprehension and destruction of notorious offenders ... whose removal will, more than anything, tend to the suppression of outrage, and to the deterring of others from violent aggressions.'[47] Executions were a daily occurrence under Thomson's lauded reign; no Indian man was safe from this purge, no matter how embedded he was in the imperial apparatus. One Indian under Thomson's command, who had

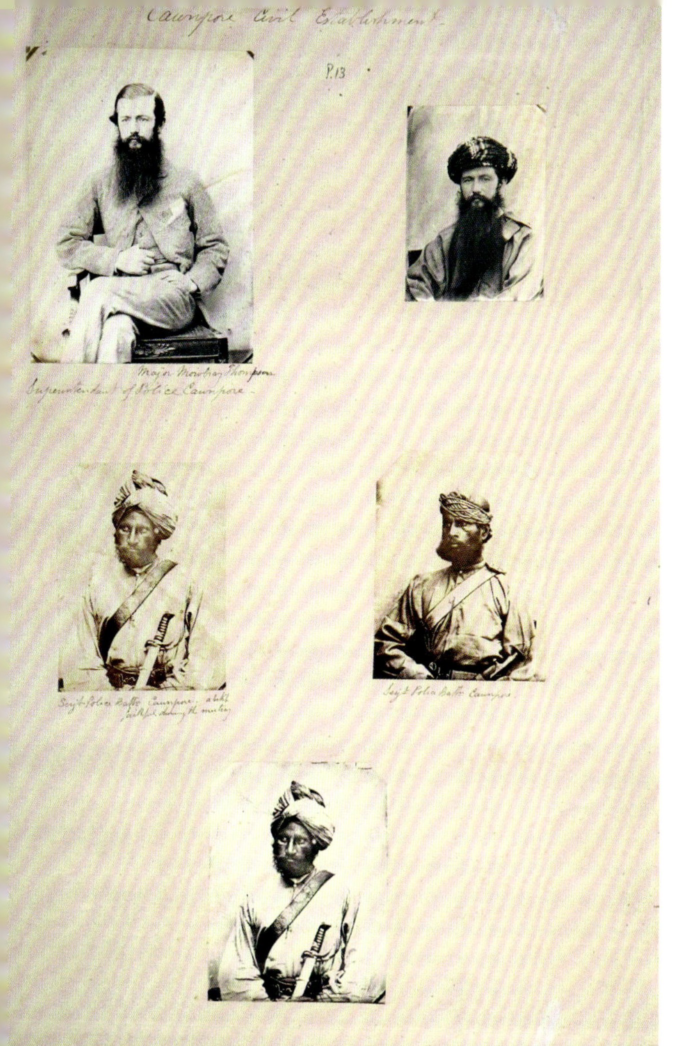

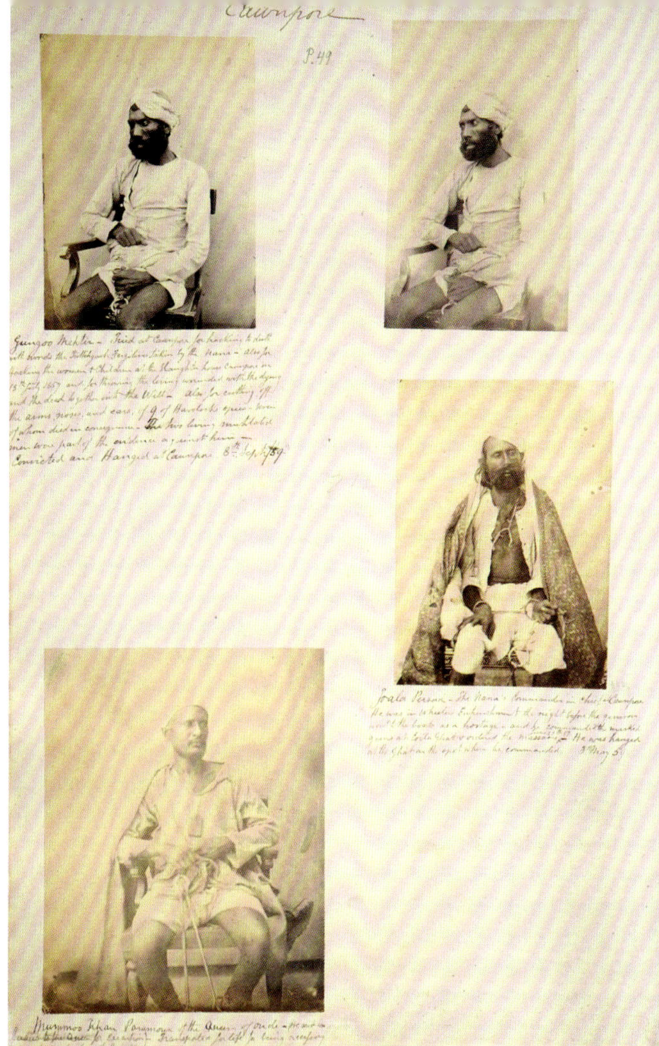

previously been instrumental in the arrests of numerous suspected insurgents, was himself accused of betraying the British, brought to trial and sentenced to three years' imprisonment. Even the Indian executioner responsible for hanging the Cawnpore rebels was ultimately suspended from his own gibbet.[48]

This climate of persecution was also registered by Tresidder, as condemned Indian men were brought to his studio in chains. It is not known whether or not the portraits of war prisoners were intended to serve as official administrative records of judicial proceedings or merely as triumphal documents of imperial retribution (such uses were of course not mutually exclusive); convict photography was however by no means a routine practice in mid-nineteenth-century India, despite official discussion regarding its potential merits.[49] Two photographs of the captive Gungoo Mehter (fig. 83) are thus remarkable in the way that they capture the downfall of a convicted war criminal, showing the thousand-yard stare of a man sentenced to death for his role in murdering British women and children. A slumped Mehter holds his restraints

82 John Nicholas Tresidder, 'Cawnpore Civil Establishment', in 'The Tresidder Album', *c.*1858–64, page 13. Albumen and salt-paper prints. Alkazi Collection of Photography, New Delhi

83 Dr John Nicholas Tresidder, 'Cawnpore', in 'The Tresidder Album', *c.*1858–64, page 49. Albumen and salt-paper prints. Alkazi Collection of Photography, New Delhi

in his hands; they trail down beneath the frame, presumably tied to Mehter's feet, as they are in a companion portrait on the same page showing Mummoo Khan, a 'Paramour of the Queen of Oude', who was condemned to 'transportation for life for [being] accessory to murder and a leader of Rebellion in 1857'. Chains aside, these images are both extremely familiar, strongly recalling those of the British and Indian professionals who were also asked to sit for Tresidder on this same chair, in this same space – thus providing a striking demonstration of Allan Sekula's maxim that 'every proper portrait has its lurking, objectifying inverse in the files of the police.'[50]

The photographer's studio thus served to stage imperial sovereignty 'with hegemony' – the liberal extension of some kind of shared citizen-status in the colonial system – and 'dominance without hegemony', in which individuals like Gungoo Mehter were identified as persons subject to state-sanctioned imprisonment and death.[51] The studio served a dual purpose: functioning 'both *honorifically* and *repressively*',[52] it anointed some Indians as professionals with a stake in the imperial system, while identifying others as what Giorgio Agamben termed 'bare life', wholly exposed to imperial violence.[53] Yet these two currents of the counter-insurgent order in Cawnpore could not be neatly separated (at least not in visual terms): the portraits of Indian prisoners implicate the poses of imperial professionalism as themselves embodiments of a certain disciplinary subjection, so that the spectres of violence and exclusion haunt the inclusive respectability that we see in the portraits of civil society.[54]

How, then, to distinguish between the 'insurgent' and the 'citizen'? Unlike the portraits that have been examined so far, the captive figure of Mehter was not identified in the album with merely a laconic caption stating his name and occupation. Instead, the portrait was incorporated into a discourse of crime and punishment, conspicuously distanced from the other Anglo-Indian portraits through a detailed account of his alleged role in the Cawnpore massacres:

> Gungoo Mehter – Tried at Cawnpore for hacking to death with swords the Futtehgarh fugitives taken by the Nana [Sahib] – also for Hacking the women & children at the Slaughter house Cawnpore on 15th July 1857 and for throwing the living wounded with the dying and the dead together into the Well – also for cutting off the arms, noses, and ears, of 9 of Havelock's spies – seven of whom died in consequence – The two living mutilated men were part of the evidence against him – Convicted and Hanged at Cawnpore 8th Sept/ 59.[55]

Tresidder thus deployed lengthy, detail-laden text to anchor Mehter's portrait in a juridical context. But on an aesthetic level, it was by no means dissimilar from common poses of harmonious imperial professionalism. Once placed in front of the photographer's lens, much-reviled Indian rebels suddenly inhabited an arena that functioned to neutralise distinctions between 'good' and 'bad' Indians – and even to some extent between coloniser and colonised – because of a shared visual language of pose and placement. The homogenising visual grammar of photography dissolved important markers of social difference.

To a certain extent, the visual slippage between convicts and colleagues appears to have been accepted by Tresidder, who could after all have placed the prisoners in an alternative manner (standing, for instance) but chose instead to abide by standard portrait conventions and merely allow for the presence of restraints and the addition of captions to recuperate relevant political distinctions. Yet, in a remarkable double-page spread in the album (fig. 84), certain anxieties about such portraiture's slipperiness do seem to emerge.

The ability – or lack thereof – to register political distinctions was ultimately framed by Tresidder as a matter of life and death. On the top right-hand side of the spread (page 48 in the album) is a photograph of an elderly Islamic cleric, who during the war had issued a decree stating it was morally right for Muslims to kill Christians. Again, this portrait mimics the bourgeois tone of the poses seen earlier, as do the two portraits beneath it, one of an Indian man called Nana Narain Rao, the other of his son. Rao had helped the British by passing them information about Nana Sahib but he was nevertheless suspected as being 'one of those double-dyed traitors who hang on the skirts of success and are driven backwards and forwards by every gust of fortune.'[56] The inclusion of his portrait (an Indian man whose allegiance to the British was uncertain) underneath the portrait of the cleric (whose antipathy to the British was known) speaks to the mortal difficulty of identifying people as 'friends' or 'enemies' – which, as Carl Schmitt's political theory has it, is the sovereign act par excellence.[57]

While seemingly content to allow Indian men to occupy a visual (although not textual) space that dramatised ambiguities of allegiance, Tresidder at the same time sought to develop a separate photographic mode to envision the unity of the British community. He substantially reworked his photographs in a manner that recuperated the very racial demarcations that his portraits of civil servants had worked to elide. Beneath the images of Rao and the insurgent cleric we find an assemblage of portraits entitled 'Cawnpore friends'. This is a photomontage of the white community, whose heads and shoulders have been cut from their bodies and arranged to create a composite negative, from which Tresidder secured a combination print.[58] Strikingly, the print is placed as

following pages

84 Dr John Nicholas Tresidder, 'Cawnpore', in 'The Tresidder Album', *c.*1858–64, pages 47–8. Albumen and salt-paper prints. Alkazi Collection of Photography, New Delhi

Cawnpore

P.47

North Burial Ground – Cawnpore –

J. Sandys Esqre. – A Celebrated lawyer of Cawnpore

Baker Ali Khan – A Celebrated Native Physician Cawnpore

Buldeo Sahai. a loyal Native of Cawnpore

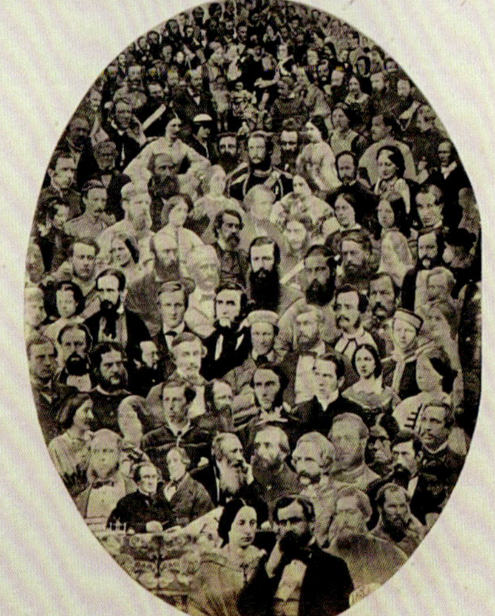

Cawnpore

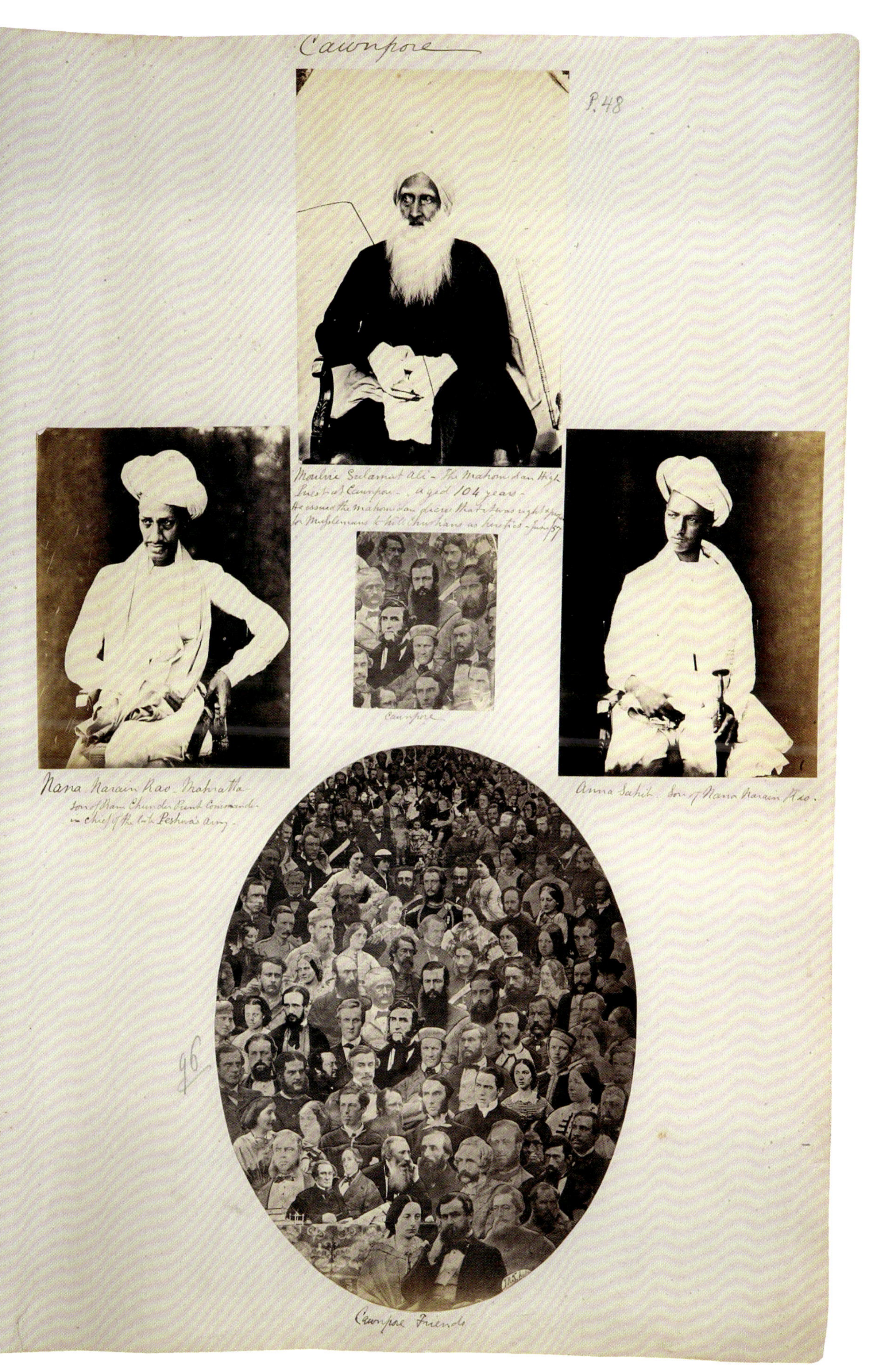
Cawnpore
P. 48
Maulvie Sulamut Ali – The Mahomedan High
Priest at Cawnpore – aged 104 years –
Cawnpore
Nana Narain Rao – Mahratta –
Commander in Chief of the Peshwa's Army –
Anna Sahib – Son of Nana Narain Rao.
Cawnpore Friends

if under siege by the enemy cleric and the possibly disloyal Indian men. Even the 'loyal native of Cawnpore' on the left-hand side of the spread is cast adrift from colonials; his unreconstructed portrait resides outside the composite image of Europeans, situated in visual relation to the insurgent preacher and the ambiguously aligned figure of Rao. Indians are thereby partitioned into 'friends' and 'enemies' according to imperial notions of loyalty – but the colonial community is seen as formally distinct from both these Indian categories.

The traumatic atmosphere of crime and punishment, paranoia and suspicion, which reigned in Cawnpore following the atrocities of 1857 therefore spurred Tresidder along inventive trajectories of portraiture production. The Caucasian unity embodied by the carefully orchestrated composite print is founded on a jointly Christian sense of loss, encapsulated by the two-part panorama 'North burial ground – Cawnpore', which unfolds to span the double-page spread. In this way the death of Europeans is made literally to hang over the post-conflict composition of Anglo-Indian relations in Cawnpore, forming the grisly backdrop to and the potential consequence of any colonial difficulties in properly distinguishing between friends and enemies in India. Under this divisive symbol of imperial mourning, Tresidder's photographic reconstruction of Cawnpore undergoes a profound shift in political emphasis, moving from a visual ordering of Anglo-Indian relations that was based on mutual participation in civic institutions, to an organisation of the community based on formally segregated groups, in which 'friends' are distinguishable above all by race. The seriality of the photographic portrait thus opened up the opportunity to envision postwar Anglo-Indian society as operating in harmonious accordance with liberal ideals of formal equality, but the de-differentiation involved in this manner of picturing British India also carried the threatening implication that allies and enemies were not always visually apparent. Such disturbing murkiness seemed to call for the reinscription of distinct social boundaries and thus a photographic mode that worked to emphasise the sanctity of race, still the clearest outward marker of political identity within the imperial imaginary.

CONCLUSION

Over and above issues regarding the military logistics of maintaining power in South Asia, the question raised by the 1857 insurrection was this: in the aftermath of extraordinary inter-racial violence, could British India still be imagined as a workable political entity? The answer given by Tresidder's photography was that, yes, such an entity could be pictured, but the visual grammar of photography articulated a colonial society that was perhaps a little too coherent, eliding cherished racial distinctions. The formal possibilities of photography were thus experimented with by Tresidder in ways that paradoxically crystallised firstly, a comforting sense of Anglo-Indian harmony in the institutions of the civil establishment, as a formal equality was compellingly rendered by the standardised photographic portrait; and secondly, a faith in the inviolate nature of the white community against an unstable Indian 'loyalty', as the standardised portrait was segmented and spliced until it could satisfy the imperial craving for racial distinction. In this double movement, the imagery serves as a visual register for one of the key ideological antagonisms of the post-1857 empire in India, 'the effort to preserve elements of an ongoing liberalism within a conception of Indian "difference"'.[59]

Tresidder's studio and album thus offered cathartic spaces where incompatible desires could be navigated. The spectre of violent insurgency created an urgent need to stabilise Anglo-Indian society but it also confronted colonials with their limited capacity to sustain a coherently liberal, socially rehabilitative mode of political and aesthetic praxis. Homi K. Bhabha identified ambivalence of this sort as a constitutive feature of political liberalism as it is expressed in the colonial context, wherein the ability for the colonised Other to 'mimic' the habits of Europe does not validate the imperial mission so much as cause deep anxiety in the coloniser, who struggles to maintain a stable sense of self, or a distinct aura of authority, that can legitimise their dominance over subject peoples.[60] Photography in particular was a potent cause of this sort of anxiety, since its own formal logic tended to raise troubling questions about the relative status of Briton and Indian under the imperial regime.

8 · THE COLOUR OF SOVEREIGNTY

Colonial Portraiture and the Coronation Durbars in British India, 1877–1911[1]

WHAT DOES IT MEAN FOR THE AESTHETICS OF A POLITICAL REGIME to fail? This is the question posed by the vast twenty-seven-foot oil painting that Valentine Cameron Prinsep (1838–1904) produced in official commemoration of the spectacular 'Imperial Assemblage' ceremony held in Delhi on 1 January 1877 (fig. 85). On the dais, cloaked in rippling blue velvet with an ermine tippet, is the Viceroy of India, Earl Edward Robert Bulwer-Lytton, his arm outstretched towards the stolid figure of Major Barnes, who comes bearing the scroll that gave rise to the fanfare that surrounds them: a proclamation heralding Queen Victoria's assumption of a new title, 'Empress of India' or *Kaisar-i-hind*.[2] The portraits of numerous South Asian rulers line the surrounding amphitheatre, many taken from studies produced by Prinsep during his year travelling through the so-called 'princely states'. Such was the size of this unprecedented imperial group portrait that it occupied an entire wall at the Royal Academy exhibition of 1880 but perceptions that it did not fit there, either spatially or artistically, permeated the reviews. For one critic, the work 'suffers terribly from its discordancy with everything in the exhibition, while it ruins the effects of every other picture, not only in its vicinity, but while the glare of its colouring haunts the vitiated eye.'[3] It seemed to launch an aggressive ocular assault on the show's visitors: 'its high colour shrieks at us in other rooms,' leaving 'the eye dazzled and the sense confounded.'[4]

Colour held a fraught and 'vertiginous' political status in the colonies.[5] This chapter argues that the tumultuous chromatics of Prinsep's *The Imperial Assemblage held at Delhi, 1 January 1877* registered as a crisis of imperial governance for Victorian viewers, disrupting the sober visual strategies that had emerged in British portraiture to secure social cohesion. A similar interpretation of the unruly significance of Prinsep's aesthetic failure at the Royal Academy was offered by a contemporary

Val Prinsep, *The Imperial Assemblage held at Delhi, 1 January 1877*, 1880 (detail of fig. 85).

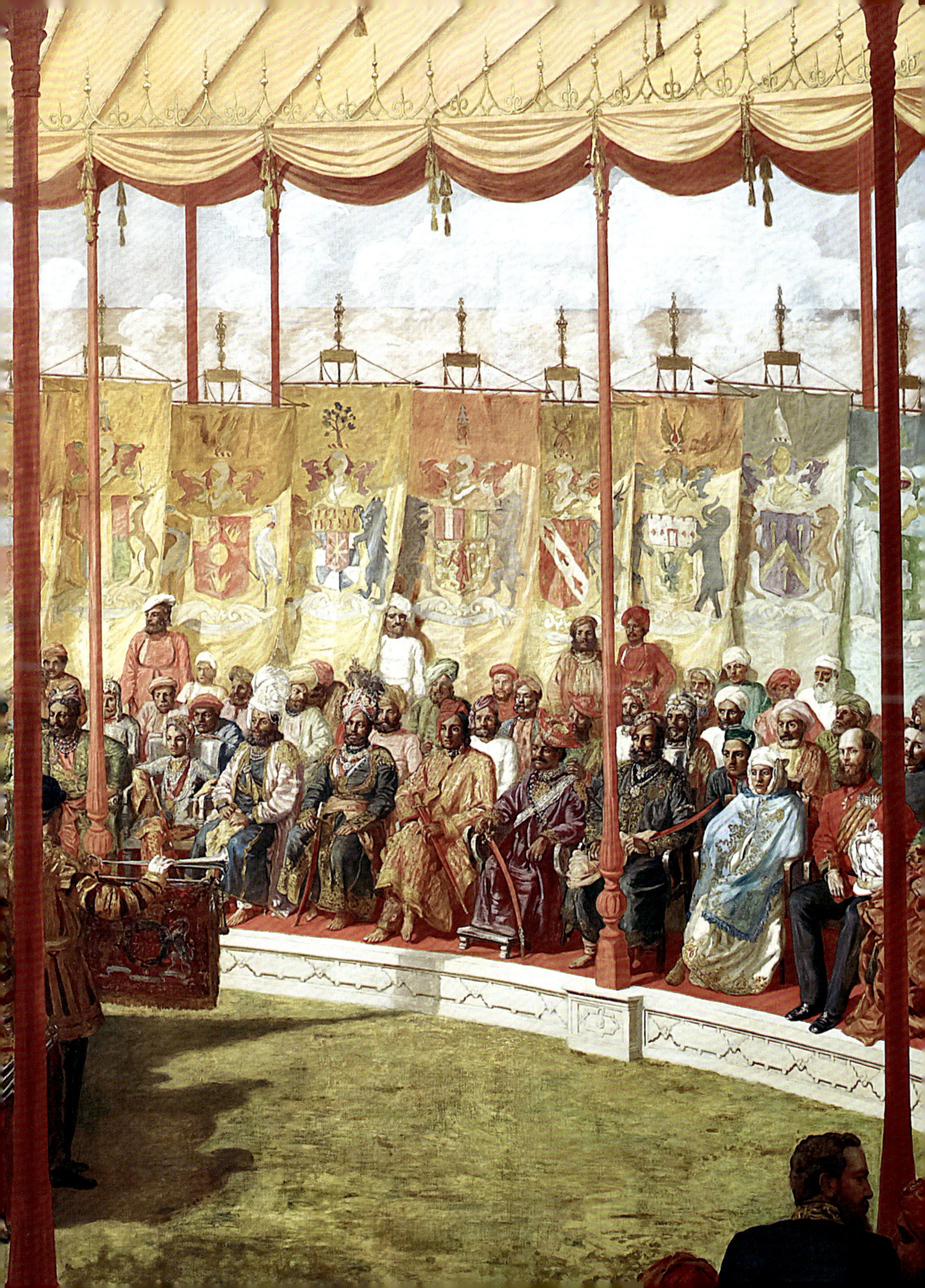

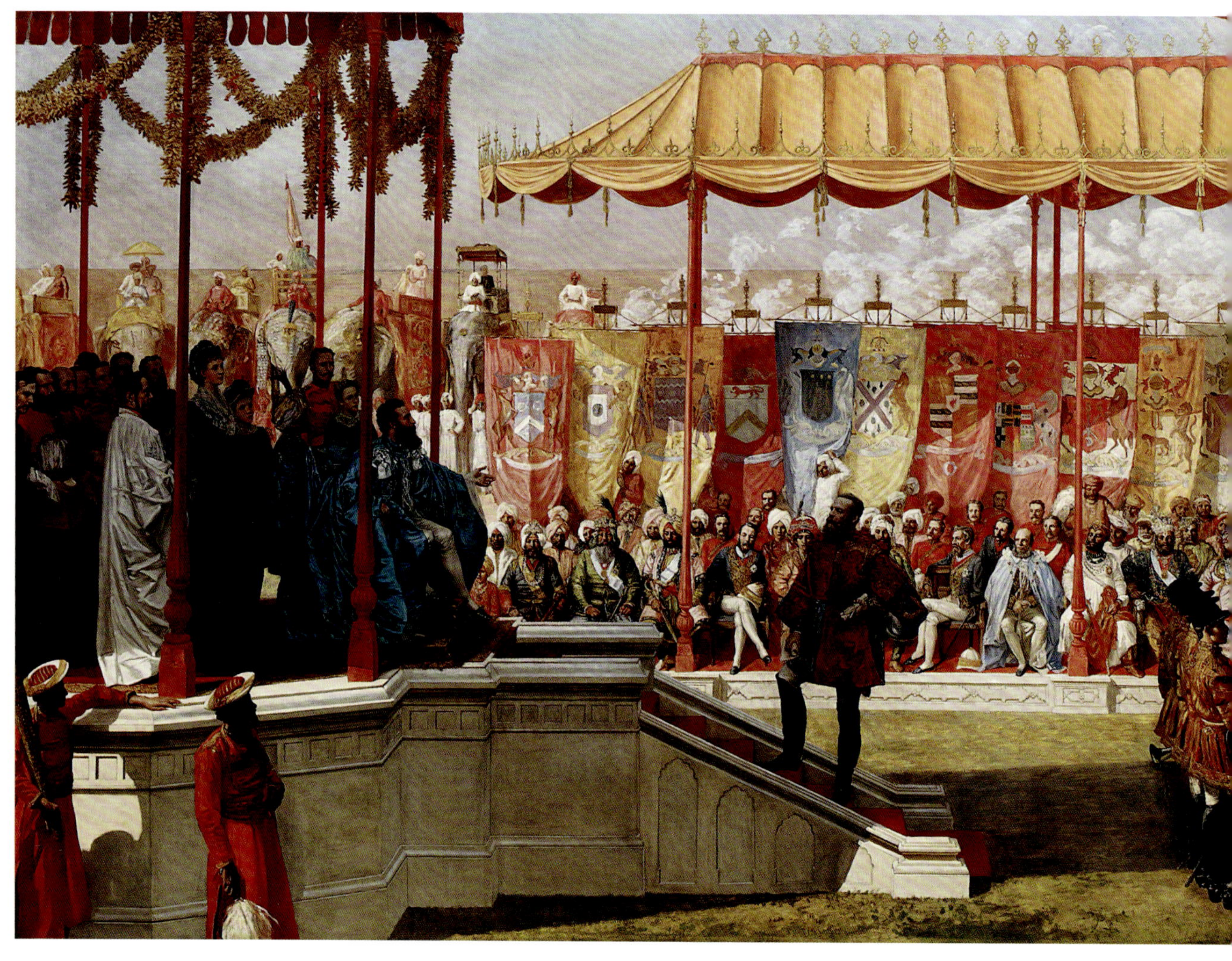

85 Val Prinsep, *The Imperial Assemblage held at Delhi, 1 January 1877*, 1880. Oil on canvas, 3 × 7.2 m (10 × 27 ft). Royal Collection © Her Majesty Queen Elizabeth II, RCIN 407181

American critic, who mused on whether the garishness of the artist's painting was actually a form of Indian retribution against the British for the subcontinent being coerced into financing the production of this work as a 'gift' for the new empress. 'Is it possible', asked the *New York Times*, 'that the inhabitants of India resented this political move, and have begun their stealthy revenge upon England's Queen by undermining her health with this terrible picture?'[6] The political antagonisms of the Raj were thus posited, albeit jestingly, as the cause of an injurious visual disharmony in Prinsep's work.

Droll criticism aside, there was a sense in contemporary British aesthetic discourse that the (dis)unity of a polity could be expressed through the formal properties of the arts. In her book on Victorian political imagery, Janice Carlisle has shown how political discourse was

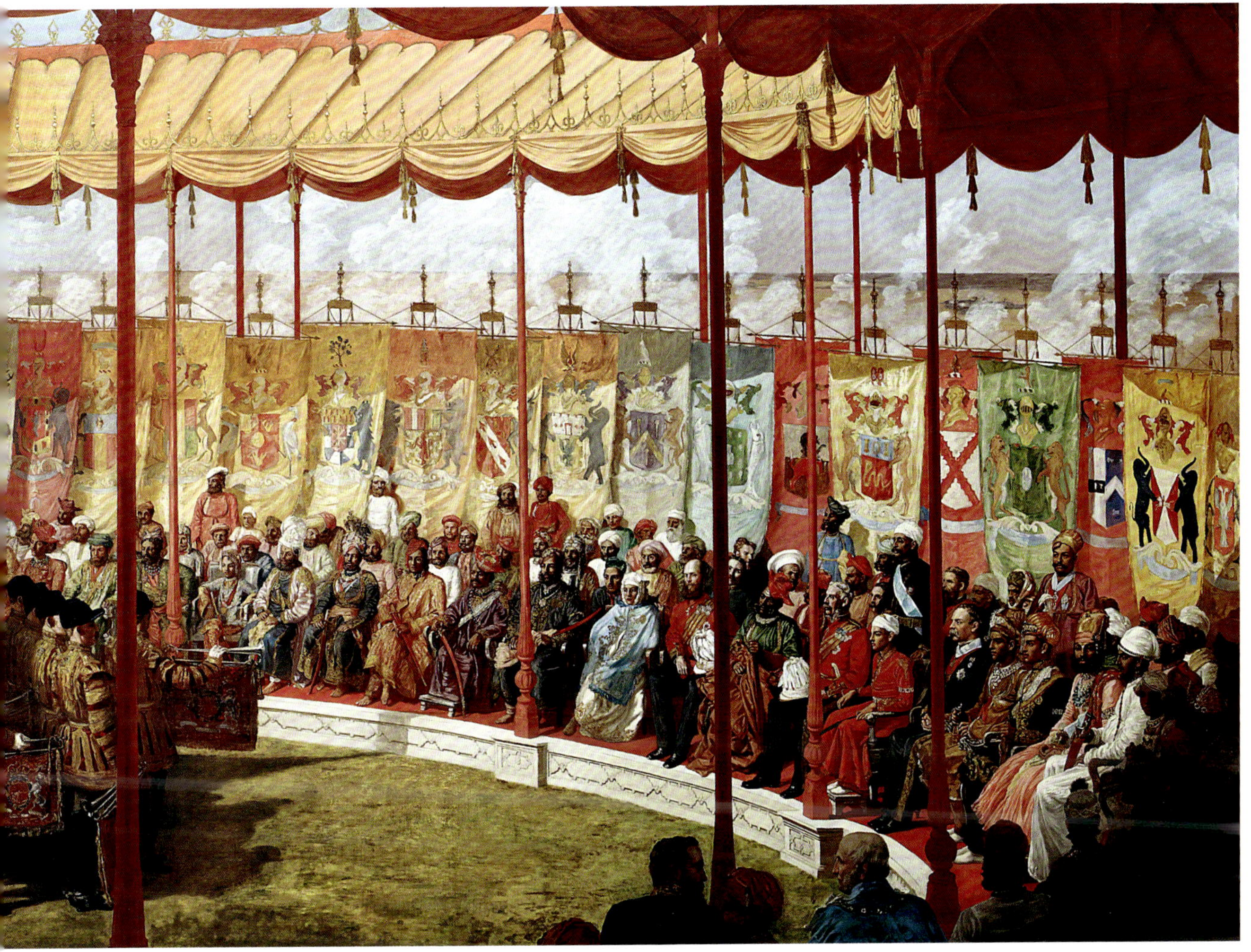

often influenced by aesthetic concepts[7] and that, for famous art critics like John Ruskin, aesthetic properties were imbued with political resonances, with composition being 'an exhibition, in order of the notes, or colours, or forms, of the advantage of perfect fellowship, discipline, and contentment.'[8] It follows, then, that compositional disorder could imply political disorder, and I suggest that the disorientating colour scheme of Prinsep's 'kaleidoscopic combinations' should indeed be read in such terms.[9] The painting's unwieldy grouping of ruling-class figures represented a wider, entangled set of political and aesthetic problematics in British India. It inadvertently signalled the acute antagonisms inherent in the aestheticised power structures of the late Victorian Raj, gesturing towards the very social fissures that the elaborately controlled spectacle of the Imperial Assemblage had sought to overlay.

The 38 Indian states are inscribed on the frame (clockwise from top left): Rajpootana, Tonk, Kerowlee, Jhallawur, Dholepore, Ulwur, Bhurtpore, Kisengurh, Boondee, Jodhpore, Jeypore, Oudeypore, Tanjore, Bombay, Bengal, Bewal, Bopal, Dorgha Dhar, Duwitta, Bumptur, Rutlum, Jowrah, Chirkaree, Puwna, Chuwterpor, Ajeyurh, Central India, Jkend, Bhawulpore, Indore, Gwalior, Cashmere, Hyderabad, Baroda, Mysore, Rampore, Nabha Sikh.

Numerous historians have pointed to the Imperial Assemblage as the expression of a new form of imperial sovereignty that was 'ornamentalist,' 'ritualised' and 'participatory' in its method of rule.[10] The 1877 event was the first of three grand 'durbars' that married aspects of Mughal Indian ceremony with the visual themes of the High Victorian medieval revival, and were held in Delhi to formalise the coronations of successive British monarchs as emperors or empresses of India, the last two of which took place in 1903 for Edward VII and in 1911 for George V. These events embodied the imperial structure that had emerged in the aftermath of the 1857 Uprising, when power in India had officially been transferred from the East India Company to the British Crown and Indian royals were promised security from future conquest in return for recognising the 'paramountcy' of the British Raj. One of numerous 'invented traditions' of the Victorian era, the post-1857 imperial framework saw the establishment not only of an honours system, the Order of the Star of India, but also of elaborate feudal-inspired protocols, whereby maharajas were accorded between nine and twenty-one gun salutes according to their prestige in the eyes of the British.[11] The Bengal civil servant Robert Taylor was even charged with designing medieval-style coats of arms for the Indian 'princely' states, thus binding a congeries of kingdoms together with shared forms of invented imagery.[12]

The legitimacy of the Raj was increasingly tied to the success of this carefully managed image-regime. While casting an eye back to feudal forms of statecraft, the spectacles of 1877, 1903 and 1911 also anticipated, writes Julie Codell, 'the mass political rallies of European totalitarianism and the aestheticisation of politics in the modern world.'[13] But such a visual turn was not without problems for the British. A recent collection of essays about the role played by photography in these imperial durbars has uncovered myriad elements of Indian resistance or ideological tension in the photographic archive; broadly, the essays locate the intersections between these events and a rising tide of anti-colonial feeling, tracing a narrative in which maharajas symbolically 'decolonised' their bodies.[14] The 1877 Assemblage has thus been cast in relative terms as less visually problematic for the British because less troubled by Indian resistance than the subsequent durbars (perhaps partly because of this it receives by far the least attention in the book). Prinsep's work is mentioned only in passing and yet, as I shall argue, it is precisely here that the aesthetic fabric of the post-1857 regime of spectacle was first seen to fray.

Born in Calcutta, Prinsep had a family history on the subcontinent but his training and career took place for the most part in Europe, seeing him active in Pre-Raphaelitism and the Holland Park Circle (even if he was always a peripheral figure within such groups).[15] The oil portrait studies, immense history painting and published account that Prinsep produced as a result of his year in India have gone virtually unstudied but they represent one of the most expansive and prestigious commissions ever issued to a painter by the colonial government.[16] This chapter first explores the context for this commission, situating the painting in the matrix of artistic strategies that had historically been mobilised by the British to project an image of their Indian empire as a legitimate political construct undergirded by treaties and diplomatic ties as much as by unilateral conquest. It then examines Prinsep's encounters with Indian royals, theorising portrait sittings as zones of discrepant sovereignties in which coercive colonial demands clashed with the countervailing agency of maharajas, whose qualified acquiescence to imperial diktat is attested by Prinsep's many abandoned canvases.

The argument can be rehearsed as follows. When, at the Royal Academy Exhibition in 1880, Prinsep's motley assembly of British and Indian figures staged their unruly visual assault on the eyes of critics, an uncomfortable political point was made. The aesthetic discord of the painting flew in the face of the visual grammar that had been established in Victorian Britain to picture stable forms of governance. And with imperial power in India increasingly exercised in, and legible through, the logic of the spectacle – whereby the social relationships of the Raj were mediated by a carefully orchestrated regime of images, a visual turn that can be traced back to the Anglo-Indian ruptures of the Uprising – aesthetic turbulence of this sort was no small matter. In fact, the representational difficulties that beset Prinsep in his attempt to situate diverse Indian rulers comprehensibly in an overarching framework of imperial sovereignty registered a wider British inability to envision (and perhaps even administer) their multiracial empire as a viable political entity.

DIPLOMATIC PORTRAITURE

Two men greet one another with gestures of civility and in doing so symbolise a historical shift in power relations before a diverse crowd of onlookers, whose witnessing works to ratify the declaration of sovereignty. These are the broad themes of Prinsep's luminous and imposing canvas, now displayed in the State Apartments at St James's Palace in London, but the basic contours of this diplomatic mise-en-scène were laid down in the eighteenth-century history paintings that chronicled the East India Company's rise to regional dominance: Benjamin Wilson's *Mir Jafar and his Son Miran delivering the Treaty of 1757 to William Watts* (1758), Francis Hayman's *Robert Clive and Mir Jafar after the Battle of Plassey* (*c.*1760; see fig. 38), Benjamin West's *Shah 'Alam conveying the Grant of the Diwani to Lord Clive* (1774; see fig. 39) and Mather Brown's *The Delivery of the Definitive Treaty by the Hostage Princes* (1794; see fig. 40). Like the art of diplomacy examined earlier in the book, Prinsep's scheme indulged in a kind of diplomatic fetishism that sublimated colonialism's violence into tropes of genteel resolution.

Significantly, though, Prinsep's scene departs from its eighteenth-century progenitors in that it removes Indian participation from the central action: all maharajas are consigned to the role of passive spectators of British supremacy here. However, while passive acceptance of British power reigns at the level of representational content, the very existence of Prinsep's populous scene was intended by the British to symbolise a more active Indian embrace of Victoria's imperial sovereignty. Unlike previous history paintings of colonial events, this one was ostensibly a gift to the queen from the Indian subjects whose portraits populate the background of the image.

The names of the thirty-eight Indian states that 'subscribed' to the painting are listed on the frame. While these included both British – and Indian-run territories, the viceroy had engineered the commission to appear as if it was specifically the Indian rulers who had spontaneously proposed it as a commemorative offering.[17] Before the Assemblage in Delhi, a circular had been sent round to Indian royalty inviting subscriptions to the painting and, while the response appears to have been muted at best,[18] Lytton nevertheless wrote to the queen claiming that her subjects were very anxious to present her with 'a pictorial record' depicting the 'utmost pomp and magnificence' of the event.[19] The Imperial Assemblage was Lytton's brainchild and he was therefore especially concerned that his turn to pomp ran smoothly and that it was perceived as having a harmonising effect on official Anglo-Indian relations. Since the maharajas involved in the Assemblage were due to receive a medallion engraved with Victoria's image during the ceremony itself, the proposed group portrait functioned to imbue the proceedings with a diplomatic sense of reciprocity.

Such coercive artistic exchange was not new. Art – in particular portraiture – had been active in episodes of diplomacy almost from the inception of Anglo-Indian relations. The sixteenth-century Mughal emperor Akbar and his successor Jahangir had both received British envoys who used artworks as gifts.[20] In the 1760s the British governor of Madras had arranged for George III to gift a portrait of himself to the Nawab of Arcot, Muhammad Ali, who in turn sent back his own portrait by Tilly Kettle (1735–1786), an expatriate English artist.[21] In a series of articles on early colonial portraiture, Natasha Eaton has described how the first Governor-General of Bengal, Warren Hastings, tried to conventionalise this practice of exchange in the 1770s and 80s, frequently gifting his own portrait and aggressively pressing European painters on Indian rulers (who, by and large, otherwise showed no enthusiasm for patronising Western art).[22]

Those maharajas who were required to receive ceremoniously and then reluctantly gift portraits during the Imperial Assemblage were partaking in a calculated act of cultural appropriation. The Mughal-derived durbar ceremony which the Imperial Assemblage adapted for British purposes was a ritual of 'incorporation' in which the person being admitted into the presence of the ruler was required to offer *nazar* (gold coins) and/or *peshkash* (valuables) in return for *khilats* (specific kinds of clothes that could also include other signifiers of authority such as animals or jewels). Offering *nazar* or *peshkash* represented an acknowledgement that the ruler was a source of wealth and wellbeing; receiving *khilat* symbolised the incorporation of the recipient into the body of the Indian sovereign and thus into the body politic.[23] Yet, in the eighteenth century, it had been the economic value of *nazar, peshkash* and *khilat* that loomed large in the British mind, with such rituals of symbolic exchange being seen merely as opportunities for bribery and extortion.[24] By inserting the portrait into this Indian custom, the British were attempting to ensure fiscal probity. For Hastings – a man whose ruthless imperial instincts were intertwined with a scholarly love of Indian culture – the portrait was the ideal object to substitute for potentially corrupting items such as coins and jewels because, according to Akbar's chronicle the *Ain-i-Akbari,* portraits were already enmeshed in the performance of Indian sovereignty and thus capable of bearing the symbolic import necessary for Indian courtly ritual.[25]

The Indian rulers on whom the portrait-gift was first imposed remained conspicuously hostile to the new hybrid practice. On occasion, the portraits that were received were given away contemptuously and even those that were kept were sometimes hung upside down and allowed to rot.[26] Acts of subversion such as this are unsurprising when one considers the scale of the usurpation that the portrait-gift had attempted to effect. The entire Mughal framework of reciprocity was being dismantled, with the East India Company expecting Indian rulers to patronise European portraitists only then to gift the resulting work back to the Company. Increasingly, Indian rulers would not even receive a portrait in return. A Mughal ritual of exchange had been transformed into a sort of tribute offered to the colonial British – an asymmetry that was revived in earnest for the image-based diplomacy of the 1877 Imperial Assemblage.[27]

By the Victorian period, however, there is evidence to suggest that portrait exchange had also gained currency in independent networks of South Asian kingship. During his time in India following the Uprising, William Simpson accompanied Viceroy Canning on a tour of the subcontinent that was aimed at consolidating British power through a series of durbars. As a correspondent for the *Illustrated London News*, Simpson was of particular use to the viceroy, who was keen that the diplomatic ceremonies being staged in India would be seen in the pages of that newspaper, presumably to redefine the narrative of British rule following two years in which journalistic accounts had been dominated by violent scenes from the recent rebellion. Palliative diplomatic spectacle was the official order of the day.

According to Simpson, the Indian royals who were visited by the viceroy kept artists in their employ whose 'principal work is to take portraits, often doing their master's portrait to send to other rajahs, and doing rajahs and chiefs for their employer's collection.' Thus when in 1860 the Maharajah of Kashmir, Ranbir Singh, was asked by Canning to sit for a portrait with Simpson during one of the viceregal durbars that would soon grace the pages of the *Illustrated London News* (fig. 86), the ruler was able to ambush the British with a reciprocal request, suddenly admitting that he had his own artist in the durbar tent 'enduring under very strange conditions' to obtain a likeness of the viceroy: he was 'concealed ... under a kind of sofa, which had been placed as nearly opposite Lord Canning's seat as it was possible.'[28] This act of diplomatic subterfuge functioned to incorporate an unwitting viceroy into an image-regime that was organised under the (covert) regal agency of the maharaja; at the same time, it situated in an economy of reciprocal exchange any portrait that the colonial artist Simpson might produce.

The scene of Simpson's that ended up in the *Illustrated London News* did not admit this reciprocity but showed the viceroy receiving a Kashmiri shawl from Singh in an act of what the article termed 'tribute' (just one item among the horses, tents, beds, arms and furs that were reportedly offered to Canning by the maharaja).[29] Yet a certain equality of status was nevertheless enforced in the encounter itself, even if it was denied in the official visual documentation. Essentially, the maharaja's revelation of his hidden portraitist also served to reveal his awareness that the portrait being requested by the British viceroy was not simply innocent; rather, it was a manoeuvre that was enmeshed in the power plays, variously clandestine and conspicuous, of diplomacy. In the spectacular mode of imperial governance that had come to hold sway in the aftermath of the Uprising's violence, control over images was an important function of sovereignty – and the maharaja knew it.

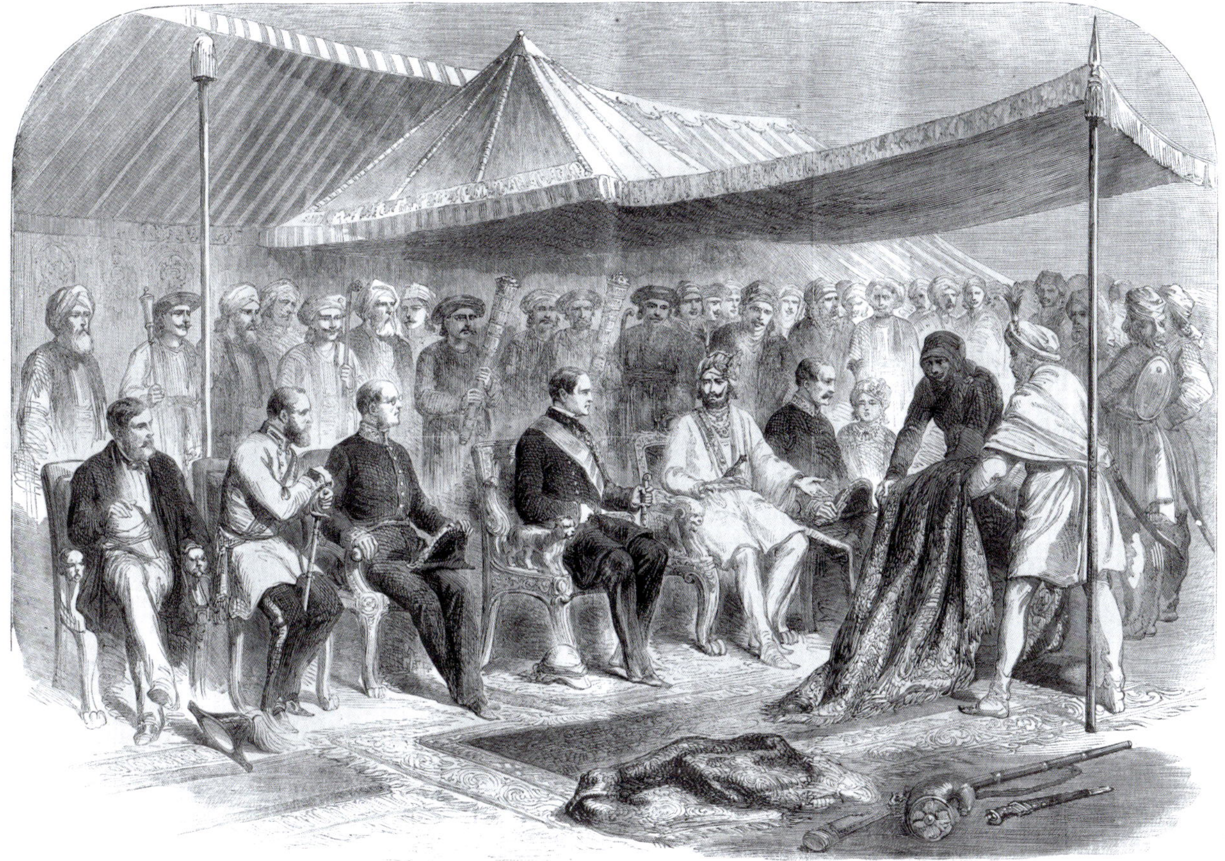

86 William Simpson, 'Lord Canning's return visit to the Maharaja of Cashmere', *Illustrated London News*, 14 July 1860. Wood engraving. © Mary Evans Picture Library

It is against this historical backdrop of overlapping British and South Asian circuits of portrait production and exchange that Prinsep's *The Imperial Assemblage held at Delhi* should be viewed. The model of image-based diplomacy for which Prinsep was made an ambassador would not have appeared altogether new to Indian rulers at the 1877 Imperial Assemblage but its particular valences were open to change depending on how those rulers responded to the demands of the portrait sitting. At least some of the Indian rulers sought to redefine the significance of the imperial proceedings, orchestrating the processes of image production in such a way as to highlight their countervailing sovereign agency.

CAPS IN THE PAINT

Prinsep used watercolour to sketch some of the less powerful maharajas in India but in the months after the coronation durbar the majority of Indian rulers sat for full-length oil portraits with the artist in their own kingdoms. All these portraits are of similar dimensions (about 100 by 80

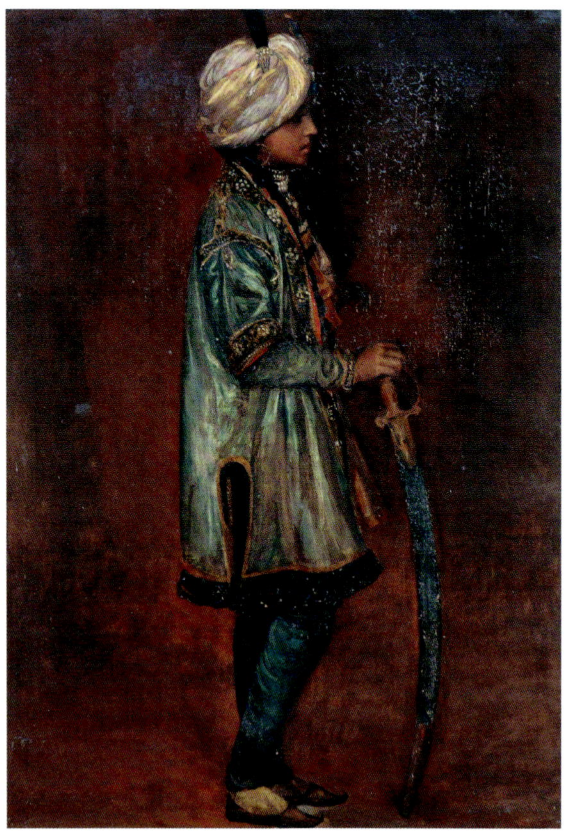

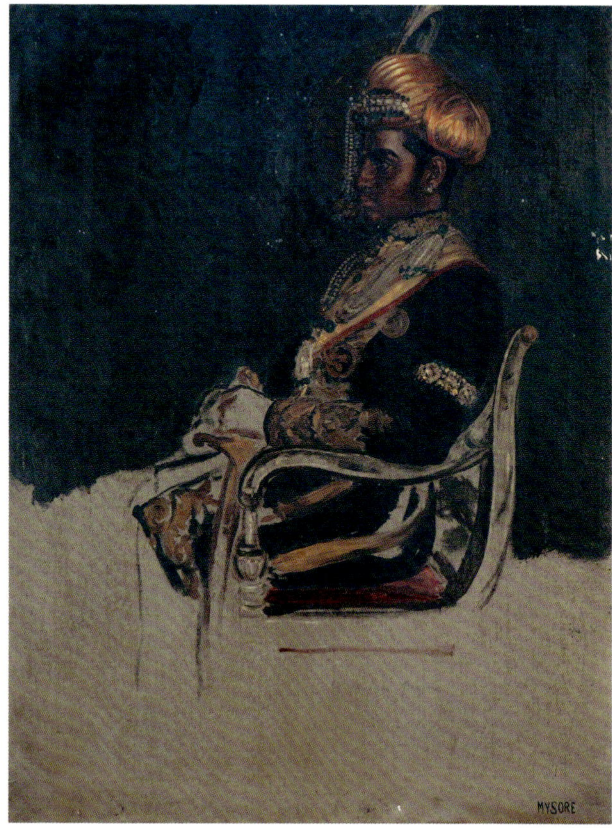

87 Val Prinsep, *Son of the Maharaja of Kashmir*, 1877. Oil on canvas, 99 × 71.1 cm. Victoria Memorial Museum, Kolkata, R2785

88 Val Prinsep, *Maharaja of Mysore*, 1877. Oil on canvas, 90.2 × 70.8 cm. Victoria Memorial Museum, Kolkata, R2779

centimetres, 39 by 31 inches) and are now held in the Victoria Memorial Museum, Kolkata, having been acquired from the Governing Committee of the Bengal Club in February 1936.[30] Each figure is shown seated, with the exception of the young son of the Maharaja of Kashmir (fig. 87), who stands in profile and can be seen as such behind Lytton in *The Imperial Assemblage held at Delhi*. In various states of incompletion, these are unloved canvases in which blank canvas (fig. 88), provisional outlines over undercoating (fig. 89) and cracked and fading paint (fig. 90) attest to a history of tensions, indifference and neglect.

How should we think about such gaps in the paint? It is not sufficient to attribute the abandoned nature of these works to the fact that they were executed as studies for a larger, prioritised history painting. For one thing, Prinsep's portrait of the Maharana of Oodeypore (Udaipur), Sajjan Singh (fig. 91), goes to the trouble of painting a wallpaper-patterned background that would have been of no use to *The Imperial Assemblage held at Delhi*, implying that the artist at one point had hopes of completing stand-alone representations of these figures. But more than this, the level of finish in the studies does not relate neatly to the prominence of the Indian rulers in the final scene. In the portrait of the young Rana of Dholpur, Nihal Singh (fig. 92), for example, the shades of cream, highlights of white and strips of gold on his bejewelled clothes have been treated with considerable painterly attention and care in comparison to the flat-toned undercoating on the Maharaja of Mysore, Chamaraja Wodeyar IX. Yet in Prinsep's finished scene it is this (significantly more politically powerful) figure whose costume is most conspicuous, while the former fades into the shadows, blocked anyway by the heads of other rulers (fig. 93).

One thing to which the gaps in the paint of these portraits attest is the consistently beleaguered conditions in which Prinsep found himself operating in India. In the painter's illustrated narrative of his travels, *Imperial India: An Artist's Journals, Illustrated by Numerous Sketches Taken at the Courts of the Principal Chiefs in India* (1879), an affected tone of bonhomie frequently gives way to moments of anger and anxiety in his attempts to deal with native royalty. He was on the front line of the British campaign to convey India's subordination: it was often left to him to deliver the message that the portrait sittings for which maharajas were paying were a 'gift' to Victoria and not something of which the rulers

89 Val Prinsep, *Sir Salar Jung*, 1877. Oil on canvas, 108.2 × 84.8 cm. Victoria Memorial Museum, Kolkata, R2776

90 Val Prinsep, *H.H. Raja Dewas*, 1877. Oil on canvas, 91.2 × 70.8 cm. Victoria Memorial Museum, Kolkata, R2777

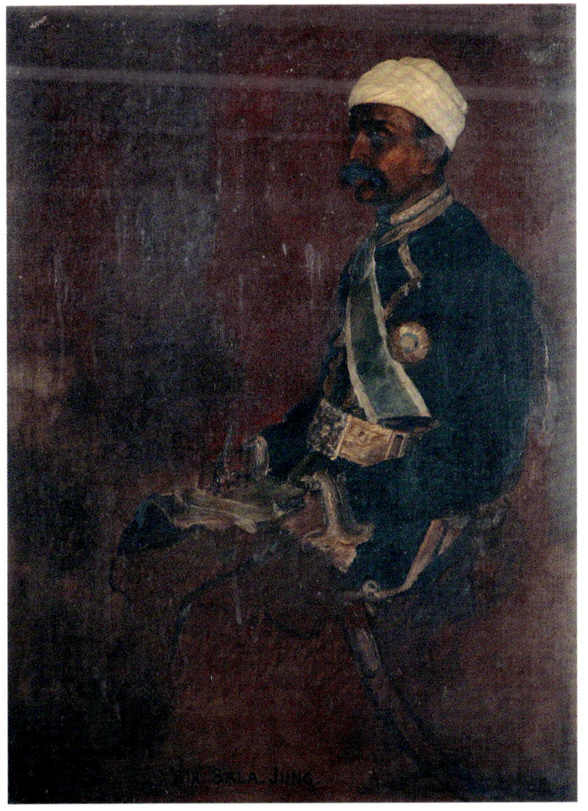

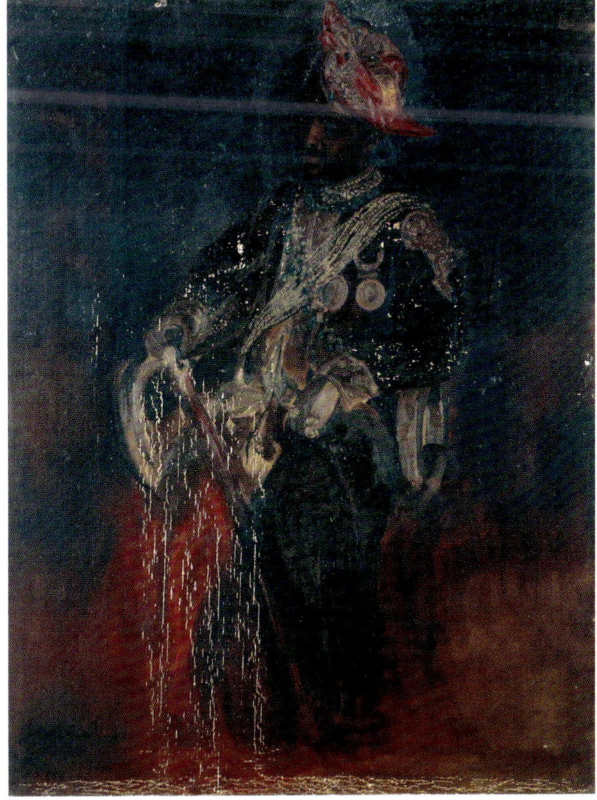

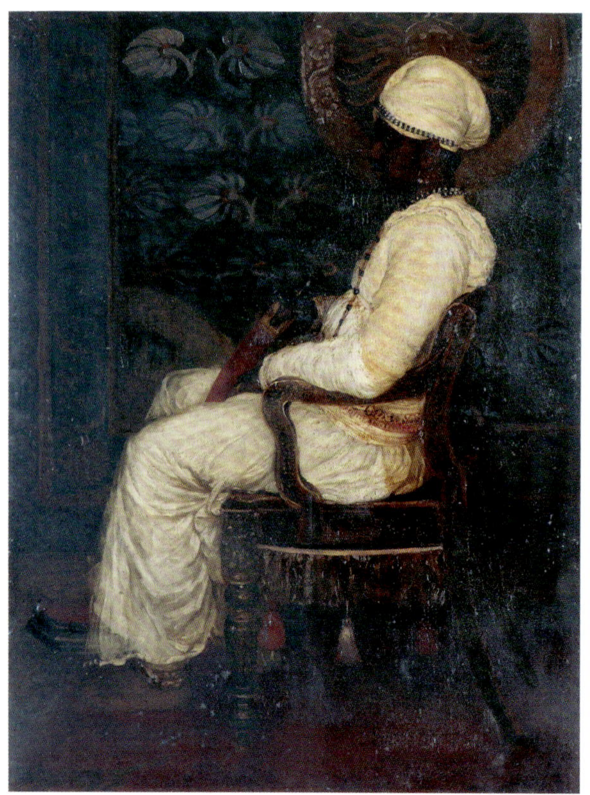

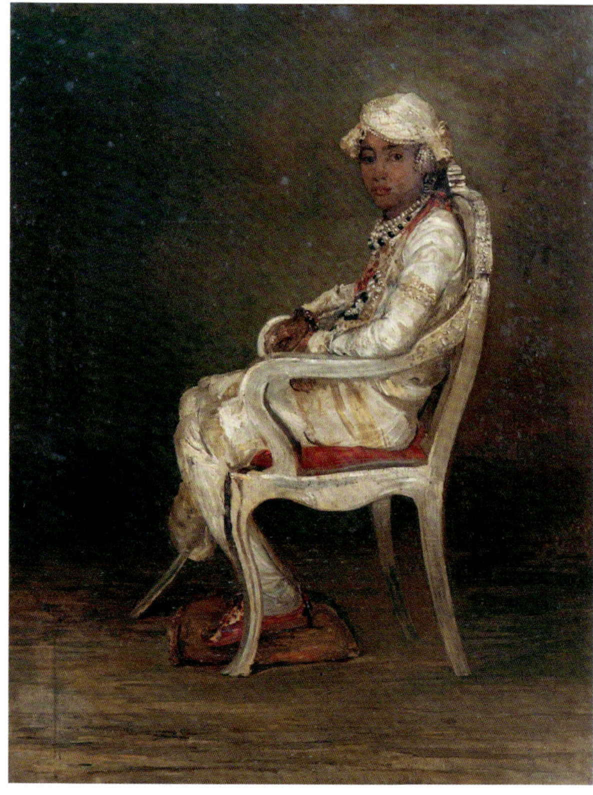

91 Val Prinsep, *Maharana of Oodeypore*, 1877. Oil on canvas, 104 × 84 cm. Victoria Memorial Museum, Kolkata, R2788

92 Val Prinsep, *Rana of Dholpur*, 1877. Oil on canvas, 90.2 × 70.8 cm. Victoria Memorial Museum, Kolkata, R2779

themselves could one day hope to see the results. Sittings were consequently fraught and fluid zones in which the dynamic of Anglo-Indian relations was renegotiated and re-performed. The artist was interrogated by subjects such as the Maharaja of Bhurtpore, who 'bothered me a great deal to know what the [colonial] Government are going to give him for sitting, whether he is to have a copy (great Heavens!) of the picture, or an engraving.' It is 'rather hard', Prinsep complained, 'that I should have to explain to them that they get nothing for their money.'[31]

It was not only the maharajas whose expectations of treatment were readjusted in these sittings. A key motif of Prinsep's narrative is his sense of pride in his status as an artist coming into conflict with the severely curtailed conditions under which Indian royals permitted him to operate. Lytton had initially thought that Prinsep could gather all the necessary portraits in the brief time that everyone was on formally British-run territory in Delhi for the Assemblage. Yet, while a number of maharajas – in particular those from the more remote or inaccessible regions of the subcontinent – were sketched or painted by Prinsep in a flurry of activity in those few days, the sheer number of sitters meant that the artist's work sprawled beyond both the durbar and the boundaries of explicitly colonial terrain. So, from the perspective of the Indian royals in whose kingdoms Prinsep found himself over the course of the following year, the portrait sitting functioned as a sort of reinscription of their subordinate status vis-à-vis an imperial suzerain. And while Prinsep might have dismissed as 'children' the rulers who viewed him with 'suspicion' on the basis of his role as an 'accredited painter to the Government', his own hunting-based analogies cast his practice as a site of antagonism. His mission was 'to track the rajah to his lair, and there "fix" him', while his first sitter was described as his 'first victim'.[32]

Still, Prinsep might play the predator but his reliance on the hospitality and cooperation of Indian rulers opened up a space for maharajas to use portrait sittings to assert countervailing narratives of native sovereignty, taking advantage of the relative autonomy they enjoyed in their own kingdoms to complicate attempts to take their likeness. Given Prinsep's rather dim and patronising view of the Indian character, it is unsurprising that maharajas appear to have gone out of their way to thwart the artist. Following the sittings, Prinsep was repeatedly required to put touches on his portraits in cramped spaces 'singularly unfit for painting-rooms' ('what room in India is suitable for a studio?' bemoaned the beleaguered artist) and was sometimes even left with nothing other than his own hot travelling tent, miles from where he was having his sittings ('painting in a tent in this climate with a shining and blazing sun is next to impossible').[33] The artist's woeful published narrative of his troubles can in some respects be seen as pre-empting criticism of his final painting by pointing to such difficult conditions of production.

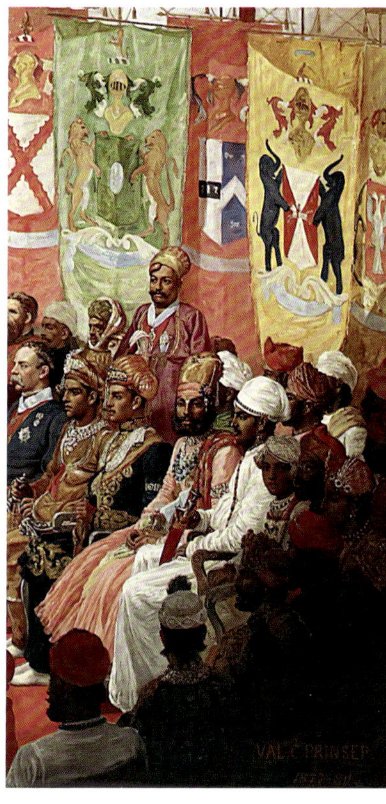

93 Val Prinsep, *The Imperial Assemblage held at Delhi*, 1880 (detail of fig. 85).

This all must have been particularly galling for a painter such as Prinsep, whose investment in the notion of the studio as a privileged environment over which he held authorial sway was demonstrated by his inclusion in Frank Dudman's series of photographs of artists in their studios in the 1880s (fig. 94). Here, he sits authoritatively in the centre of a capacious and sumptuous room filled with dozens of paintings, his gaze fixed on the viewer and his palette and brushes held in prominent view. Ironically, the artist had commissioned the luxurious room in which we see him here immediately prior to travelling to the decidedly less propitious spaces of India, having agreed to pay the architect Philip Webb up to £850 to make the necessary alterations to his house.[34]

Yet Prinsep's authorial privilege was undermined in India even before the rulers consigned him to insulting studio environments. The artist tended not to find willing sitters and had to negotiate continuously with the hostility or indifference of maharajas towards the mere prospect of a portrait sitting with him. In a typical lamentation, Prinsep complained that 'the Rajah is late again, later than ever ... Confound all Rajahs! – Ah!

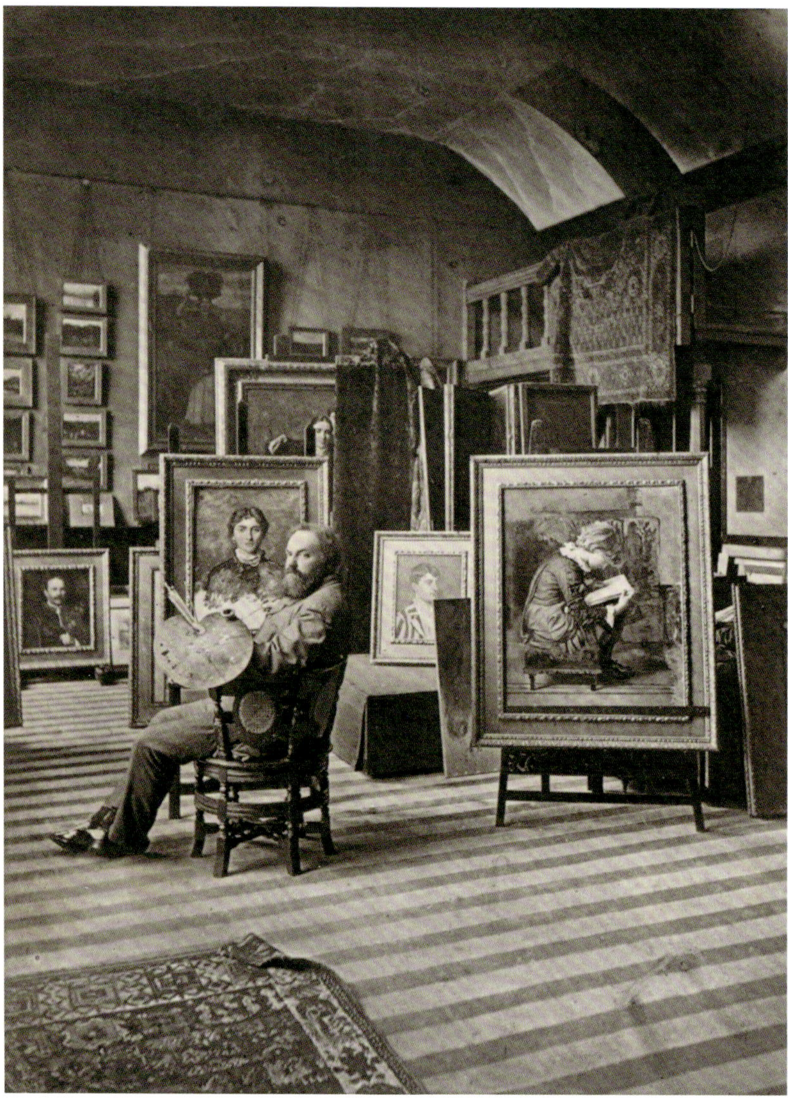

94 Frank Dudman, *Val Prinsep* ARA, 1883. Photogravure. © National Portrait Gallery, London, NPG Ax27817

here he comes! I must smile and be happy, with black rage at my heart.' On one occasion, the artist was kept waiting for days for a sitting that was ultimately cancelled altogether. Prinsep interpreted such tardiness through his preconceived and racist notions of Indian ineptitude, claiming that the rulers had 'no more idea of time than sitting hens'.[35] But it is interesting to note that a common motif of Mughal paintings of royalty had once been an hourglass indicating control of time and thus, while Prinsep's European aesthetic conventions meant that signifiers of this sort were unavailable to the maharajas in their portraits, the temporal mastery of an Indian sovereign could nonetheless be asserted through calculated belatedness in regards to the portrait sittings.[36]

Gaps in the paint of Prinsep's portraits therefore indexed fissures in Anglo-Indian relations. The state of finish was inextricably tied up with the difficulties that assailed Prinsep in India, with rulers hampering the portrait sitting in order to inscribe the colonial artist's practice with a sense of Indian independence. As a rule, then, the most incomplete portraits stand as testament to the assertion of a disruptive Indian sovereign agency. Prinsep's least finished painting was of his 'worst sitter', the Maharaja of Gwalior, Jayajirao Scindia (fig. 95), who also happened to be one of the most powerful. Scindia had sided with the British during the Uprising and by all accounts seemed more or less content with his situation under British rule; yet his deference had its limits. As Prinsep reported after the Imperial Assemblage, '[Scindia] had behaved very

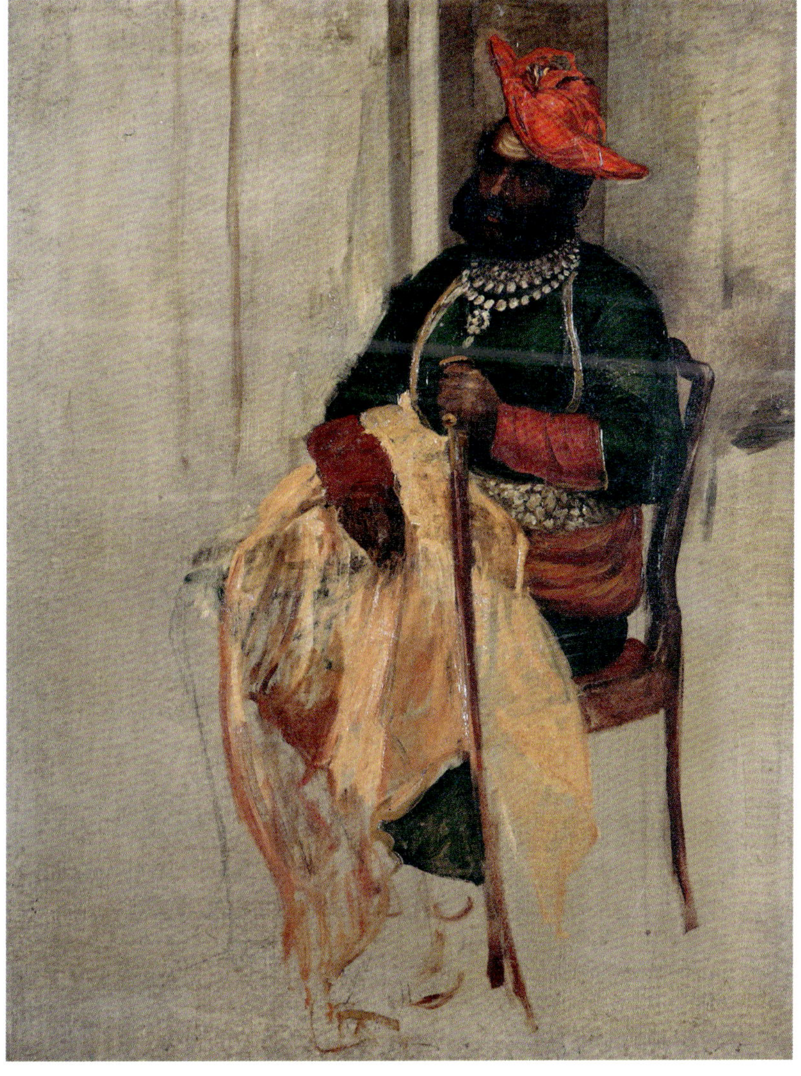

95 Val Prinsep, *Maharaja of Scindia* (the Maharaja of Gwalior, Jayajirao Scindia), 1877. Oil on canvas, 104 × 84 cm. Victoria Memorial Museum, Kolkata, R2783

badly the day before to the Viceroy, who made him Chancellor of the Empire, an English general, and gave him the title of Sword of the Empire, and twenty-one guns [in salute]; for all which Master Sindia forgot to say "thank you".'[37] Scindia's interaction with the British was therefore layered: on the one hand, he was a highly decorated model of militarily useful 'loyalty' but on the other, he rejected the sort of etiquette of respect that the British craved.

Such a rejection was made particularly manifest during Scindia's dealings with Prinsep, which were used by the maharaja to recuperate a sense of his autonomy while going along minimally with British demands. In Delhi during the Assemblage, Prinsep had had an appointment for a sitting with Scindia but the maharaja never turned up. On another occasion, when the artist did manage to secure a sitting, Scindia left after only fifteen minutes, 'whereupon he invited me to Gwalior; and I shall have to go, bad luck to it!' In Gwalior, though, the maharaja moved constantly during Prinsep's attempts to paint him and said explicitly that if the British resident Sir Henry Daly had not personally asked him to do so, he 'wouldn't sit at all ... after all what is the use? I don't get anything by it.'[38] The artist's practice was thus caught between the imperial sovereignty of the resident and the native sovereignty of the maharaja, with the portrait sitting becoming a stage for the latter's ambivalent display of deference to an imperial suzerain.

Prinsep was eventually compelled to end the session when it became 'impossible to keep him [Scindia] any longer'.[39] He even had difficulty acquiring a set of the recalcitrant maharaja's clothes from which to make independent studies (although the artist did ultimately manage to get some via Scindia's son).[40] This clash over the maharaja's clothing was especially fraught. Previous accounts of the visual culture of the coronation durbars of 1877, 1903 and 1911 have tended to locate anti-colonial feeling only in the portraits from the last two events, since by that time Indian assertions of independence were finding visual expression in the attire that sitters were choosing to wear for their (photographic) portraits. As scholars such as Bernard S. Cohn and Joanne Punzo Waghorne showed in depth, Indian dress was a heavily coded, historically resonant aspect of regional kingship.[41] Yet, while extravagantly bejewelled items had once been key to the self-fashioning of South Asian royalty, under the Raj these same items began to signify a lack of modernity to British eyes and they consequently functioned to shore up imperial claims to supremacy. The British expected traditional dress to be worn at events like the coronation durbars, with the ornate Indian body increasingly functioning as what Romita Ray terms 'an imperial masquerade, whose assertions of wealth and dynastic privileges flaunted the lineage and traditions of

Indian royals on the one hand, while cementing the currency of British imperial rule on the other.'[42]

Scindia ultimately fell prey to this sartorial snare. His constant thwarting of Prinsep's attempts to get a decent sitting obliged him in the end to 'put on his jewels' and sit instead for his amateur photographer son, Bulwant Singh.[43] A photograph was therefore offered to the artist in lieu of the physical presence of the maharaja. Notably, by relocating the sitting in the realm of photography, the maharaja arrogated an amount of control over the conditions of his pose, keeping the image-making event within the family, and mobilising a medium that was emblematic of the very modernity that the British sought to deny him by their stress on traditional dress. He was not the only ruler to do this: Prinsep was repeatedly given photographic portraits when he failed to capture likenesses during the sittings which were rationed to him, with the Maharaja of Jeypore (Jaipur) and the Maharaja of Dhar in particular making a point of their fluency with the practice.

The use of photography to explore alternative aesthetic trajectories for Indian royal identity is made tangible in a carte-de-visite portrait that Scindia had done in the 1870s by the popular colonial photography studio Bourne & Shepherd, in which the maharaja eschewed ornate attire in favour of simple white Maratha dress (fig. 96). This hints at the growing divergence between the maharajas and the British with regard to the fashioning of kingly authority. The imperial investment in seeing elaborate 'exotic' costumes on Indian rulers meant that these costumes only had to be visually denied to the British in order to start disrupting colonial assumptions of rule. Julie Codell has shown that maharajas accordingly 'decolonised their bodies' in the 1903 and 1911 durbars by 'wearing simpler, martial clothes ... and assuming masculine postures' in the official photographs.[44]

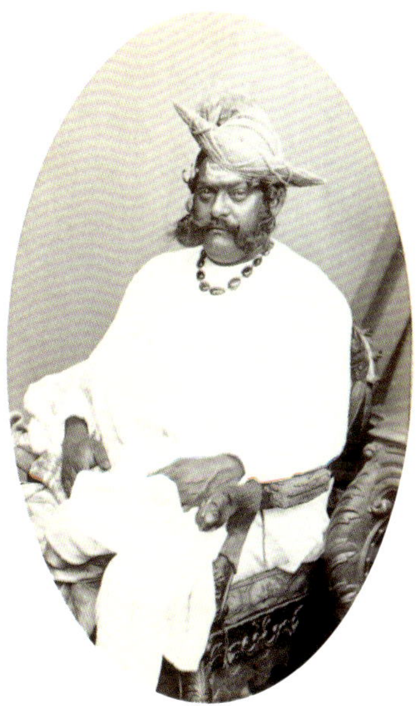

96 Bourne & Shepherd, *Maharaja of Gwalior*, *c.*1876. Albumen print, 10.3 × 6.3 cm. Alkazi Collection of Photography, New Delhi, 96.04.002 00016/1

Unlike these later rulers, Scindia did not disrupt the official imagery of the Assemblage with his plain attire. Still his reluctance to be painted on Prinsep's terms meant that a commission based on a crude British notion of the portrait as gift was reconstituted as a fluid image-making encounter in which an overarching framework of imperial suzerainty harboured the countervailing assertion of South Asian sovereignties. Prinsep felt insulted by Scindia, writing that he 'does not know what is due to an artist who has come a hundred miles for a sitting.' Yet the maharaja was obviously not unfamiliar with the procedure: the room in which the sitting occurred was adorned with both Indian and European-painted portraits of the ruler. Prinsep was unable to attribute Scindia's restless movement to ignorance of etiquette and was forced instead to appreciate it as an undercurrent of self-asserting agency in the wider framework of feudal subordination embodied by the ruler's acceptance of dressing up, sitting and gifting. As another maharaja later told the artist, 'It was not sitting Scindia found so unpleasant, it was being obliged to sit.'[45] The image-making event thus opened up a space for a resistant sovereign agency that is perhaps not immediately apparent at the level of representational content, legible only through the gaps in the surface of the paint – indices of imperial failure to properly mobilise Indian rulers for this exercise in imperial hegemony.

COMPOSING POWER

However hard Indian rulers like Scindia might have tried to hijack the significance of the portrait sittings, Prinsep was always going to have the last word. The high finish of the artist's *Imperial Assemblage* served to paint over those cracks in colonial relations that had been registered by the interstices of the individual portraits. Yet I want to suggest that something of these maharajas' potential unruliness did smuggle itself into the vast and ill-received rainbow-coloured canvas that Prinsep spent two years working on following his return to England in 1878. At the Royal Academy exhibition in 1880 there was a near-unanimous critical recoiling from a scene that functioned as 'an historical rememberancer' (sic) but which 'as a work of contemporary art ... has nothing to commend it.'[46] Yet there was also sympathy with Prinsep for having been dealt such a 'thankless task'.[47] It was noted that the 'tinselled ceremony' of the coronation durbar was itself 'a fiasco artistically', meaning that there was little scope for 'art-treatment'.[48] (Certainly, this was how Prinsep saw the matter. His reaction to the ceremony was unequivocal: 'Oh, horror! what have I to paint?'[49]) The voices of the art establishment, the *Art Journal* and *The Athenaeum*, were particularly sympathetic to Prinsep's plight. They offered the most (faint) praise – or at least the most tempered criticism – of what was a 'good picture in many respects', a critical sensitivity that was possibly due to Prinsep's personal popularity within establishment circles.[50]

Such was the size of Prinsep's painting that is difficult to find precedent for it. However, judging from the similarity of the figures in the bottom-left corner of the scene and those in Frederic Leighton's *The Syracusan Bride* (fig. 97), it seems that Prinsep had his neighbour and friend Leighton's work in mind – a work which was noted for its scale by critics when it was displayed in 1866 but was still only half the size of *The Imperial Assemblage*. Generally speaking, it was classical subject matter of the sort that Leighton's scene addressed that predominated in large paintings: another possible point of comparison for Prinsep's scene was Paolo Veronese's *The Family of Darius before Alexander* (fig. 98),

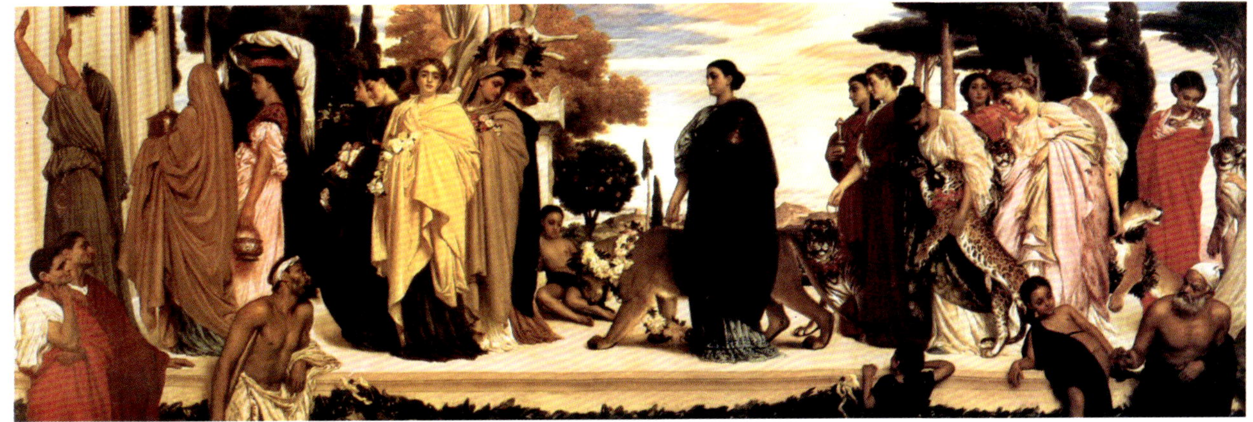

fifteen feet long, which had been bought for the National Gallery in London in 1857 (but, again, only about half the size of Prinsep's).[51] In terms of scale, then, Prinsep's scene laid claim to an illustrious classical pedigree for Britain's Raj. Yet if such connections were made, they were made silently; mostly the critics responded to the painting in terms of its role as a group portrait – an 'intractable multitude' of Indian rulers, military men, British governors, wives and daughters.[52] The notion that the congeries of figures did not make aesthetic sense permeated the reviews.

97 Frederic Leighton, *The Syracusan Bride*, 1866. Oil on canvas, 134.7 × 424.3 cm. Private collection. Wikimedia Commons

Recalling Ruskin's belief that good composition in the arts was bound up with 'the great laws of Divine government and human polity', it seems significant that numerous critics located the compositional failings of

98 Paolo Veronese, *The Family of Darius before Alexander*, c.1567. Oil on canvas, 236.2 × 474.9 cm. National Gallery, London, NG294

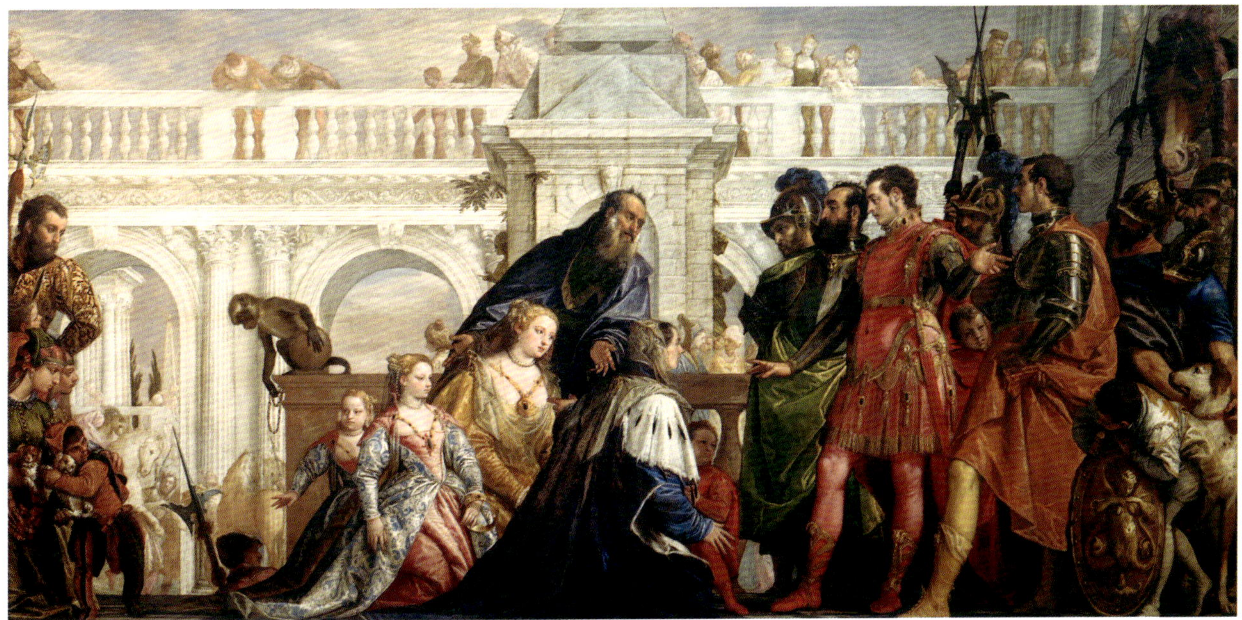

99 Bourne & Shepherd, *Lord Lytton, Viceroy and Governor-General of India, Grand Master of the Star of India*. Woodburytype print. Getty Open Content Program

Prinsep's scene precisely in the constitution of the Anglo-Indian polity that was represented at the Assemblage.[53] Critics believed that 'by marshalling the many-tinted actors in his drama Mr. Prinsep has been compelled by the immutable exigencies of etiquette and precedence to violate a good many laws and ordinances governing the juxtaposition of tones, the distribution of light and shade, and the symmetries of composition.'[54] The political makeup of the Raj and its expression at the coronation durbar were therefore viewed as visually problematic.

For the *Illustrated London News*, aesthetic failure was basically inevitable given the political constitution of the subject matter:

> how gaudy, under the Indian sun, *must* be this painted open-air pageant of rajahs, maharajahs, and British governors seated in one expansive semicircle (though not nearly so large as it in fact was), dressed in their gorgeous native or European costume, each backed by his banner given by the Queen, and each banner emblazoned with the grotesque and anachronistic heraldry of the British College of Arms.[55]

Such an attack on the heraldry (which was made specially for the Assemblage) appears in numerous reviews and meant that even Britain's attempt to render the 'intractable multitude' visually comprehensible as a political network bound together by shared forms of imagery is seen to offer nothing more than further convolution. In other words, the entire aesthetics of empire – from the clashing variety of luminous costumes expected of the maharajas, to the heraldic backdrops that gave feudal contours to imperial relations, and the artistic status of Prinsep's history painting – all of this was seen to jar or to falter.

In part, such critical recoiling from the aesthetics of *The Imperial Assemblage* can be read as a marker of the ambivalence with which the British approached ostentatious ceremony per se. Britain's self-perception as a Protestant country of ascetic values defined against the supposed lavish despotism of Catholicism and the Orient meant that there was a distinct sense of unease about the fanfare-and-trumpets form of imperialism that began to emerge in this period. Tracy Anderson's work on the late Victorian viceregal portrait has shown that representations of Lytton around the time of the Assemblage consequently imbued him with a 'dual body' on which the spectacular feudal mode of imperial rule existed in tension with more sober-minded civic ideals of progressive colonial governance. This tension registered sartorially in an interplay between (effete) ostentation and (manly) sobriety in colonial British dress. In commemorative photographs of Lytton such as Bourne & Shepherd's *Lord Lytton, Viceroy and Governor-General of India, Grand Master of the Star of India* (fig. 99), for instance, the ostentation of the attire is undercut by 'a sense of

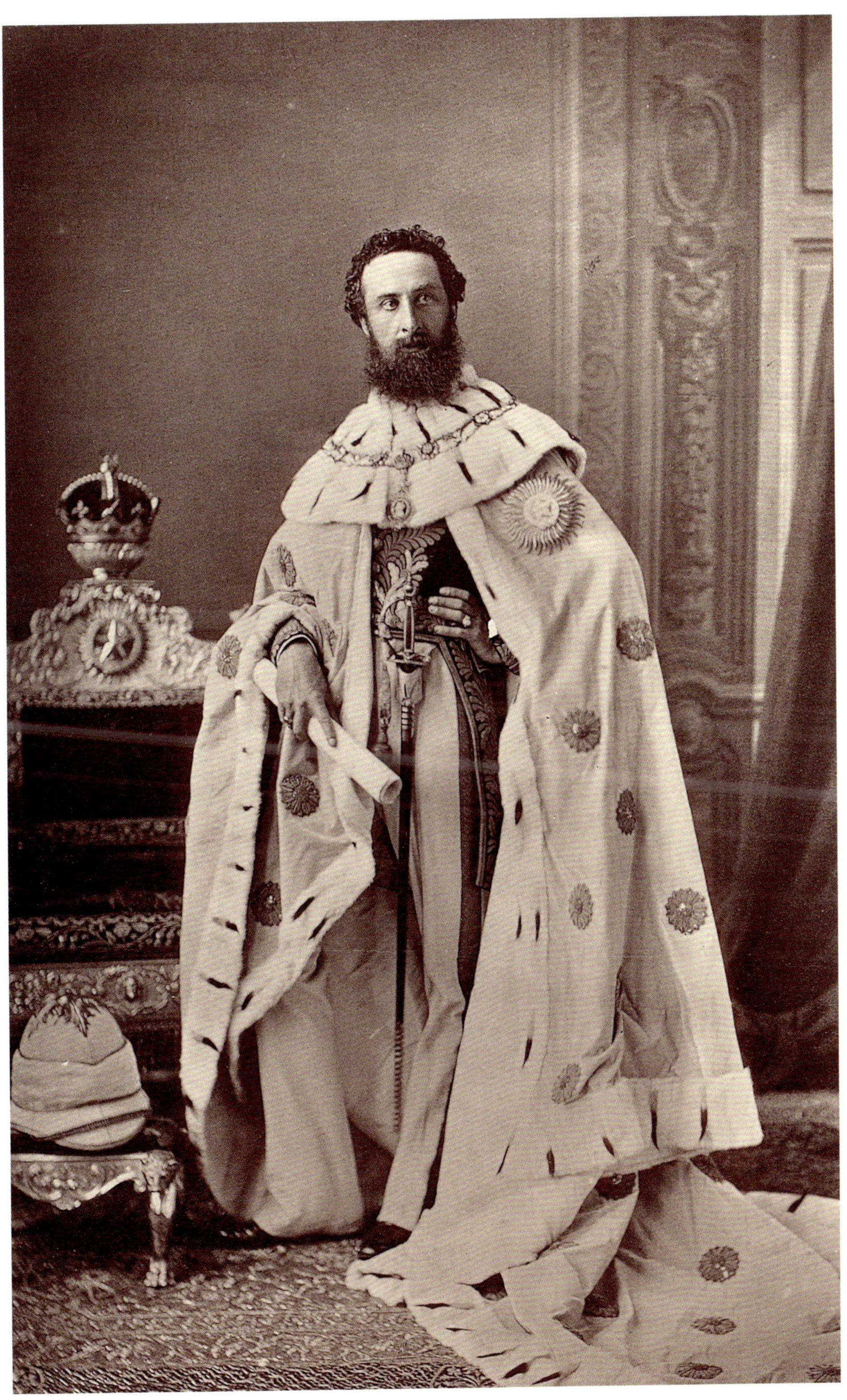

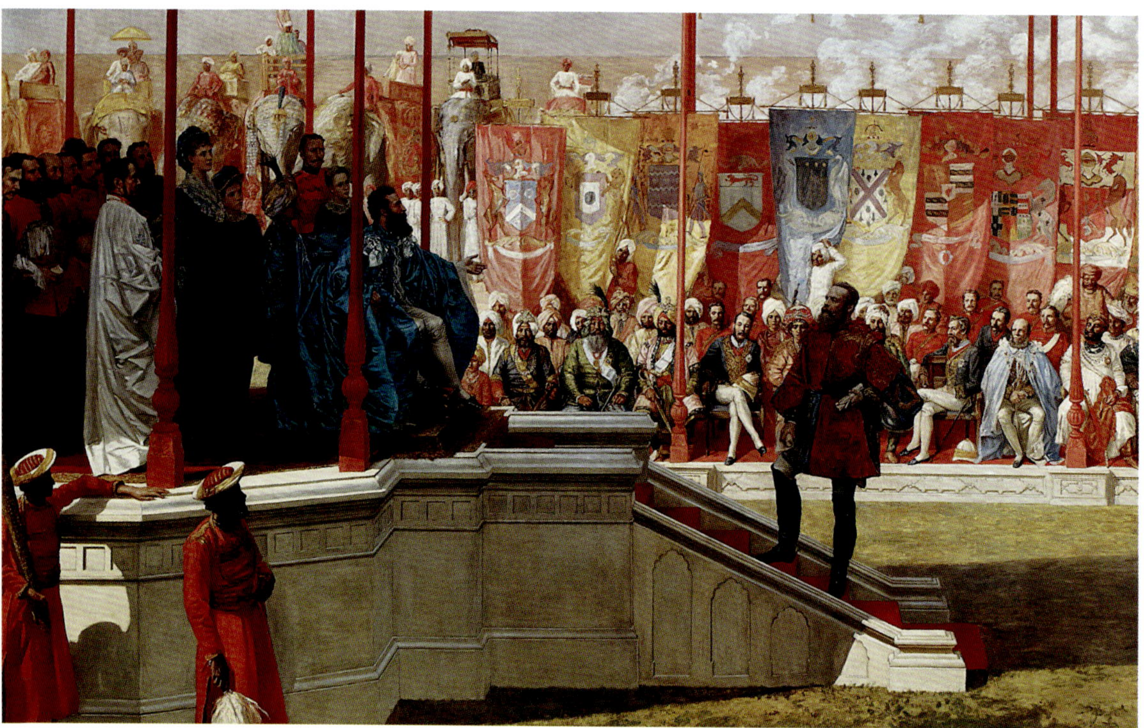

100 Val Prinsep, *The Imperial Assemblage held at Delhi*, 1880 (detail of fig. 85).

discomfort, a metaphorical nakedness of the imperial body beneath this would-be emperor's new clothes.'[56]

Prinsep hinted at contemporary British anxieties over the imperial body becoming feminised due to the exigencies of ornate fashion in India by creating a shared palette of blue for Lytton's wife and daughter, the young Indian prince and the viceroy himself (fig. 100). This unmanning of Lytton was seemingly not lost on the reviewers of Prinsep's painting, who singled him out for particular criticism, while praising the masculine bearing of the blood-red figure of Barnes.[57] Visually, however, it is not the case that the viceroy's effete portrait fails properly to bear imperial authority whereas the imposing masculinity of the major succeeds. The gravitas of the entire encounter between these two men is rendered unstable by the pair of languid Indian servants in the bottom left-hand corner of the image, whose poses offer casual visual echoes of the gestures of both Lytton and Barnes. On the far left, an outstretched arm draped indolently along the platform undercuts the solemnity of the viceroy's equivalent motion; on the right, the figure offers a slouched approximation of the major's martial stance. This slippage between mimicry and mockery compromises both poles of imperial self-fashioning: extravagant pomp and staid masculinity both have their efficacy as signifiers of power challenged by these enervated reiterations in subaltern figures.[58]

SUBLIME ASSAULT

The imperial entity envisioned by Prinsep was therefore politically and aesthetically unstable: the main colonial protagonists strike highly discrepant postures of power in front of a discordantly heterogeneous crowd. In showing British rule personified with such varied sartorial properties in the diversely attired figures of Lytton and Barnes, Prinsep played on contemporary anxieties over fashions 're-tailoring identities'.[59] But more than this, the lack of formal cohesion among the British ruling classes in India meant that the artist had exploded the visual grammar that had emerged in Victorian art to situate individuals within a politically stable collective. Mass group portraits of political events like this were rare but the stress that critics placed on the tumultuous polychrome of the myriad sitters' costumes and the staccato iconography of the banners in the background positions *The Imperial Assemblage* in more or less antithetical relation to one of the few comparable paintings of the period.

George Hayter's immense group portrait of 375 Tory and Whig MPs and peers passing the Great Reform Act of 1832, *The House of Commons, 1833* (fig. 101), approached similar compositional difficulties to Prinsep in terms of collating numerous portrait studies of individual political figures into a visually comprehensible unit.[60] Completed in 1843 and bought by the Tory party for the recently established National Portrait

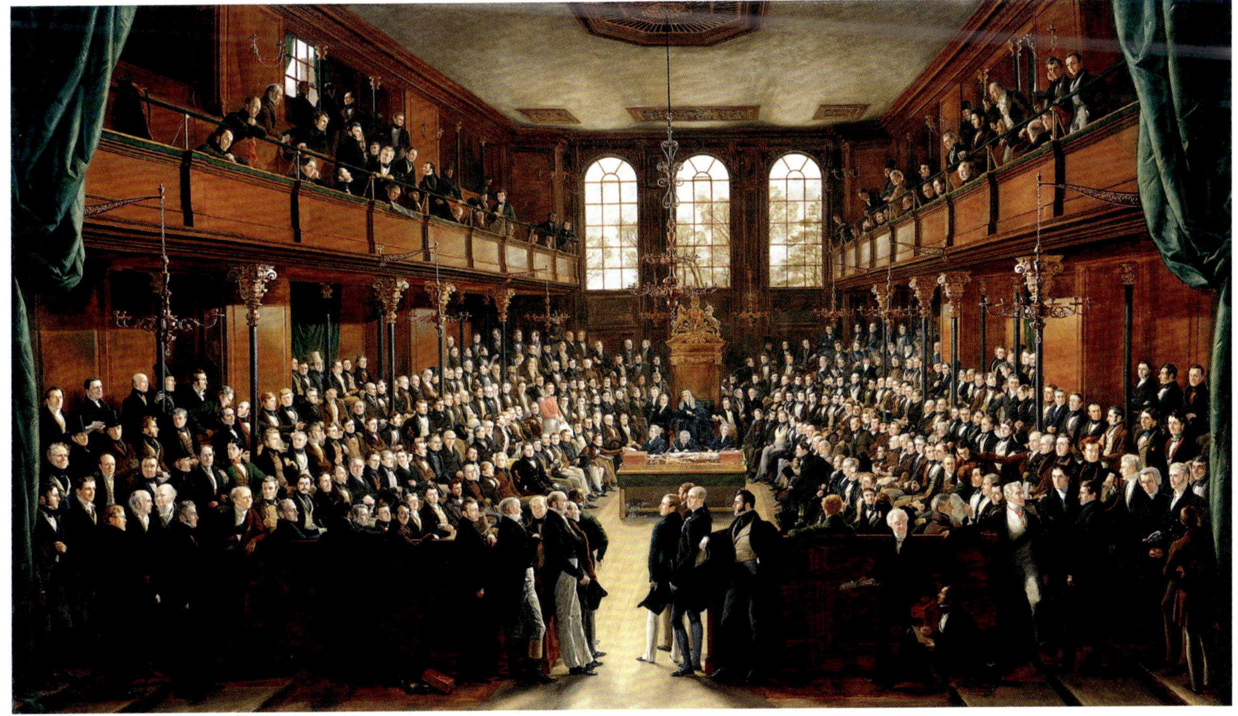

101 George Hayter, *The House of Commons, 1833*, 1843. Oil on canvas, 5.42 × 3.46 m. © National Portrait Gallery, London, NPG 54

Gallery in 1858, Hayter's *The House of Commons* was consequently on public view when Prinsep came to paint his imperial group. Unlike Prinsep's work, however, Hayter's scene had been the subject of significant critical praise.[61] Rows of monotonously clad men recede into the chamber, framed by the uniformly plain brown panelling of the political architecture. The 'uncompromising sameness' of the politicians' 'heavy and dusky' clothes might have been seen by both Hayter and the critic of the *Illustrated London News* as an artistic difficulty to be overcome but the effect of this unvarying sartorial palette is that the partisan nature of these men can be visualised in a unified space.[62] What Hayter's scene managed to achieve was to situate the political agency of individual people and parties within a cohesive collective framework.

The aesthetics of politics in Victorian Britain were a thoroughly sober affair, in other words, and stood in marked contrast to the vibrancy of Indian attire. Interestingly, the deep brown of Hayter's Commons chamber, which does much to contain the myriad figures in a coherent political space – and can also be seen performing a similar function in later paintings of the chamber which was built following the 1843 fire – is a hue that also came to dominate the backdrop of the political portrait.[63] The classical trappings of the sort of mise-en-scène associated with the grand manner of portraiture that had been popular in the eighteenth and early nineteenth century increasingly gave way to decontextualised monochromatic spaces in the Victorian era. In the 1840s the Prime Minister Robert Peel's instructions about portraits he had commissioned of his colleagues made clear the importance of modern dress and the absence of adornment.[64] This austere style was able to mediate between political polarities: when John Everett Millais came to paint William Gladstone (fig. 102) and Benjamin Disraeli (fig. 103) in the late 1870s and 1880s, he arranged these parliamentary opponents so that, when seen together, they could face one another as rivals. And yet these portraits are so similar in stance, dress and chromatics that such political antagonism takes place under a unifying horizon.[65] The monochromatic palette was therefore active in visualising adversarial parliamentary politics in terms of a wider cohesive system.

Monochrome's politically stabilising effects should be borne in mind when reading that Prinsep's polychromatic painting was 'inartistic' because 'the gorgeous dresses of the Indian chiefs, placed against a background of gaudy banners' amounted to 'kaleidoscopic combinations' – a metaphor of restless colour that refuses to be fixed and one which occurs in more than one review.[66] Note particularly how dresses that are individually 'gorgeous' become offensive when seen as a group. The artistic appeal of lavishly ornamented Indian costumes to the British

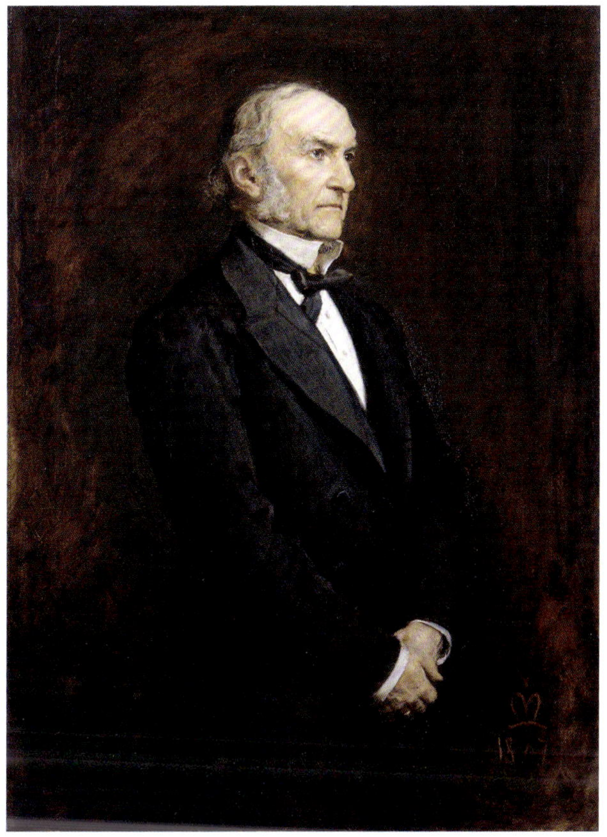

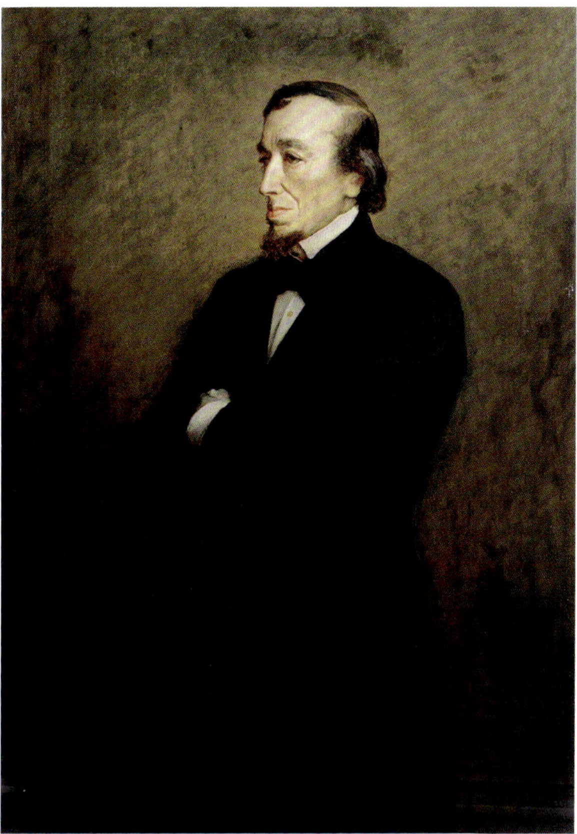

102 Sir John Everett Millais, *William Ewart Gladstone*, 1879. Oil on canvas, 125.7 × 91.4 cm. National Portrait Gallery, London, NPG 3637

103 Sir John Everett Millais, *Benjamin Disraeli, Earl of Beaconsfield*, 1881. Oil on canvas, 127.6 × 93.1. National Portrait Gallery, London, NPG 3241

was well established by the Victorian period, thoroughly enmeshed in the 'picturesque' registers of colonial viewing that had developed in the eighteenth century.[67] The costume of a maharaja did not in itself present any insurmountable problems for the British. In his individual portraits of the maharajas, Prinsep sometimes positioned them against the same sober backdrop that was then prevalent in contemporary portraits by Millais, G. F. Watts (1817–1904) and James Abbott McNeill Whistler (1834–1903). A mode of Indian dress that appeared 'medieval' to the colonial eye was, it seems, easily assimilated into the emerging portrait forms of Victorian modernity.

Yet when seen en masse and as part of an imperial polity, maharajas began to mount an aesthetic challenge to the British. To a Victorian audience for whom a staid style of portraiture secured a sense of cohesion among partisan individuals, the riotous colour of the Raj could speak to dangerous political ferment. An account that sheds some light on the visual difficulties thrown up by the sheer colourful force of India's royal splendour was offered by another colonial artist at another coronation durbar, Mortimer Menpes at Edward VII's official proclamation

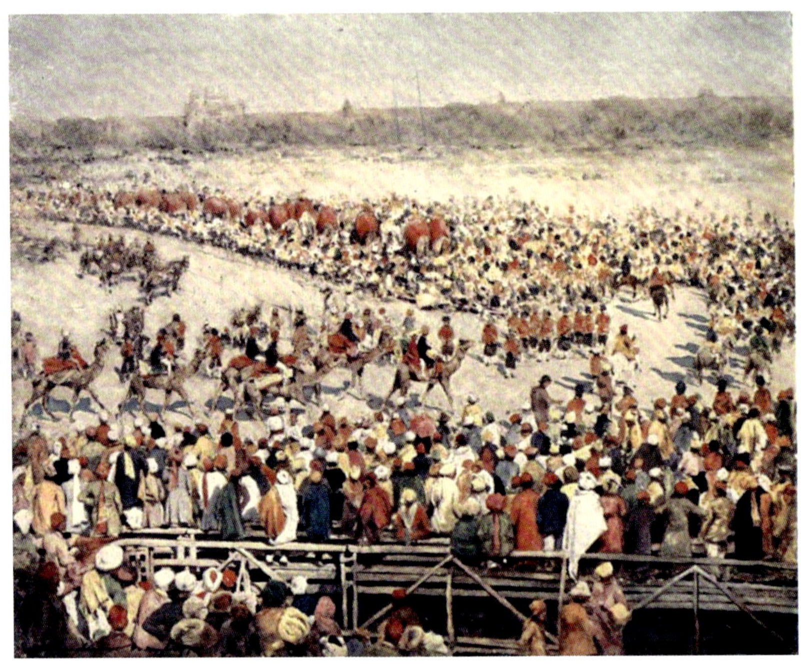

104 Mortimer Menpes, 'State Entry as seen from the Jumma Masjid', in Mortimer Menpes (transcribed by Dorothy Menpes), *The Durbar* (London: Adam & Charles Black, 1903), plate 15, page 28. Internet Archive

as emperor in 1903. Menpes gave this description of watching the maharajas enter Delhi:

> I feasted my eye on each elephant; I gloated over each magnificent combination and each harmony, the emerald greens, the carmines, the violets, the golds, and the vermilions; and the result was that, before I had passed more than half the glittering throng, my sense of colour was exhausted. I was satiated: I had seen too much. Then I realised that here in India, to avoid the danger of becoming colour-blind, one should nurse one's eyes, not stare and exhaust oneself in colour, but always keep some strength in reserve.[68]

Such enervating ocular effects strikingly recall earlier comments made about Prinsep's painting ('the glare of its colouring haunts the vitiated eye'; 'the eye [is left] dazzled and the sense confounded'). Indeed, if one reads Menpes's 1903 account alongside the 1880 reviews of *The Imperial Assemblage*, it seems that Prinsep was remarkably successful in reproducing the violently disorientating visual impact of multiple maharajas on the colonial eye.

Exactly why was the sight of multiple maharajas so confounding for the British? For Menpes, this was partly a problem of representation, as the injurious chromatic overload of maharaja costume confronted him with the limits of his medium. Repeatedly, the artist's account swings from the visual excess of India to the stubborn materiality of painting: 'I took out my paint-box and blushed. The folly of it, the absolute futility!

Here I was standing before a scene which no artist save Turner should ever have attempted to paint, calmly unfolding a stupid little paint-box and squeezing out tubes of Reeves's water-colour, pigment which, compared with the glowing tones around me, looked like mud.'[69] In the face of this insufficiency, Menpes grasps around for representational practices that lay outside the predominant techniques of the Western artistic canon, something that might meet the challenge of conveying the 'blaze of colour' before him:

> Rembrandt couldn't have painted this scene ... Then one felt the value of precious stones to work with, or something very different from ordinary pigment. It must be painted in the jewel-like, gem-like manner, and bit by bit, facet by facet. To attempt to paint it in flowing watercolour were to reproduce a sunset in silhouette. The crowd was a mosaic, and the people were like living tapestry.[70]

Those technologies of vision traditionally familiar to the West are thus shown to be moribund in the Indian context. As Saloni Mathur has noted, the imagery that Menpes consequently produced (figs 104 and 105)

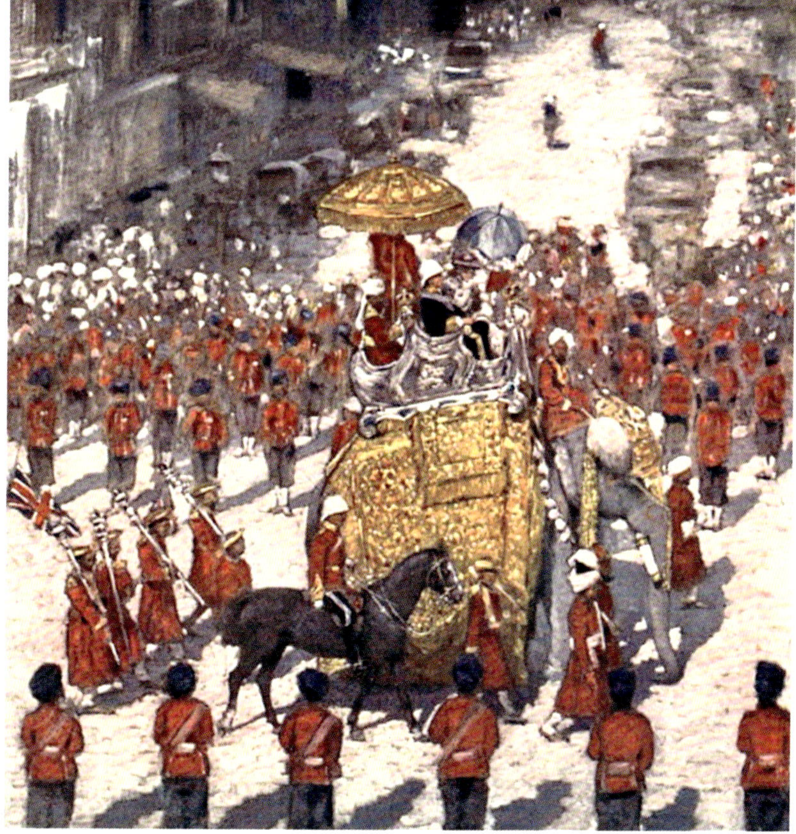

105 Mortimer Menpes, 'Lord and Lady Curzon Entering Delhi', in Mortimer Menpes (transcribed by Dorothy Menpes), *The Durbar* (London: Adam & Charles Black, 1903), plate 23, page 44. Internet Archive

articulated his anxiety about the epistemological status of his medium by adopting points of view that demonstrate 'a unique self-awareness about the position of the viewer and its implication for knowledge': his scenes of the durbar tend to dwell more on the differential perspectives of the crowd than on the spectacle itself.[71] No (failed) attempt is made, au Prinsep, to convey the maharajas as a totality. They are glimpsed only in impressionistic flashes of colour.

My readings of Prinsep's and Menpes's artistic struggles indicate that, in the framework of colonial aesthetics, the colourful diversity of Indian rulers simply could not be seen as a coherent totality. This artistic failure was something that implicitly destabilised the political structures of the Raj, undergirded as those were at this time by the image-based logic of the spectacle. There is an unspoken aesthetic category that haunts Menpes's visceral account of the 'blinding colour' of this royal Indian parade. His description of representational breakdown, belief in the injurious affective power of the scene ('like looking at the sun') and contention that Turner 'was the only man to paint this procession of native rulers', all situate the Indian parade in the sphere of 'the sublime', a concept that had once been key to British artistic discourse.[72] Turner's work has been widely recognised for its encapsulation of the effect of boundlessness that eighteenth-century philosophers had attributed to the sublime, the currency of which dealt in ineffable vastness and uncontrollable threat.[73] With notable exceptions, after about 1850 this aesthetic category had become marginal to mainstream British art; Menpes's relationship to the concept was therefore indirect but the challenge that the sublime launched – 'to paint the unpaintable' – is clearly at work here for the artist and frames the procession of Indian royals as a spectacle of power beyond colonial capture or control.[74] The political difficulty of composing diverse rulers into a workable political unit is thus sublimated into the aesthetic problematic of the sublime.

CONCLUSION

The myriad hues of an Indian crowd can be seen to constitute a sublime visual force for the British, one beyond the representational capacities of European aesthetics and even coded as injurious to the colonial eye. Although the British actively encouraged maharajas to wear ornate dress, the effect of this was to create scenes that could not be assimilated to the sober visual grammar that worked to picture a viable ruling class in Britain. True, the positioning of maharajas outside such grammar functioned to deny them a form of political agency that was recognisable to the British (hence their increasing rejection of ostentation, as traced by Julie Codell, over the course of the coronation durbars). So too could talk of Indian rulers appearing as a fragmentary chromatic flux dovetail with imperial claims to legitimacy as a stable overlord pacifying inherently atomised and bellicose Indian kingdoms. At a visual level, however, British rule was not seen as stable or even coherent. The sartorial dislocation between the ostentatious Lord Lytton and the sober Major Barnes in Prinsep's painting mirrors the discontinuities between the maharajas, as the aesthetics of British power are split to meet the exigencies of an imperial rule that believed some splendour was necessary to carry authority in India, while at the same time fretting about no-frills manliness. A sense of political stability was necessarily lost in the process of translating the visuals of British power to the Indian context.

There could be no secure spectacle of imperial power for the British. The monochromatic visual idioms that characterised (and stabilised) the domestic political theatre of the age simply had no purchase in an empire that was heterogeneously colourful, diversely attired and multiracial. The post-1857 regime of spectacle in India therefore failed on its own terms; to the British eye, it was a chaotic and combustible-looking visual construct in which could be glimpsed the very limits of imperial authority over a region that was characterised above all by diversity and difference.

CONCLUSION

William Simpson, 'The Ameer Yakoob Khan and Major Cavagnari signing the Treaty of Gundamuk', *Illustrated London News*, 27 September 1879 (detail of fig. 50).

'THE VICTORIAN AGE HAS BEEN ONE OF PEACE', WROTE THE *WESTERN Gazette* in 1896, the year Queen Victoria became the longest reigning monarch in British history. The article then added this extraordinary qualification:

> but scarcely a twelvemonth period has passed during her Majesty's reign without finding our country at war in some part of the world. The following is a list of them: – Afghan war 1838–40, first Chinese war 1841, Sikh war 1845, Kaffir war 1846, second war with China, second Afghan war, 1849, second Sikh war 1848–9, Burmese war 1850, second Kaffir war 1851–52, second Burmese war 1852–53, Crimea 1854, third war with China 1856–58, Indian Mutiny 1857, Maori war 1860–61, more wars with China 1860 and 1862, second Maori war 1863–65, Ashantee war 1864, war in Bhootan 1864, Abyssinia war 1867–68, war with the Bazotees 1868 [people on the North-West Frontier of India], third Maori war 1873–4, third Kaffir war 1877, Zulu war 1878–79, third Afghan war 1878–80, war in Basutoland 1879–81, Transvaal war, 1879–81, Egyptian war 1882, Soudan 1885–89, third Burma war 1885–92, Zanzibar 1890, India 1890, Matabele wars, 1894 and 1896, Chitral campaign 1895, third Ashantee campaign 1895, second Soudan campaign 1896.[1]

Just how could this relentless chronicle of conflict – 'World War Zero', as Dan Hicks has recently termed it – be described as an era of 'peace'?[2]

Such cognitive dissonance was, I have argued, fundamental to the imperial imagination. The Victorians envisioned their global role via three key modes of visual spectacle: an ethnographic complex, in which the Other and their objects were documented and displayed according to colonial taxonomies; a diplomatic complex, in which international sovereignties were composed according to aesthetic criteria; and a military

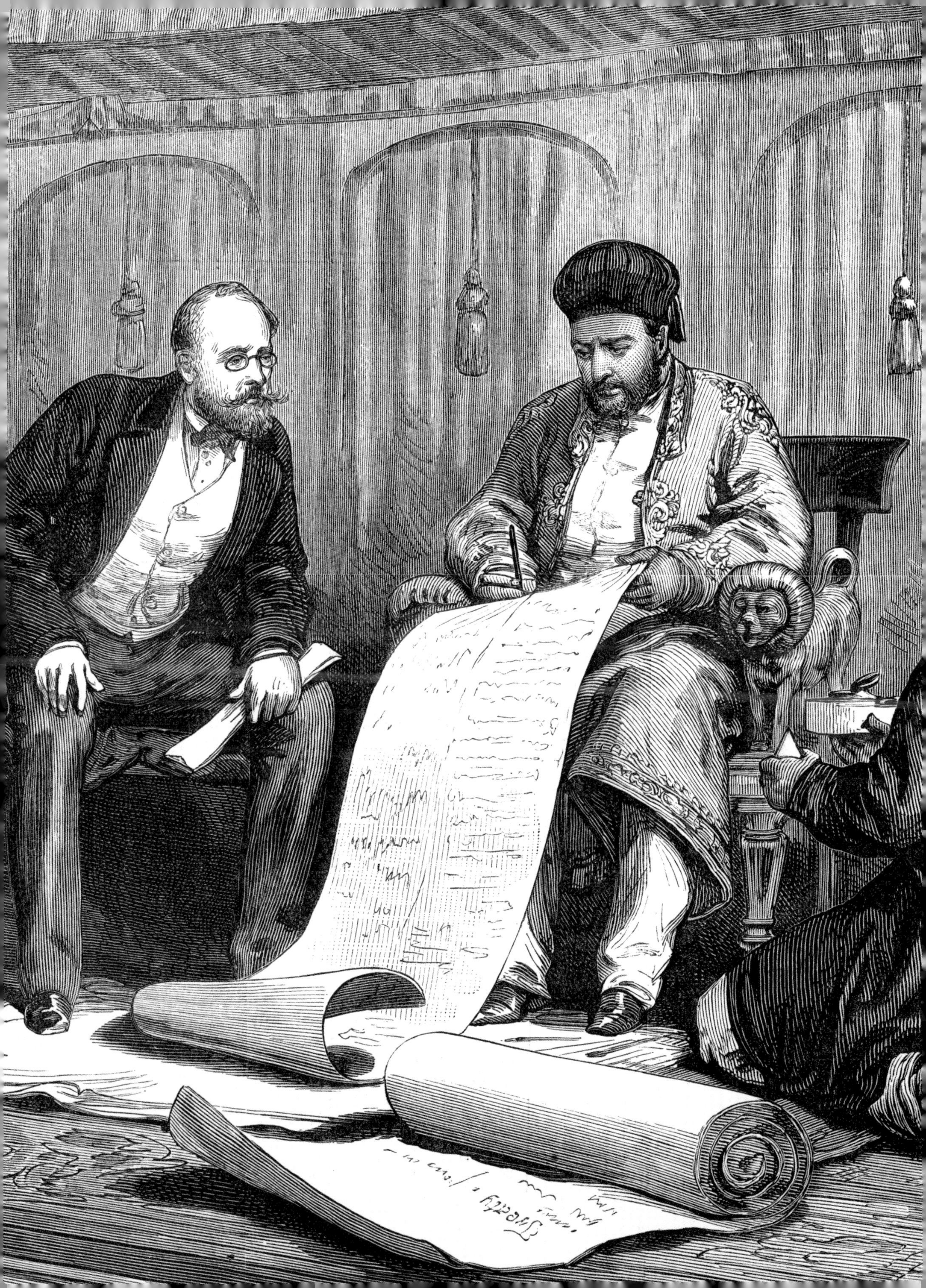

complex, whereby warfare was waged and consumed with an eye to its dramatic impact. The British Empire was thus frequently rendered into a spectacle of 'peace': exhibitions of the arts and crafts of world cultures; theatricalised political rituals that presented colonial relations as gentlemanly, legalistic and consensual; visions of citizenship that posited a hegemonic ideal of imperial unity; elaborate coronation events that strove to impose a viable visual identity onto a fractious polity. Yet all this occurred against the drumbeat of incessant colonial war – campaigns which, far from being ignored, were in fact unprecedentedly visible in the cultural forms of Victorian society.

This study has suggested that Victorian Britain's self-perception (or self-deception) as a pacific force in the world – a fact proudly proclaimed at the Great Exhibition of 1851 – calls for an approach that considers visual cultures of geopolitical violence alongside their apparent opposite, the 'arts of peace'. More research is needed to situate the Victorians' vexed aestheticisation of warfare in terms of broader shifts in cultural sensibilities regarding the picturing and witnessing of violence in nineteenth-century Britain. Public executions, for example, were abolished in 1868; such displays were 'inconceivably awful', as Charles Dickens had written in 1849.[3] At the same time, however, the *Illustrated Police News*, founded in 1864, was running graphic coverage of criminal violence and, at times, front-page renderings of the state executions that were now happening behind closed doors. This sensationalist imagery of villainy had an estimated circulation of 300,000 by 1888 (the same as the *Illustrated London News* at its 1860s peak).[4] Victorian images of violence thus navigated complex and evolving moral and legal landscapes, shaping the contours of both domestic criminality and global conflict.

The proliferation of such images occurred in a fast-transforming media ecosystem. The coterminous rise of the popular illustrated press and photographic technologies was part of a broader revolution in the efficiency of imperial communications – 'that divine progress', as the photographer John Thomson put it, 'which by a thousand telegraphs, railways and industries, is tending more and more to bind the nations of the earth together'.[5] Any account of the colonial experience in this period is incomplete without understanding something of the nature of this international traffic in text and image, via which artists, photographers, correspondents and ethnographers operating 'on the spot' of the 'periphery' sent their work back to the 'metropole' and thereby fostered new modes of mass spectatorship for imperial events, especially for the military and diplomatic crises that defined the Victorian empire. I have analysed this traffic not merely in terms of the circulation and consumption of finished pictures but as the global dissemination of various image-making processes and techniques: particular modes of spatial occupation, intersubjective relations and styles of perception and comportment. The Victorian imperial subject was constituted by the transmissions, tropes and temporalities of such networks.

This book's central argument has been that Victorian visions of war and peace were structured by the technical procedures and aesthetic conventions of modern visual practices: the plein air pencil sketches produced by 'adventurous' special artists; the woodcut engravings produced after such sketches, which were published in visual serials in the illustrated press; and the labour-intensive early photographic technologies like the calotype and, more commonly, the glass-plate wet-collodion process. The 1850s – the decade with which this study began – was thus a pivotal moment in the emergence of a distinctly Victorian experience of empire because it established many of its formal and material preconditions: the first World's Fair at the Crystal Palace in 1851; the invention of the collodion photographic process by Frederick Scott Archer that same year; the subsequent rise of a new breed of photographer venturing into the 'field' to experiment with the glass-plates and chemical mixtures of Archer's method; and the popularisation and professionalisation of the role of the special artist, whose coverage of international events was situating visual ephemera at the heart of the Victorian public sphere.

So, as colonials increasingly invested their faith in the efficacy of spectacle – not only attempting to consume empire as an exotic visual treat but also to compose it as a regime of images – these visual practices accrued considerable geopolitical agency. They shaped the contours of imperial sovereignty and established many of the aesthetic and ethical registers through which colonial violence was confronted.

COLONIAL VIOLENCE AND THE VISUAL ARCHIVE

This book was finished during a time of increasing calls to 'decolonise' the discipline of art history.[6] Between submitting the manuscript for review and receiving the reader reports, the issue of decolonisation became more pressing than it had been at any time since I first began researching colonial archives for my doctorate in 2010. Global protests associated with the Black Lives Matter movement, galvanised by public revulsion at the footage of the murder of George Floyd by a white US policeman, ultimately led to the toppling of the statue of the eighteenth-century slave trader Edward Colston in Bristol on 7 June 2020. In their introduction to a multi-authored decolonial intervention in the journal *Art History*, Catherine Grant and Dorothy Price write that, when public sculpture catalyses political debate in this way (they were referring to the Rhodes Must Fall campaign but the point holds), 'It serves to remind us of the centrality of the discipline in promoting and maintaining dominant cultural values; and yet it also enables us to interrogate them as historically located and subject to inevitable temporal mutation.'[7]

The imagery in this book is far from such public sculpture; the issue is not that it has enjoyed too much prominence or visibility within our society but too little. As numerous art historians have noted, 'decolonisation' in the context of the discipline of art history is something of a misnomer: what is needed is the 'recolonisation' of art history, a problematisation of insular national canons through a more sustained critical engagement with the visual archives of empire and a greater appreciation of the diverse cultural agencies that have constituted British artistic traditions.[8] I have worked with the broadest definition of 'art' in this study, incorporating both 'high' and 'low' forms of visual culture, in order to demonstrate art history's central role in structuring the imperialistic visions that structured (and to a degree continue to structure) the modern world. In highlighting the importance of both empire and racialised colonial violence to the visual culture of the Victorians, this book responds to a fraught history of white supremacy, the spectre of which continues to haunt the public square.

There is a vexed ethics to engaging with the visual archives of empire. These images could be thorny for the Victorians themselves and they remain so for the institutions that hold this material and the scholars who study it (or, indeed, ignore it). As the Victorians grew increasingly accustomed to being spectators of military violence in the illustrated press and at exhibitions of photography and art, the nature of that violence was changing, reconstituted by the exigencies of 'small wars' and the racial animus that stoked them. The artists and photographers embedded in military campaigns were not confronting the traditional 'civilised' methods of warfare that had characterised intra-European conflict – standing armies and set-piece battles that could be conceived of in terms of aristocratic values – but were witnesses to an emerging colonial military doctrine of counter-insurgency that relied on spectacular displays of 'demonstrative' violence.[9] While Victorian discourses on race helped to render this kind of violence against non-Europeans acceptable, the characteristic excesses of 'savage warfare' could nevertheless threaten to disturb the Victorian's self-image as a decent, moderate and humane people.

This was particularly an issue for photographers, whose medium was less adept than the artist's pencil at making mass killing conform to the light-hearted conventions of the imperial romance. Explicit photographs of colonial violence are therefore rare in the imperial archive; in consequence they are liable to be overlooked or dismissed as anomalous in a manner that reinforces a popular vision of the British Empire as a historical phenomenon whose 'positive' attributes (railways, trade, pageantry and so on) can be separated from the occasional 'regrettable' massacre. Yet such rarity is not evidence of the general benignity of the imperial project or the restraint of its military methods but, rather, of what the Victorian journalist Gratton Geary called the 'pharasaical' morals of his compatriots when it came to their colonial wars: 'a spirit which revolts at the operation of photographing a batch of men at the moment of their execution, when their execution in batches is accepted as an ordinary incident in the subjugation of a conquered people.'[10] Colonial violence was thus both increasingly visible in Victorian culture – through the acceptably heroic tropes of the pictorial press and the fine arts – and also strangely absent.

Yet, while they might appear as shocking outliers in an imperial visual culture dominated by picturesque landscapes, regal portraiture and ethnographic studies, photographs of death and destruction point to the intimate entanglement of that very culture with the colonial violence it seemingly omits. The proximity – temporal, aesthetic, authorial and archival – between photographs of stark violence and photographs of its absence prompt a reconsideration of what visual evidence of 'colonial violence' looks like. My thinking here has been informed by Ann Stoler's question in 2016, 'Can we provide an adequate vocabulary to identify what a "colonial presence" looks like? Is it lodged in the figure of the stateless migrant, the killing machine of the drone, ashen landscape, or the global philanthropic industry?'[11] Ariella Azoulay, too, has engaged with such a task when writing of how to conceptualise the absence of any photographs of the mass rape that occurred in Occupied Berlin in 1945: 'many photographs were dissociated from what happened in the places where they were taken, and it is this dissociation that we ought to unlearn'.[12]

Staged photographs of slaughtered enemies are perhaps easily recognisable as grisly war trophies. Yet they were not alone in performing this function. When a troop of British Orientalists descended on Burma in the aftermath of a colonial invasion to document sacred sites that had once been off limits to them, the ethnographic documentation that ensued doubled as displays of military triumphalism; and when a 'diplomatic' expedition to Tibet forced entry into Lhasa and let scores of cameras loose on the city, the resulting photographs were as much war trophies as the goods that had been pilfered from slain Tibetan corpses along the way. This is not to say that the images did not also have aesthetic and scholarly value to the Victorians as depictions of architecture, landscapes or peoples. Yet in reading these pictures not merely in terms of their manifest representational content but as artefacts of image-making events, the imagery's dependence on and performance of violent imperial dispossession becomes clear. Colonial violence is rendered palpable as the very 'ether' of these images.[13]

At the same time, however, I have tried to be careful not to reproduce uncritically the Victorians' own violent photographic fantasies about the camera serving as a surrogate for the cannon. The camera-as-gun trope is often left unpacked, a vague analogy between different sorts of 'shooting'. My account of photography's intimidating aspects is thoroughly contextual, sensitive to how the camera shadowed violence and fixed colonised bodies and attention on it; in this respect, I suggest, the artist's pencil could also serve to channel violence. Unlike the gun, the early camera was intrinsically fragile and its complicated and sensitive procedures created spaces of political encounter that were not reducible to the straightforward subject–object Cartesianism that has traditionally been attributed to the imperial gaze. The materialities and temporalities of such processes were characterised by a dynamic and unpredictable openness, what Kaja Silverman terms 'liquid intelligence'.[14] Victorian rhetoric about ballistic camerawork thus belied the vulnerability and relationality of operating with paper and glass-plate negatives 'in the field'.

Throughout this book I have attended to both photography and other artistic practices in terms of their status as dynamic intersubjective processes rather than as finished and fixed images; this, I have argued, was how visual media was encountered by coloniser and colonised in the imperial field. By definition such visual theatre was inconclusive, its final products – static and captioned prints – only ever posited during the initial corporeal performance of image-making. The aesthetic, anthropological and geopolitical categories through which Victorians subsequently read the figures in such images – picturesque staffage, imperial subjects, anthropological specimens and so on – were not necessarily the categories that structured the experiences of those involved in the image-making event itself. That tended to harbour a much more diverse array of affects, agencies and sovereignties.

My account has therefore been motivated in part by a desire to recuperate some aspect of the experience of those whose positionality in imperial regimes was constituted, at least to a degree, by colonial visual technologies. Such recuperative hermeneutics can be seen as futile in the context of imperial archives, since many of the figures found therein are what Zeb Tortorici calls 'indexical absences': their existence is indexed by these images but only as spectral presences that point to a more substantial loss, an archival lacuna: no names, no testimony, just darkened forms on a fading photograph.[15] As Anjali Arondekar has noted, just because 'a body is found' in the archive does not mean that 'a subject can be recovered.'[16] Her observation can be frustratingly on the mark when one confronts the procession of anonymous and shadowy Indian figures – 'picturesque staffage' – in nineteenth-century colonial photographs.[17]

This book has often circled round such colonised bodies, honing in on moments when some information about their conditions or experience flashes up in the general archival gloom, while attempting to reconstruct the often violent contexts in which they sat for, or witnessed, colonial photographers and artists operating in the 'contact zone' of conflict. And if, ultimately, much of this experience is lost – or approachable only asymptotically, via colonial accounts and speculation – it nevertheless seems insufficient to me to engage with these figures merely as colonial motifs. The visual archive of empire is haunted by other agencies: glimpsed in the colonial rumours that formed round the photographs of an Indian rebel, in the negative archives of colonial photographers and in the gaps in the paint of abandoned portraits.

NEW TECHNOLOGIES, NEW TERRITORIES

The visual technologies that shaped Victorian imperialism remained reasonably constant until the invention of the Kodak camera in 1888 and the contemporaneous rise of the halftone printing process, which enabled newspapers to print directly from photographs. There was now no need for the extensive apparatus, convoluted chemical procedures and beasts of burden that had characterised earlier photographic methods in the imperial field. This radically expanded the spread of the camera and its images in fin-de-siècle imperial societies. When Mortimer Menpes arrived in India to paint the 1903 Coronation Durbar, for instance, he wrote of how 'Nearly every one had a kodak, even many of the natives themselves; and there was the sound of ping! ping! ping! all over the place, and the buzz of the cinematograph.'[18] More than ever, the camera's operations were fully a part of the imperial spectacle they were there to record. 'A closer look at the durbar's photographic archive begins to reveal an interesting pattern', writes Saloni Mathur of the 1903 event: 'The more one looks for these "photographers looking", the more one finds their presence in the frame: men and women, Europeans and Indians, professionals and amateurs.'[19]

By the time that Menpes wrote of the 'kodak fiend' at the Delhi Durbar of 1903, however, the mode of imperial sovereignty being captured by the snapshot-happy audience was in decline. While diplomatic fetishism, demonstrative violence and ethnographic spoils remained essential elements of the imperial endeavour, the elaborate neo-feudal aesthetics of Britain's formal empire in Asia found little purchase in newer colonies. The closing decades of the century saw an imperial pivot to Africa, in which, following the Berlin Conference of 1885, European powers 'scrambled' for territory on the 'dark' continent.

British imperial activity in Africa around the turn of the century increasingly embodied what Hicks, dissatisfied with the term 'informal empire', has called 'corporate militarist colonialism'.[20] This came with its own issues of how to conceptualise imperial sovereignty. 'I do not use the word "protectorate"', wrote George Goldie, Governor of the Royal Niger Company, in 1899, 'I very much like the term sphere of influence'.[21] The Royal Niger Company's motto attests the continuing centrality of an ideology of 'peace' to the politics of colonial war in the late Victorian era – *Pax, Jus, Ars* (peace, justice, art). British visual reportage from the region was increasingly animated by notions of humane Christian intervention, invoking colonial tropes about Africa – human sacrifice, cannibalism and 'fetish' worship – that 'signalled the beginning of militarist humanitarianism: the use of a "human rights" justification for unprovoked regime change.'[22]

Much of this imagery remains little studied. Further research is needed to show how late Victorian visions of their military interventions and diplomatic coups adapted in response to the new possibilities of graphic and photographic media, as well as the particular demands of different phases and modalities of imperialism. Due to a virulent anti-blackness in Victorian thought and the imputation to Africans of an especially aggressive barbarism, images of colonial and anti-colonial violence on the 'dark continent' could signify in highly different ways from equivalent pictures emerging from imperial activity in Asia.

By the turn of the century, then, a series of technological developments and geopolitical shifts had begun to reconstitute the aesthetics of empire. The rise of the handheld camera had particularly profound implications for the political agency of photography; it began to register more as a 'poison' than a 'cure' for colonial governance.[23] Increasingly mobile, the camera came to operate in what Christopher Pinney has termed a 'disseminated field of unexpected effects', increasingly deployed by agents critical of the imperial project. If, as this book has shown, photography had always stoked the political and ethical anxieties of empire, then these anxieties were increasingly acute from the early twentieth century onwards, as colonials came to the 'deep and disturbing realisation that control of photography and its evidential protocols had now irretrievably slipped from the hands of the state.'[24] From the British concentration camps of Bloemfontein, South Africa, in 1901 to the infamous massacre at Amritsar in 1919, the handheld camera was becoming an inconvenient witness to the imperial atrocities that sprang from the pitiless and paranoid logics of counter-insurgency warfare.[25]

Official anxieties were not limited to the Kodak, however, but were increasingly clustering round pictorial reportage as such. There had been no quick or easy substitution of the photographer for the artist in the pages of the illustrated press, even as the handheld camera freed the former from earlier technological constraints. The special artists maintained much of their cultural authority throughout the final decades of the nineteenth century; the South African War, like the Crimean War fifty years earlier, featured extensively in the illustrated press through pencil sketches produced 'on the spot'. Yet in the heat of this particularly vicious and controversial military campaign of white-on-white violence, relations between the press and the military were souring. *The Graphic* complained, 'a certain restriction continues to be imposed on war correspondents by wire with an eye, mainly, to the mystification of the enemy's Intelligence Department, if they have such a thing ... the "fog of war" has again descended on the theatre of hostilities from Mafeking to Maritzburg.'[26]

I do not cite this to assert a hard distinction between an earlier 'truthful' free press and a modern regime of censorship. The military had always sought to censor images, even if there were no legal inhibitions on such publications back in Britain; and anyway, as Tom Gretton has noted, artists had a 'more or less well-internalised self-censorship ... a reticence, a reluctance, a protectiveness of the delicacy of their bourgeois family public.'[27] But an increasingly strict military censorship began to curtail the artists' movements on campaigns in the early years of the new century, altering what it meant to be 'on the spot'.

This situation only intensified in the First World War, when the use of propaganda as an instrument of British foreign policy became systematic.[28] Such direct government supervision and its associated legal constraints led to the disillusionment of veteran Victorian specials like Frederic Villiers: 'I resented being so scurvily treated by my own folk', he wrote, 'when through forty years of British war I had been persona grata with generals like Wolseley, Roberts, Methuan, Browne and Buller.'[29] If the emergence of official state propaganda projects signalled a continuing faith in the power of images to aid the business of imperial statecraft, it was a faith that was increasingly contingent on a strict centralised authority controlling production. Villiers was mourning the Victorian era's more informal structures of media-management. Then, barring exceptional although highly revealing controversies, the benefit of having artists and photographers on campaigns was more or less taken for granted, part of the habitus of empire. In the transformed techno-media landscape of the early twentieth century, in which the British confronted cataclysmic intra-European violence, such an approach was no longer tenable.

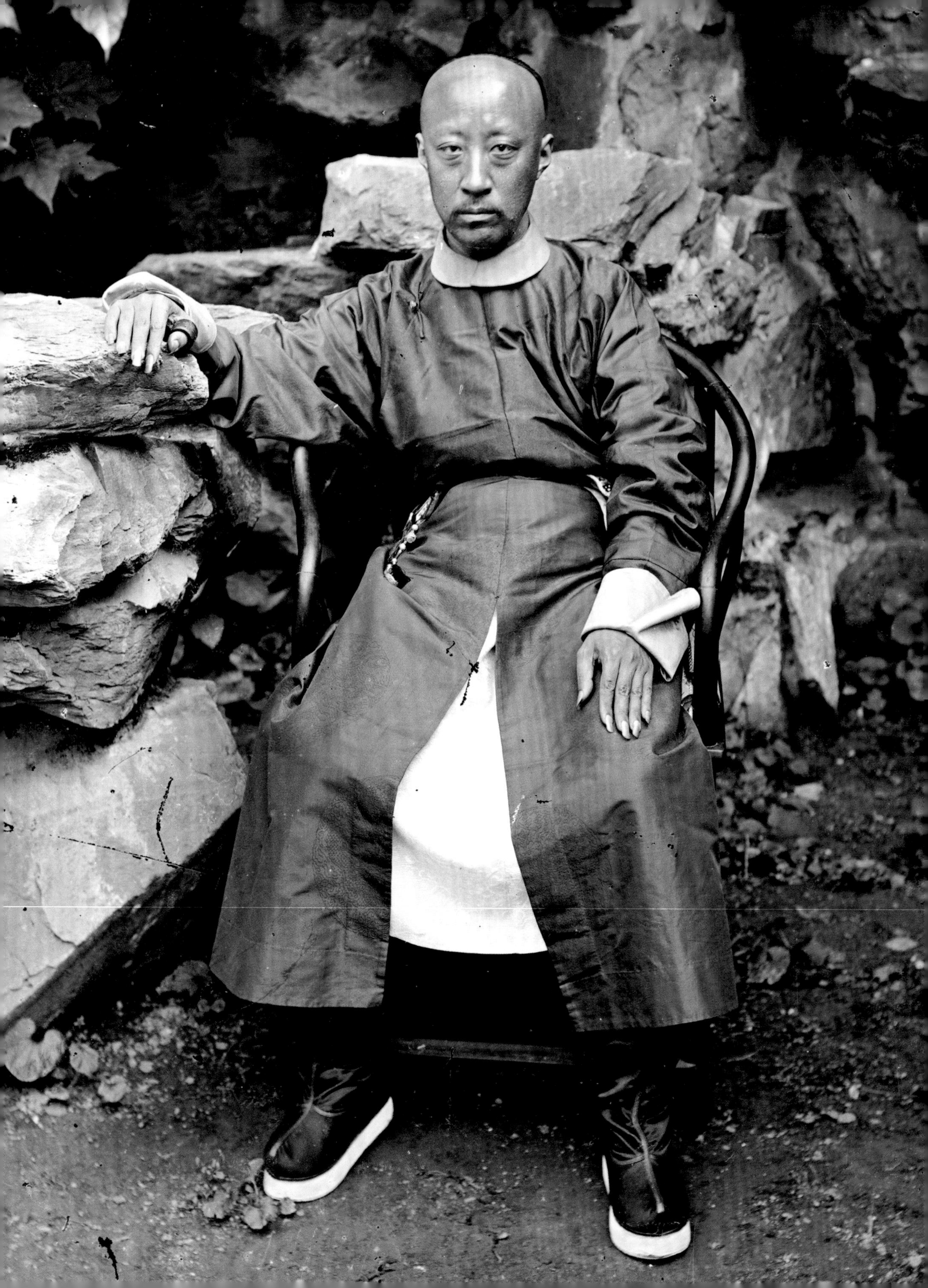

Notes

John Thomson, *Prince Kung*, 1872 (detail of fig. 44).

INTRODUCTION

1 *Illustrated London News*, 14 June 1862. For other images depicting the British engagement with the military court at the International Exhibition, see 'Birmingham Small Arms Trophy', *Illustrated London News*, 14 June 1862; 'The Armstrong Gun Trophy', *Cassell's Illustrated Family Paper Exhibitor: Containing About Three Hundred Illustrations, with Letter Press Descriptions of all the Principal Objects in the International Exhibition of 1862* (London: Cassell, Petter and Galpin, 1862); 'The Armstrong Gun Trophy', in Tal. P. Shaffner, *The Illustrated Record of the International Exhibition of the Industrial Arts and Manufactures, and the Fine Arts, of All Nations, in 1862* (London and New York: London Printing and Publishing Company, 1862).

2 'At the Great Exhibition', *Cornhill Magazine*, 5 (1862), 677; emphasis in original.

3 See William Laurence Burn, *The Age of Equipoise: A Study of the Mid-Victorian Generation* (New York: Norton and Co., 1964).

4 Rudyard Kipling, *The Light that Failed* (1891; Auckland, NZ: Floating Press, 2016), 57.

5 Tim Barringer, 'The South Kensington Museum and the Colonial Project', in Tim Barringer and Tom Flynn, eds, *Colonialism and the Object: Empire, Material Culture and the Museum* (London and New York: Routledge, 1998), 12.

6 See Timothy Mitchell, 'The World as Exhibition', *Comparative Studies in Society and History*, vol. 31, no. 2 (April 1989), 222. See also Jeffrey A. Auerbach and Peter H. Hoffenberg, *Britain, the Empire, and the World at the Great Exhibition* (Abingdon and New York: Routledge, 2016).

7 Mitchell, 'World as Exhibition', 228.

8 The fire at Varna is the most likely candidate out of the newspaper's wartime covers; *Illustrated London News*, 2 September 1854.

9 See Daniel J. Rycroft, *Representing Rebellion: Visual Aspects of Counter-insurgency in Colonial India* (New Delhi: Oxford University Press, 2006).

10 See Peter Harrington, 'The Defence of Kars: Paintings by William Simpson and Thomas Jones Barker', *Journal of the Society for Army Historical Research*, vol. 69, no. 277 (Spring 1991): 22–8; Harrington, 'The First True War Artist', *MHQ: The Quarterly Journal of Military History*, vol. 9, no. 1 (Autumn 1996): 100–09; Peter Johnson, *Front Line Artists* (London: Cassell, 1978).

11 Patrick Collier, 'Imperial/Modernist Forms in the *Illustrated London News*', *Modernism/modernity*, vol. 19, no. 3 (September 2012), 489.

12 'Our Address', *Illustrated London News*, 14 May 1842.

13 *The Graphic*, 24 July 1886.

14 Collier, 'Imperial/Modernist Forms', 502.

15 Chandrika Kaul, *Reporting the Raj: The British Press and India, c.1880–1922* (Manchester and New York: Manchester University Press, 2003), 3.

16 E. S. Dallas, *The Gay Science*, 2 vols (London: Chapman and Hall, 1866), vol. 2, 312.

17 Christopher GoGwilt, *The Fiction of Geopolitics: Afterimages of Culture, from Wilkie Collins to Alfred Hitchcock* (Stanford, Cal: Stanford University Press, 2000), 11.

18 Lauren M. E. Goodlad, *The Victorian Geopolitical Aesthetic: Realism, Sovereignty and Transnational Experience* (Oxford: Oxford University Press, 2015), 11.

19 Ann Laura Stoler, 'On Degrees of Imperial Sovereignty', *Public Culture*, vol. 18, no. 1 (December 2006), 128; see Giorgio Agamben, *Homo Sacer: Sovereign Power and Bare Life* (Stanford: Stanford University Press, 1998).

20 Agamben, *Homo Sacer*.

21 Stoler, 'On Degrees of Imperial Sovereignty', 139.

22 GoGwilt, *Fiction of Geopolitics*, 46.

23 Frederic Jameson, *The Geopolitical Aesthetic: Cinema and Space in the World*

System (Bloomington and Indianapolis: Indiana University Press, 1992).

24 Goodlad, *Victorian Geopolitical Aesthetic*, 2.

25 Lauren M. E. Goodlad, 'Cosmopolitanism's Actually Existing Beyond: Toward a Victorian Geopolitical Aesthetic', *Victorian Literature and Culture*, vol. 38, no. 2 (2010), 406, 400.

26 Susan Buck-Morss, 'Aesthetics and Anesthetics: Walter Benjamin's Artwork Essay Reconsidered', *October*, vol. 62 (Autumn 1992), 6; see also Zahid R. Chaudhary, *Afterimage of Empire: Photography in Nineteenth-Century India* (Minneapolis: University of Minnesota Press, 2012); Walter Mignolo and Rolando Vazquez, 'Decolonial AestheSis: Colonial Wounds/Decolonial Healings', *Social Text* (July 2013), https://socialtextjournal.org/periscope_article/decolonial-aesthesis-colonial-woundsdecolonial-healings/, accessed 30 January 2019.

27 Walter Mignolo, 'The Geopolitics of Sensing and Knowing: On (de) Coloniality, Border Thinking, and Epistemic Disobedience', *Confero*, vol. 1, no. 1 (2013), 132.

28 Walter Mignolo and Catherine Walsh, *On Decoloniality: Concepts, Analytics, Praxis* (Durham, N.C., and London: Duke University Press, 2018), 195.

29 Mignolo, 'Geopolitics of Sensing and Knowing'.

30 Jameson, *Geopolitical Aesthetic*, 10.

31 Lord Lytton quoted in Bernard S. Cohn, 'Representing Authority in Victorian India', in Eric Hobsbawm and Terence Ranger, eds, *The Invention of Tradition* (Cambridge and New York: Cambridge University Press, 1983), 192.

32 See Nicholas B. Dirks, *The Scandal of Empire: India and the Creation of Imperial Britain* (Cambridge, Mass., and London: Harvard University Press, 2008).

33 See, e.g., Zahid R. Chaudhary, *Afterimage of Empire: Photography in Nineteenth-Century India* (Minneapolis: University of Minnesota Press, 2012); John Falconer, *India: Pioneering Photographers, 1850–1900* (London: British Library Publishing, 2001); John Fraser, 'Beato's Photograph of the Interior of the Sikanderbagh at Lucknow', *Journal of the Society for Army Historical Research*, vol. 59, no. 237 (1981); Christopher Pinney, *The Coming of Photography in India* (London: British Library, 2008); James R. Ryan, *Picturing Empire: Photography and the Visualization of the British Empire* (London: Reaktion Books, 1997).

34 See Mildred Archer, *India and British Portraiture, 1770–1825* (London: Sotheby Parke Bernet, 1979).

35 G. D. S. Beechey, *The Eighth Child: George Duncan Beechey, 1797–1852, Royal Portrait Painter to the Last Four Kings of Oudh* (London: Excalibur Press, 1994), 35.

36 'Papers regarding William Florio Hutchisson', British Library, Mss Eur F236/478.

37 See Natasha Eaton, 'The Art of Colonial Despotism: Portraits, Politics, and Empire in South Asia, 1750–1795', *Cultural Critique*, vol. 70 (Fall 2008), 63–93; Eaton, 'Between Mimesis and Alterity: Art, Gift and Diplomacy in Colonial India, 1770–1800', *Comparative Studies in Society and History*, vol. 46 (2006), 816–44; Eaton, 'Critical Cosmopolitanism: Gifting and Collecting Art at Lucknow, 1775–97', in Timothy Barringer, Geoff Quilley and Douglas Fordham, eds, *Art and the British Empire* (Manchester and New York: Manchester University Press, 2007), 189–204.

38 *India Review*, 1830s, quoted in Peary Chand Mittra, *Life of Colesworthy Grant, Founder and Late Honourable Secretary of the Calcutta Society for the Prevention of Cruelty to Animals* (Calcutta: I. C. Bose & Co., 1881), 5. While a good source of information on Grant's early career, Mittra's work – as the title implies – was motivated by Grant's later achievements in preventing animal cruelty rather than by his activities as an artist.

39 Colesworthy Grant, *An Anglo-Indian Domestic Sketch: A Letter from an Artist in India to his Mother in England* (Calcutta: Thacker & Co., 1849), v.

40 Mittra, *Life of Grant*, 10–14.

41 The exception is Mildred Archer's discussion of Grant's work in a short article for a popular history magazine: 'Mission to Burma, 1855', *History Today* (October 1963), 691–9.

42 Colesworthy Grant, *Dost Muhummud Khan, and the Recent Events in Caubool* (London: Thacker & Co., 1842).

43 All the 106 watercolours that Grant ultimately produced on the Burma mission are now mounted one-to-a-page in a large leather-bound album in the India Office Collection of the British Library: Colesworthy Grant, 'Album of 106 Drawings of Landscapes and Portraits of Burmese and Europeans made in Burma during Major Phayre's Mission to the Court of Ava in 1855', PDP/WD540.

44 Colesworthy Grant, *Rough Pencillings of a Rough Trip to Rangoon in 1846* (Calcutta, London and Bombay: Thacker, Spink and Co., 1853), v.

45 Bernard Porter, *The Absent-Minded Imperialists: Empire, Society and Culture in Britain* (Oxford and New York: Oxford University Press, 2004), 107.

46 See Nicholas B. Dirks, 'Guiltless Spoliations: Picturesque Beauty, Colonial Knowledge, and Colin Mackenzie's Survey of India', in Catherine B. Asher and Thomas R. Metcalf, eds, *Perceptions of South Asia's Visual Past* (New Delhi, Mumbai and Kolkata: Oxford and IBH Publishing Co., 1994), 211–32; Matthew H. Edney, *Mapping an Empire: The Geographical Construction of British India, 1765–1843* (London and Chicago: University of Chicago Press, 1997); Jennifer Howes, *Illustrating India: The Early Colonial Investigations of Colin Mackenzie (1784–1821)* (Oxford and New York: Oxford University Press, 2010).

47 Edward Said, *Culture and Imperialism* (New York: Alfred A. Knopf, 1993), 7.

48 Deborah Poole, *Vision, Race, and Modernity: A Visual Economy of the Andean*

Image World (Princeton: Princeton University Press, 1997), 10.

49 Kim Wagner, 'Savage Warfare: Violence and the Rule of Colonial Difference in Early British Counterinsurgency', *History Workshop Journal*, vol. 85 (Spring 2018), 217–37.

50 Natasha Eaton, '"Enchanted Traps?" The Historiography of Art and Colonialism in Eighteenth-century India', *Literature Compass*, vol. 9, no. 1 (January 2012), 15.

51 See the following by Mildred Archer: *British Drawings in the India Office Library* (London: HMSO, 1969); *Company Drawings in the India Office Library* (London: HMSO, 1972); *Company Paintings: Indian Paintings of the British Period* (London: Victoria and Albert Museum with Mapin Publishing, 1992); *Early Views of India: The Picturesque Journeys of Thomas and William Daniell, 1786–1794* (London and New York: Thames and Hudson, 1980); *India and British Portraiture*; *India Observed: India as Viewed by British Artists, 1760–1860: An Exhibition* (London: V&A Museum and Trefoil, 1982); *Indian Architecture and the British* (Feltham: Country Life, 1968); *The Indian Collection of Paintings and Sculpture* (London: British Library, 1986); *Indian Popular Painting in the India Office Library* (London: HMSO, 1977); *Natural History Drawings in the India Office Library* (London: HMSO, 1962).

52 Barringer, Quilley and Fordham, *Art and the British Empire*, 9 (emphasis in original), 2.

53 See Julie Codell, ed., *Transculturation in British Art, 1770–1930* (Aldershot: Ashgate, 2012); and Julie Codell and D. S. Macleod, eds, *Orientalism Transposed: The Impact of the Colonies on British Culture* (Aldershot: Ashgate, 1998); Jason Edwards, 'Introduction: From the East India Company to the West Indies and Beyond: The World of British Sculpture, *c.*1757–1947', *Visual Culture in Britain*, vol. 11, no. 2 (2010): 147–72; Susheila Nasta, ed., *India in Britain: South Asian Networks and Connections, 1858–1950* (Basingstoke and New York: Palgrave Macmillan, 2013); Sarah Victoria Turner, 'The "Essential Quality of Things": E. B. Havell, Ananda Coomaraswamy, Indian Art and Sculpture in Britain, *c.*1910–14', *Visual Culture in Britain*, vol. 11, no. 2 (2010): 239–64.

54 See Barringer and Flynn, *Colonialism and the Object*.

55 See Arindam Dutta, *The Bureaucracy of Beauty: Design in the Age of its Global Reproducibility* (London and New York: Routledge, 2006).

56 On colonial art schools, see ibid; Tapati Guha-Thakurta, *The Making of a New 'Indian' Art: Artists, Aesthetics and Nationalism in Bengal, c.1850–1920* (Cambridge and New York: Cambridge University Press, 1992); Partha Mitter, *Art and Nationalism in Colonial India, 1850–1922: Occidental Orientations* (Cambridge: Cambridge University Press, 1994); Mahrukh Tarapor, 'John Lockwood Kipling and British Art Education in India', *Victorian Studies*, vol. 24, no. 1 (Autumn 1980): 53–81.

57 See Natasha Eaton, *Mimesis across Empires: Artworks and Networks in India, 1765–1860* (Durham, N.C., and London: Duke University Press, 2013).

58 See Pheroza Godrej and Pauline Rohatgi, eds, *Scenic Splendours: India through the Printed Image* (London: British Library, 1989); Godrej and Rohatgi, eds, *Under the Indian Sun: British Landscape Artists* (Bombay: Marg Publications, 1995); Graham Parlett and Pauline Rohatgi, eds, *Indian Life and Landscape by Western Artists: Paintings and Drawings from the Victoria and Albert Museum, 17th to the Early 20th Century* (London: V&A Museum; Mumbai: Chatrapati Shivaji Maharaj Vastu Sangrahalaya, 2008); Pratapaditya Pal, *From Merchants to Emperors: British Artists in India, 1757–1930* (Ithaca and London: Cornell University Press, 1986).

59 Romita Ray, *Under the Banyan Tree: Relocating the Picturesque in British India* (New Haven and London: Yale University Press, 2013), 7.

60 Ibid., 2.

61 See Lauren Berlant, *Cruel Optimism* (Durham, N.C: Duke University Press, 2011), 5.

62 Ibid., 6.

63 Anjali Arondekar, *For the Record: On Sexuality and the Colonial Archive in India* (Durham, N.C., and London: Duke University Press, 2009), 6.

64 See Ariella Azoulay, *The Civil Contract of Photography* (New York: Zone Books, 2008).

65 Julie F. Codell, 'Photography and the Delhi Durbars: 1877, 1903, 1911', in Julie F. Codell, ed., *Power and Resistance: The Delhi Coronation Durbars* (New Delhi: Mapin Publishing with the Alkazi Collection of Photography, 2012), 17.

1 · EXHIBITING GLOBAL CONFLICT

1 Sir Henry Maine, *International Law: A Series of Lectures Delivered Before the University of Cambridge, 1887* (London: John Murray, 1888), 3–4.

2 On the cultural significance of the Great Exhibition, see Jeffrey A. Auerbach, *The Great Exhibition of 1851: A Nation on Display* (New Haven and London: Yale University Press, 1999); Kate Nichols and Sarah Victoria Turner, *After 1851: The Material and Visual Cultures of the Crystal Palace at Sydenham* (Manchester: Manchester University Press, 2017).

3 Maine, *International Law*, 6.

4 Tony Bennet, *The Birth of the Museum: History, Theory, Politics* (London: Routledge, 1995), 60–61, 67.

5 Peter H. Hoffenberg, *An Empire on Display: English, Indian and Australian Exhibitions from the Crystal Palace to the Great War* (Berkeley, Los Angeles and London: University of California Press, 2001), 71.

6 Chris Otter, *The Victorian Eye: A Political History of Light and Vision in Britain, 1800–1900* (Chicago and London: University of Chicago Press, 2008), 47–8.

7 Jordan Bear, *Disillusioned: Victorian Photography and the Discerning Subject*

(University Park: Pennsylvania State University Press, 2015), 31.

8 Ulrich Keller, *The Ultimate Spectacle: A Visual History of the Crimean War* (Amsterdam: Gordon and Breach Publishers, 2001), 10.

9 Editorial, *Journal of the Photographic Society of London*, 21 March 1854, 177.

10 *A Guide to the Great Exhibition; Contains a Description of Every Principle Object of Interest* (London: George Routledge and Co., 1851), 11.

11 John Ruskin, 'War', *Crown of Wild Olive: Four Lectures on Industry and War* (Orpington: George Allen, 1882), 105, 112.

12 See Keller, *Ultimate Spectacle.*

13 *Punch*, 1854, quoted in ibid., 10.

14 Denis Judd, *The Crimean War* (London: Hart-Davis and MacGibbon, 1975), 7.

15 Yakup Bektas, 'The Crimean War as a Technological Enterprise', *Notes and Records*, vol. 71, no. 3 (September 2017), 233–62.

16 Helen Groth, 'Technological Mediations and the Public Sphere: Roger Fenton's Crimea Exhibition and "The Charge of the Light Brigade"', *Victorian Literature and Culture*, vol. 30, no. 2 (September 2002), 562.

17 *The Athenaeum*, no. 1457, 29 September 1855, 1118.

18 Phillip Knightley, *The First Casualty, from the Crimea to Vietnam: The War Correspondent as Hero, Propagandist, and Myth Maker* (San Diego, Cal: Harcourt Brace Jovanovich, 1975), 15.

19 William Howard Russell, 'The British Expedition', *The Times*, 18 December 1854.

20 *The Athenaeum*, 29 September 1855, 1118.

21 Jennifer Green-Lewis, *Framing the Victorians: Photography and the Culture of Realism* (Ithaca and London: Cornell University Press, 1996), 102.

22 *Art Journal*, 'Photographs from Sebastopol', 1 October 1855, 285.

23 Rachel Teukolsky, 'Novels, Newspapers, and Global War: New Realisms in the 1850s', *Novel: A Forum on Fiction*, vol. 45, no. 1 (2012), 33.

24 Nancy Armstrong, *Fiction in the Age of Photography: The Legacy of British Realism* (Cambridge, Mass., and London: Harvard University Press, 1999), 7.

25 *The Athenaeum*, 29 September 1855, 1118.

26 Green-Lewis, *Framing the Victorians*, 120.

27 Bear, *Disillusioned*, 31.

28 See Daniel J. Rycroft, *Representing Rebellion: Visual Aspects of Counter-insurgency in Colonial India* (New Delhi: Oxford University Press, 2006).

29 Don Randall, 'Autumn 1857: The Making of the Indian "Mutiny"', *Victorian Literature and Culture*, vol. 31, no. 1 (2003), 4.

30 *Illustrated London News*, 3 October 1857, quoted in ibid., 5.

31 Christopher Herbert, *War of No Pity: The Indian Mutiny and Victorian Trauma* (Princeton and Oxford: Princeton University Press, 2008), 22.

32 Murray has been dealt with summarily by scholars, with the exception of the military historian John Fraser's well-researched, if somewhat hagiographic, unpublished biography, 'Dr John Murray of Agra' (*c.*1980), National Army Museum, 2010-11-11-1. Also see: John Fraser, 'Dr John Murray of Agra', *PhotoHistorian*, No. 132, (Nov. 2000), 13–15.

33 The success of Murray's work was also partly due to its novelty: photographs of India were still rare in London and his were then 'among the largest landscapes that the camera has ... produced'; *Morning Post*, 14 November 1857.

34 John Murray, *Photographic Views in Agra and its Vicinity* (London: J. Hogarth, 1857), India Office Records, British Library, London, Photo 101; John Murray, *Picturesque Views in the North-Western Provinces of India* (London: J. Hogarth, 1859).

35 *Saturday Review*, 9 March 1861, 245.

36 Hering started selling Beato's photographs from the Indian Uprising (and photographs taken during the war in China) in 1862; Henry Hering, 'A Magnificent Collection of Photographic Views and Panoramas taken by Signor Beato, During the Indian Mutiny in 1857–58, and the late War in China, of Lucknow, Cawnpore, Delhi, Agra, Benares, & Punjab, Hong, the Peiho Forts, Pekin, the Summer Palace, and Canton', British Library, Photo 6(13): 1860.

37 *The Athenaeum*, no. 1582, 20 February 1858, 246.

38 'Photographs of Indian Cities &c.', *Art Journal*, vol. 19 (December 1857), 386.

39 Herbert, *War of No Pity*, 2.

40 See Alison Blunt, 'Embodying War: British Women and Domestic Defilement in the Indian "Mutiny", 1857–8', *Journal of Historical Geography*, vol. 26, no. 3 (2000), 403–28; Pamela Fletcher, '"To Wipe Away a Manly Tear": The Aesthetics of Emotion in Victorian Narrative Painting', *Victorian Studies*, vol. 51, no. 3 (Spring 2009): 457–69; Julia Thomas, *Pictorial Victorians: The Inscription of Values in Word and Image* (Athens: Ohio University Press, 2004), 125–44, 'A Tale of Two Stories: Joseph Noel Paton's *In Memoriam*'.

41 For a detailed account of the Cawnpore siege and massacre, see Andrew Ward, *Our Bones are Scattered: The Cawnpore Massacres and the Indian Mutiny of 1857* (London: John Murray, 2004).

42 'The Royal Academy', *Art Journal*, vol. 4 (London and New York: James S. Virtue, 1858), 169.

43 French critic of Paton's *In Memoriam* quoted in Thomas, *Pictorial Victorians*, 128.

44 *Morning Advertiser*, 9 November 1857.

45 *Morning Post*, 14 November 1857.

46 Steve Edwards, *The Making of English Photography: Allegories* (University Park: Pennsylvania State University Press, 2006), 59.

47 J. Middleton's entry for Agra Fort, in Murray, *Photographic Views*, unpaginated.

48 *Morning Post*, 14 November 1857.

49 *Morning Advertiser*, 9 November 1857.

50 *Morning Post*, 14 November 1857.

51 *Literary Gazette*, vol. 3 (7 November 1857), 1075.

52 'Photographs of Indian Cities &c.', *Art Journal*, vol. 19 (December 1857), 386.

53 *Morning Advertiser*, 9 November 1857.

54 John Ruskin, 'The Deteriotive Power of Conventional Art Over Nations', inaugural lecture at the South Kensington Museum, London, January 1858, in *The Two Paths: Being Lectures on Art, and its Application to Decoration and Manufacture, delivered in 1858–9* (London: Smith, Elder, and Co., 1859), 16.

55 Ibid., 19.

56 Tim Barringer, *Men at Work: Art and Labour in Victorian Britain* (New Haven and London: Yale University Press for the Paul Mellon Centre for British Art, 2005), 267.

57 Ruskin, 'Deteriotive Power', 18.

58 See John Ruskin, *Modern Painters*, 4 vols (London: Smith, Elder, and Co., 1848–56), vol. 1.

59 Ruskin, 'Deteriotive Power', 18.

60 Ibid., 12, 14–15.

61 Ibid., 15.

62 Ibid., 47; emphasis added.

63 Ibid., 7.

64 'The Jurors Report', quoted in Colonel Tal P. Shaffner and the Rev. W. Owens, eds, *The Illustrated Record of the International Exhibition of the Industrial Arts and Manufactures, and Fine Arts, of All Nations, in 1862* (London and New York: London Printing and Publishing Company, 1862), 101.

65 Critic of 1862 exhibition quoted in Hoffenberg, *Empire on Display*, 201.

2 · MUTINOUS VISION

1 Alexander Duff, *The Indian Rebellion: Its Causes and Results* (New York: Robert Cater & Brothers, 1858), 17.

2 See Kim Wagner, *The Great Fear of 1857: Rumours, Conspiracies and the Making of the Indian Uprising* (Witney: Peter Lang, 2010).

3 See Sophie Gordon, 'Monumental Visions: Architectural Photography in India, 1840–1901', PhD thesis, School of Oriental and African Studies, University of London, 2010, 122.

4 *Daily News*, 30 March 1858.

5 *The Englishman*, 17 February 1859.

6 Ahmad Ali Khan, 'The Lucknow Album' (*c.*1856), British Library, London, Photo 269/1.

7 William Howard Russell, 'The War in India', *The Times*, 5 April 1858.

8 Alison Blunt, 'Home and Empire: Photographs of British Families in the 'Lucknow Album', 1856–57', in James Ryan, ed., *Picturing Place: Photography and the Geographical Imagination* (New York: I. B. Tauris, 2006), 243–60.

9 *The Englishman*, 19 February 1858.

10 Jonathan Crary, *Techniques of the Observer: On Vision and Modernity in the Nineteenth Century* (Cambridge, Mass: MIT Press, 1992; 1998), 30.

11 *Bengal Hurkaru*, 23 February 1858.

12 Zahid R. Chaudhary, *Afterimage of Empire: Photography in Nineteenth-Century India* (Minneapolis: University of Minnesota Press, 2012), 29–30.

13 Christopher Pinney, *The Coming of Photography in India* (London: British Library, 2008), 9.

14 The Rev. Joseph Mullins, October 1856, quoted in John Falconer, '"A Pure Labour of Love": A Publishing History of *The People of India*', in Eleanor M. Hight and Gary D. Sampson, eds, *Colonialist Photography: Imag(in)ing Race and Place* (London and New York: Routledge, 2013), 51–83.

15 See Walter D. Mignolo, 'Geopolitics of Sensing and Knowing: On (De) Coloniality, Border Thinking and Epistemic Disobedience', *Postcolonial Studies*, vol. 14, no. 3 (2011), 273–83.

16 See Thomas Metcalf, *The Aftermath of Revolt: India, 1857–1870* (Princeton: Princeton University Press, 1964), 46–92, 'The Mutiny and its Causes'.

17 Pinney, *Coming of Photography*, 106.

18 Indian soldier on telegraphy, quoted in Christopher Pinney, 'The Colonial Dromosphere: Speed, Transmission, and Prosthesis in Colonial India', in J. Carlos Viana Ferreira and Teresa de Ataíde Malafaia, eds, *The British Empire: Ideology, Perspectives, Perceptions* (Lisbon: University of Lisbon, Centre for English Studies, 2010), 117.

19 *Journal of the Photographic Society of London*, 21 April 1854, 189.

20 See Chaudhary, *Afterimage of Empire*, 131–9; Pinney, *Coming of Photography*, 133. Khan's photographs for Wajid Ali Shah are now held in the British Library, 'Miscellaneous Portraits of the Royal Family of Oudh and other Sitters', PDP/ Photo 500.

21 *Daily News*, 30 March 1858; the same report was published in the *Sheffield & Rotherham Independent*, 3 April 1858, and the *Illustrated Times*, 15 May 1858.

22 See Stéphanie Roy Bharath, 'Recording South Indian Architecture: Linnaeus Tripe and Edmund David Lyon', in *South Asian Studies*, vol. 26, no. 2 (2010): 97–118.

23 Sophie Gordon, 'A City of Mourning: The Representation of Lucknow, India in Nineteenth-Century Photography', *History of Photography*, vol. 30, no. 1 (2006), 86.

24 Mary Louise Pratt, *Imperial Eyes: Travel Writing and Transculturation* (London and New York: Routledge, 1992; 2008), 1–12.

25 See Blunt, 'Home and Empire'.

26 The Rev. E. and Rev. T. S. Polehampton, eds, *A Memoir: Letters, and Diary, of Rev. Henry S. Polehampton, M. A. Chaplain of Lucknow* (London: Richard Bentley, 1858), 141–2.

27 Ibid., 224, 142.

28 Ibid., 225.

29 Captain John Arthur Bayley quoted in Fraser, 'The Indian Mutiny in Photographs', 18.

30 *Bengal Hurkaru*, 23 February 1858.

31 In drawing on the notion of a 'habitus', Pinney, *Coming of Photography*, 30, is following Bourdieu.

32 Jacques Derrida, 'Plato's Pharmacy', trans. Barbara Johnson, in *Dissemination* (Chicago: University of Chicago Press, 1981).

33 Pinney, *Coming of Photography*, 17.

34 Nicholas Mirzoeff, *The Right to Look: A Counterhistory of Visuality* (Durham, N.C., and London: Duke University Press, 2011), 8.

35 For accounts of colonial art schools in India, see Arindam Dutta, *The Bureaucracy of Beauty: Design in the Age of its Global Reproducibility* (London and New York: Routledge, 2006); Tapati Guha-Thakurta, *The Making of a New 'Indian' Art: Artists, Aesthetics and Nationalism in Bengal, c.1850–1920* (Cambridge and New York: Cambridge University Press, 1992); Partha Mitter, *Art and Nationalism in Colonial India, 1850–1922: Occidental Orientations* (Cambridge: Cambridge University Press, 1994); Mahrukh Tarapor, 'John Lockwood Kipling and British Art Education in India', *Victorian Studies*, vol. 24, no. 1 (Autumn 1980), 53–81.

36 Christopher Pinney, *'Photos of the Gods': The Printed Image and Political Struggle in India* (London: Reaktion Books, 2004), 19.

37 Thomas Babington Macaulay, 'Minute on Indian Education' [2 February 1835], *Speeches by Lord Macaulay with his Minute on Indian Education*, ed. G. M. Young (London: Oxford University Press, 1979), 345–61.

38 Sir Richard Temple, *Oriental Experience: A selection of essays and addresses delivered on various occasions* (London: John Murray, 1883), 485.

39 John Ruskin, 'The Deteriotive Power of Conventional Art Over Nations', in *The Two Paths: Being Lectures on Art, and its Application to Decoration and Manufacture, delivered in 1858–9* (London: Smith, Elder, and Co., 1859), 19.

40 Sir Henry Yule, *A Narrative of the Mission sent by the Governor-General of India to the Court of Ava in 1855* (London: Smith, Elder, and Co., 1858), 89.

41 Sir James Fergusson, 1869, quoted in Pinney, *Coming of Photography*, 73.

42 R. H. Thouless, 1933, quoted in Natasha Eaton, *Colour, Art and Empire: Visual Culture and the Nomadism of Representation* (London: I. B. Tauris, 2013), 130.

43 *The Englishman*, 19 February 1858.

44 Suren Lalvani, *Photography, Vision, and the Production of Modern Bodies* (Albany: State University of New York Press, 1996), 2.

45 Martin Jay locates Cartesian perspectivalism as one of three scopic regimes of modernity; 'Scopic Regimes of Modernity', in Hal Foster, ed., *Vision and Visuality* (Seattle: Bay Press, 1988), 3–23.

46 John Wylie, 'Depths and Folds: On Landscape and the Gazing Subject', *Environment and Planning: Society and Space*, vol. 24, no. 4 (2006), 522.

47 *Report of the commissioners appointed to consider the best mode of re-organizing the system for training officers for the Scientific Corps; together with an account of foreign and other military education* (London: George E. Eyre & William Spottiswoode, 1857), 405, 267.

48 Theodore Henry Fielding, *Synopsis of Practical Perspective, Linear and Aerial* (London: W. H. Allen & Co., 1836), 29. A book on perspective was also published by a later teacher of drawing at Addiscombe; see Aaron Penley, *The Elements of Perspective: Illustrated by Numerous Examples and Diagrams* (London: Windsor and Newton, 1866).

49 Ranajit Guha, *Dominance without Hegemony: History and Power in Colonial India* (Cambridge, Mass: Harvard University Press, 1997).

50 Daniel J. Rycroft, *Representing Rebellion: Visual Aspects of Counter-insurgency in Colonial India* (New Delhi: Oxford University Press, 2006), 147, 166.

51 Peter H. Hoffenberg, *An Empire on Display: English, Indian and Australian Exhibitions from the Crystal Palace to the Great War* (Berkeley, Los Angeles and London: University of California Press, 2001), 71–3.

52 *The Englishman*, 24 April 1857.

53 Rycroft, *Representing Rebellion*, 53.

54 For an account of Rajendralal Mitra's career as a scholar in India, as well as his reincorporation into British colonial society, see Malavika Karlekar, *Re-Visioning the Past: Early Photography in Bengal, 1875–1915* (Oxford and New York: Oxford University Press, 2005), 134–48.

55 For accounts of the politics of pigment production in India, see Jordanna Bailkin, 'Indian Yellow: Making and Breaking the Imperial Palette', *Journal of Material Culture*, vol. 10, no. 2 (July 2005), 197–214; Natasha Eaton, 'Nomadism of Colour: Painting and Waste in the Chromo-Zones of Colonial India, *c.*1765–*c.*1860', *Journal of Material Culture*, vol. 17, no. 1 (March 2012): 61–81; Michael Taussig, 'Redeeming Indigo', *Theory, Culture & Society*, vol. 25, no. 3 (May 2008), 1–15.

56 *To the Members of the Photographic Society of Bengal* [An address, signed 'A Member', opposing an intended resolution to expel Rajendralal Mitra for speaking against the Indigo Planters at a public meeting] (Calcutta: J. Thomas, 1857).

57 *The Englishman*, 17 July 1857.

58 Ibid.

59 *To the Members*, 7.

60 *Bengal Hurkaru*, 23 August 1857.

61 Ibid., 15 December 1857.

62 Gordon, 'A City of Mourning', 82.

63 *The Englishman*, 19 February 1858.

64 Michael Taussig, *Mimesis and Alterity: A Particular History of the Senses* (London and New York: Routledge, 1993), 8.

65 Homi K. Bhabha, *The Location of Culture* (London and New York: Routledge, 1994), 129.

66 *The Englishman*, 9 July 1857.

3 · 'ADDITIONAL HORRORS'

1 Colonel Charles Edward Callwell, *Small Wars: Their Principle and Practice* (London: HMSO, 1896).

2 'Why Did the Indian Mutiny Happen?', National Army Museum, London, https://www.nam.ac.uk/explore/why-did-indian-mutiny-happen, accessed 22 February 2021.

3 Anne Lacoste, *Felice Beato: A Photographer on the Eastern Road* (Los Angeles: J. Paul Getty Museum, 2010), 2.

4 Kim Wagner, '"Calculated to Strike Terror": The Amritsar Massacre and the Spectacle of Colonial Violence', *Past and Present*, vol. 233, no. 1 (November 2016), 197.

5 Ibid., 205.

6 Kim Wagner, 'Savage Warfare: Violence and the Rule of Colonial Difference in Early British Counterinsurgency', *History Workshop Journal*, vol. 85 (Spring 2018), 220.

7 Susan Sontag, *On Photography* (Harmondsworth and New York: Penguin Books, 1978), 3.

8 John Ruskin, *Modern Painters*, vol. 4 (London: Smith, Elder, and Co., 1856), 1.

9 Ibid., 9; emphasis in original. My reading of Ruskin's critique of the picturesque as 'the origin of a modern perceptualist culture' is indebted to John Macarthur, 'The Heartlessness of the Picturesque: Sympathy and Disgust in Ruskin's Aesthetics', *Assemblage*, no. 32 (April 1997), 139.

10 Malcolm Andrews, *The Search for the Picturesque: Landscape Aesthetics and Tourism in Britain, 1760–1800* (Stanford, Cal: Stanford University Press, 1989), 5.

11 John Ruskin to his parents, from Parma, Italy, July 1845, quoted in Robert Hewison, 'Ruskin and the Picturesque', in *John Ruskin: The Argument of the Eye* (Princeton, N.J: Princeton University Press, 1976), http://www.victorianweb.org/authors/ruskin/hewison/2.html, accessed 7 January 2019.

12 Zahid R. Chaudhary, *Afterimage of Empire: Photography in Nineteenth-Century India* (Minneapolis: University of Minnesota Press, 2012), 73–107.

13 Ibid., 116.

14 Henry A. Giroux, 'Disturbing Pleasures: Murderous Images and the Aesthetics of Depravity', *Third Text*, vol. 26, no. 3 (2012), 259–73.

15 Christopher Pinney, *The Coming of Photography in India* (London: British Library, 2008), 123.

16 Chaudhary, *Afterimage of Empire*, 77.

17 Callwell, *Small Wars*, 26–7, 228.

18 Lord Canning to Queen Victoria, 25 September 1857, quoted in William Dalrymple, *The Last Mughal: The Fall of a Dynasty, Delhi, 1857* (London, New York and Berlin: Bloomsbury Publishing, 2006), 402.

19 Bhonlanauth Chunder, *The Travels of a Hindoo to various parts of Bengal and Upper India*, 2 vols (London: N. Trubner & Co., 1869), vol. 1, 335.

20 Dr John Murray, diary, 1 January 1858, British Library, London, Western Manuscripts, RP9617.

21 J. Murray, Esquire, M. D., to C. Beadon, Esquire, Secretary to the Government of India, 20 March 1858, British Library, IOR/P/188/52.

22 Murray, diary, 22 February 1858.

23 Ibid., 27 February 1858.

24 No. 68. From C. BEADON, Esquire, Secretary to the Government of India, to J. MURRAY, Esquire, M.D., No. 176, 22 January 1858, IOR/P/188/49.

25 Murray, diary, 18 January 1858; emphasis added.

26 Anne McClintock, 'Imperial Ghosting and National Tragedy: Revenants from Hiroshima and Indian Country in the War on Terror', *PMLA*, vol. 129, no. 4 (October 2014), 821.

27 Beato's *Interior of the Secundrabagh after the Slaughter of 2000 Rebels*, but not the photograph of the hanging, appears in the following albums: Sir Edward Bosc Sladen, 'Views at Lucknow and Cawnpore by Felice Beato, taken after the Indian Mutiny', British Library, London, Visual Arts, Photo 1100; 'Album of views of military, religious, and secular architecture, portraits and topography, India and Egypt', Canadian Centre for Architecture, Montreal, PH1987:1084:001–147; 'The Tresidder Album', Alkazi Foundation for the Arts, New Delhi. More commonly, however, both these photographs are omitted. Significant collections of colonial photography from this time include numerous Beato scenes from the Uprising but not his most explicitly violent views, e.g. Sir Richard Carnac Temple Collection: Views of India, China and England, British Library, Visual Arts, Photo 125; Montgomerie Collection: Views in India, ibid., Photo 25.

28 See National Army Museum, London, 1962-11-63-23; Victoria and Albert Museum, London, 3219–1955.

29 Arthur Moffat Lang, *Lahore to Lucknow: The Indian Mutiny Journal of Arthur Moffat Lang*, ed. David Blomfield (London: Leo Cooper, 1992), 139.

30 Arthur Moffat Lang to his brother Matthew Lang, 21 June 1858, British Library, Add. Ms 43822, fol. 100. I am indebted to John Fraser's meticulous early research on photography in India for this and other Lang references; John Fraser, 'Beato's Photograph of the Interior of the Sikanderbagh at Lucknow', *Journal of the Society for Army Historical Research*, vol. 59, no. 237 (1981), 51–5; 'Some Pre-Mutiny Photographs', *Journal of the Society for Army Historical Research*, vol. 58, no. 234 (1980), 134–47; 'The Indian Mutiny in Photographs', *c.*1986, 33, NAM, 2010-11-11-2-1.

31 Nathan K. Hensley, *Forms of Empire: The Poetics of Victorian Sovereignty* (Oxford and New York: Oxford University Press, 2016), 24, 26.

32 Arthur Moffat Lang, diary, 21 June 1858, Add. Ms 43825, fol. 36.

33 Anne Radcliffe, 'The Supernatural in Poetry', *New Monthly Magazine and Literary Journal*, Vol. 16, no. 1 (1826), 149.

34 Lang, *Lahore to Lucknow*, 139.

35 Ibid.

36 Pinney, *Coming of Photography*, 126.

37 Hensley, *Forms of Empire*, 29.

38 Pinney, 'Seven Theses on Photography', *Thesis Eleven*, vol. 113, no. 1 (2012), 144.

39 Judith Butler, *Frames of War: When is Life Grievable?* (London and New York: Verso, 2009), 25.

40 Chunder, *Travels of a Hindoo*, vol. 1, 321–2.

41 Tina Campt, *Image Matters: Archive, Photography, and the African Diaspora in Europe* (Durham, N.C., and London: Duke University Press, 2012), 60.

42 See Sean Willcock, 'Aesthetic Bodies: Posing on Sites of Violence in India, 1857–1900', *History of Photography*, vol. 39, no. 2 (2015), 142–59.

43 Elizabeth Edwards, *Raw Histories: Photography, Anthropology, and Museums* (Oxford and New York: Berg, 2001), 18.

44 Giorgio Agamben, *Homo Sacer: Sovereign Power and Bare Life* (Stanford, Cal: Stanford University Press, 1998), 122.

45 Richard Wendorf, *Sir Joshua Reynolds: The Painter in Society* (Cambridge, Mass: Harvard University Press, 1996), 135; emphasis in original.

46 Wagner, '"Calculated to Strike Terror"', 218.

47 Alex Tickell, *Terrorism, Insurgency and Indian-English Literature, 1830–1947* (London and New York: Routledge, 2012), 92.

48 Chaudhary, *Afterimage of Empire*, 77.

49 Giles Tillotson, *The Artificial Empire: The Indian Landscapes of William Hodges* (Richmond, Surrey: Curzon Press, 2000).

50 Jeffrey Auerbach, 'The Picturesque and the Homogenization of Empire', *British Art Journal*, vol. 5, no. 1 (2004), 283–305.

51 Both Chaudhary and Anne Lacoste locate Beato at the intersection of 'picturesque' and 'documentary' modes of practice; Chaudhary, *Afterimage of Empire*, 80; Lacoste, *Felice Beato*, 5.

52 Ruskin, *Modern Painters*, vol. 4, 10.

53 Chaudhary, *Afterimage of Empire*, 80.

54 Dr David Field Rennie, 1864, quoted in David Harris, *Of Battle and Beauty: Felice Beato's Photographs of China* (Santa Barbara, Cal: Santa Barbara Museum of Art, 1999), 29.

55 Chaudhary, *Afterimage of Empire*, 77.

56 Ibid. 110.

57 Ruskin to his parents, from Parma, Italy, July 1845, quoted in Hewison, 'Ruskin and the Picturesque'.

58 Ibid.

59 Sontag's views on photography famously changed from her 1977 essays in *On Photography* to her later meditation on images of suffering, *Regarding the Pain of Others* (London and New York: Penguin, 2003). I speak mostly of her earlier views here, taking them as emblematic of a particular but prominent strain of photographic theory that has been characterised by an extreme level of anxiety over the ethical quandary of photography; for a critical overview of such scholarship, see Susie Linfield, *Cruel Radiance: Photography and Political Violence* (Chicago: University of Chicago Press, 2010), 3–32.

60 Chaudhary, *Afterimage of Empire*, 90, 97.

61 Susan Buck-Morss, 'Aesthetics and Anesthetics: Walter Benjamin's Artwork Essay Reconsidered', *October*, vol. 62 (Autumn 1992), 3–41.

62 Ruskin, *Modern Painters*, vol. 4, 9.

63 Macarthur, 'Heartlessness of the Picturesque', 136.

64 Sir George Campbell, *Memoirs of my Indian Career*, ed. Sir Charles E. Bernard, 2 vols (London: Macmillan and Co., 1893), vol. 2, 4, emphasis added; 37.

65 Macarthur, 'Heartlessness of the Picturesque', 139.

66 Pierre Bourdieu quoted in Chaudhary, *Afterimage of Empire*, 121.

67 Ibid., 110.

68 Pinney, *Coming of Photography*, 23.

69 Ibid., 30.

70 Wagner, '"Calculated to Strike Terror"', 212.

71 Frederick Bailey, 1903, quoted in Simeon Koole, 'Photography as Event: Power, the Kodak Camera and Territoriality in Early Twentieth-Century Tibet', *Comparative Studies in Society and History*, vol. 59, no. 2 (2017), 340.

72 See John Falconer, 'Willoughby Wallace Hooper: "A Craze about Photography"', *Photographic Collector*, vol. 4, no. 3 (Winter 1983), 258–85.

73 'No. 14, Letter from Viceroy Dufferin to Lord Randolph Churchill (extract), January 24 1886', *Telegraphic Correspondence relating to Military Executions and Dacoity in Burmah* (London: Eyre and Spottiswoode, 1886), 8.

74 Falconer, 'Willoughby Wallace Hooper', 243.

75 Dufferin to Randolph Churchill, 26 January 1886, quoted in ibid., 258.

76 For Hooper's second photograph of the execution, see Christie's, London, 31 May 2007, Auction 7395, 'Photo Books', lot 5, https://www.christies.com/lot/lot-lieut-col-ww-hooper-4914374/?from=salesummary&intObjectID=4914374&lid=1, accessed 23 February 2021.

77 Christopher Pinney, 'The Colonial Dromosphere: Speed, Transmission and Prosthesis in Colonial India', in J. Carlos Viana Ferreira and Teresa de Ataíde Malafaia, eds, *The British Empire: Ideology, Perspectives, Perceptions* (Lisbon: University of Lisbon, Centre for English Studies, 2010), 128.

78 Grattan Geary, *Burma, After the Conquest: Viewed in its Political, Social, and Commercial Aspects from Mandalay* (London: Sampson Low, Marston, Searle & Rivington, 1886), 243.

79 *The Times*, 29 January 1886.

80 Geary, *Burma*, 243.

81 See Jane Lydon, *Photography, Humanitarianism, Empire* (London and New York: Routledge, 2016); Sharon Sliwinski, 'The Childhood of Human Rights: The Kodak on the Congo', *Journal of Visual Culture*, vol. 5, no. 3 (2006), 333–63.

82 Geary, *Burma*, 241.

83 *The Times*, 21 January 1886.

84 'No. 19. Telegram from Viceroy Dufferin to Lord Randolph Churchill, 2 February 1886', *Telegraphic Correspondence*, 9.

85 Willoughby Wallace Hooper, letter to *The Times*, 4 March 1886.

86 *The Times*, 21 January 1886.

87 Geary, *Burma*, 261.

88 Lee Ann Fujii, 'The Puzzle of Extra Lethal Violence', *Perspectives on Politics*, vol. 11, no. 2 (June 2013), 411.

89 Slavoj Žižek, 'What Rumsfeld doesn't know that He knows about Abu Ghraib', *In These Times*, 21 May 2004.

90 Lieutenant-Colonel Willoughby Wallace Hooper, *Burmah: One hundred photographs, illustrating incidents connected with the British Expeditionary Force to that country, from Embarkation at Madras, 1st Nov. 1885, to the capture of King Theebaw, with many views of Mandalay and surrounding country, native life and industries, and most interesting descriptive notes* (London: J. A. Lugard; Calcutta: Thacker, Spink and Co., 1887); see British Library, Visual Arts, Photo 312.

91 Christie's, Auction 7395, lot 5, https://www.christies.com/lot/lot-lieut-col-ww-hooper-4914374/?from=salesummary&intObjectID=4914374&lid=1, accessed 26 February 2021.

4 · SKETCHING 'ON THE SPOT'

1 Mortimer Menpes, *War Impressions: Being a Record in Colour by Mortimer Menpes*, transcr. Dorothy Menpes (London: Adam & Charles Black, 1901), 140. As with many of Menpes's books, the text is billed as being 'by Dorothy Menpes', his daughter, and scholars have thus usually cited her as the author. Yet the first-person voice deployed in the narrative is from Mortimer's perspective and an obituary of him claimed that his daughter was his amanuensis; *Sydney Morning Herald*, 9 April 1938. I therefore cite Mortimer as the author throughout.

2 Menpes, *War Impressions*, 138.

3 Roger T. Stearn, 'War Correspondents and Colonial War, *c.*1870–1900', in John M. MacKenzie, ed., *Popular Imperialism and the Military: 1850–1950* (Manchester and New York: Manchester University Press, 1992), 141.

4 Rudyard Kipling, *The Light that Failed* (London and New York: Macmillan and Co.,1895), 70.

5 See Andrew Griffiths, *The New Journalism, the New Imperialism and the Fiction of Empire, 1870–1900* (Houndmills, Basingstoke: Palgrave Macmillan, 2015); Catherine Waters, *Special Correspondence and the Newspaper Press in Victorian Print Culture, 1850–1886* (Houndmills, Basingstoke: Palgrave Macmillan, 2019).

6 Hitherto, when written about at all, the 'special artist' has been the preserve of military historians. This chapter is indebted to their research. It has benefited in particular from Peter Harrington's meticulous archival work on William Simpson at the Anne S. K. Brown Military Collection, Brown University, Providence, R.I., and I am most grateful for his generous help during my research visit to the collection; see e.g. Peter Harrington, ed., *William Simpson's Afghanistan: Travels of a Special Artist and Antiquarian during the Second Afghan War, 1878–1879* (Solihull: Helion, 2016). This chapter has also benefited greatly from Peter Johnson's highly readable early popular study *Front Line Artists* (London: Cassell, 1978) and Roger T. Stearn's research; see e.g. Stearn, 'War Correspondents and Colonial War' and 'War and the Media in the Nineteenth Century: Victorian Military Artists and the Image of War, 1870–1914', RUSI Journal, vol. 131, no. 3 (1986): 55–62. .

7 Tom Gretton, 'Richard Caton Woodville (1856–1927) at the *Illustrated London News*', *Victorian Periodicals Review*, vol. 48, no. 1 (Spring 2015), 87–120.

8 'The Doyen of Special War Artists: Mr William Simpson, F. R. G. S.', *Illustrated Naval and Military Magazine*, vol. 1 (July–December 1884), 309.

9 *Illustrated London News*, 4 January 1879.

10 Mason Jackson, *The Pictorial Press: Its Origin and Progress* (London: Hurst and Blackett, 1885), 341.

11 Christine Ferguson, 'Sensational Dependence: Prosthesis and Affect in Dickens and Braddon', *Literature Interpretation Theory*, vol. 19, no. 1, (2008), 1.

12 Martin Green, *Dreams of Adventure, Deeds of Empire* (New York: Basic Books, 1979), 70.

13 'Photographs from the Crimea', *The Athenaeum*, no. 1457, 29 September 1855, 1117.

14 'Mr. Fenton's Photographic Pictures of the Crimea', *Daily News*, 20 September 1855.

15 'American Photographs', *The Times*, 30 August 1862.

16 William Simpson, *Illustrated London News*, 28 December 1878.

17 Lieut.-Colonel J. Baillie, 'Photography Applied to Military Science', *Journal of the Royal United Service Institution*, vol. 13 (London: W. Mitchell and Co., 1870), 454.

18 Lorraine Daston and Peter Galison, 'The Image of Objectivity', *Representations*, 40, Autumn 1992, 81–128.

19 Jennifer Green-Lewis, *Framing the Victorians: Photography and the Culture of Realism* (Ithaca and London: Cornell University Press, 1996), 97.

20 Christopher Pinney, *The Coming of Photography in India* (London: British Library, 2008), 28.

21 See Mary Louise Pratt, *Imperial Eyes: Travel Writing and Transculturation* (London and New York: Routledge, 1992; 2008).

22 Samuel Bourne, 'Ten Weeks with a Camera in the Himalayas', *British Journal of Photography*, vol. 11, no. 208 (February 1864), 69–70.

23 Pinney, *Coming of Photography*, 29.

24 Daniela Bleichmar, *Visible Empire: Botanical Expeditions and Visual Culture in the Hispanic Enlightenment* (Chicago and London: University of Chicago Press, 2012), 45.

25 Henry V. Barnett, 'The Special Artist', *Magazine of Art*, vol. 6 (1883), 166.

26 On the ethical component of on the spot practice, see Sarah Thomas's work on artists and abolitionism: *Witnessing Slavery: Art and Travel in the Age of Abolition* (New Haven and London: Yale University Press, 2019).

27 See Claudio Greppi, '"On the Spot": Traveling Artists and the Iconographic Inventory of the World, 1769–1859', in Felix Driver and Luciana Martins, eds, *Tropical Visions in an Age of Empire* (Chicago and London: University of Chicago Press, 2005), 23–42; Sarah Thomas, '"On the spot": Travelling Artists and Abolitionism, 1770–1830', *Atlantic Studies*, vol. 8, issue 2 (2011), 213–32.

28 See Bernard Smith, 'William Hodges and English Plein Air Painting', *Art History*, vol. 6, no. 2 (June 1983), 143–53.

29 Admiralty Board to Matthew Flinders, 1801, quoted in Michael Charlesworth, 'The Picturesque, William Hodges, Photography, and Some Problems in Recent Interpretations of Images of India', *Word & Image: A Journal of Verbal/Visual Enquiry*, vol. 23, no. 3 (2007), 379.

30 Ibid.

31 Greppi, '"On the Spot"', 32.

32 Charles Baudelaire, *The Painter of Modern Life and Other Essays*, trans. P. E. Charvet (London: Penguin, 2010), 13.

33 Ibid., 9.

34 Jackson, *Pictorial Press*, 354.

35 'The Rise and Fall of the War Correspondent', *Macmillan's Magazine*, vol. 90 (August 1904), 301, quoted in Waters, *Special Correspondence*, 92.

36 Romita Ray, *Under the Banyan Tree: Relocating the Picturesque in British India* (New Haven and London: Yale University Press, 2013), 7.

37 Nancy Forgione, 'Everyday Life in Motion: The Art of Walking in Late Nineteenth-Century Paris', *Art Bulletin*, vol. 87, no. 4 (December 2005), 665.

38 Nicholas Daly, *Modernism, Romance and the Fin de Siècle: Popular Fiction and British Culture* (Cambridge and New York: Cambridge University Press, 2004), 156.

39 Jackson, *Pictorial Press*, 332.

40 Ibid., 332–6.

41 See also William Simpson, 'The War: Arrest of English Correspondent at Metz', *Illustrated London News*, 20 August 1870.

42 John O. Springall, '"Up Guards and at Them": British Imperialism and Popular Art, 1880–1914', in John M. Mackenzie, ed., *Imperialism and Popular Culture* (Manchester and New York: Manchester University Press, 1986), 60.

43 Crystal Palace, London, exhibition catalogue quoted in *The Times*, 3 October 1870.

44 'The War Sketches at the Crystal Palace', ibid.

45 Forgione, 'Everyday Life in Motion', 21.

46 Natasha Eaton, *Mimesis across Empires: Artworks and Networks in India, 1765–1860* (Durham, N.C., and London: Duke University Press, 2013), 212.

47 Luciana Martins and Felix Driver, 'John Septimus Roe and the Art of Navigation, *c.*1815–30', in Tim Barringer, Geoff Quilley and Douglas Fordham, eds, *Art and the British Empire* (Manchester and New York: Manchester University Press, 2007), 64–5; see also Driver and Martins, *Tropical Visions*.

48 Martins and Driver, 'John Septimus Roe', 65.

49 Jessica Dubow, '"From a View on the World to a Point of View in It": Rethinking Sight, Space and the Colonial Subject', *Interventions*, vol. 2, no. 1 (2000), 100.

50 Patrick Bratlinger, *Victorian Literature and Postcolonial Studies* (Edinburgh: Edinburgh University Press, 2009), 33.

51 Griffiths, *New Journalism*, 52.

52 Ralph Crane and Lisa Fletcher, 'Picturing the Empire in India: Illustrating Henty', *English Literature in Transition, 1880–1902*, vol. 55, no. 2 (2012), 165–6, 163, 169.

53 Alfred Baker, 1890, quoted in Waters, *Special Correspondence*, 7.

54 From Villiers's obituary in *The Times*, quoted in Springall, '"Up Guards and at Them"', 54.

55 *Illustrated London News*, 5 November 1910, quoted in Jane Carruthers, *Melton Prior: War Artist in Southern Africa, 1895–1900* (Johannesburg: Brenthurst Press, 1987), 39.

56 William Simpson, *The Autobiography of William Simpson, R.I. (Crimean Simpson)*, ed. George Eyre-Todd (London: T. Fisher Unwin, 1903), 26.

57 William Simpson, 'In the Trenches before Sebastopol', *English Illustrated Magazine*, vol. 14 (December 1895), 232.

58 Ibid.

59 Eve Kosofsky Sedgwick, *Touching Feeling: Affect, Pedagogy, Performativity* (Durham, N.C., and London: Duke University Press, 2003), 69.

60 Slavoj Žižek, *The Sublime Object of Ideology* (London and New York: Verso, 1989), 113.

61 William Simpson, 'Experiences', Mitchell Library, Glasgow, 12840a, 6.

62 William Simpson in Fort Dakka to W. Harry Rylands of Lincoln's Inn Fields, London, 28 November 1878, in Harrington, *William Simpson's Afghanistan*, 235.

63 'Celebrities at Home', *The World*, 13 June 1894.

64 Simpson is an important and under-studied figure in the history of colonial ethnography; see these articles and lectures by him: 'The architecture of India', RIBA *Trans.* (Royal Institute of British Architects) (May 1862), 165–78; 'Arkite Ceremonies in the Himalayas', *Good Words* (1866), 601–8; 'Praying Machines', *Good Words* (1867), 845–50; 'Church Architecture of Abyssinia', RIBA *Trans.* (1869), 234–46; 'The Royal Quarries', *Palestine Exploration Fund* (1870), 373–9; 'Jerusalem', *Society for Biblical Archaeology* (1872), 310–27; 'The Architecture of China', RIBA *Trans.* (1873), 33–50; 'China's Future Place in Philology', *Macmillan's Magazine* (November 1873), 45–8; 'Gangootre', *Alpine Journal* (May 1874), 385–97; 'Symbolism of Oriental Ornament', *Royal Society of the Arts Journal*, vol. 22 (1874), 488–94; 'The Modoc Region', *Royal Geographical Society Proceedings*, vol. 19 (1874–5), 292–302; 'Ark-Shrines of Japan', *Society for Biblical Archaeology* (1877), 550–54.

65 See Jennifer Howes, *Illustrating India: The Early Colonial Investigations of Colin Mackenzie (1784–1821)* (Oxford and New York: Oxford University Press, 2010).

66 William Simpson, 'Notes and Recollections of my life to my dear daughter Ann Penelope Simpson', *c.*1890 (partial transcription by Paul Bucherer-Dietschi, Foundation Bibliotheca Afganica), National Library of Scotland, Edinburgh, Acc. 11877 (ii).

67 Priyamvada Gopal, *Insurgent Empire: Anticolonial Resistance and British Dissent* (London and New York: Verso, 2019), 59.

68 Zahid R. Chaudhary, 'Phantasmagoric Aesthetics: Colonial Violence and the Management of Perception', *Cultural Critique*, no. 59 (Winter 2005), 105.

69 Trooper quoted in Christopher Hibbert, *The Great Mutiny: India, 1857* (London: Allen Lane; New York: Viking, 1978), 295.

70 *Illustrated London News*, 10 October 1857.

71 Henry A. Giroux, 'Disturbing Pleasures: Murderous Images and the Aesthetics of Depravity', *Third Text*, vol. 26, no. 3 (2012), 264.

72 William Michael Rossetti quoted in Joan Winifred Martin Hichberger, *Images of the Army: The Military in British Art, 1815–1914* (Manchester and New York: Manchester University Press, 1988), 69.

73 Ibid., 71.

74 Paul Usherwood, *Elizabeth Butler: Battle Artist* (London: Sutton, 1987), 15.

75 Giroux, 'Disturbing Pleasures', 272.

76 Ibid., 268.

5 · 'SAVE ME FROM MY FRIENDS!'

1 General Carl von Clausewitz, *On War*, trans. J. J. Graham (London: Kegan Paul, Trench, Trubner & Co., 1908), xxiii.

2 Thomas Richards, *The Imperial Archive: Knowledge and the Fantasy of Empire* (London and New York: Verso, 1993), 21.

3 Walter Bagehot, *The English Constitution* (London: Chapman & Hall, 1867; Boston, Mass: Little, Brown, and Company, 1870), 184.

4 Robin Wagner-Pacifici, *The Art of Surrender: Decomposing Sovereignty at Conflict's End* (Chicago and London: University of Chicago Press, 2005), 129.

5 Eduardo Cadava, *Words of Light: Theses on the Photography of History* (Princeton, N.J: Princeton University Press, 1998), xxii, xxiii.

6 See Wagner-Pacifici, *Art of Surrender*.

7 Romita Ray, 'Baron of Bengal: Robert Clive and the Birth of an Imperial Image', in Julie Codell, ed., *Transculturation in British Art, 1770–1930* (London and New York: Routledge, 2012), 24.

8 See Turan Kayaoglu, 'Westphalian Eurocentrism in International Relations Theory', *International Studies Review*, vol. 12, no. 2 (2010), 193–217.

9 Jennifer Pitts, 'Boundaries of International Law', in Duncan Bell, ed., *Victorian Visions of Global Order: Empire and International Relations in Nineteenth-Century Political Thought* (Cambridge, New York and Delhi: Cambridge University Press, 2007), 68.

10 Mayer & Pierson, *Galerie des Plénipotentiares au Congrès de Paris* (Paris: Ernest Bourdin, 1856), Royal Collection Trust, RCIN 1045758.

11 Kayaoglu, 'Westphalian Eurocentrism', 195.

12 Bagehot, *English Constitution*, 184.

13 *Allen's India Mail*, no. 13, 16 August 1855, 441.

14 See Sir Henry Yule, *A Narrative of the Mission sent by the Governor-General of India to the Court of Ava in 1855* (London: Smith, Elder, and Co., 1858).

15 See Oliver B. Pollak, 'A Mid-Victorian Cover up: The Case of the "Combustible Commodore" and the Second Anglo-Burmese War, 1851–52', *Albion*, vol. 10, no. 2 (Summer 1978), 171–83.

16 Richard Cobden, *How Wars Are Got Up in India: The Origin of the Burmese War* (London: William & Frederick G. Cash, 1853). This pamphlet warranted a response from John Clark Marshman, *How Wars Arise in India: Observations on Mr. Cobden's Pamphlet* (London: W. H. Allen & Co., 1853).

17 'Private Journal of Arthur Phayre', in Henry Yule, *Mission to the Court of Ava in 1855* (repr. of Yule, *Narrative*; London and New York: Oxford University Press, 1968), xxvi.

18 *The Bengal Hurkaru*, 27 August 1855.

19 Yule, *Narrative*, 83.

20 Ibid.

21 Wagner-Pacifici, *Art of Surrender*, 61.

22 Yule, *Narrative*, 79.

23 Ibid., 95.

24 Ibid.

25 Allan Sekula, 'The Body and the Archive', *October*, vol. 39 (Winter 1986), 7.

26 Wagner-Pacifici, *Art of Surrender*, 4.

27 *Times of India*, 24 April 1884, 2.

28 John Thomson, *Through China with a Camera* (London and New York: Harper & Brothers, 1899), 252.

29 'Thomson's Photographs of China', *Saturday Review of Politics, Literature, Science and Art*, 19 July 1873, 93.

30 Wagner-Pacifici, *Art of Surrender*, 13.

31 For an account of Burke's career, see Omar Khan, *From Kashmir to Kabul: The Photographs of John Burke and William Baker, 1860–1900* (Ahmedabad: Mapin Publishing; Munich: Prestel, 2002).

32 John O. Springall, '"Up Guards and at Them": British Imperialism and Popular Art, 1880–1914', in John M. Mackenzie, ed., *Imperialism and Popular Culture* (Manchester and New York: Manchester University Press, 1986), 51.

33 Wagner-Pacifici, *Art of Surrender*, 51.

34 Ariella Azoulay, *The Civil Contract of Photography* (New York: Zone Books, 2012), 112.

35 Ibid., 110–12.

36 Ibid., 112.

37 Sir Henry Maine, 1862, quoted in Barbara Ramusack, *The New Cambridge History of India*, vol. 3, pt 6: *The Indian Princes and their States* (Cambridge and New York: Cambridge University Press, 2004), 94.

38 David Strang, 'Contested Sovereignty: The Social Construction of Colonial Imperialism', in Thomas J. Biersteker, ed., *State Sovereignty as Social Construct* (Cambridge: Cambridge University Press, 2011), 26.

39 Simeon Koole, 'Photography as Event: Power, the Kodak Camera, and Territoriality in Early Twentieth-Century Tibet', *Comparative Studies in Society and History*, vol. 59, no. 2 (2017), 311, 315.

40 William Simpson, 'An Interview with Yakoob Khan', *Daily News*, 10 June 1879.

41 John B. Thomson, *Media and Modernity: A Social Theory of the Media* (Cambridge: Polity Press with Blackwell Publishing, 1995), 148.

42 William Simpson, 'Photographing the Ameer', *Daily News*, 18 June 1879.

43 Elizabeth Edwards, *Raw Histories: Photographs, Anthropology, Museums* (Oxford and New York: Berg, 2001), 6.

44 John Thomson, 'Practical Photography in Tropical Regions', *British Journal of Photography*, vol. 13, no. 335 (3 October 1866), 472–3.

45 Oliver Wendell Holmes, 'Doings of the Sunbeam', *The Atlantic* (July 1863), 240.

46 Ulrich Baer, *Spectral Evidence: The Photography of Trauma* (Cambridge, Mass., and London: MIT Press, 2002), 13.

47 Ibid., 7.

48 Walter Benjamin, *The Work of Art in the Age of Its Technological Reproducibility, and Other Writings on Media* (Cambridge, Mass., and London: Belknap Press of Harvard University Press, 2008), 33.

49 Major Pierre Louis Napoleon Cavagnari quoted in Karl Meyer and Shareen Brysac, *Tournament of Shadows: The Great Game and the Race for Empire in Asia* (London: Abacus, 2001), 189.

50 Ibid., 192.

51 *The Graphic*, 13 September 1879.

52 Cavagnari to Peshawar, 2 September 1879, quoted in Meyer and Brysac, *Tournament of Shadows*, 192.

53 Yaqub Khan to Peshawar, September 1879, quoted in ibid.

54 Baer, *Spectral Evidence*, 7.

55 General Roberts, 1880, quoted in Meyer and Brysac, *Tournament of Shadows*, 199.

6 · NEGATIVE HISTORIES

1 Sir Francis Younghusband, *India and Tibet: A History of the Relations which have Subsisted between the Two Countries from the Time of Warren Hastings to 1910; with a Particular Account of the Mission to Lhasa of 1904* (London: John Murray, 1910), 303.

2 Ibid., 238.

3 Edmund Chandler, *The Unveiling of Lhasa* (London: Edward Arnold, 1905).

4 Perceval Landon, *The Opening of Tibet: An Account of Lhasa and the Country and People of Central Tibet and of the Progress of the Mission Sent there by the English Government in the Year 1903–4* (New York: Doubleday, Page & Co., 1905), 285.

5 Samuel Bourne, 'Photography in the East', *British Journal of Photography* (1 July 1863), 268.

6 For an extended consideration of the camera-cannon analogy, see James R. Ryan, *Picturing Empire: Photography and the Visualization of the British Empire* (London: Reaktion Books, 1997), 99–139.

7 Elizabeth Edwards, *Raw Histories: Photographs, Anthropology, and Museums* (Oxford and New York: Berg, 2001); Edwards, Chris Gosden and Ruth B. Phillips, eds, *Sensible Objects: Colonialism, Museums and Material Culture* (Oxford and New York: Berg, 2006).

8 Elizabeth Edwards, 'Some Thoughts on Photographs as History', in Clare Harris and Tsering Shakya, eds, *Seeing Lhasa: British Depictions of the Tibetan Capital, 1936–1947* (Chicago: Serindia Publications, 2003), 133.

9 Geoffrey Batchen, *Negative/Positive: A History of Photography* (London and New York: Routledge, 2020), 3.

10 See Susan E. Cook, *Victorian Negatives: Literary Culture and the Dark Side of Photography in the Nineteenth Century* (New York: SUNY Press, 2019).

11 Ali Behdad, *Camera Orientalis: Reflections on Photography of the Middle East* (Chicago and London: University of Chicago Press, 2016), 65.

12 Edwards, *Raw Histories*, 2.

13 Mark Knight and Lesley McFadyen, '"At Any Given Moment": Duration in Archaeology and Photography', in Lesley McFadyen and Dan Hicks, eds, *Archaeology and Photography: Time, Objectivity and Archive* (London, New York, New Delhi and Sydney: Bloomsbury Visual Arts, 2020), 55–72.

14 Nicholas Thomas, *Entangled Objects: Exchange, Material Culture, and Colonialism in the Pacific* (Cambridge, Mass., and London: Harvard University Press, 1991), 126.

15 Rudyard Kipling, *From Sea to Sea and Other Sketches: Letters of Travel*, 4 vols (London: Macmillan and Co., 1914), vol. 2, 16.

16 Minute by Governor-General Dalhousie, 12 April 1855, British Library, London, IOR/P/SEC/IND/191.

17 Johannes Fabian, *Time and the Other: How Anthropology Makes its Object* (New York: Columbia University Press, 2014), 122.

18 Dan Hicks, *The Brutish Museums: The Benin Bronzes, Colonial Violence and Cultural Restitution* (London: Pluto Press, 2020), 56.

19 Thomas Richards, *The Imperial Archive: Knowledge and the Fantasy of Empire* (London and New York: Verso, 1993), 21.

20 See Janet Dewan, *The Photographs of Linnaeus Tripe: A Catalogue Raisonné* (Toronto: Art Gallery of Ontario, 2003); Andrew Jarvis, '"The Myriad-Pencil of the Photographer": Seeing, Mapping and Situating Burma in 1855', *Modern Asian Studies*, vol. 45, no. 4 (July 2011), 791–823; Roger Taylor and Crispin Branfoot, *Captain Linnaeus Tripe: Photographer of India and Burma, 1852–1860* (Washington D.C: National Gallery of Art, 2014).

21 Sir Henry Yule, *A Narrative of the Mission sent by the Governor-General of India to the Court of Ava in 1855* (London: Smith, Elder, and Co., 1858), 28.

22 Colesworthy Grant, 'Notes Explanatory of a Series of Views taken in Burmah during Major Phayre's Mission to the Court of Ava in 1855', 1856, British Library, London, PDP/WD540, 11.

23 Ibid.

24 Christopher Pinney, *'Photos of the Gods': The Printed Image and Political Struggle in India* (London: Reaktion Books, 2004), 34.

25 Grant, 'Notes Explanatory', 15.

26 Yule, *Narrative of the Mission*, 89.

27 Linnaeus Tripe, 'Views in Burma taken during the Mission to Ava' (1857), British Library, Photo 61.

28 Tina M. Campt, *Image Matters: Archive, Photography, and the African Diaspora in Europe* (Durham, N.C., and London: Duke University Press, 2012), 128.

29 Cook, *Victorian Negatives*, xxviii.

30 Thomas Ruff, 'Thomas Ruff Reimagines 1850s India and Burma', IndiaArtFair, https://web.archive.org/web/20200814204458/http://indiaartfair.in/thomas-ruff-reimagines-1850s-india-and-burma, accessed 20 December 2020.

31 Serpil Oppermann, 'Material Ecocriticism', in Iris van der Turin, ed., *Gender: Nature* (New York: Macmillan, 2016), 90.

32 Caitlin DeSilvey, 'Observed Decay: Telling Stories with Mutable Things', *Journal of Material Culture*, vol. 11, no. 3 (2006), 323.

33 Miles Ogborn, 'Archives', in Stephen Harrison, Steve Pile and Nigel Thrift, eds, *Patterned Ground: Entanglements of Nature and Culture* (Chicago: University of Chicago Press, 2004), 240.

34 Jarvis, '"Myriad-Pencil of the Photographer"', 807.

35 Linda Tuhiwai Smith, *Decolonizing Methodologies: Research and Indigenous Peoples* (London and New York: Zed Books; Dunedin: University of Otago Press, 2008), 2.

36 Yule, *Narrative of the Mission*, 89.

37 Ibid.

38 In the 1857 Madras Exhibition jury report, Tripe's calotype was said to be 'remarkable both as regards the beauty of its detail and the picturesqueness of its effect'; quoted in Jarvis, '"Myriad-Pencil of the Photographer"', 807.

39 *The Englishman*, 13 July 1855.

40 Minute by the Honourable J. P. Grant, dated 28 April 1855, No. 38, 3 July 1855, British Library, IOR/L/PS/5/224.

41 Major A. P. Phayre to Cecil Beadon, 30 April 1855, ibid.

42 *The Bengal Hurkaru*, 8 October 1855.

43 Colesworthy Grant, *Rough Pencillings of a Rough Trip to Rangoon in 1846* (Calcutta, London and Bombay: Thacker, Spink and Co., 1853), 43–4, 28.

44 Jarvis, '"Myriad-Pencil of the Photographer"', 810.

45 Walter Mignolo, 'The Moveable Center: Geographical Discourses and Territoriality during the Expansion of the Spanish Empire', in Ana del Sarto, Alicia Rios and Abril Trigo, eds, *The Latin American Cultural Studies Reader* (Durham, N.C: Duke University Press, 2004), 262.

46 Tim Barringer, 'Landscape Then and Now', *British Art Studies*, issue 10 (November 2018), https://www.britishartstudies.ac.uk/doi/445/p9, accessed 12 March 2021.

47 The camera was often interwoven with wider networks of modern infrastructure: see Simone Natale, 'Photography and Communication Media in the Nineteenth Century', *History of Photography*, vol. 36, no. 4 (2012), 451–6.

48 Major Phayre to Cecil Beadon, 30 April 1855, p. 187, IOR/L/PS/5/224.

49 Christopher Pinney, *The Coming of Photography in India* (London: British Library, 2008), 25.

50 Kaja Silverman, *The Miracle of Analogy: or, The History of Photography, Part 1* (Stanford, Cal: Stanford University Press, 2015), 69.

51 Lesley McFadyen and Dan Hicks, 'Introduction: From Archaeography to Photology', in McFadyen and Hicks, *Archaeology and Photography*, 7.

52 David Griffiths and Deanna K. Kriesel, 'Introduction: Open Ecologies', *Victorian Literature and Culture*, vol. 48, no. 1 (Spring 2020), 1–28.

53 Deborah Poole, *Vision, Race, and Modernity: A Visual Economy of the Andean Image World* (Princeton, N.J: Princeton University Press, 1997), 9–13.

54 John Thomson, 'Practical Photography in Tropical Regions', *British Photography Journal*, vol. 13, no. 329 (24 August 1866), 404.

55 John Thomson, 'Practical Photography in Tropical Regions', *British Photography Journal*, vol. 13, no. 327 (10 August 1866), 380.

56 John Thomson, 'Practical Photography in Tropical Regions', VI, *British Photography Journal*, vol. 13, no. 336 (12 October 1866), 487.

57 John Thomson, *Through China with a Camera* (London and New York: Harper & Brothers, 1899), 253.

58 Felix Driver, *Geography Militant: Cultures of Exploration and Empire* (Oxford: Blackwell, 2001), 63.

59 Ryan, *Picturing Empire*, 165–6.

60 Fabian, *Time and the Other*, 144.

61 Christopher Pinney, 'The Colonial Dromosphere: Speed, Transmission and Prosthesis in Colonial India', in J. Carlos Viana Ferreira and Teresa de Ataíde Malafaia, eds, *The British Empire: Ideology, Perspectives, Perceptions* (Lisbon: University of Lisbon, Centre for English Studies, 2010), 128.

62 Edwards, *Raw Histories*; John Falconer, '"A Pure Labour of Love": A Publishing History of *The People of India*', in Eleanor M. Hight and Gary D. Sampson, eds, *Colonialist Photography: Imag(in)ing Race and Place* (Abingdon and New York: Routledge, 2013), 17–62; Christopher Pinney, *Photography and Anthropology* (London: Reaktion Books, 2011), 50–62.

63 https://wellcomelibrary.org/collections/digital-collections/john-thomson-photographs/.

64 I went to see 'China and Siam: Through the Lens of John Thomson'

at the Brunei Gallery, SOAS, London (12 April–22 June 2018). For a full list of venues from 2009 to the present, see http://www.johnthomsonexhibition.org/venues, accessed 22 August 2018.

65 See Phaisān Pīammēttāwat, ed., *Siam: Through the Lens of John Thomson, 1865–66* (Bangkok: River Books, 2015); Betty Yao, ed., *China: Through the Lens of John Thomson, 1868–1872* (Bangkok: River Books, 2015).

66 See Mirjam Brusius, 'Impreciseness in Julia Margaret Cameron's Portrait Photographs', *History of Photography*, vol. 34, no. 4 (2010), 342–55.

67 http://www.johnthomsonexhibition.org/john-thomson-annie-liebovitz-19th-century-china-siam-phuong-lecocq, accessed 22 August 2018.

68 Allan Sekula, 'Traffic in Photographs', *Photography Against the Grain: Essays and Photo Works, 1973–1983* (Halifax: Press of Nova Scotia College of Art and Design, 1984; London: Mack Books, 2016), 79.

69 See John Thomson, *Illustrations of China and its People: A Series of Two Hundred Photographs, with Letterpress Descriptive of the Places and People Represented*, 4 vols (London: Sampson, Low, Marston, Low & Searle, 1873–4).

70 Geoffrey Belknap, 'Through the Looking Glass: Photography, Science and Imperial Motivations in John Thomson's Photographic Expeditions', *History of Science*, vol. 52, no. 1 (2014), 73–97.

71 Edwards, *Raw Histories*, 123–4.

72 Christopher Pinney, 'Seven Theses on Photography', *Thesis Eleven*, vol. 113, no. 1 (2012), 149.

73 John Thomson, *The Straits of Malacca, Indo-China and China; or Ten Years' Travels, Adventures and Residence Abroad* (London: Sampson, Low, Marston, Low & Searle, 1875), 521.

74 Oliver Wendell Holmes, 'Doings of the Sunbeam', *The Atlantic* (July 1863), 240.

75 Silverman, *Miracle of Analogy*, 75.

76 Ibid., 73.

77 Ariella Aïsha Azoulay, *Potential History: Unlearning Imperialism* (Verso: London: New York, 2019).

78 http://www.johnthomsonexhibition.org/john-thomson-annie-liebovitz-19th-century-china-siam-phuong-lecocq, accessed 22 August 2018.

79 http://www.johnthomsonexhibition.org/grave-restoration, accessed 22 August 2018.

80 E. M. Estabrooke, *Photography in the Studio and in the Field* (New York: E. & H. T. Anthony & Co., 1887), 140.

81 Simeon Koole, 'Photography as Event: Power, the Kodak Camera, and Territoriality in Early Twentieth-Century Tibet', *Comparative Studies in Society and History*, vol. 59, no. 2 (2017), 314.

82 Patrick French, *Younghusband: The Last Great Imperial Adventurer* (London: HarperCollins, 1994).

83 Clare E. Harris, *The Museum on the Roof of the World: Art, Politics, and the Representation of Tibet* (Chicago and London: University of Chicago Press, 2014), 52–4.

84 Landon, *Opening of Tibet*, 416.

85 Harris, *Museum on the Roof of the World*, 108.

86 Silverman, *Miracle of Analogy*, 83.

87 Koole, 'Photography as Event', 318, 344.

88 Ibid., 340.

89 Ibid., 318.

90 Harris, *Museum on the Roof of the World*, 109.

91 Dibyesh Anand, 'Strategic Hypocrisy: The British Imperial Scripting of Tibet's Geopolitical Identity', *Journal of Asian Studies*, vol. 68, no. 1 (February 2009), 234.

92 Dawa Norbu, *China's Tibet Policy* (Padstow: Curzon Press, 2001), 155.

93 Landon, *Opening of Tibet*, 253.

94 Ingrid Pollard quoted in Campt, *Image Matters*, 128.

95 John Falconer writes: 'The firm, in fact, not only appear to have printed White's work but also to have purchased the negatives and thereby acquired the copyright ... Like so many glass negatives, they are unlikely to have survived intact the rigours of the succeeding 100 years, and although Johnston and Hoffman stayed in business until the early 1950s, the fate of their negatives has not been discovered'; quoted in Kurt Meyer and Pamela Deuel Meyer, *In the Shadow of the Himalayas: Tibet, Bhutan, Nepal, Sikkim: A Photographic Record of John Claude White, 1883–1908* (Ahmedabad: Mapin Publishing, 2005), 9.

96 Campt, *Image Matters*, 36.

97 Geoffrey Batchen, *Each Wild Idea: Writing, Photography, History* (Cambridge, Mass., and London: MIT Press, 2000), 83.

98 MacFayden and Hicks, 'From Archaeography to Photology', 29.

7 · SPECIMENS, SUSPECTS, CITIZENS

1 *Copies of the Proclamation of the King, Emperor of India, to the Princes and Peoples of India, of the 2nd day of November 1908, and the Proclamation of the late Queen Victoria of the 1st day of November 1858, to the Princes, Chiefs, and People of India* (London: Eyre and Spottiswoode, 1908), 2.

2 Christopher Pinney, 'Seven Theses on Photography', *Thesis Eleven*, vol. 113, no. 1 (2012), 141–56.

3 See e.g. Liam Buckley, 'Studio Photography and the Aesthetics of Citizenship in The Gambia, West Africa', in Elizabeth Edwards, Chris Gosden and Ruth B. Phillips, eds, *Sensible Objects: Colonialism, Museums and Material Culture* (Oxford and New York: Berg, 2006), 61–86; Lily Cho, 'Intimacy among Strangers: Anticipating Citizenship in Chinese Head Tax Photographs', *Interventions*, vol. 15, no. 1 (2013), 10–23; Thy Phu, *Picturing Model Citizens: Civility in Asian American Visual Culture* (Philadelphia: Temple University Press, 2012); Lorena Rizzo, 'Visual Aperture: Bureaucratic Systems of Identification, Photography and Personhood in Colonial Southern Africa', *History of Photography*, vol. 37, no. 3 (2013), 263–82.

4 Rizzo, 'Visual Aperture', 263.

5 The Tresidder Album is now held along with the doctor's medical diary in the Alkazi Foundation for the Arts, New Delhi.

6 Rashmi Viswanathan, 'The Tresidder Album: A Case Study of a Private "Ethnography"', *Self and Nation*, vol. 7, no. 1 (Autumn 2016), https://quod.lib.umich.edu/t/tap/7977573.0007.104/--tresidder-album-a-case-study-of-a-private-ethnography?rgn=main;view=fulltext, accessed 5 March 2021.

7 For a detailed account of the Cawnpore siege and massacre, see Andrew Ward, *Our Bones are Scattered: The Cawnpore Massacres and the Indian Mutiny of 1857* (London: John Murray, 2004).

8 George Dodd, *The History of the Indian Revolt and of the Expeditions to Persia, China, and Japan, 1856–7–8, with Maps, Plans, and Wood Engravings* (London: W. & R. Chambers, 1859), 144.

9 Thomas Stevens, *Around the World on a Bicycle*, vol. 2: *From Teheran to Yokohama* (New York: Charles Scribner's Sons, 1889), 340.

10 See Sean Willcock, 'Aesthetic Bodies: Posing on Sites of Violence in India, 1857–1900', *History of Photography*, vol. 39, no. 2 (2015), 142–59.

11 Manu Goswami, '"Englishness" on the Imperial Circuit: Mutiny Tours in Colonial South Asia', *Journal of Historical Sociology*, vol. 9, no. 1 (March 1996), 54; Ian Baucom, *Out of Place: Englishness, Empire, and the Locations of Identity* (Princeton, N.J: Princeton University Press, 1999), 107.

12 See Gary D. Sampson, 'Unmasking the Colonial Picturesque: Samuel Bourne's Photographs of Barrackpore Park', in Eleanor M. Hight and Gary D. Sampson, eds, *Colonialist Photography: Imag(in)ing Race and Place* (Abingdon and New York: Routledge, 2004), 84–106; Willcock, 'Aesthetic Bodies'.

13 Sometimes spelled 'Tressider'; the captions in the album read 'Tresidder', a spelling that I have had confirmed in conversation with Robert Haskins, one of Tresidder's descendants, and a family historian.

14 Nicholas B. Dirks, *Castes of Mind: Colonialism and the Making of Modern India* (Princeton and Oxford: Princeton University Press, 2001), 149.

15 Christopher Pinney, *Photography and Anthropology* (London: Reaktion Books, 2011), 17.

16 Sir John William Kaye and John Forbes Watson, *The People of India: A Series of Photographic Illustrations, with Descriptive Letterpress, of the Races and Tribes of Hindustan*, 8 vols (London: India Museum, 1868–75); see John Falconer, '"A Pure Labour of Love": A Publishing History of *The People of India*', in Hight and Sampson, *Colonialist Photography*, 17–62.

17 Christopher Pinney, *Camera Indica: The Social Life of Indian Photographs* (London: Reaktion Books, 1997), 34.

18 *The Economist*, vol. 15 (26 September 1857), 1062; emphasis in original.

19 For an account of the ideology of liberalism in British India, see Thomas R. Metcalf, *The New Cambridge History of India*, vol. 3.4: *Ideologies of the Raj* (Cambridge and New York: Cambridge University Press, 1994).

20 Sukanya Banerjee, *Becoming Imperial Citizens: Indians in the Late-Victorian Empire* (Durham, N.C: Duke University Press, 2010), 23.

21 Metcalf, *Ideologies of the Raj*, 59.

22 See Lara Perry, 'The Carte de Visite in the 1860s and the Serial Dynamic of Photographic Likeness', *Art History*, vol. 35, no. 4 (September 2012), 728–49.

23 *Allen's Indian Mail*, vol. 14, January–December 1856 (London: W. H. Allen and Co., 1856), 66.

24 Andrew Winter, ed., *The British Medical Journal, Being the Journal of the British Medical Association* (London: Thomas John Honeyman, 1857), 724.

25 *Allen's Indian Mail*, vol. 15, January–December 1857 (London: W. H. Allen and Co., 1857), 304 (19 May 1857).

26 Sir Edward Arthur Henry Blunt, *List of Inscriptions on Christian Tombs and Tablets of Historical Interest in the United Provinces of Agra and Oudh* (Allahabad: W. C. Abel, Govt. Press, 1911), 114.

27 Mowbray Thomson, *The Story of Cawnpore* (London: Richard Bentley, 1859), 252.

28 Christopher Pinney, *The Coming of Photography in India* (London: British Library, 2008), 122–3; see also Zahid R. Chaudhary, *Afterimage of Empire: Photography in Nineteenth-Century India* (Minneapolis: University of Minnesota Press, 2012), 37–72, 'Death and the Rhetoric of Photography: × Marks the Spot'.

29 Pinney, *Coming of Photography*, 122.

30 For an account of the importance of the figure of the British woman in accounts of the Uprising, see Jane Robinson, *Angels of Albion: Women of the Indian Mutiny* (London: Viking Press, 1996).

31 I thank Robert Haskins for this information.

32 Tresidder's initials can be seen in the portrait of 'Native Doctor Jail Hospital – Cawnpore', 'Tresidder Album', p. 9.

33 Perry, 'Carte de Visite', 729, 730; see also Geoffrey Batchen, 'Dreams of Ordinary Life: Cartes-de-Visite and the Bourgeois Imagination', in J. J. Long, Andrea Noble and Edward Welch, eds, *Photography: Theoretical Snapshots* (Oxford and New York: Routledge, 2009), 80–97.

34 Malavika Karlekar, *Re-visioning the Past: Early Photography in Bengal, 1875–1915* (Oxford and New York: Oxford University Press, 2005), 71.

35 Ibid., 86.

36 Judith Butler, *Frames of War: When is Life Grievable?* (London and New York: Verso, 2009), 140.

37 Banerjee, *Becoming Imperial Citizens*, 5.

38 Sorabji Jehangir, *Representative Men of India: A Collection of Memoirs, with Portraits, of Indian Princes, Nobles, Statesmen, Philanthropists, Officials, and Eminent Citizens*, intro. George Birdwood (London: W. H. Allen & Co., 1889), v.

39 Pinney, *Camera Indica*, 97.

40 Banerjee, *Becoming Imperial Citizens*, 23.

41 Batchen, 'Dreams of Ordinary Life', 87.

42 Gabrielle Moser, *Projecting Citizenship: Photography and Belonging in the British Empire* (University Park, Penn: Penn State University Press, 2019), 41, 37.

43 James R. Ryan, *Picturing Empire: Photography and the Visualization of the British Empire* (London: Reaktion Books, 1997), 191.

44 Pinney, *Coming of Photography*, 38.

45 Ibid., 114.

46 Mowbray Thomson, *Story of Cawnpore*, 206.

47 *Report of Police Administration in the North Western Provinces, for 1861* (Allahabad: Government Press, 1862), 30.

48 Mowbray Thomson, *Story of Cawnpore*, 247–8, 246.

49 Pinney, *Coming of Photography*, 63.

50 Allan Sekula, 'The Body and the Archive', *October*, vol. 39 (Winter 1986), 7.

51 See Ranajit Guha, *Dominance without Hegemony: History and Power in Colonial India* (Cambridge, Mass., and London: Harvard University Press, 1997). For a discussion of how 'hegemony' and its absence were visualised by the British in the *Illustrated London News* before the 1857 Uprising, see Daniel J. Rycroft, *Representing Rebellion: Visual Aspects of Counter-insurgency in Colonial India* (New Delhi: Oxford University Press, 2006).

52 Sekula, 'Body and the Archive', 6; emphasis in original.

53 See Giorgio Agamben, *Homo Sacer: Sovereign Power and Bare Life* (Stanford, Cal: Stanford University Press, 1998).

54 Jeannene M. Przyblyski, 'Revolution at a Standstill: Photography and the Paris Commune of 1871', *Yale French Studies*, vol. 101 (2001), 65.

55 Tresidder, 'Tresidder Album', 49.

56 John William Kaye, *A History of the Sepoy War in India, 1857–58*, 2 vols (London: W. H. Allen, 1870), vol. 2, 393.

57 Carl Schmitt, *The Concept of the Political* (Chicago and London: University of Chicago Press, 1996).

58 Earlier in the album, Tresidder had executed a similar combination print using the portraits of his Indian domestic servants, whose Indianness was contained in a single collage, effectively segregated from the surrounding photographs of white colonial domesticity (see fig. 79).

59 Metcalf, *Ideologies of the Raj*, 49.

60 For an account of the ambivalence of colonial discourse, see Homi K. Bhabha, 'Of Mimicry and Man: The Ambivalence of Colonial Discourse', *October*, vol. 28, Discipleship: A Special Issue on Psychoanalysis (Spring 1984), 125–33.

8 · THE COLOUR OF SOVEREIGNTY

1 A version of this chapter was originally published as 'Composing the Spectacle: Colonial Portraiture and the Coronation Durbars of British India, 1877–1911', *Art History*, vol. 40, issue 1 (2017), 132–55.

2 *Kaisar-i-Hind* was a title used to describe Victoria's status that maintained its imperial resonance across several languages, all derived from Latin *Caesar*: in Hindi *Qaisar* and in Urdu *Kaisar*.

3 *Illustrated London News*, 1 May 1880.

4 *Hampshire Telegraph and Sussex Chronicle*, 3 May 1880.

5 See Natasha Eaton, *Colour, Art and Empire: Visual Culture and the Nomadism of Representation* (London: I. B. Tauris, 2013).

6 *New York Times*, 3 June 1880.

7 Janice Carlisle, *Picturing Reform in Victorian Britain* (Cambridge and New York: Cambridge University Press, 2012), 33.

8 John Ruskin, *The Elements of Drawing* (London: George Allen, 1857), 245.

9 *Bury and Norwich Post, and Suffolk Herald*, 18 May 1880.

10 David Cannadine, *Ornamentalism: How the British saw their Empire* (Oxford and New York: Oxford University Press, 2002); Alan Trevithick, 'Some Structural and Sequential Aspects of the British Imperial Assemblages at Delhi: 1877–1911', *Modern Asian Studies*, vol. 24, no. 3 (July 1990), 561–78; Jim Masselos, 'The Great Durbar Crowds: The Participant Audience', in Julie F. Codell, ed., *Power and Resistance: The Delhi Coronation Durbars* (New Delhi: Mapin Publishing with the Alkazi Collection of Photography, 2012), 177–203; see also Pramod K. Nayar, 'Empire Communications, Inc.: Nineteenth-Century Imperial Pageantry and the Politics of Display', *Journal of Creative Communications*, vol. 5, no. 2 (July 2010), 75–87.

11 See Bernard S. Cohn, 'Representing Authority in Victorian India', in Eric Hobsbawm and Terence Ranger, eds, *The Invention of Tradition* (Cambridge and New York: Cambridge University Press, 1983), 165–210.

12 Robert Taylor, *The Princely Armory: Being a Display of the Arms of the Ruling Chiefs of India After Their Banners as Prepared for the Imperial Assemblage Held at Delhi on the First Day of January 1877* (Calcutta: Government Central Printing Office, 1877).

13 Julie F. Codell, 'Photography and the Delhi Durbars: 1877, 1903, 1911', in Codell, *Power and Resistance*.

14 See Julie F. Codell, 'Photographic Interventions and Identities: Colonising and Decolonising the Royal Body', in Codell, *Power and Resistance*, 110–41.

15 See Caroline Dakers, *The Holland Park Circle: Artists and Victorian Society* (New Haven and London: Yale University Press, 1999); Jan Marsh, *The Pre-Raphaelite Circle* (London: National Portrait Gallery, 2005).

16 It was thought by the artist Luke Fildes that Prinsep would be knighted for his efforts; Dakers, *Holland Park Circle*, 207.

17 'Summary of Correspondence Respecting Mr. Prinsep's Picture of the Imperial Assemblage', 1876, India Office Records, British Library, IOR DIEK 035/43, 1.

18 The notable silence of the Indian rulers in the official summary of correspondence regarding the commission is telling. Lytton first asked political agents to make inquiries

about the likelihood of Indian rulers subscribing to the commission. He hoped to be able to write to Victoria about 'the anxiety of the Native Chiefs to be allowed to present Her with a large oil picture' but, as the report records, he 'does not appear [to have written] as promised.' Ultimately, a circular was sent round stating that 'a desire was expressed on the part of many Chiefs and Princes, to commemorate [the Assemblage] by a painting to be presented to the Queen.' But the author of the report admits to not having actually seen any Indian replies on the matter; see ibid., 2.

19 Lord Lytton quoted in online catalogue for the Royal Collections, http://www.royalcollection.org.uk/collection/407181/the-imperial-assemblage-held-at-delhi-1-january-1877, accessed 9 March 2021.

20 See Natasha Eaton, 'Between Mimesis and Alterity: Art, Gift and Diplomacy in Colonial India, 1770–1800', *Comparative Studies in Society and History*, vol. 46, no. 4 (October 2006), 821.

21 See Natasha Eaton, 'The Art of Colonial Despotism: Portraits, Politics and Empire in South Asia, 1750–1795', *Cultural Critique*, vol. 70 (Autumn 2008), 63–93.

22 See ibid. and 'Between Mimesis and Alterity'.

23 Caroline Keen, *Princely India and the British: Political Development and the Operation of Empire* (London, New York, New Delhi and Sydney: Bloomsbury, 2012), 176. This sartorial induction into the political system was arguably present in inverted form during the Assemblage, when Lytton presented Indian rulers with the Queen Victoria medallion, an item to be worn.

24 Eaton, 'Between Mimesis and Alterity', 819.

25 As Akbar's chronicler, Ab'l Fazl, recorded, 'His Majesty himself sat for his likeness and also ordered to have the likenesses taken of all of the grandees in the realm. An immense album was thus formed; those who had passed away have received new life and those who are still alive have immortality promised them'; quoted in Eaton, 'Mimesis and Alterity', 822.

26 Ibid., 822.

27 See ibid.

28 William Simpson, 'Notes and Recollections of my life', *c.*1890, National Library of Scotland, Edinburgh, Acc. 11877, 125.

29 *Illustrated London News*, 14 July 1860.

30 My thanks to Jayanta Sengupta at the Victoria Memorial Museum for this information.

31 Valentine Cameron Prinsep, *Imperial India: An Artist's Journals, Illustrated by Numerous Sketches Taken at the Courts of the Principal Chiefs in India* (London: Chapman & Co., 1879), 85.

32 Ibid., 74, 3, 30.

33 Ibid., 284, 234, 31.

34 See Dakers, *Holland Park Circle*, 207.

35 Prinsep, *Imperial India*, 126, 104, 126.

36 Barbara Ramusack, *The New Cambridge History of India*, vol. 3, pt 6: *The Indian Princes and their States* (Cambridge and New York: Cambridge University Press, 2004), 147.

37 Prinsep, *Imperial India*, 32.

38 Ibid., 39, 66.

39 Ibid., 66.

40 'The Adventures of an A.R.A.', *Los Angeles Herald*, 24 January 1897, 17.

41 Bernard S. Cohn, *Colonialism and its Forms of Knowledge: The British in India* (Princeton, N.J: Princeton University Press, 1996), 106–62, 'Cloth, Clothes, and Colonialism'; Joanne Punzo Waghorne, *The Raja's Magic Clothes: Re-Visioning Kingship and Divinity in England's India* (University Park: Penn State University Press, 1994).

42 Romita Ray, *Under the Banyan Tree: Relocating the Picturesque in British India* (New Haven and London: Yale University Press, 2013), 154.

43 Prinsep, *Imperial India*, 73.

44 Codell, 'Photographic Interventions and Identities', 133.

45 Prinsep, *Imperial India*, 67, 74.

46 *Newcastle Courant*, 30 April 1880.

47 *Art Journal*, vol. 6 (1880), 218.

48 *Illustrated London News*, 1 May 1880.

49 Prinsep, *Imperial India*, 20.

50 *The Athenaeum*, 1 May 1880, 572.

51 This scene was suggested to me in the helpful response which I received to a paper on Prinsep given at the Paul Mellon Centre for Studies in British Art, London, 22 November 2013.

52 *Illustrated London News*, 1 May 1880.

53 Ruskin, *Elements of Drawing*, 247.

54 *Bristol Mercury and Daily Post*, 3 May 1880.

55 *Illustrated London News*, 1 May 1880.

56 Tracy Anderson, 'Fashioning the Viceroy: Portraits of Edward Robert Bulwer-Lytton (1831–91)', *Visual Culture in Britain*, vol. 12, no. 3 (2011), 300, 293.

57 Ibid., 302.

58 For an account of the slippages between mimicry and mockery in colonial discourse, see Homi K. Bhabha, 'Of Mimicry and Man: The Ambivalence of Colonial Discourse', *October*, vol. 28, Discipleship: A Special Issue on Psychoanalysis (Spring 1984), 125–33.

59 See Julie Codell, 'Victorian Portraits: Re-Tailoring Identities', *Nineteenth-Century Contexts: An Interdisciplinary Journal*, vol. 34, no. 5 (2012), 493–516.

60 See Carlisle, *Picturing Reform*, for a detailed analysis of the history of Hayter's painting.

61 Ibid., 74.

62 *Illustrated London News*, 27 May 1843. In his introduction to the 1843 exhibition catalogue, Hayter wrote: 'The colour of European costume cannot be considered favourable to an artist; the colours worn are nearly all the same, and, from the material of which they are composed, are less calculated to reflect light than silks or satins. These were some of the unyielding materials of such a work'; quoted in Richard Ormond, *Early Victorian Portraits* (London: HMSO, 1973), 527.

63 See Henry Barraud, *Lionel Nathan de Rothschild introduced in the House of Commons on 26 July 1858 by Lord John Russell and Mr Abel Smith* (1872; Rothschild Archive, London).

64 See H. C. G. Matthew, 'Portraits of Men: Millais and Victorian Public Life', in Peter Funnell and Malcolm Warner, eds, *Millais: Portraits* (London: National Portrait Gallery, 1999), 143.

65 While commissioned separately and thus not intended for display together, the portraits of Gladstone and Disraeli were frequently sold in engraving as a pair; ibid., 155.

66 *Bury and Norwich Post, and Suffolk Herald*, 18 May 1880.

67 See Ray, *Under the Banyan Tree*, 153–200, 'Imperial Phantoms'.

68 Mortimer Menpes, *The Durbar*, transcr. Dorothy Menpes (London: Adam & Charles Black, 1903), 35.

69 Ibid., 39.

70 Ibid., 41–2.

71 Saloni Mathur, 'The Durbar and the Visual Arts: Revisiting the Picture Archive', in Codell, *Power and Resistance*, 84–5.

72 Menpes, *The Durbar*, 46.

73 See Alison Smith, 'The Sublime in Crisis: Landscape Painting after Turner', in Nigel Llewellyn and Christine Riding, eds, *The Art of the Sublime*, January 2013, http://www.tate.org.uk/art/research-publications/the-sublime/alison-smith-the-sublime-in-crisis-landscape-painting-after-turner-r1109220, accessed 5 October 2013.

74 Christine Riding and Nigel Llewellyn, 'British Art and the Sublime', in ibid., accessed 5 October 2013.

CONCLUSION

1 *Western Gazette*, 25 September 1896, quoted in Dan Hicks, *Brutish Museums: The Benin Bronzes, Colonial Violence and Cultural Restitution* (London: Pluto Press, 2020), 51.

2 Ibid., 49.

3 Charles Dickens, 'Mr. Charles Dickens and the Execution of the Mannings', *The Times*, 13 November 1849.

4 Alice Smalley, 'Representations of Crime, Justice and Punishment in the Popular Press: A Study of the Illustrated Police News, 1864–1938', PhD thesis, Open University, 2017, 13.

5 John Thomson, *Through China with a Camera* (London and New York: Harper & Brothers, 1899), 227.

6 See Catherine Grant and Dorothy Price, 'Decolonizing Art History', *Art History*, vol. 43, no. 1 (Feb. 2020), 8–66.

7 Ibid., 9.

8 See Tim Barringer and David Bindman entries in ibid., 11, 17.

9 See Kim Wagner, 'Savage Warfare: Violence and the Rule of Colonial Difference in Early British Counterinsurgency', *History Workshop Journal*, vol. 85 (Spring 2018), 217–37.

10 Grattan Geary, *Burmah, After the Conquest: Viewed in its Political, Social, and Commercial Aspects from Mandalay* (London: Sampson Low, Marston, Searle & Rivington, 1886), 243.

11 Ann Laura Stoler, *Imperial Duress* (Durham, N.C., and London: Duke University Press, 2016), 26.

12 Ariella Azoulay, *Potential History: Unlearning Imperialism* (London and New York: Verso, 2019), 240.

13 Ibid., 246.

14 Kaja Silverman, *The Miracle of Analogy: or, The History of Photography, Part 1* (Stanford, Cal: Stanford University Press, 2015), 67.

15 Zeb Tortorici, 'Archival Seduction: Indexical Absences and Historiographical Ghosts', *Archive Journal* (November 2015), http://www.archivejournal.net/essays/archival-seduction/, accessed 10 March 2021.

16 Anjali Arondekar, *For the Record: On Sexuality and the Colonial Archive in India* (Durham, N.C., and London: Duke University Press, 2009), 3.

17 For more on the anonymity and absence of 'native' bodies in colonial archives, see Christina Riggs, *Photographing Tutankhamun: Archaeology, Ancient Egypt, and the Archive* (London and New York: Bloomsbury, 2019), 141–71.

18 Mortimer Menpes, *The Durbar*, transcr. Dorothy Menpes (London: Adam & Charles Black, 1903), 60.

19 Saloni Mathur, 'The Durbar and the Visual Arts: Revisiting the Pictorial Archive', in Julie Codell, ed., *Power and Resistance: The Delhi Coronation Durbars* (New Delhi: Mapin Publishing with the Alkazi Collection of Photography, 2012), 75.

20 Hicks, *Brutish Museums*, 55.

21 George Goldie, 1899, quoted in ibid., 58.

22 Ibid.

23 Christopher Pinney, *The Coming of Photography in India* (London: British Library, 2008), 17.

24 Christopher Pinney, 'The Line and the Curve: Spatiality and Ambivalence in the 1903 Delhi Coronation Durbar', in Codell, *Power and Resistance*, 214.

25 See Michael Godby, 'Confronting Horror: Emily Hobhouse and the Concentration Camp Photographs of the South African War', in Maria Pia Di Bella and James Elkins, eds, *Representations of Pain in Art and Visual Culture* (London and New York: Routledge, 2012), 157–70; Pinney, *Coming of Photography*, 83–5; Sean Willcock, 'Guilt in the Archive: Photography and the Amritsar Massacre of 1919', *History of Photography*, vol. 43, no. 1 (2019): 47–59.

26 *The Graphic*, 31 March 1900, quoted in Peter Johnson, *Front Line Artists* (London: Cassell, 1978), 162.

27 Tom Gretton, '"Elegant and Dignified Military Operations in the Present Age": The Imperfect Invisibility of Collateral Damage in Late Nineteenth Century Metropolitan Illustrated Magazines', 2009, http://www.melton-priorinstitut.org/pages/textarchive.php5?view=print&ID=202&language=English, accessed 10 March 2021.

28 Kaul, *Reporting the Raj: The British Press and India, c.1880–1922* (Manchester and New York: Manchester University Press, 2003), 12.

29 Frederic Villiers, *Villiers: His Five Decades of Adventure*, 2 vols (New York and London: Harper & Brothers, 1920), vol. 2, 309.

Bibliography

NEWSPAPERS AND PERIODICALS

Allen's Indian Mail
Art Journal
The Athenaeum
The Atlantic
Bengal Hurkaru
Bristol Mercury and Daily Post
British Journal of Photography
British Medical Journal, Being the Journal of the British Medical Association
Bury and Norwich Post, and Suffolk Herald
Cornhill Magazine
Daily News
The Economist
English Illustrated Magazine
The Englishman
The Graphic
Hampshire Telegraph and Sussex Chronicle
Illustrated London News
Illustrated Naval and Military Magazine
Illustrated Times
Journal of the Photographic Society of London
Literary Gazette
Los Angeles Herald
Morning Advertiser
Morning Post
Newcastle Courant
New York Times
Punch, or the London Charivari
Saturday Review of Politics, Literature, Science and Art
Sheffield & Rotherham Independent
Sydney Morning Herald
The Times
Times of India
Western Gazette
The World

PERIOD SOURCES

BAGEHOT, Walter. *The English Constitution*. London: Chapman & Hall, 1867; Boston, Mass: Little, Brown, and Company, 1870

BAILLIE, J., Lieut.-Colonel. 'Photography Applied to Military Science', *Journal of the Royal United Service Institution*, vol. 13. London: W. Mitchell and Co., 1870

BARNETT, Henry V. 'The Special Artist', *Magazine of Art*, vol. 6 (1883): 163–70

BAUDELAIRE, Charles. *The Painter of Modern Life and Other Essays*, trans. P. E. Charvet. London: Penguin, 2010

BLUNT, Sir Edward Arthur Henry. *List of Inscriptions on Christian Tombs and Tablets of Historical Interest in the United Provinces of Agra and Oudh*. Allahabad: W. C. Abel, Govt. Press, 1911

BOURNE, Samuel. 'Narrative of a Photographic Trip to Kashmir (Cashmere) and Adjacent Districts', I, *British Journal of Photography*, vol. 14, no. 335 (5 October 1866): 474–5

——. 'Narrative of a Photographic Trip to Kashmir (Cashmere) and Adjacent Districts', II, *British Journal of Photography*, vol. 14, no. 337 (19 October 1866): 498–9

——. 'Narrative of a Photographic Trip to Kashmir (Cashmere) and Adjacent Districts', III, *British Journal of Photography*, vol. 14, no. 342 (23 November 1866): 359–60

——. 'Narrative of a Photographic Trip to Kashmir (Cashmere) and Adjacent Districts', IV, *British Journal of Photography*, vol. 14, no. 347 (28 December 1866): 617–19

——. 'Photography in the East', *British Journal of Photography* (1 July 1863): VOL? NO.? PAGES?

——. 'Ten Weeks with a Camera in the Himalayas', *British Journal of Photography*, vol. 11, no. 208 (February 1864): 69–70

CALLWELL, Charles Edward, Colonel. *Small Wars: Their Principles and Practice*. London: HMSO, 1896

CAMPBELL, Sir George. *Memoirs of my Indian Career*, ed. Sir Charles E. Bernard, 2 vols. London: Macmillan and Co., 1893

CHANDLER, Edmund. *The Unveiling of Lhasa*. London: Edward Arnold, 1905

CHUNDER, Bholanauth. *The Travels of a Hindoo to various parts of Bengal and Upper India*. 2 vols. London: N. Trubner & Co., 1869

CLAUSEWITZ, General Carl von. *On War*, trans. J. J. Graham. London: Kegan Paul, Trench, Trubner & Co., 1908

COBDEN, Richard. *How Wars Are Got Up in India: The Origin of the Burmese War*. London: William & Frederick G. Cash, 1853

Copies of the Proclamation of the King, Emperor of India, to the Princes and Peoples of India, of the 2nd day of November 1908, and the Proclamation of the late Queen Victoria of the 1st day of November 1858, to the Princes, Chiefs, and People of India. London: Eyre and Spottiswoode, 1908

DALLAS, E. S. *The Gay Science*, 2 vols. London: Chapman and Hall, 1866

DODD, George. *The History of the Indian Revolt and of the Expeditions to Persia, China, and Japan, 1856–7–8, with Maps, Plans, and Wood Engravings*. London: W. & R. Chambers, 1859

DUFF, Alexander. *The Indian Rebellion: Its Causes and Results*. New York: Robert Cater & Brothers, 1858

ESTABROOKE, E. M. *Photography in the Studio and in the Field*. New York: E. & H. T. Anthony & Co., 1887

FIELDING, Theodore Henry. *Synopsis of Practical Perspective, Linear and Aerial*. London: W. H. Allen & Co., 1836

GEARY, Grattan. *Burmah, After the Conquest: Viewed in its Political, Social, and Commercial Aspects from Mandalay*. London: Sampson Low, Marston, Searle & Rivington, 1886

GRANT, Colesworthy. *An Anglo-Indian Domestic Sketch: A Letter from an Artist in India to his Mother in England*. Calcutta: Thacker & Co., 1849

——. *Dost Muhummud Khan, and the Recent Events in Caubool*. London: Thacker & Co., 1842

——. *Rough Pencillings of a Rough Trip to Rangoon in 1846*. Calcutta, London and Bombay: Thacker, Spink and Co., 1853

——. 'Album of 106 Drawings of Landscapes and Portraits of Burmese and Europeans made in Burma during Major Phayre's Mission to the Court of Ava in 1855'. British Library, London, PDP/WD540

——. 'Notes Explanatory of a Series of Views taken in Burmah during Major Phayre's Mission to the Court of Ava in 1855', 1856. British Library, London, PDP/WD540

A Guide to the Great Exhibition; Contains a Description of Every Principle Object of Interest. London: George Routledge and Co., 1851

HATTON, Joseph. *Journalistic London: Being a series of sketches of famous pens and papers of the day*. London: Sampson Low, Marston, Searle & Rivington, 1882

HERING, Henry. *A Magnificent Collection of Photographic Views and Panoramas taken by Signor Beato during the Indian Mutiny in 1857–58 and the late War in China*, sale cat. London, 1862

HOLMES, Oliver Wendell. 'Doings of the Sunbeam', *The Atlantic* (July 1863): 1–15?

HOOPER, Willoughby Wallace, Lieutenant-Colonel. *Burmah: One hundred photographs, illustrating incidents connected with the British Expeditionary Force to that country, from Embarkation at Madras, 1st Nov. 1885, to the capture of King Theebaw, with many views of Mandalay and surrounding country, native life and industries, and most interesting descriptive notes*. London: J. A. Lugard; Calcutta: Thacker, Spink and Co., 1887

JACKSON, Mason. *The Pictorial Press: Its Origin and Progress*. London: Hurst and Blackett, 1885

JEHANGIR, Sorabji. *Representative Men of India: A Collection of Memoirs, with Portraits, of Indian Princes, Nobles, Statesmen, Philanthropists, Officials, and Eminent Citizens*, intro. George Birdwood. London: W. H. Allen & Co., 1889

KAYE, John William. *A History of the Sepoy War in India, 1857–58*, 2 vols. London: W. H. Allen, 1870

KAYE, Sir John William, and John Forbes Watson. *The People of India: A Series of Photographic Illustrations, with Descriptive Letterpress, of the Races and Tribes of Hindustan*, 8 vols. London: India Museum, 1868–75

KIPLING, Rudyard. *From Sea to Sea and Other Sketches: Letters of Travel*, 4 vols. London: Macmillan and Co., 1914

——. *The Light that Failed* (1891). Auckland, NZ: Floating Press, 2016

LANDON, Perceval. *The Opening of Tibet: An Account of Lhasa and the Country and People of Central Tibet and of the Progress of the Mission Sent there by the English Government in the Year 1903–4*. New York: Doubleday, Page & Co., 1905

LANG, Arthur Moffat. *Lahore to Lucknow: The Indian Mutiny Journal of Arthur Moffat Lang*, ed. David Blomfield. London: Leo Cooper, 1992

——. Diary. British Library, London, Add. MS 43825

——. Letters. British Library, London, Add. MS 43822

MACAULAY, Thomas Babington. *Speeches by Lord Macaulay with his Minute on Indian Education*, ed. G. M. Young. London: Oxford University Press, 1979

MAINE, Sir Henry. *International Law: A Series of Lectures Delivered Before the University of Cambridge, 1887*. London: John Murray, 1888

MARSHMAN, John Clark. *How Wars Arise in India: Observations on Mr. Cobden's Pamphlet*. London: W. H. Allen & Co., 1853

MENPES, Mortimer. *The Durbar*, transcr. Dorothy Menpes. London: Adam & Charles Black, 1903

——. *War Impressions: Being a Record in Colour by Mortimer Menpes*, transcr. Dorothy Menpes. London: Adam & Charles Black, 1901

MITTRA, Peary Chand. *Life of Colesworthy Grant, Founder and Late Honourable Secretary of the Calcutta Society for the Prevention of Cruelty to Animals*. Calcutta: I. C. Bose & Co., 1881

MURRAY, John. *Photographic Views in Agra and its Vicinity*. London: J. Hogarth, 1857

——. *Picturesque Views in the North-Western Provinces of India*. London: J. Hogarth, 1859

——. Collection of Dr John Murray's miscellaneous papers and personal memorabilia. British Library, London, Western Manuscripts, RP9617

PENLEY, Aaron. *The Elements of Perspective: Illustrated by Numerous Examples and Diagrams*. London: Windsor and Newton, 1866

POLEHAMPTON, the Rev. E. and Rev. T. S., eds. *A Memoir: Letters, and Diary, of Rev. Henry S. Polehampton, M. A. Chaplain of Lucknow*. London: Richard Bentley, 1858

PRINSEP, Valentine Cameron. *Imperial India: An Artist's Journals, Illustrated by Numerous Sketches Taken at the Courts of the Principal Chiefs in India*. London: Chapman & Co., 1879

PRIOR, Melton. *Campaigns of a War Correspondent*. London: Edward Arnold, 1912

RADCLIFFE, Anne. 'The Supernatural in Poetry', *New Monthly Magazine and Literary Journal*, Vol. 16, no. 1 (1826): 145–52

Report of the commissioners appointed to consider the best mode of re-organizing the system for training officers for the Scientific Corps; together with an account of foreign and other military education. London: George E. Eyre & William Spottiswoode, 1857

Report of Police Administration in the North Western Provinces, for 1861. Allahabad: Government Press, 1862

RUSKIN, John. *Crown of Wild Olive: Four Lectures on Industry and War*. Orpington: George Allen, 1882

——. *The Elements of Drawing*. London: George Allen, 1857

——. *Modern Painters*, 4 vols. London: Smith, Elder, and Co., 1848–56

——. *The Two Paths: Being Lectures on Art, and its Application to Decoration and Manufacture, delivered in 1858–9*. London: Smith, Elder, and Co., 1859

SHAFFNER, Colonel Tal P., and the Rev. W. Owens, eds. *The Illustrated Record of the International Exhibition of the Industrial Arts and Manufactures, and Fine Arts, of All Nations, in 1862*. London and New York: London Printing and Publishing Company, 1862

SIMPSON, William. *The Autobiography of William Simpson, R.I. (Crimean Simpson)*, ed. George Eyre-Todd. London: T. Fisher Unwin, 1903

——. *Meeting the Sun: A Journey all round the World through Egypt, China, Japan, and California*. London: Longmans, Green, Reader, and Dyer, 1874

——. Diary kept during campaign in Afghanistan, 1878–9, Anne S. K. Brown Military Collection, Brown University, Providence, R.I., DS364, S567 1878

——. 'Experiences', Ms. Mitchell Library, Glasgow, 12840a

——. 'Notes and Recollections of my life to my dear daughter Ann Penelope Simpson', *c.*1890 (partial transcription by Paul Bucherer-Dietschi, Foundation Bibliotheca Afganica). National Library of Scotland, Edinburgh, Acc. 11877 (ii)

——. William Simpson Archive, Anne S. K. Brown Military Collection, Brown University, Providence, R.I.

STEVENS, Thomas. *Around the World on a Bicycle*, vol. 2: *From Teheran to Yokohama*. New York: Charles Scribner's Sons, 1889

TAYLOR, Robert. *The Princely Armory: Being a Display of the Arms of the Ruling Chiefs of India After Their Banners as Prepared for the Imperial Assemblage Held at Delhi on the First Day of January 1877*. Calcutta: Government Central Printing Office, 1877

Telegraphic Correspondence relating to Military Executions and Dacoity in Burmah. London: Eyre and Spottiswoode, 1886

TEMPLE, Sir Richard. *Oriental Experience: A selection of essays and addresses delivered on various occasions*. London: John Murray, 1883

THOMSON, John. *Illustrations of China and its People: A Series of Two Hundred Photographs, with Letterpress Descriptive of the Places and People Represented*, 4 vols. London: Sampson, Low, Marston, Low & Searle, 1873–4

——. *The Straits of Malacca, Indo-China and China; or Ten Years' Travels, Adventures and Residence Abroad*. London: Sampson, Low, Marston, Low & Searle, 1875

——. *Through China with a Camera*. London and New York: Harper & Brothers, 1899

——. 'Practical Photography in Tropical Regions', *British Photography Journal*, vol. 13, no. 327 (10 August 1866): 380

——. 'Practical Photography in Tropical Regions', II, *British Photography Journal*, vol. 13, no. 328 (17 August 1866): 393

——. 'Practical Photography in Tropical Regions', III, *British Photography Journal*, vol. 13, no. 329 (24 August 1866): 404

——. 'Practical Photography in Tropical Regions', IV, *British Photography Journal*, vol. 13, no. 330 (14 September 1866): 436

——. 'Practical Photography in Tropical Regions', V, *British Photography Journal*, vol. 13, no. 335 (5 October 1866): 472–3

——. 'Practical Photography in Tropical Regions', VI, *British Photography Journal*, vol. 13, no. 336 (12 October 1866): 487

THOMSON, Mowbray. *The Story of Cawnpore*. London: Richard Bentley, 1859

To the Members of the Photographic Society of Bengal. Calcutta: J. Thomas, 1857

TRIPE, Linnaeus. 'Views in Burma taken during the Mission to Ava' (1857). British Library, London, Photo 61: 1855

VILLIERS, Frederic. *Peaceful Personalities and Warriors Bold*. London and New York: Harper & Brothers, 1907

——. *Villiers: His Five Decades of Adventure*, 2 vols. New York and London: Harper & Brothers, 1920

WINTER, Andrew, ed. *The British Medical Journal, Being the Journal of the British Medical Association*. London: Thomas John Honeyman, 1857

YOUNGHUSBAND, Sir Francis. *India and Tibet: A History of the Relations which have Subsisted between the Two Countries from the Time of Warren Hastings to 1910; with a Particular Account of the Mission to Lhasa of 1904*. London: John Murray, 1910

Yule, Sir Henry. *A Narrative of the Mission sent by the Governor-General of India to the Court of Ava in 1855*. London: Smith, Elder, and Co., 1858; repr. *Mission to the Court of Ava in 1855*. London and New York: Oxford University Press, 1968

SECONDARY SOURCES

Agamben, Giorgio. *Homo Sacer: Sovereign Power and Bare Life*. Stanford, Cal: Stanford University Press, 1998

Anand, Dibyesh. 'Strategic Hypocrisy: The British Imperial Scripting of Tibet's Geopolitical Identity', *Journal of Asian Studies*, vol. 68, no. 1 (February 2009): 227–52

Anderson, Tracy. 'Fashioning the Viceroy: Portraits of Edward Robert Bulwer-Lytton (1831–91)', *Visual Culture in Britain*, vol. 12, no. 3 (2011): 293–311

Andrews, Malcolm. *The Search for the Picturesque: Landscape Aesthetics and Tourism in Britain, 1760–1800*. Stanford, Cal: Stanford University Press, 1989

Archer, Mildred. *British Drawings in the India Office Library*. London: HMSO, 1969

——. *Company Drawings in the India Office Library*. London: HMSO, 1972

——. *Company Paintings: Indian Paintings of the British Period*. London: Victoria and Albert Museum with Mapin Publishing, 1992

——. *Early Views of India: The Picturesque Journeys of Thomas and William Daniell, 1786–1794*. London and New York: Thames and Hudson, 1980

——. *India and British Portraiture, 1770–1825*. London: Sotheby Parke Bernet, 1979

——. *India Observed: India as Viewed by British Artists, 1760–1860: An Exhibition*. London: V&A Museum and Trefoil, 1982

——. *Indian Architecture and the British*. Feltham: Country Life, 1968

——. *The Indian Collection of Paintings and Sculpture*. London: British Library, 1986

——. *Indian Popular Painting in the India Office Library*. London: HMSO, 1977

——. *Natural History Drawings in the India Office Library*. London: HMSO, 1962

——. 'Mission to Burma, 1855', *History Today*, vol. 13, 10 (October 1963): 691–9

Armstrong, Nancy. *Fiction in the Age of Photography: The Legacy of British Realism*. Cambridge, Mass., and London: Harvard University Press, 1999

Arondekar, Anjali. *For the Record: On Sexuality and the Colonial Archive in India*. Durham, N.C., and London: Duke University Press, 2009

Auerbach, Jeffrey A. *The Great Exhibition of 1851: A Nation on Display*. New Haven and London: Yale University Press, 1999

——. 'The Picturesque and the Homogenization of Empire', *British Art Journal*, vol. 5, no. 1 (2004): 283–305

——, and Peter H. Hoffenberg. *Britain, the Empire, and the World at the Great Exhibition*. Abingdon and New York: Routledge, 2016

Azoulay, Ariella. *The Civil Contract of Photography*. New York: Zone Books, 2008

——. *Potential History: Unlearning Imperialism*. London and New York: Verso, 2019

Baer, Ulrich. *Spectral Evidence: The Photography of Trauma*. Cambridge, Mass., and London: MIT Press, 2002

Bailkin, Jordanna. 'Indian Yellow: Making and Breaking the Imperial Palette', *Journal of Material Culture*, vol. 10, no. 2 (July 2005), 197–214

Banerjee, Sukanya. *Becoming Imperial Citizens: Indians in the Late-Victorian Empire*. Durham, N.C: Duke University Press, 2010

Barringer, Tim. *Men at Work: Art and Labour in Victorian Britain*. New Haven and London: Yale University Press for the Paul Mellon Centre for British Art, 2005

——. 'Landscape Then and Now', *British Art Studies*, issue 10 (November 2018): https://www.britishartstudies.ac.uk/doi/445/p9

——. 'The South Kensington Museum and the Colonial Project', in Tim Barringer and Tom Flynn, eds, *Colonialism and the Object: Empire, Material Culture and the Museum*. London and New York: Routledge, 1998, 11–30

——, and Tom Flynn, eds, *Colonialism and the Object: Empire, Material Culture and the Museum*. London and New York: Routledge, 1998

——, Geoff Quilley and Douglas Fordham, eds. *Art and the British Empire*. Manchester and New York: Manchester University Press, 2007

Batchen, Geoffrey. *Each Wild Idea: Writing, Photography, History*. Cambridge, Mass., and London: MIT Press, 2000

——. *Negative/Positive: A History of Photography*. London and New York: Routledge, 2020

——. 'Dreams of Ordinary Life: Cartes-de-Visite and the Bourgeois Imagination', in J. J. Long, Andrea Noble, and Edward Welch, eds, *Photography: Theoretical Snapshots*. Oxford and New York: Routledge, 2009, 80–97

Baucom, Ian. *Out of Place: Englishness, Empire, and the Locations of Identity*. Princeton, N.J: Princeton University Press, 1999

Bear, Jordan. *Disillusioned: Victorian Photography and the Discerning Subject*. University Park: Pennsylvania State University Press, 2015

Beechey, G. D. S. *The Eighth Child: George Duncan Beechey, 1797–1852, Royal Portrait Painter to the Last Four Kings of Oudh*. London: Excalibur Press, 1994

Behdad, Ali. *Camera Orientalis: Reflections on Photography of the Middle East*. Chicago and London: University of Chicago Press, 2016

Bektas, Yakup. 'The Crimean War as a Technological Enterprise', *Notes and Records*, vol. 71, no. 3 (September 2017): 233–62

Belknap, Geoffrey. 'Through the Looking Glass: Photography, Science and Imperial Motivations in John Thomson's Photographic Expeditions', *History of Science*, vol. 52, no. 1 (2014): 73–97

Benjamin, Walter. *The Work of Art in the Age of Its Technological Reproducibility, and Other Writings on Media*, trans. Edmund Jephcott, Rodney Livingstone, Howard

Eiland et al. Cambridge, Mass., and London: Belknap Press of Harvard University Press, 2008

Bennet, Tony. *The Birth of the Museum: History, Theory, Politics*. London: Routledge, 1995

Berlant, Lauren. *Cruel Optimism*. Durham, N.C: Duke University Press, 2011

Bhabha, Homi K. *The Location of Culture*. London and New York: Routledge, 1994

——. 'Of Mimicry and Man: The Ambivalence of Colonial Discourse', *October*, vol. 28, Discipleship: A Special Issue on Psychoanalysis (Spring 1984): 125–33

Bharath, Stéphanie Roy. 'Recording South Indian Architecture: Linnaeus Tripe and Edmund David Lyon', in *South Asian Studies*, vol. 26, no. 2 (2010): 97–118

Bleichmar, Daniela. *Visible Empire: Botanical Expeditions and Visual Culture in the Hispanic Enlightenment*. Chicago and London: University of Chicago Press, 2012

Blunt, Alison. 'Embodying War: British Women and Domestic Defilement in the Indian "Mutiny", 1857–8', *Journal of Historical Geography*, vol. 26, no. 3 (2000): 403–28

——. 'Home and Empire: Photographs of British Families in the Lucknow Album, 1856–57', in James Ryan, ed., *Picturing Place: Photography and the Geographical Imagination*. New York: I. B. Tauris, 2006, 243–60

Bratlinger, Patrick. *Victorian Literature and Postcolonial Studies*. Edinburgh: Edinburgh University Press, 2009

Brusius, Mirjam. 'Impreciseness in Julia Margaret Cameron's Portrait Photographs', *History of Photography*, vol. 34, no. 4 (2010): 342–55

Buck-Morss, Susan. 'Aesthetics and Anesthetics: Walter Benjamin's Artwork Essay Reconsidered', *October*, vol. 62 (Autumn 1992): 3–41

Buckley, Liam. 'Studio Photography and the Aesthetics of Citizenship in The Gambia, West Africa', in Elizabeth Edwards, Chris Gosden and Ruth B. Phillips, eds. *Sensible Objects: Colonialism, Museums and Material Culture*. Oxford and New York: Berg, 2006, 61–86

Burn, William Laurence. *The Age of Equipoise: A Study of the Mid-Victorian Generation*. New York: Norton and Co., 1964

Butler, Judith. *Frames of War: When is Life Grievable?* London and New York: Verso, 2009

Cadava, Eduardo. *Words of Light: Theses on the Photography of History*. Princeton, N.J: Princeton University Press, 1998

Campt, Tina. *Image Matters: Archive, Photography, and the African Diaspora in Europe*. Durham, N.C., and London: Duke University Press, 2012

Cannadine, David. *Ornamentalism: How the British saw their Empire*. Oxford and New York: Oxford University Press, 2002

Carlisle, Janice. *Picturing Reform in Victorian Britain*. Cambridge and New York: Cambridge University Press, 2012

Carruthers, Jane. *Melton Prior: War Artist in Southern Africa, 1895–1900*. Johannesburg: Brenthurst Press, 1987

Charlesworth, Michael. 'The Picturesque, William Hodges, Photography, and Some Problems in Recent Interpretations of Images of India', *Word & Image: A Journal of Verbal/Visual Enquiry*, vol. 23, no. 3 (2007): 376–380

Chaudhary, Zahid R. *Afterimage of Empire: Photography in Nineteenth-Century India*. Minneapolis: University of Minnesota Press, 2012

——. 'Phantasmagoric Aesthetics: Colonial Violence and the Management of Perception', *Cultural Critique*, no. 59 (Winter 2005): 63–119

Cho, Lily. 'Intimacy among Strangers: Anticipating Citizenship in Chinese Head Tax Photographs', *Interventions*, vol. 15, no. 1 (2013): 10–23

Codell, Julie F. 'Photographic Interventions and Identities: Colonising and Decolonising the Royal Body', in Codell, *Power and Resistance*, 110–41

——. 'Photography and the Delhi Durbars: 1877, 1903, 1911', in Codell, *Power and Resistance*, 16–45

——. 'Victorian Portraits: Re-Tailoring Identities', *Nineteenth-Century Contexts: An Interdisciplinary Journal*, vol. 34, no. 5 (2012): 493–516

——, ed. *Power and Resistance: The Delhi Coronation Durbars*. New Delhi: Mapin Publishing with the Alkazi Collection of Photography, 2012

——, ed. *Transculturation in British Art, 1770–1930*. Aldershot: Ashgate, 2012

——, and D. S. Macleod, eds. *Orientalism Transposed: The Impact of the Colonies on British Culture*. Aldershot: Ashgate, 1998

Cohn, Bernard S. *Colonialism and its Forms of Knowledge: The British in India*. Princeton, N.J: Princeton University Press, 1996

——. 'Representing Authority in Victorian India', in Eric Hobsbawm and Terence Ranger, eds. *The Invention of Tradition*. Cambridge and New York: Cambridge University Press, 1983, 165–210

Collier, Patrick. 'Imperial/Modernist Forms in the *Illustrated London News*', *Modernism/modernity*, vol. 19, no. 3 (September 2012): 487–514

Company Paintings: Indian Paintings of the British Period. London: Victoria and Albert Museum and Mapin Publishing, 1992

Cook, Susan E. *Victorian Negatives: Literary Culture and the Dark Side of Photography in the Nineteenth Century*. New York: SUNY Press, 2019

Crane, Ralph, and Lisa Fletcher. 'Picturing the Empire in India: Illustrating Henty', *English Literature in Transition, 1880–1902*, vol. 55, no. 2 (2012): 155–75

Crary, Jonathan. *Techniques of the Observer: On Vision and Modernity in the Nineteenth Century*. Cambridge, Mass: MIT Press, 1992; 1998

Dakers, Caroline. *The Holland Park Circle: Artists and Victorian Society*. New Haven and London: Yale University Press, 1999

Dalrymple, William. *The Last Mughal: The Fall of a Dynasty, Delhi, 1857*. London, New York and Berlin: Bloomsbury Publishing, 2006

Daly, Nicholas. *Modernism, Romance and the Fin de Siècle: Popular Fiction and British Culture*. Cambridge and New York: Cambridge University Press, 2004

Daston, Lorraine, and Peter Galison. 'The Image of Objectivity', *Representations*, no. 40 (Autumn 1992): 81–128

Derrida, Jacques. 'Plato's Pharmacy', trans. Barbara Johnson, in *Dissemination*. Chicago: University of Chicago Press, 1981

DeSilvey, Caitlin. 'Observed Decay: Telling Stories with Mutable Things', *Journal of Material Culture*, vol. 11, no. 3 (2006): 318–38

Dewan, Janet. *The Photographs of Linnaeus Tripe: A Catalogue Raisonné*. Toronto: Art Gallery of Ontario, 2003

DiBello, Patrizia. *Women's Albums and Photography in Victorian England: 'Ladies, Mothers and Flirts'*. London and New York: Routledge, 2016

Dirks, Nicholas B. *Castes of Mind: Colonialism and the Making of Modern India*. Princeton and Oxford: Princeton University Press, 2001

——. *The Scandal of Empire: India and the Creation of Imperial Britain*. Cambridge, Mass., and London: Harvard University Press, 2008

——. 'Guiltless Spoliations: Picturesque Beauty, Colonial Knowledge, and Colin Mackenzie's Survey of India', in Catherine B. Asher and Thomas R. Metcalf, eds, *Perceptions of South Asia's Visual Past*. New Delhi, Mumbai and Kolkata: Oxford: IBH Publishing Co., 1994, 211–32

Driver, Felix. *Geography Militant: Cultures of Exploration and Empire*. Oxford: Blackwell, 2001

——, and Luciana Martins (eds). *Tropical Visions in the Age of Empire*. Chicago and London: University of Chicago Press, 2005

Dubow, Jessica. '"From a View on the World to a Point of View in It": Rethinking Sight, Space and the Colonial Subject', *Interventions*, vol. 2, no. 1 (2000): 87–102

Dutta, Arindam. *The Bureaucracy of Beauty: Design in the Age of its Global Reproducibility*. London and New York: Routledge, 2006

Eaton, Natasha. *Colour, Art and Empire: Visual Culture and the Nomadism of Representation*. London: I. B. Tauris, 2013

——. *Mimesis across Empires: Artworks and Networks in India, 1765–1860*. Durham, N.C., and London: Duke University Press, 2013

——. 'The Art of Colonial Despotism: Portraits, Politics and Empire in South Asia, 1750–1795', *Cultural Critique*, vol. 70 (Autumn 2008): 63–93

——. 'Between Mimesis and Alterity: Art, Gift and Diplomacy in Colonial India, 1770–1800', *Comparative Studies in Society and History*, vol. 46, no. 4 (October 2006): 816–44

——. 'Critical Cosmopolitanism: Gifting and Collecting Art at Lucknow, 1775–97', in Timothy Barringer, Geoff Quilley and Douglas Fordham, eds, *Art and the British Empire*. Manchester and New York: Manchester University Press, 2007, 189–204

——. '"Enchanted Traps?" The Historiography of Art and Colonialism in Eighteenth-century India', *Literature Compass*, vol. 9, no. 1 (January 2012): 15–33

——. 'Nomadism of Colour: Painting and Waste in the Chromo-Zones of Colonial India, *c*.1765–*c*.1860', *Journal of Material Culture*, vol. 17, no. 1 (March 2012): 61–81

Edney, Matthew H. *Mapping an Empire: The Geographical Construction of British India, 1765–1843*. London and Chicago: University of Chicago Press, 1997

Edwards, Elizabeth, *Raw Histories: Photographs, Anthropology, and Museums*. Oxford and New York: Berg, 2001

——. 'Some Thoughts on Photographs as History', in Clare Harris and Tsering Shakya, eds. *Seeing Lhasa: British Depictions of the Tibetan Capital, 1936–1947*. Chicago: Serindia Publications, 2003

——, Chris Gosden and Ruth B. Phillips. eds. *Sensible Objects: Colonialism, Museums and Material Culture*. Oxford and New York: Berg, 2006

Edwards, Jason. 'Introduction: From the East India Company to the West Indies and Beyond: The World of British Sculpture, *c*.1757–1947', *Visual Culture in Britain*, vol. 11, no. 2 (2010): 147–72

Edwards, Steve. *The Making of English Photography: Allegories*. University Park: Pennsylvania State University Press, 2006

Fabian, Johannes. *Time and the Other: How Anthropology Makes Its Object*. New York: Columbia University Press, 2014

Falconer, John. *India: Pioneering Photographers, 1850–1900*. London: British Library Publishing, 2001

——. 'Willoughby Wallace Hooper: "A Craze about Photography"', *Photographic Collector*, vol. 4, no. 3 (Winter 1983): 258–85

——. '"A Pure Labour of Love": A Publishing History of *The People of India*', in Eleanor M. Hight and Gary D. Sampson, eds. *Colonialist Photography: Imag(in)ing Race and Place*. Abingdon and New York: Routledge, 2013, 17–62

Ferguson, Christine. 'Sensational Dependence: Prosthesis and Affect in Dickens and Braddon', *Literature Interpretation Theory*, vol. 19, no. 1 (2008): 1–25

Fletcher, Pamela. '"To Wipe Away a Manly Tear": The Aesthetics of Emotion in Victorian Narrative Painting', *Victorian Studies*, vol. 51, no. 3 (Spring 2009): 457–69

Forgione, Nancy. 'Everyday Life in Motion: The Art of Walking in Late Nineteenth-Century Paris', *Art Bulletin*, vol. 87, no. 4 (December 2005): 664–87

Foster, Hal, ed. *Vision and Visuality*. Seattle: Bay Press, 1988

Fraser, John. 'Beato's Photograph of the Interior of the Sikanderbagh at Lucknow', *Journal of the Society for Army Historical Research*, vol. 59, no. 237 (1981): 51–5

——. 'The Indian Mutiny in Photographs', *c.*1986, National Army Museum, London, 2010-11-11-2-1

——. 'Some Pre-Mutiny Photographs', *Journal of the Society for Army Historical Research*, vol. 58, no. 234 (1980), 134–47

French, Patrick. *Younghusband: The Last Great Imperial Adventurer*. London: HarperCollins, 1994

Fujii, Lee Ann. 'The Puzzle of Extra Lethal Violence', *Perspectives on Politics*, vol. 11, no. 2 (June 2013), 410–26

Giroux, Henry A. 'Disturbing Pleasures: Murderous Images and the Aesthetics of Depravity', *Third Text*, vol. 26, no. 3 (2012): 259–73

Godby, Michael. 'Confronting Horror: Emily Hobhouse and the Concentration Camp Photographs of the South African War', in Maria Pia Di Bella and James Elkins, eds. *Representations of Pain in Art and Visual Culture*. London and New York: Routledge, 2012, 157–70

Godrej, Pheroza, and Pauline Rohatgi, eds. *Scenic Splendours: India through the Printed Image*. London: British Library, 1989

—— and ——, eds. *Under the Indian Sun: British Landscape Artists*. Bombay: Marg Publications, 1995

GoGwilt, Christopher. *The Fiction of Geopolitics: Afterimages of Culture, from Wilkie Collins to Alfred Hitchcock*. Stanford, Cal: Stanford University Press, 2000

Goodlad, Lauren M. E. *The Victorian Geopolitical Aesthetic: Realism, Sovereignty, and Transnational Experience*. Oxford: Oxford University Press, 2015

——. 'Cosmopolitanism's Actually Existing Beyond: Toward a Victorian Geopolitical Aesthetic', *Victorian Literature and Culture*, vol. 38, no. 2 (2010): 399–411

Gopal, Priyamvada. *Insurgent Empire: Anticolonial Resistance and British Dissent*. London and New York: Verso, 2019

Gordon, Sophie. 'A City of Mourning: The Representation of Lucknow, India in Nineteenth-Century Photography', *History of Photography*, vol. 30, no. 1 (2006), 80–91

——. 'Monumental Visions: Architectural Photography in India, 1840–1901'. PhD thesis. School of Oriental and African Studies, London University, 2010

Goswami, Manu. "Englishness' on the Imperial Circuit: Mutiny Tours in Colonial South Asia', *Journal of Historical Sociology*, vol. 9, no. 1 (March 1996): 54–84

Grant, Catherine, and Dorothy Price. 'Decolonizing Art History', *Art History*, vol. 43, no. 1 (February 2020): 8–66

Green, Martin. *Dreams of Adventure, Deeds of Empire*. New York: Basic Books, 1979

Green-Lewis, Jennifer. *Framing the Victorians: Photography and the Culture of Realism*. Ithaca and London: Cornell University Press, 1996

Greppi, Claudio. '"On the Spot": Traveling Artists and the Iconographic Inventory of the World, 1769–1859', in Felix Driver and Luciana Martins, eds, *Tropical Visions in an Age of Empire*. Chicago and London: University of Chicago Press, 2005, 23–42

Gretton, Tom. '"Elegant and Dignified Military Operations in the Present Age": The Imperfect Invisibility of Collateral Damage in Late Nineteenth Century Metropolitan Illustrated Magazines', 2009, http://www.meltonpriorinstitut.org/pages/textarchive.php5?view=print&ID=202&language=English

——. 'Richard Caton Woodville (1856–1927) at the *Illustrated London News*', *Victorian Periodicals Review*, vol. 48, no. 1 (Spring 2015): 87–120

Griffiths, Andrew. *The New Journalism, the New Imperialism and the Fiction of Empire, 1870–1900*. Houndmills, Basingstoke: Palgrave Macmillan, 2015

Griffiths, David, and Deanna K. Kriesel. 'Introduction: Open Ecologies', *Victorian Literature and Culture*, vol. 48, no. 1 (Spring 2020): 1–28

Groth, Helen. 'Technological Mediations and the Public Sphere: Roger Fenton's Crimea Exhibition and "The Charge of the Light Brigade"', *Victorian Literature and Culture*, vol. 30, no. 2 (September 2002): 553–70

Guha, Ranajit. *Dominance without Hegemony: History and Power in Colonial India*. Cambridge, Mass., and London: Harvard University Press, 1997

Guha-Thakurta, Tapati. *The Making of a New 'Indian' Art: Artists, Aesthetics and Nationalism in Bengal, c.1850–1920*. Cambridge and New York: Cambridge University Press, 1992

Harrington, Peter. *William Simpson's Afghanistan: Travels of a Special Artist and Antiquarian during the Second Afghan War, 1878–1879*. Solihull: Helion, 2016

——. 'The Defence of Kars: Paintings by William Simpson and Thomas Jones Barker', *Journal of the Society for Army Historical Research*, vol. 69, no. 277 (Spring 1991): 22–8

——. 'The First True War Artist', *MHQ: The Quarterly Journal of Military History*, vol. 9, no. 1 (Autumn 1996): 100–09

Harris, Clare E. *The Museum on the Roof of the World: Art, Politics, and the Representation of Tibet*. Chicago and London: University of Chicago Press, 2014

——. *Photography and Tibet*. London: Reaktion Books, 2016

Harris, David. *Of Battle and Beauty: Felice Beato's Photographs of China*. Santa Barbara, Cal: Santa Barbara Museum of Art, 1999

Hensley, Nathan K. *Forms of Empire: The Poetics of Victorian Sovereignty*. Oxford and New York: Oxford University Press, 2016

Herbert, Christopher. *War of No Pity: The Indian Mutiny and Victorian Trauma*. Princeton and Oxford: Princeton University Press, 2008

Hewison, Robert. *John Ruskin: The Argument of the Eye*. Princeton, N.J: Princeton University Press, 1976

HIBBERT, Christopher. *The Great Mutiny: India, 1857*. London: Allen Lane; New York: Viking, 1978

HICHBERGER, Joan Winifred Martin. *Images of the Army: The Military in British Art, 1815–1914*. Manchester and New York: Manchester University Press, 1988

HICKS, Dan. *The Brutish Museums: The Benin Bronzes, Colonial Violence and Cultural Restitution*. London: Pluto Press, 2020

HIGHT, Eleanor M., and Gary D. Sampson, eds. *Colonialist Photography: Imag(in)ing Race and Place*. Abingdon and New York: Routledge, 2004

HOFFENBERG, Peter H. *An Empire on Display: English, Indian and Australian Exhibitions from the Crystal Palace to the Great War*. Berkeley, Los Angeles and London: University of California Press, 2001

HOWES, Jennifer. *Illustrating India: The Early Colonial Investigations of Colin Mackenzie (1784–1821)*. Oxford and New York: Oxford University Press, 2010

JAMESON, Frederic. *The Geopolitical Aesthetic: Cinema and Space in the World System*. Bloomington and Indianapolis: Indiana University Press, 1992

JARVIS, Andrew. '"The Myriad-Pencil of the Photographer": Seeing, Mapping and Situating Burma in 1855', *Modern Asian Studies*, vol. 45, no. 4 (July 2011): 791–823

JAY, Martin. 'Scopic Regimes of Modernity', in Hal Foster, ed. *Vision and Visuality*. Seattle: Bay Press, 1988, 3–23

JOHNSON, Peter. *Front Line Artists*. London: Cassell, 1978

JUDD, Denis. *The Crimean War*. London: Hart-Davis and MacGibbon, 1975

KARLEKAR, Malavika. *Re-Visioning the Past: Early Photography in Bengal, 1875–1915*. Oxford and New York: Oxford University Press, 2005

KAUL, Chandrika. *Reporting the Raj: The British Press and India, c.1880–1922*. Manchester and New York: Manchester University Press, 2003

KAYAOGLU, Turan. 'Westphalian Eurocentrism in International Relations Theory', *International Studies Review*, vol. 12, no. 2 (2010): 193–217

KEEN, Caroline. *Princely India and the British: Political Development and the Operation of Empire*. London, New York, New Delhi and Sydney: Bloomsbury, 2012

KELLER, Ulrich. *The Ultimate Spectacle: A Visual History of the Crimean War*. Amsterdam: Gordon and Breach Publishers, 2001

KHAN, Omar. *From Kashmir to Kabul: The Photographs of John Burke and William Baker, 1860–1900*. Ahmedabad: Mapin Publishing; Munich: Prestel, 2002

KNIGHT, Mark, and Lesley McFadyen. '"At Any Given Moment": Duration in Archaeology and Photography', in Lesley McFadyen and Dan Hicks, eds, *Archaeology and Photography: Time, Objectivity and Archive*. London, New York, New Delhi and Sydney: Bloomsbury Visual Arts, 2020, 55–72

KNIGHTLEY, Phillip. *The First Casualty, from the Crimea to Vietnam: The War Correspondent as Hero, Propagandist, and Myth Maker*. San Diego, Cal: Harcourt Brace Jovanovich, 1975

KOOLE, Simeon. 'Photography as Event: Power, the Kodak Camera, and Territoriality in Early Twentieth-Century Tibet', *Comparative Studies in Society and History*, vol. 59, no. 2 (2017): 310–45

LACOSTE, Anne. *Felice Beato: A Photographer on the Eastern Road*. Los Angeles: J. Paul Getty Museum, 2010

LALVANI, Suren. *Photography, Vision, and the Production of Modern Bodies*. Albany: State University of New York Press, 1996

LINFIELD, Susie. *Cruel Radiance: Photography and Political Violence*. Chicago: University of Chicago Press, 2010

LYDON, Jane. *Photography, Humanitarianism, Empire*. London and New York: Routledge, 2016

MACARTHUR, John. 'The Heartlessness of the Picturesque: Sympathy and Disgust in Ruskin's Aesthetics', *Assemblage*, no. 32 (April 1997): 126–41

MCCLINTOCK, Anne. 'Imperial Ghosting and National Tragedy: Revenants from Hiroshima and Indian Country in the War on Terror', *PMLA*, vol. 129, no. 4 (October 2014): 821

MCFADYEN, Lesley, and Dan Hicks, eds. *Archaeology and Photography: Time, Objectivity and Archive*. London, New York and New Delhi: Bloomsbury Visual Arts, 2019

MARSH, Jan. *The Pre-Raphaelite Circle*. London: National Portrait Gallery, 2005

MARTINS, Luciana, and Felix Driver. 'John Septimus Roe and the Art of Navigation, *c*.1815–30', in Tim Barringer, Geoff Quilley and Douglas Fordham, eds, *Art and the British Empire*, Manchester and New York: Manchester University Press, 2007, 53–66

MASSELOS, Jim. 'The Great Durbar Crowds: The Participant Audience', in Codell, *Power and Resistance*, 177–203

MATHUR, Saloni. *India by Design: Colonial History and Cultural Display*. Los Angeles and London: University of California Press, 2007

——. 'The Durbar and the Visual Arts: Revisiting the Picture Archive', in Codell, *Power and Resistance*, 70–93

MATTHEW, H. C. G. 'Portraits of Men: Millais and Victorian Public Life', in Peter Funnell and Malcolm Warner, eds, *Millais: Portraits*. London: National Portrait Gallery, 1999, 137–61

METCALF, Thomas R. *The Aftermath of Revolt: India, 1857–1870*. Princeton: Princeton University Press, 1964

——. *The New Cambridge History of India*, vol. 3.4: *Ideologies of the Raj*. Cambridge and New York: Cambridge University Press, 1994

MEYER, Karl, and Shareen Brysac. *Tournament of Shadows: The Great Game and the Race for Empire in Asia*. London: Abacus, 2001

MEYER, Kurt, and Pamela Deuel Meyer. *In the Shadow of the Himalayas: Tibet, Bhutan, Nepal, Sikkim: A Photographic Record of John Claude White, 1883–1908*. Ahmedabad: Mapin Publishing, 2005

MIGNOLO, Walter. 'Geopolitics of Sensing and Knowing: On (De)Coloniality, Border Thinking and Epistemic

Disobedience', *Postcolonial Studies*, vol. 14, no. 3 (2011): 273–83

——. 'The Geopolitics of Sensing and Knowing: On (de)Coloniality, Border Thinking, and Epistemic Disobedience', *Confero*, vol. 1, no. 1 (2013): 129–50

——. 'The Moveable Center: Geographical Discourses and Territoriality during the Expansion of the Spanish Empire', in Ana del Sarto, Alicia Rios and Abril Trigo, eds, *The Latin American Cultural Studies Reader*. Durham, N.C: Duke University Press, 2004

——, and Catherine Walsh. *On Decoloniality: Concepts, Analytics, Praxis*. Durham, N.C, and London: Duke University Press, 2018

Mignolo, Walter, and Rolando Vazquez. 'Decolonial AestheSis: Colonial Wounds/Decolonial Healings', *Social Text* (July 2013), https://socialtextjournal.org/periscope_article/decolonial-aesthesis-colonial-woundsdecolonial-healings/

Mirzoeff, Nicholas. *The Right to Look: A Counterhistory of Visuality*. Durham, N.C., and London: Duke University Press, 2011

Mitchell, Timothy. 'The World as Exhibition', *Comparative Studies in Society and History*, vol. 31, no. 2 (April 1989): 217–32

Mitter, Partha. *Art and Nationalism in Colonial India, 1850–1922: Occidental Orientations*. Cambridge: Cambridge University Press, 1994

Moser, Gabrielle. *Projecting Citizenship: Photography and Belonging in the British Empire*. University Park: Penn State University Press, 2019

Nasta, Susheila, ed. *India in Britain: South Asian Networks and Connections, 1858–1950*. Basingstoke and New York: Palgrave Macmillan, 2013

Natale, Simone. 'Photography and Communication Media in the Nineteenth Century', *History of Photography*, vol. 36, no. 4 (2012): 451–6

Nayar, Pramod K. 'Empire Communications, Inc.: Nineteenth-Century Imperial Pageantry and the Politics of Display', *Journal of Creative Communications*, vol. 5, no. 2 (July 2010): 75–87

Nichols, Kate, and Sarah Victoria Turner. *After 1851: The Material and Visual Cultures of the Crystal Palace at Sydenham*. Manchester: Manchester University Press, 2017

Norbu, Dawa. *China's Tibet Policy*. Padstow: Curzon Press, 2001

Ogborn, Miles. 'Archives', in Stephen Harrison, Steve Pile and Nigel Thrift, eds, *Patterned Ground: Entanglements of Nature and Culture*. Chicago: University of Chicago Press, 2004

Oppermann, Serpil. 'Material Ecocriticism', in Iris van der Turin, ed., *Gender: Nature*. New York: Macmillan, 2016, 89–102

Ormond, Richard. *Early Victorian Portraits*. London: HMSO, 1973

Otter, Chris. *The Victorian Eye: A Political History of Light and Vision in Britain, 1800–1900*. Chicago and London: University of Chicago Press, 2008

Pal, Pratapaditya. *From Merchants to Emperors: British Artists in India, 1757–1930*. Ithaca and London: Cornell University Press, 1986

Parlett, Graham, and Pauline Rohatgi, eds. *Indian Life and Landscape by Western Artists: Paintings and Drawings from the Victoria and Albert Museum, 17th to the Early 20th Century*. London: V&A Museum; Mumbai: Chatrapati Shivaji Maharaj Vastu Sangrahalaya, 2008

Perry, Lara. 'The Carte de Visite in the 1860s and the Serial Dynamic of Photographic Likeness', *Art History*, vol. 35, no. 4 (September 2012): 728–49

Phu, Thy. *Picturing Model Citizens: Civility in Asian American Visual Culture*. Philadelphia: Temple University Press, 2012

Pīammēttāwat, Phaisān, ed. *Siam: Through the Lens of John Thomson, 1865–66*. Bangkok: River Books, 2015

Pinney, Christopher. *Camera Indica: The Social Life of Indian Photographs*. London: Reaktion Books, 1997

——. *The Coming of Photography in India*. London: British Library, 2008

——. *Photography and Anthropology*. London: Reaktion Books, 2011

——. *'Photos of the Gods': The Printed Image and Political Struggle in India*. London: Reaktion Books, 2004

——. 'The Colonial Dromosphere: Speed, Transmission and Prosthesis in Colonial India', in J. Carlos Viana Ferreira and Teresa de Ataíde Malafaia, eds, *The British Empire: Ideology, Perspectives, Perceptions*. Lisbon: University of Lisbon, Centre for English Studies, 2010, 115–36

——. 'The Line and the Curve: Spatiality and Ambivalence in the 1903 Delhi Coronation Durbar', in Codell, *Power and Resistance*, 204–15

——. 'Seven Theses on Photography', *Thesis Eleven*, vol. 113, no. 1 (2012): 141–56

Pitts, Jennifer. 'Boundaries of International Law', in Duncan Bell, ed., *Victorian Visions of Global Order: Empire and International Relations in Nineteenth-Century Political Thought*. Cambridge, New York and Delhi: Cambridge University Press, 2007

Pollak, Oliver B. 'A Mid-Victorian Cover up: The Case of the "Combustible Commodore" and the Second Anglo-Burmese War, 1851–52', *Albion*, vol. 10, no. 2 (Summer 1978): 171–83

Poole, Deborah. *Vision, Race, and Modernity: A Visual Economy of the Andean Image World*. Princeton, N.J: Princeton University Press, 1997

Porter, Bernard. *The Absent-Minded Imperialists: Empire, Society and Culture in Britain*. Oxford and New York: Oxford University Press, 2004

Pratt, Mary Louise. *Imperial Eyes: Travel Writing and Transculturation*. London and New York: Routledge, 1992; 2008

Przyblyski, Jeannene M. 'Revolution at a Standstill: Photography and the Paris Commune of 1871', *Yale French Studies*, vol. 101 (2001): 54–78

Ramusack, Barbara. *The New Cambridge History of India*, vol. 3, pt 6: *The Indian Princes and their States*. Cambridge and New York: Cambridge University Press, 2004

Randall, Don. 'Autumn 1857: The Making of the Indian "Mutiny"', *Victorian Literature and Culture*, vol. 31, no. 1 (2003): 3–17

Ray, Romita. *Under the Banyan Tree: Relocating the Picturesque in British India*. New Haven and London: Yale University Press, 2013

——. 'Baron of Bengal: Robert Clive and the Birth of an Imperial Image', in Julie Codell, ed. *Transculturation in British Art, 1770–1930*. London and New York: Routledge, 2012, 21–38

Richards, Thomas. *The Imperial Archive: Knowledge and the Fantasy of Empire*. London and New York: Verso, 1993

Riding, Christine, and Nigel Llewellyn. 'British Art and the Sublime', in Nigel Llewellyn and Christine Riding, eds. *The Art of the Sublime*, January 2013, http://www.tate.org.uk/art/research-publications/the-sublime/christine-riding-and-nigel-llewellyn-british-art-and-the-sublime-r1109418

Rizzo, Lorena. 'Visual Aperture: Bureaucratic Systems of Identification, Photography and Personhood in Colonial Southern Africa', *History of Photography*, vol. 37, no. 3 (2013): 263–82

Robinson, Jane. *Angels of Albion: Women of the Indian Mutiny*. London: Viking Press, 1996

Thomas Ruff. 'Thomas Ruff Reimagines 1850s India and Burma', IndiaArtFair, https://web.archive.org/web/20200814204458/http://indiaartfair.in/thomas-ruff-reimagines-1850s-india-and-burma

Ryan, James R. *Picturing Empire: Photography and the Visualization of the British Empire*. London: Reaktion Books, 1997

Rycroft, Daniel J. *Representing Rebellion: Visual Aspects of Counter-insurgency in Colonial India*. New Delhi: Oxford University Press, 2006

Said, Edward. *Culture and Imperialism*. New York: Alfred A. Knopf, 1993

——. *Orientalism: Western Conceptions of the Orient*. Harmondsworth and New York: Penguin, 1979

Sampson, Gary D. 'Unmasking the Colonial Picturesque: Samuel Bourne's Photographs of Barrackpore Park', in Eleanor M. Hight and Gary D. Sampson, eds. *Colonialist Photography: Imag(in)ing Race and Place*. Abingdon and New York: Routledge, 2004, 84–106

Schmitt, Carl. *The Concept of the Political*. Chicago and London: University of Chicago Press, 1996

Sedgwick, Eve Kosofsky. *Touching Feeling: Affect, Pedagogy, Performativity*. Durham, N.C., and London: Duke University Press, 2003

Sekula, Allan. *Photography Against the Grain: Essays and Photo Works, 1973–1983*. Halifax: Press of Nova Scotia College of Art and Design, 1984; London: Mack Books, 2016

——. 'The Body and the Archive', *October*, vol. 39 (Winter 1986): 3–64

Silverman, Kaja. *The Miracle of Analogy: or, The History of Photography, Part 1*. Stanford, Cal: Stanford University Press, 2015

Sliwinski, Sharon. 'The Childhood of Human Rights: The Kodak on the Congo', *Journal of Visual Culture*, vol. 5, no. 3 (2006): 333–63

Smalley, Alice. 'Representations of Crime, Justice and Punishment in the Popular Press: A Study of the Illustrated Police News, 1864–1938', PhD thesis, Open University, 2017

Smith, Alison. 'The Sublime in Crisis: Landscape Painting after Turner', in Nigel Llewellyn and Christine Riding, eds. *The Art of the Sublime*, January 2013, http://www.tate.org.uk/art/research-publications/the-sublime/alison-smith-the-sublime-in-crisis-landscape-painting-after-turner-r1109220

Smith, Bernard. 'William Hodges and English Plein Air Painting', *Art History*, vol. 6, no. 2 (June 1983): 143–53

Smith, Linda Tuhiwai. *Decolonizing Methodologies: Research and Indigenous Peoples*. London and New York: Zed Books; Dunedin: University of Otago Press, 2008

Sontag, Susan. *On Photography*. Harmondsworth and New York: Penguin Books, 1978

——. *Regarding the Pain of Others*. London and New York: Penguin, 2003

Springall, John O. '"Up Guards and at Them": British Imperialism and Popular Art, 1880–1914', in John M. Mackenzie, ed., *Imperialism and Popular Culture*. Manchester and New York: Manchester University Press, 1986, 49–72

Stearn, Roger T. 'War Correspondents and Colonial War, *c*.1870–1900', in John M. MacKenzie, ed. *Popular Imperialism and the Military: 1850–1950*. Manchester and New York: Manchester University Press, 1992, 139–61

Stoler, Ann Laura. *Imperial Duress*. Durham, N.C., and London: Duke University Press, 2016

——. 'On Degrees of Imperial Sovereignty', *Public Culture*, vol. 18, no. 1 (December 2006): 125–46

Strang, David. 'Contested Sovereignty: The Social Construction of Colonial Imperialism', in Thomas J. Biersteker, ed. *State Sovereignty as Social Construct*. Cambridge: Cambridge University Press, 2011, 22–49

Tagg, John. *The Burden of Representation: Essays on Photographies and Histories*. Minneapolis: University of Minnesota Press, 1993

Tarapor, Mahrukh. 'John Lockwood Kipling and British Art Education in India', *Victorian Studies*, vol. 24, no. 1 (Autumn 1980): 53–81

Taussig, Michael. *Mimesis and Alterity: A Particular History of the Senses*. London and New York: Routledge, 1993

——. 'Redeeming Indigo', *Theory, Culture & Society*, vol. 25, no. 3 (May 2008): 1–15

Taylor, Roger, and Crispin Branfoot. *Captain Linnaeus Tripe: Photographer of India and Burma, 1852–1860*. Washington D.C: National Gallery of Art, 2014

Teukolsky, Rachel. 'Novels, Newspapers, and Global War: New Realisms in the 1850s', *Novel: A Forum on Fiction*, vol. 45, no. 1 (2012): 31–55

Thomas, Julia. *Pictorial Victorians: The Inscription of Values in Word and Image*. Athens: Ohio University Press, 2004

Thomas, Nicholas. *Entangled Objects: Exchange, Material Culture, and Colonialism in the Pacific*. Cambridge, Mass., and London: Harvard University Press, 1991

Thomas, Sarah. *Witnessing Slavery: Art and Travel in the Age of Abolition*. New Haven and London: Yale University Press, 2019

——. '"On the spot": Travelling Artists and Abolitionism, 1770–1830', *Atlantic Studies*, vol. 8, issue 2 (2011): 213–32

Thomson, John B. *Media and Modernity: A Social Theory of the Media*. Cambridge: Polity Press with Blackwell Publishing, 1995

Tickell, Alex. *Terrorism, Insurgency and Indian-English Literature, 1830–1947*. London and New York: Routledge, 2012

Tillotson, Giles. *The Artificial Empire: The Indian Landscapes of William Hodges*. Richmond, Surrey: Curzon Press, 2000

Tortorici, Zeb. 'Archival Seduction: Indexical Absences and Historiographical Ghosts', *Archive Journal* (November 2015), http://www.archivejournal.net/essays/archival-seduction/

Trevithick, Alan. 'Some Structural and Sequential Aspects of the British Imperial Assemblages at Delhi: 1877–1911', *Modern Asian Studies*, vol. 24, no. 3 (July 1990): 561–78

Turner, Sarah Victoria. 'The "Essential Quality of Things": E. B. Havell, Ananda Coomaraswamy, Indian Art and Sculpture in Britain, *c.*1910–14', *Visual Culture in Britain*, vol. 11, no. 2 (2010): 239–64

Usherwood, Paul. *Elizabeth Butler: Battle Artist*. London: Sutton, 1987

Viswanathan, Rashmi. 'The Tresidder Album: A Case Study of a Private "Ethnography"', *Self and Nation*, vol. 7, no. 1 (Autumn 2016), https://quod.lib.umich.edu/t/tap/7977573.0007.104/--tresidder-album-a-case-study-of-a-private-ethnography?rgn=main;view=fulltext

Waghorne, Joanne Punzo. *The Raja's Magic Clothes: Re-Visioning Kingship and Divinity in England's India*. University Park: Penn State University Press, 1994

Wagner, Kim. *The Great Fear of 1857: Rumours, Conspiracies and the Making of the Indian Uprising*. Witney: Peter Lang, 2010

——. '"Calculated to Strike Terror": The Amritsar Massacre and the Spectacle of Colonial Violence', *Past and Present*, vol. 233, no. 1 (November 2016): 185–225

——. 'Savage Warfare: Violence and the Rule of Colonial Difference in Early British Counterinsurgency', *History Workshop Journal*, vol. 85 (Spring 2018): 217–37

Wagner-Pacifici, Robin. *The Art of Surrender: Decomposing Sovereignty at Conflict's End*. Chicago and London: University of Chicago Press, 2005

Ward, Andrew. *Our Bones are Scattered: The Cawnpore Massacres and the Indian Mutiny of 1857*. London: John Murray, 2004

Waters, Catherine. *Special Correspondence and the Newspaper Press in Victorian Print Culture, 1850–1886*. Houndmills, Basingstoke: Palgrave Macmillan, 2019

Wendorf, Richard. *Sir Joshua Reynolds: The Painter in Society*. Cambridge, Mass: Harvard University Press, 1996

Willcock, Sean. 'Aesthetic Bodies: Posing on Sites of Violence in India, 1857–1900', *History of Photography*, vol. 39, no. 2 (2015): 142–59

——. 'Aesthetics of the Negative: Orientalist Portraiture in the Digitised Wet Collodion Prints of John Thomson (1837–1921)', *Photoresearcher*, No. 30 (Autumn 2018): 96–110

——. 'Composing the Spectacle: Colonial Portraiture and the Coronation Durbars of British India, 1877–1911', *Art History*, vol. 40, issue 1 (2017): 132–55

——. 'Guilt in the Archive: Photography and the Amritsar Massacre of 1919', *History of Photography*, vol. 43, no. 1 (2019): 47–59

——. 'Insurgent Citizenship: Dr John Nicholas Tresidder's Photographs of War and Peace in British India, *c.*1857–1862', *British Art Studies*, Issue 4 (Autumn 2016)

——. 'Picturesque Conflict: Photography and the Aesthetics of Violence in the Nineteenth-Century British Empire, *c.*1857–1900', in Juliet Hacking (ed), *Photography and the Arts: Essays on 19th Century Practices and Debates*. London, New York, New Delhi and Sydney: Bloomsbury Visual Arts, 2020, 85–98

Wylie, John. 'Depths and Folds: On Landscape and the Gazing Subject', *Environment and Planning: Society and Space*, vol. 24, no. 4 (2006): 519–35

Yao, Betty, ed. *China: Through the Lens of John Thomson, 1868–1872*. Bangkok: River Books, 2015

Žižek, Slavoj. *The Sublime Object of Ideology*. London and New York: Verso, 1989

——. 'What Rumsfeld doesn't know that He knows about Abu Ghraib', *In These Times*, 21 May 2004

Index

Page numbers in *italics* indicate illustrations